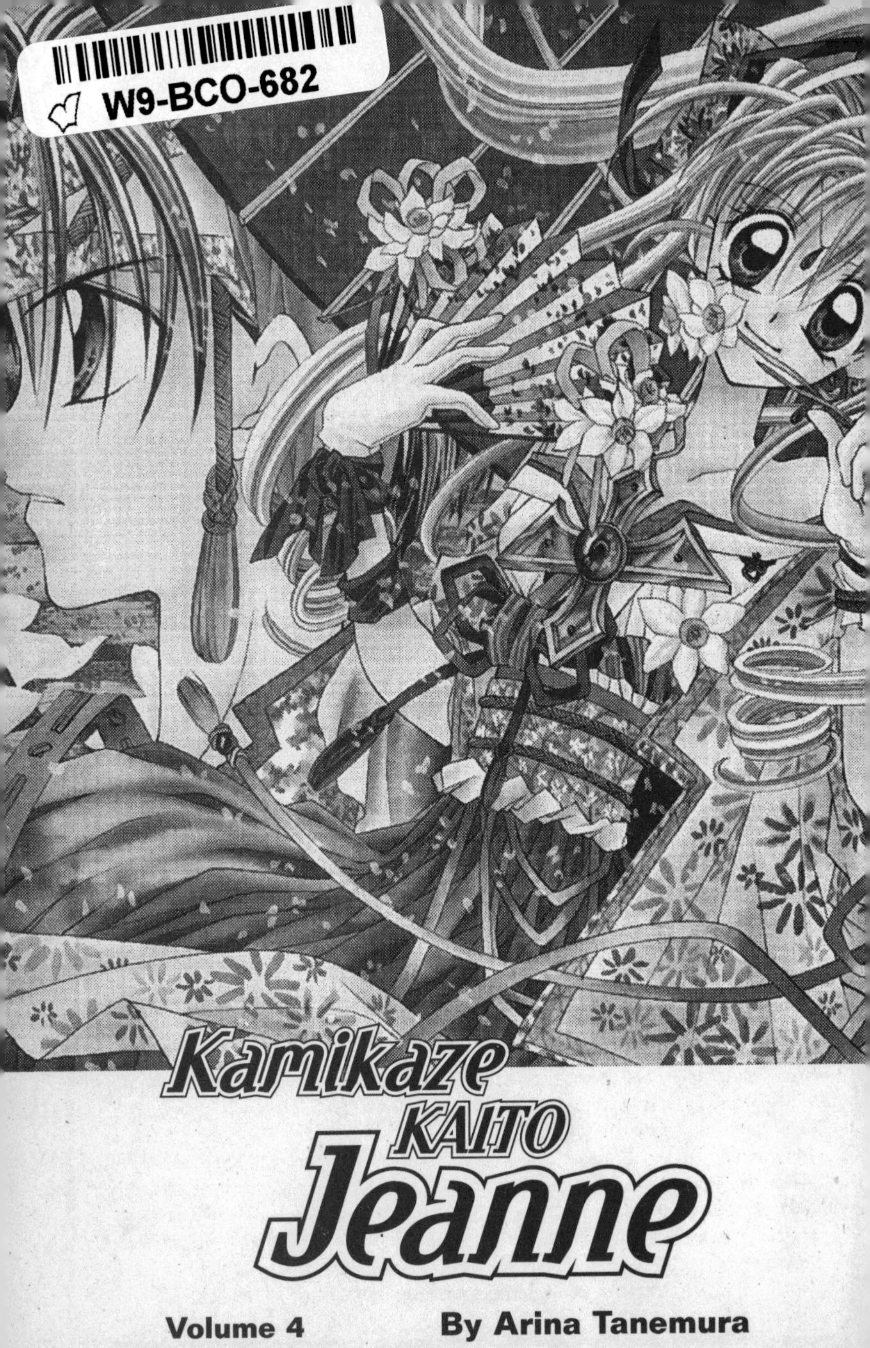

Kamikaze Kaito Jeanne

Volume 4

By Arina Tanemura

KUSAKABE MARON
Cheerful, energetic 16-year-old. Jeanne's true identity.
TODAIJI MIYAKO
Maron's friend since childhood. Jeanne-hunter.
NAGOYA CHIAKI
Mysterious transfer student who constantly hits on Maron.
KAITO SINBAD and ACCESS.
KAMIKAZE KAITO JEANNE and semi-angel FINN.

Main Character Introduction

Kamikaze Kaito Jeanne

Previously...

Maron is an average 16-year-old girl who is active in her high school's rhythmic gymnastics club. But as the reincarnation of Jeanne D'Arc, she has inherited heavenly powers, which she uses to collect demons that lie hidden inside paintings. This is Maron's other identity, Kamikaze Kaito Jeanne!!
Recently, Maron received news of her parents' intention to divorce, the shock of which made her cast her Jeanne duties aside and take off on her own, until Chiaki's words of encouragement set her back on course. Actually, Chiaki too, has a dual identity, as Jeanne's rival, Kaito Sinbad but somewhere along the line, Maron realized that, enemy or not, she had fallen in love with him...

Maron was on a roll, though, capturing one demon after another until one night when her transformation from Jeanne back to Maron was observed by a stranger! A nervous wreck, Maron still went to school the next day, half-expecting the police to be waiting, but instead was stunned to meet the man who saw her change the previous night--Momokuri High's new teacher! Whether or not the jig is up for Maron's secret identity, though, remains to be seen...

Kamikaze KAITO

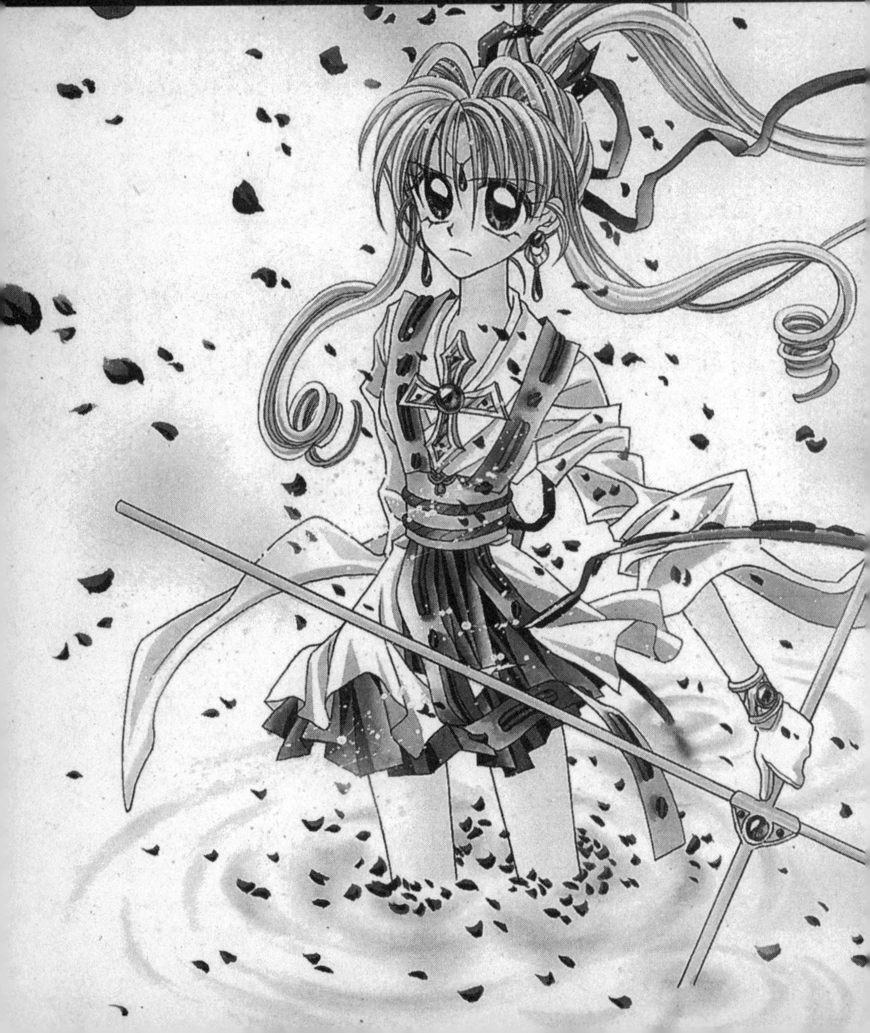

Tell us, o wise ones!!

YAY!! HEAVENLY COUPLE ACCESS AND FINN HERE!
WE'RE NOT A COUPLE!
THIS TIME, WE'LL TELL YOU A LITTLE ABOUT HOW JEANNE AND SINBAD DO THEIR TRANS-FORMING!
FWIP
ALL JEANNE HAS TO DO TO CHANGE BACK INTO MARON IS REMOVE THE RIBBON FROM HER HAIR!
AND SINBAD NEED ONLY TAKE OFF HIS BANDANA AND HE'S BACK TO BEING CHIAKI!
FWIP
HMMMM... FOLLOWING THIS LOGIC, IF WE UNDID HIS PONYTAIL, DO YOU THINK HE'D TRANS-FORM INTO SOMETHING?
TALKING ABOUT THE NEW TEACHER...
SOME-THING FISHY ABOUT HIM...
TO FIND THE ANSWER TO THAT, READ ON!

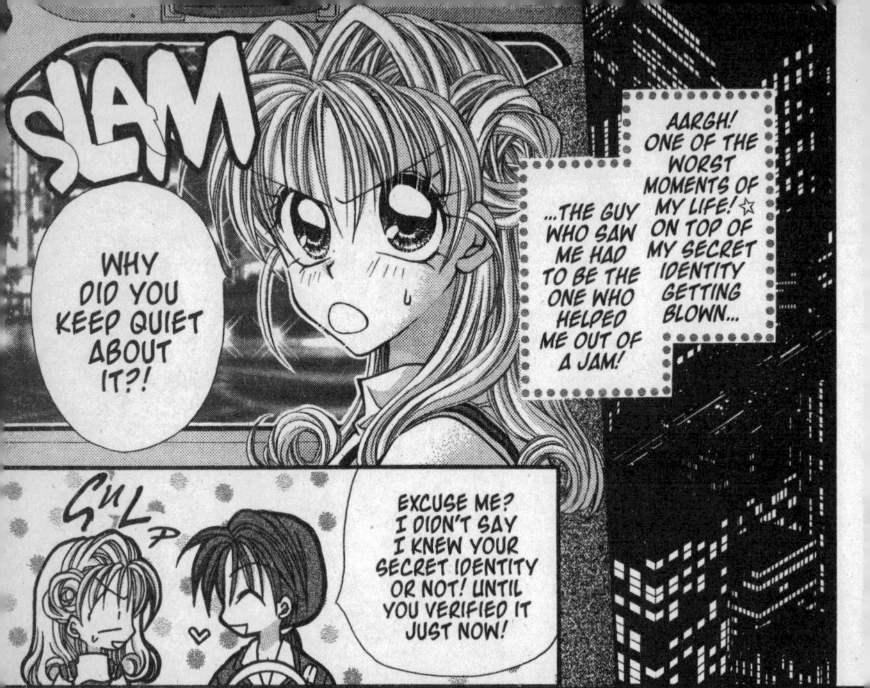
AARGH! ONE OF THE WORST MOMENTS OF MY LIFE! ☆ ON TOP OF MY SECRET IDENTITY GETTING BLOWN...
...THE GUY WHO SAW ME HAD TO BE THE ONE WHO HELPED ME OUT OF A JAM!
SLAM
WHY DID YOU KEEP QUIET ABOUT IT?!
EXCUSE ME? I DIDN'T SAY I KNEW YOUR SECRET IDENTITY OR NOT! UNTIL YOU VERIFIED IT JUST NOW!
GULP

Episode 14: "DID YOU EAT THE POPPY SEED FLOATING IN KINDNESS?"

Out of all the title page illustrations that I've done in color, this one is the absolute worst (in other words, it totally stinks). Speaking frankly, I drew it during a slumping period and I had zero ideas when it came to coloring it...and so, it looks awful. The only thing that made me feel a little better was getting the response "it looks cool♡" from a reader. Other than that, well, please accept my apologies. As to the story itself, this marks the first appearances of Zen-kun and Noin. One thing I want to clarify for readers of the magazine is that on page 14, where Maron-chan and Zen-kun meet, that "THUMP" sound effect is supposed to be the beat of Zen-kun's heart. (The reason I'm explaining it is that after the story was published in the magazine, I got a lot of fiery letters from readers, protesting that "the **only** person who should be able to make Maron's heart beat faster is Chiaki!" Poor Zen-kun!) So breathe easy, folks! Actually, though, I intended the "THUMP" to be unclear as to whose heart dealt it so that Zen-kun's initial appearance would have some impact to it! (So looking at it this way, all of you played right into my hands!) Sorry, Maron-chan...

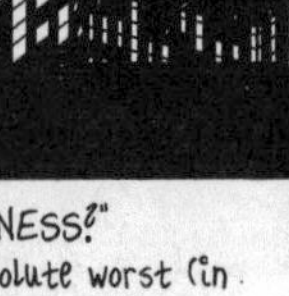
CHIAKI IS THE ONLY MAN FOR ME!

The meaning of the title is...um...about Maron's slightly agitated state of mind as she responds to Hijiri-sensei's kindness...and whether or not she's going to fall for that kindness. Am I stretching it? My favorite "shot" in this episode (apologies for forgetting to tell you last episode) is on page 30, panel 3, with the SILENCE above Jeanne shot from behind as she goes "I am number one!!!" See, I'm bad at drawing characters from behind...(Well, okay, I'm bad at drawing far too many poses.) But for once, I drew her from behind and she looked cute!♡

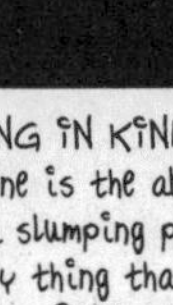
BLUSH

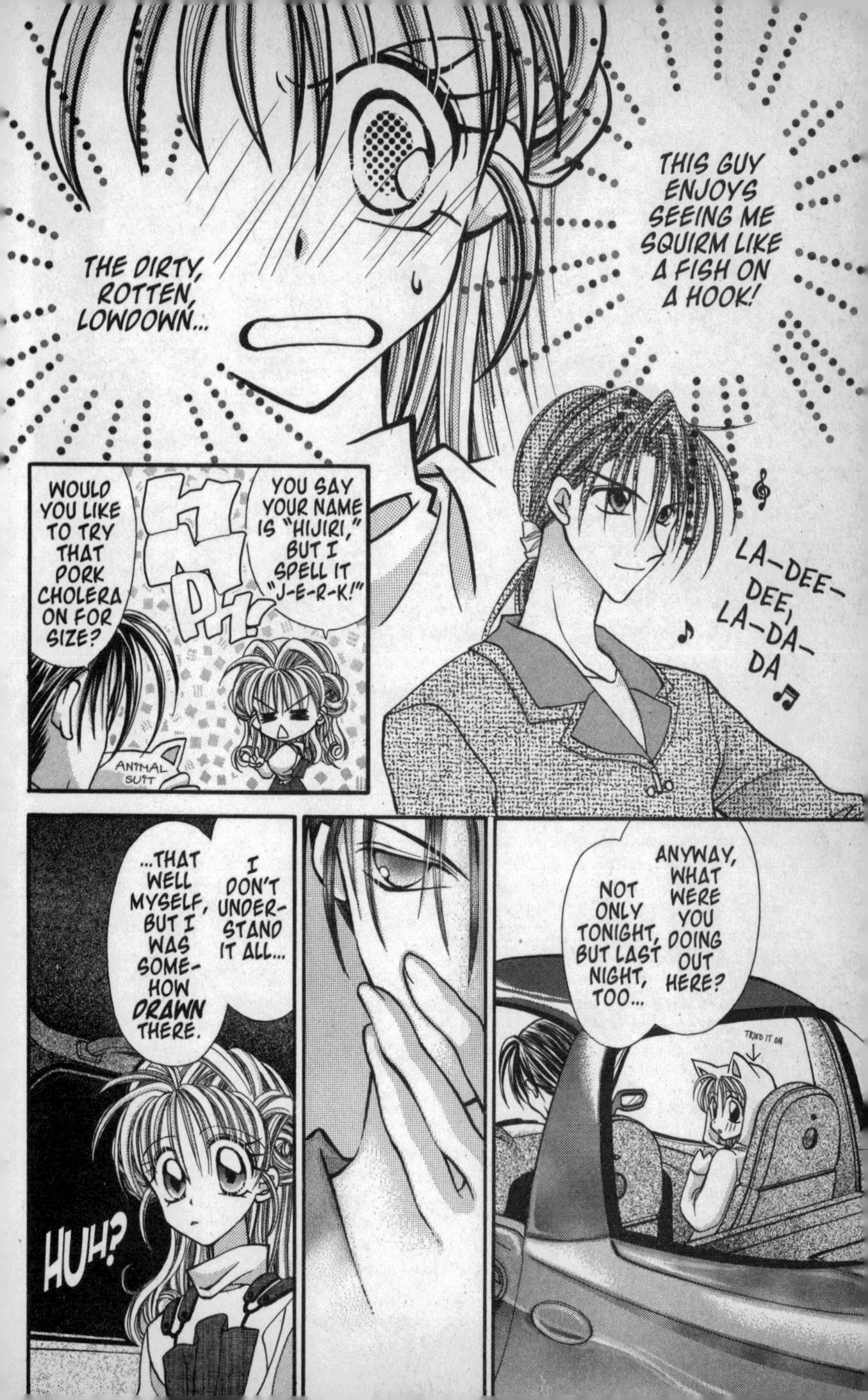
THIS GUY ENJOYS SEEING ME SQUIRM LIKE A FISH ON A HOOK!
THE DIRTY, ROTTEN, LOWDOWN...
LA-DEE-DEE, LA-DA-DA
YOU SAY YOUR NAME IS "HIJIRI," BUT I SPELL IT "J-E-R-K!"
WOULD YOU LIKE TO TRY THAT PORK CHOLERA ON FOR SIZE?
ANIMAL SUIT
ANYWAY, WHAT WERE YOU DOING OUT HERE?
NOT ONLY TONIGHT, BUT LAST NIGHT, TOO...
TRIED IT ON
I DON'T UNDER-STAND IT ALL...
...THAT WELL MYSELF, BUT I WAS SOME-HOW DRAWN THERE.
HUH?

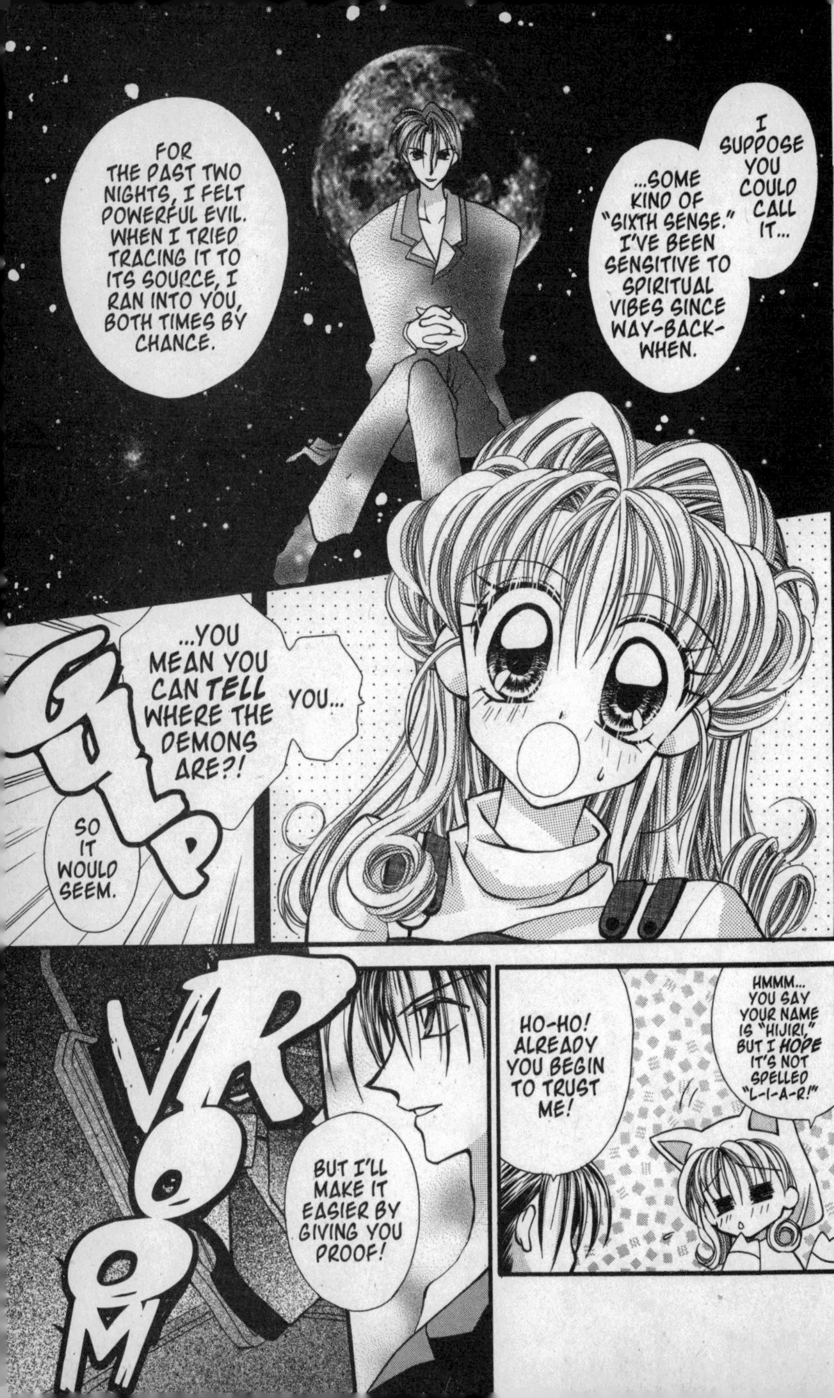
I SUPPOSE YOU COULD CALL IT...
...SOME KIND OF "SIXTH SENSE." I'VE BEEN SENSITIVE TO SPIRITUAL VIBES SINCE WAY-BACK-WHEN.
FOR THE PAST TWO NIGHTS, I FELT POWERFUL EVIL. WHEN I TRIED TRACING IT TO ITS SOURCE, I RAN INTO YOU, BOTH TIMES BY CHANCE.
YOU...
...YOU MEAN YOU CAN *TELL* WHERE THE DEMONS ARE?!
GULP
SO IT WOULD SEEM.
HMMM... YOU SAY YOUR NAME IS "HIJIRI," BUT I *HOPE* IT'S NOT SPELLED "L-I-A-R!"
HO-HO! ALREADY YOU BEGIN TO TRUST ME!
VROOM
BUT I'LL MAKE IT EASIER BY GIVING YOU PROOF!

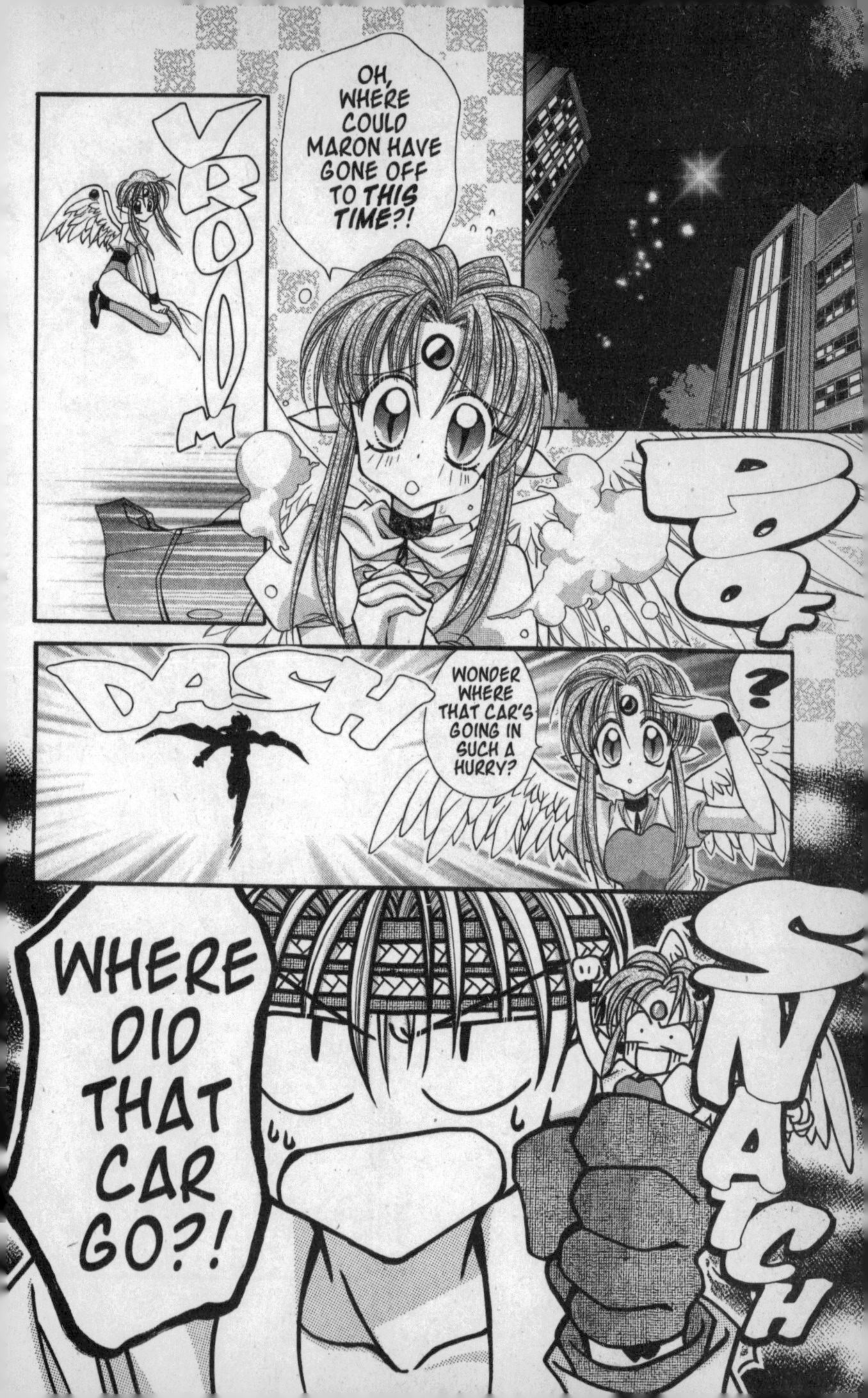
OH, WHERE COULD MARON HAVE GONE OFF TO THIS TIME?!
POOF
VROOM
?
WONDER WHERE THAT CAR'S GOING IN SUCH A HURRY?
DASH
SNATCH
WHERE DID THAT CAR GO?!

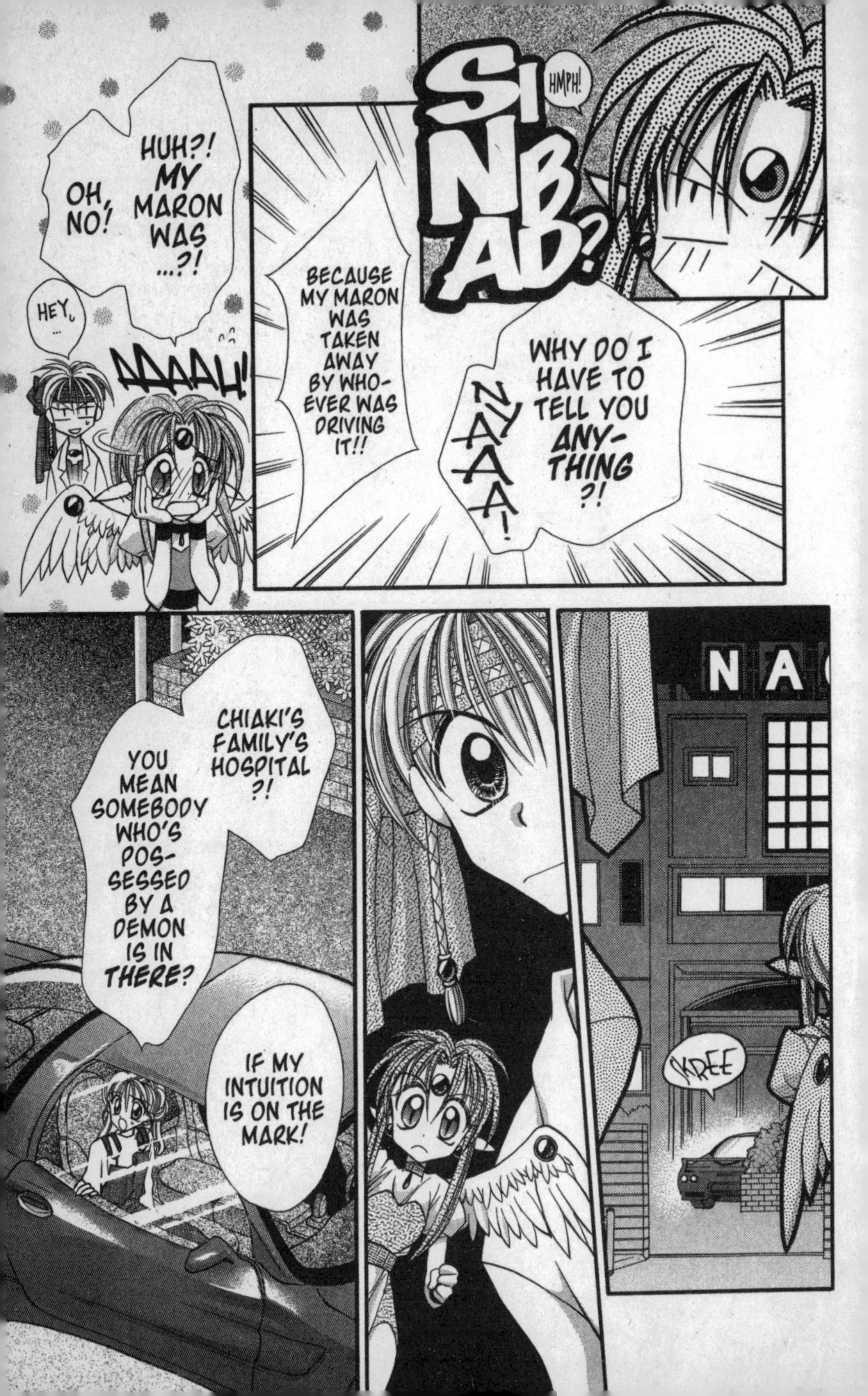
SINBAD?
HMPH!
WHY DO I HAVE TO TELL YOU ANYTHING ?!
NYAAA!
BECAUSE MY MARON WAS TAKEN AWAY BY WHO-EVER WAS DRIVING IT!!
HUH?! MY MARON WAS ...?!
OH, NO!
HEY, ...
AAAAH!
NA
SKREE
CHIAKI'S FAMILY'S HOSPITAL ?!
YOU MEAN SOMEBODY WHO'S POS-SESSED BY A DEMON IS IN THERE?
IF MY INTUITION IS ON THE MARK!

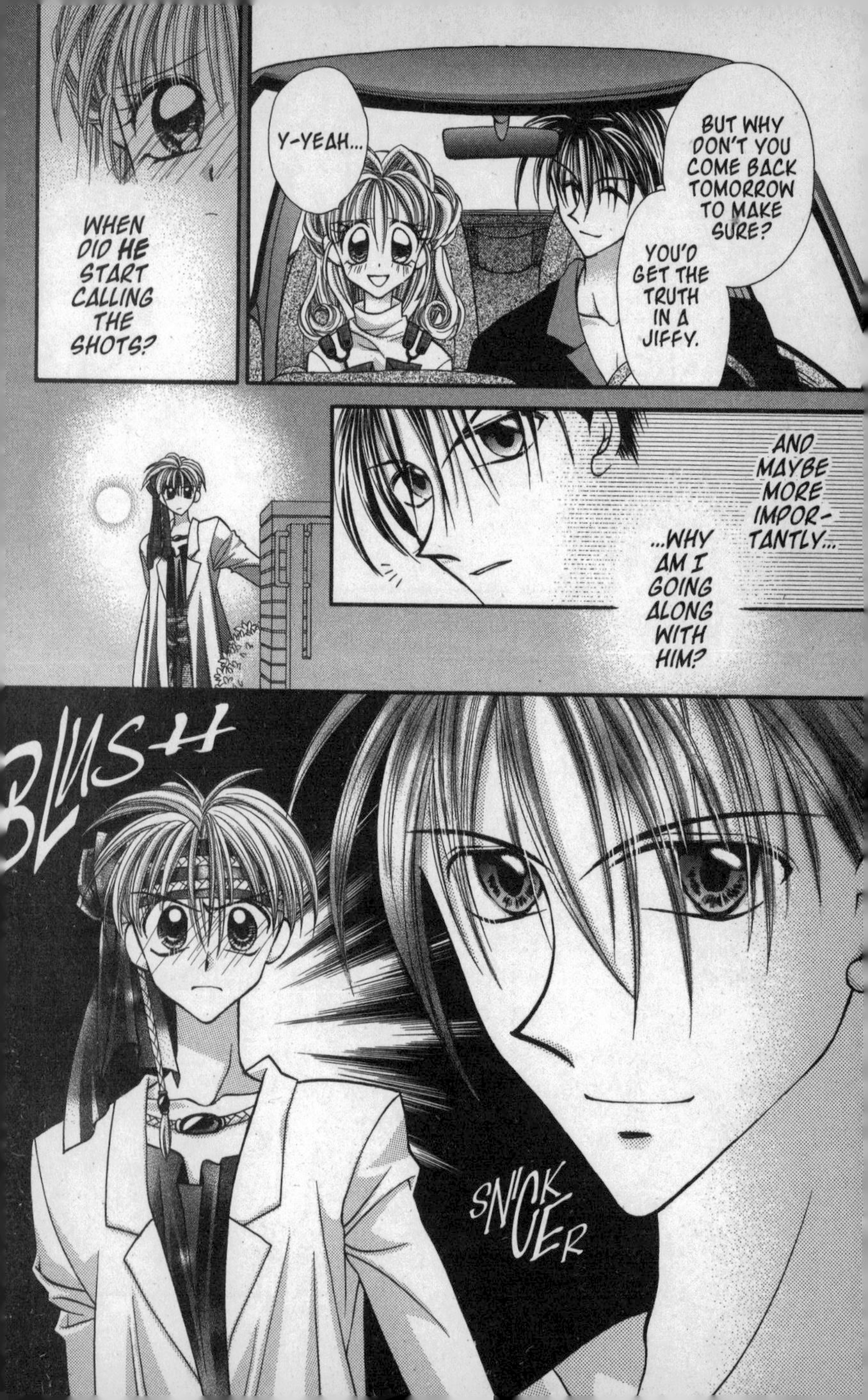
BUT WHY DON'T YOU COME BACK TOMORROW TO MAKE SURE?
YOU'D GET THE TRUTH IN A JIFFY.
Y-YEAH...
WHEN DID HE START CALLING THE SHOTS?
AND MAYBE MORE IMPOR-TANTLY...
...WHY AM I GOING ALONG WITH HIM?
BLUSH
SNICKER

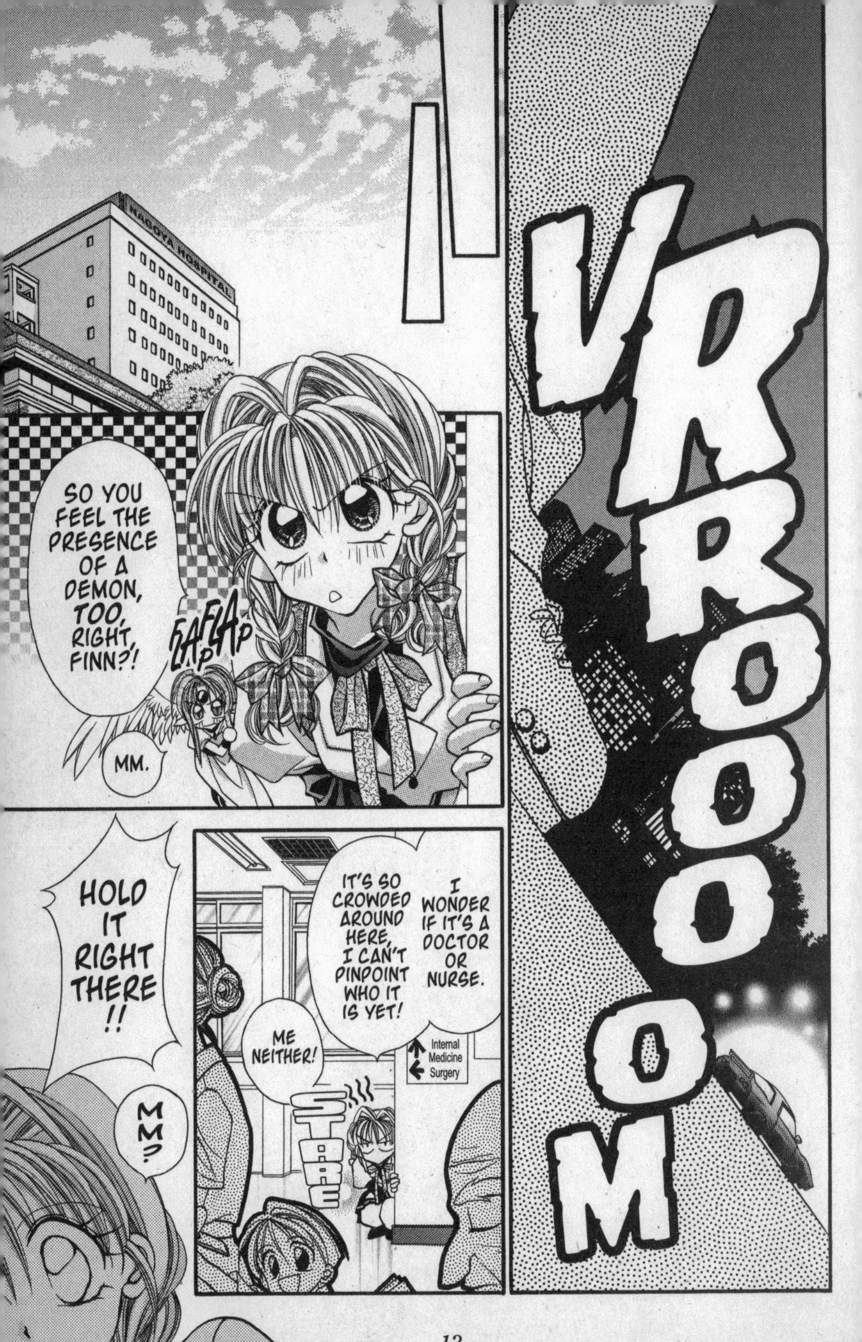
VROOOOM
NAGOYA HOSPITAL
SO YOU FEEL THE PRESENCE OF A DEMON, TOO, RIGHT, FINN?!
FLAP FLAP
MM.
I WONDER IF IT'S A DOCTOR OR NURSE.
IT'S SO CROWDED AROUND HERE, I CAN'T PINPOINT WHO IT IS YET!
ME NEITHER!
Internal Medicine
Surgery
STARE
HOLD IT RIGHT THERE!!
MM?

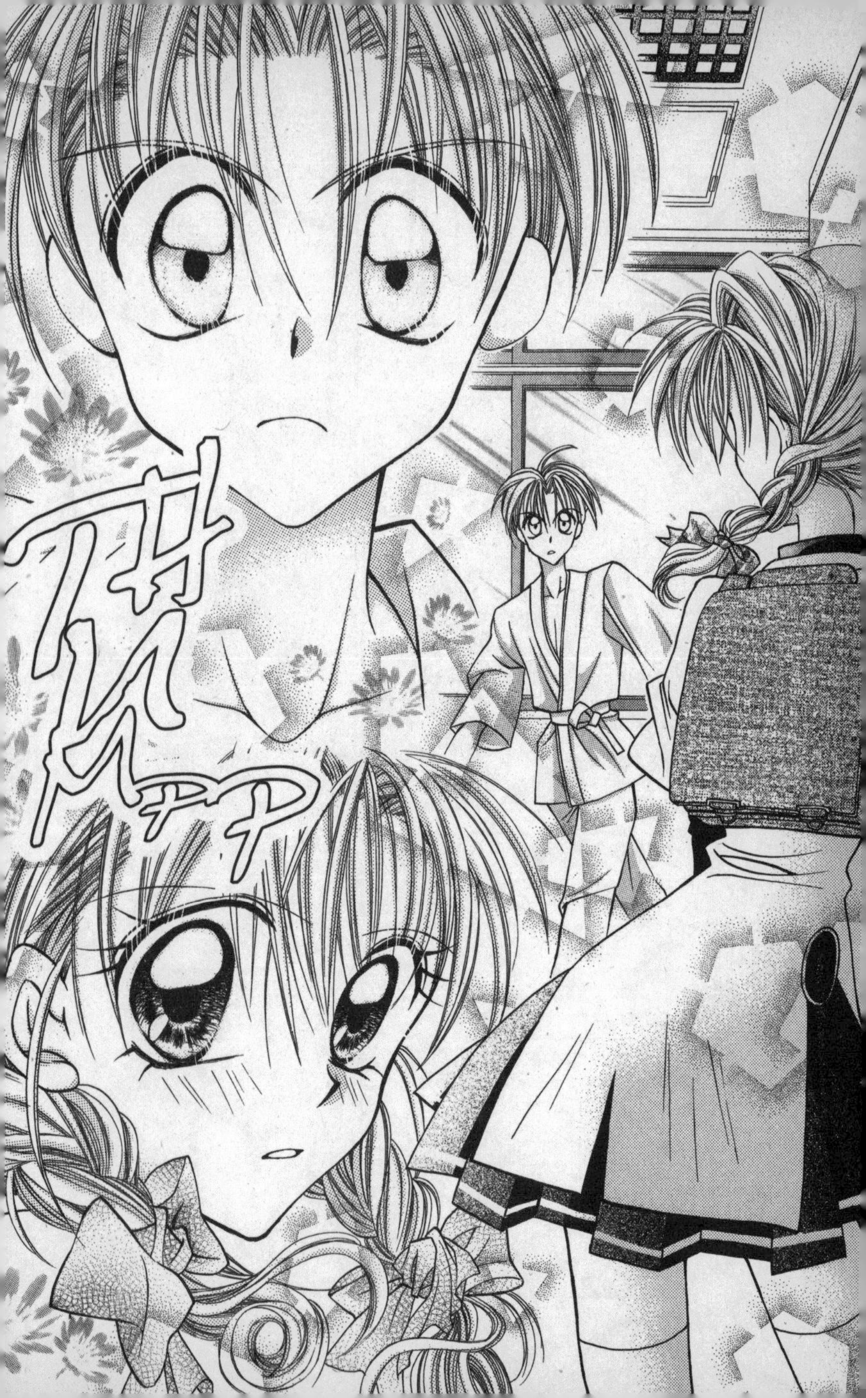

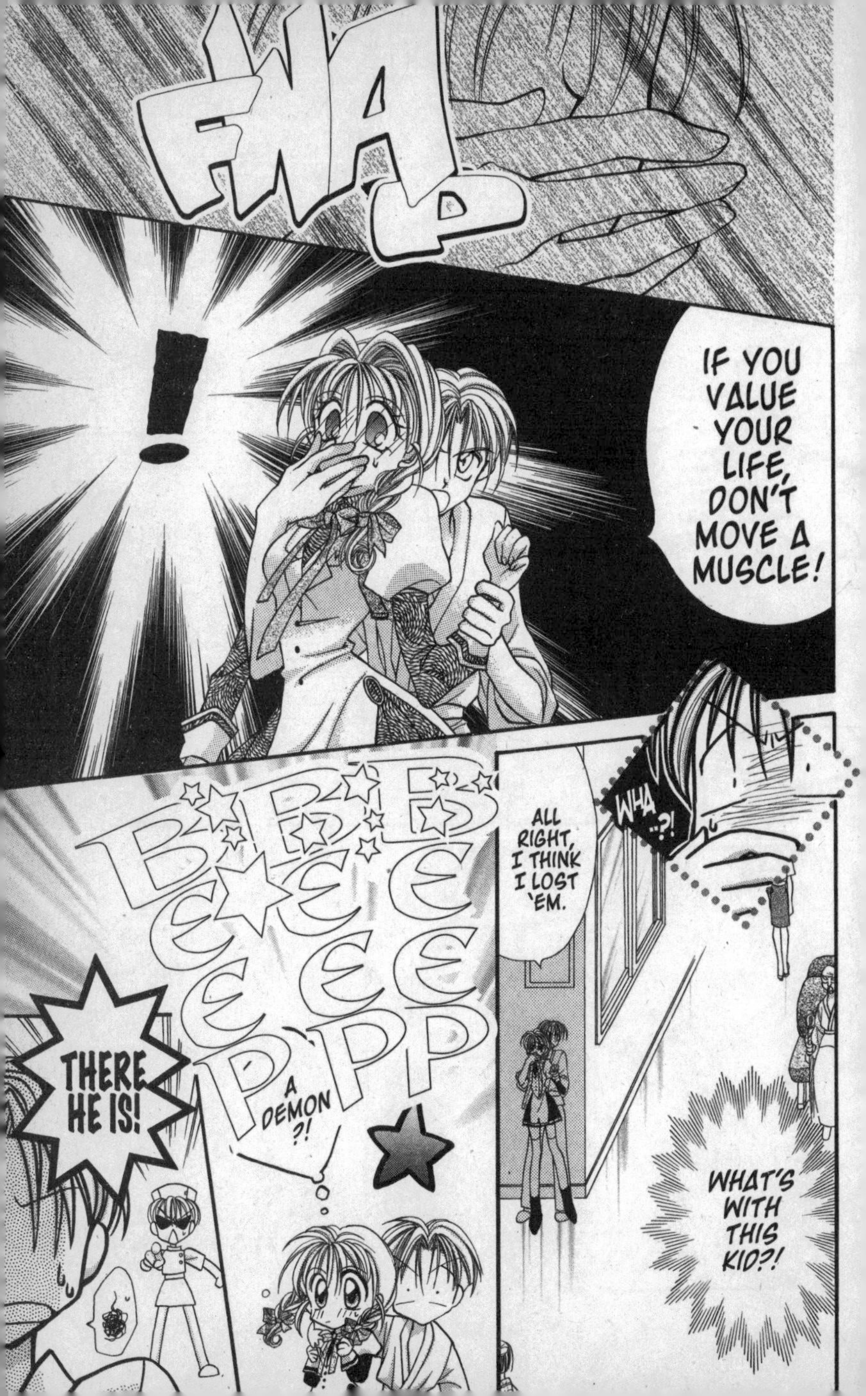
FWAP
IF YOU VALUE YOUR LIFE, DON'T MOVE A MUSCLE!
!
WHA...?!
ALL RIGHT, I THINK I LOST 'EM.
WHAT'S WITH THIS KID?!
BEEEP BEEEP BEEEP
A DEMON?!
THERE HE IS!

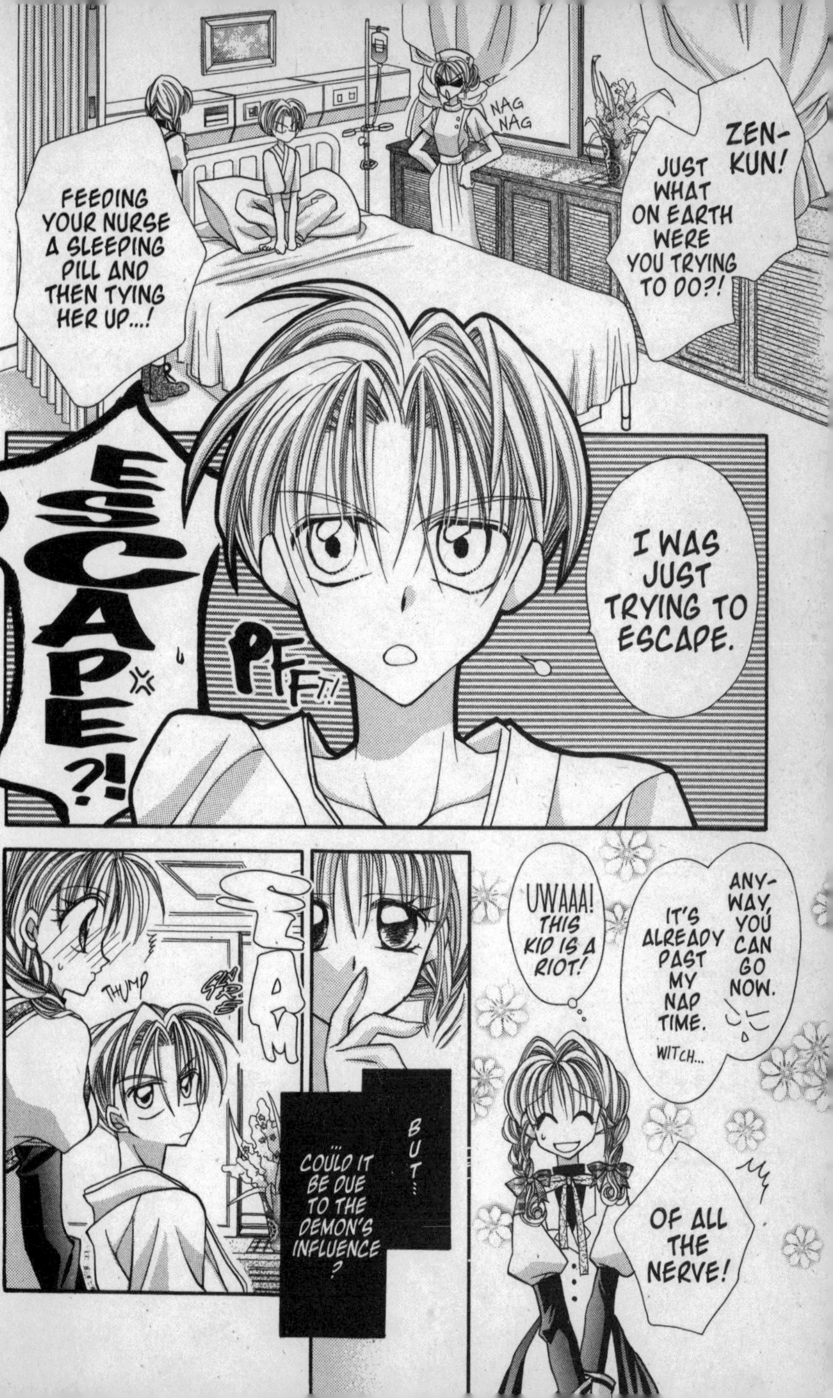
ZEN-KUN! JUST WHAT ON EARTH WERE YOU TRYING TO DO?!
NAG NAG
FEEDING YOUR NURSE A SLEEPING PILL AND THEN TYING HER UP...!
I WAS JUST TRYING TO ESCAPE.
PFFT!
ESCAPE?!
ANYWAY, YOU CAN GO NOW.
IT'S ALREADY PAST MY NAP TIME.
WITCH...
UWAAA! THIS KID IS A RIOT!
OF ALL THE NERVE!
BUT...
...COULD IT BE DUE TO THE DEMON'S INFLUENCE?
SLAM
THUMP

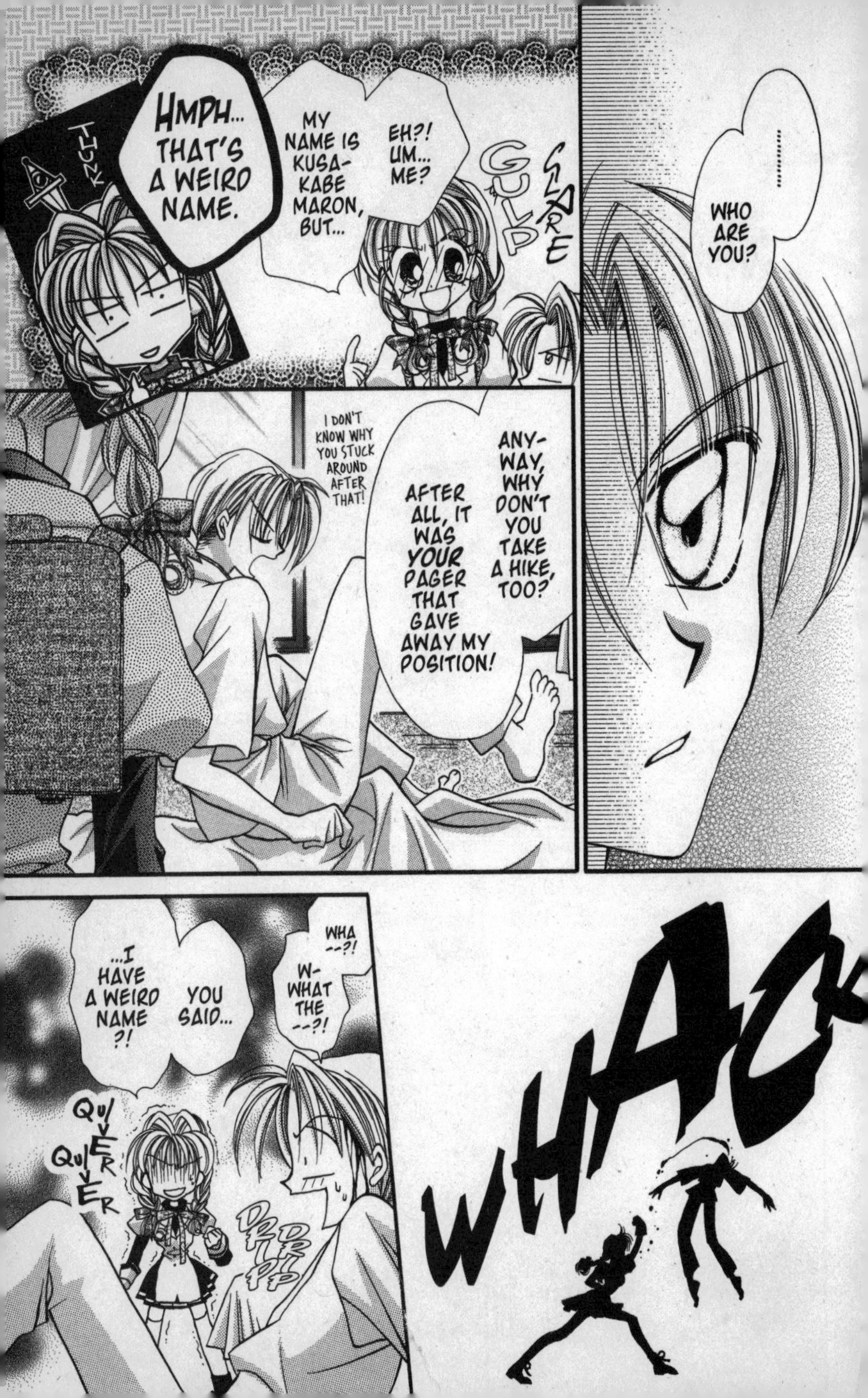
....
WHO ARE YOU?
EH?! UM... ME?
MY NAME IS KUSAKABE MARON, BUT...
GLARE
GULP
HMPH... THAT'S A WEIRD NAME.
THUNK
ANY-WAY, WHY DON'T YOU TAKE A HIKE, TOO?
AFTER ALL, IT WAS YOUR PAGER THAT GAVE AWAY MY POSITION!
I DON'T KNOW WHY YOU STUCK AROUND AFTER THAT!
WHAC
WHA--?!
W-WHAT THE--?!
YOU SAID...
...I HAVE A WEIRD NAME?!
QUIVER QUIVER
DRIP DRIP

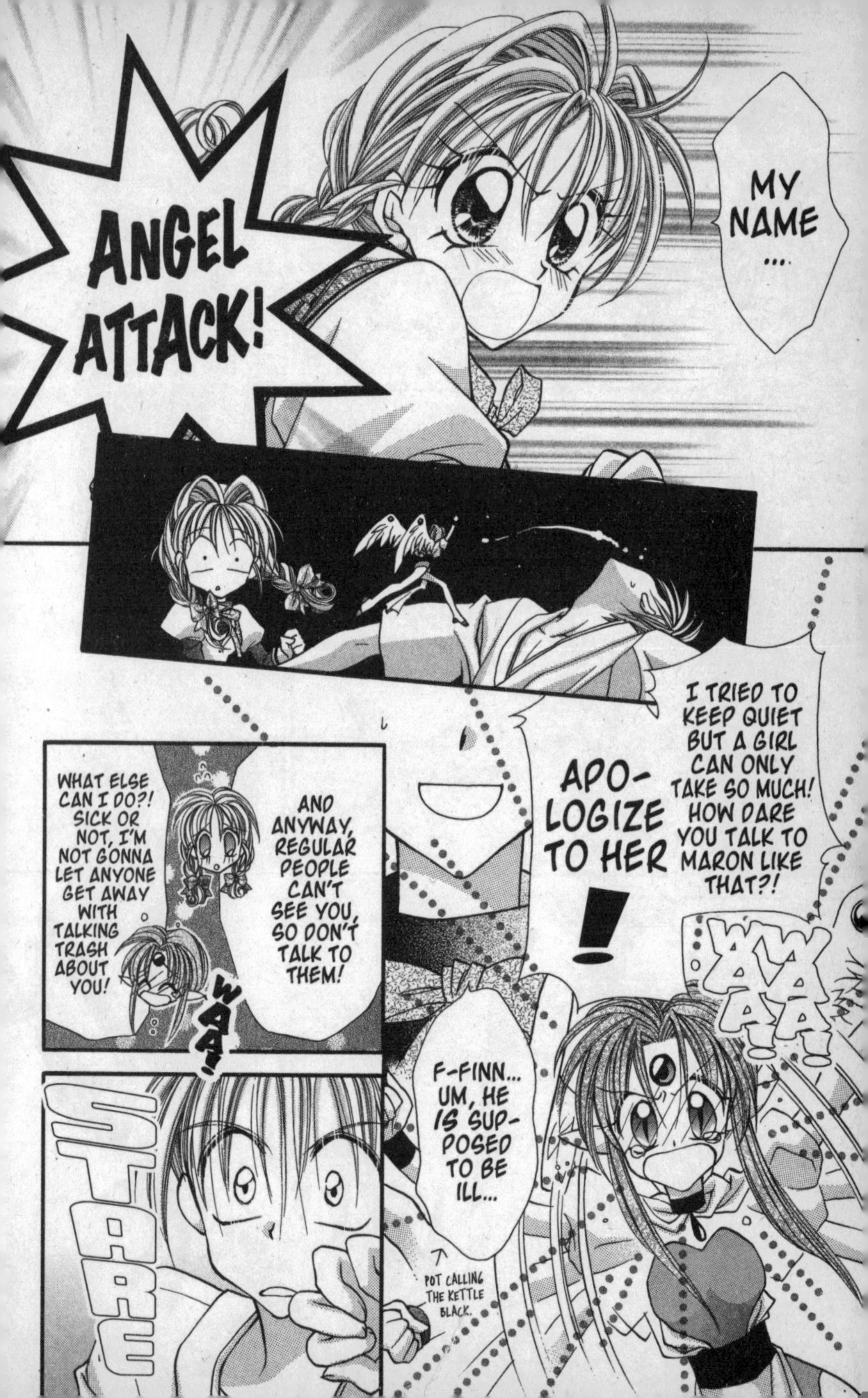
MY NAME ....
ANGEL ATTACK!
I TRIED TO KEEP QUIET BUT A GIRL CAN ONLY TAKE SO MUCH! HOW DARE YOU TALK TO MARON LIKE THAT?!
APO-LOGIZE TO HER!
WAAAA!
F-FINN... UM, HE IS SUP-POSED TO BE ILL...
POT CALLING THE KETTLE BLACK.
AND ANYWAY, REGULAR PEOPLE CAN'T SEE YOU, SO DON'T TALK TO THEM!
WHAT ELSE CAN I DO?! SICK OR NOT, I'M NOT GONNA LET ANYONE GET AWAY WITH TALKING TRASH ABOUT YOU!
WAA!
STARE

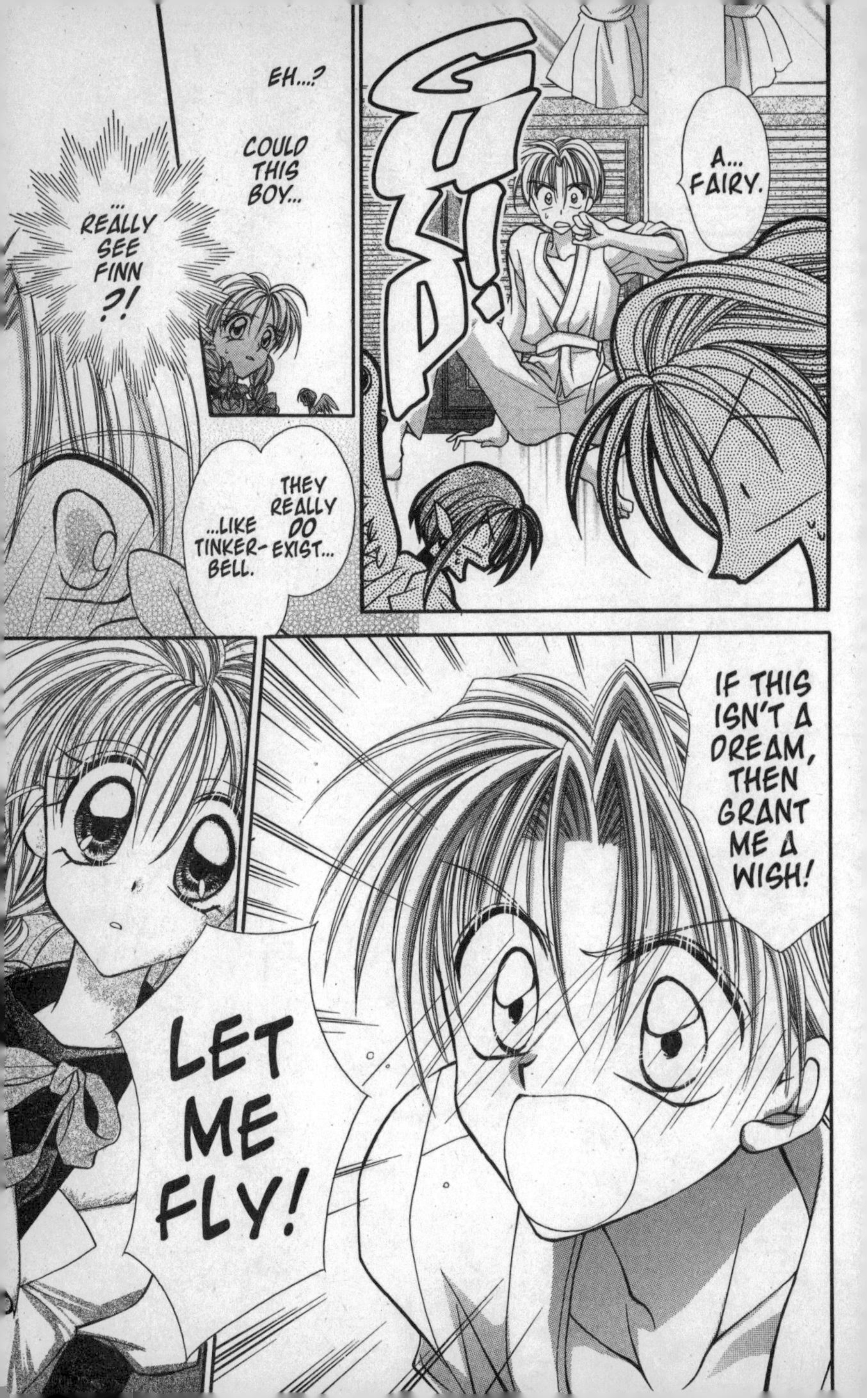

GASP!
A... FAIRY.
THEY REALLY DO EXIST...
...LIKE TINKER-BELL.
EH...?
COULD THIS BOY...
...REALLY SEE FINN?!
IF THIS ISN'T A DREAM, THEN GRANT ME A WISH!
LET ME FLY!

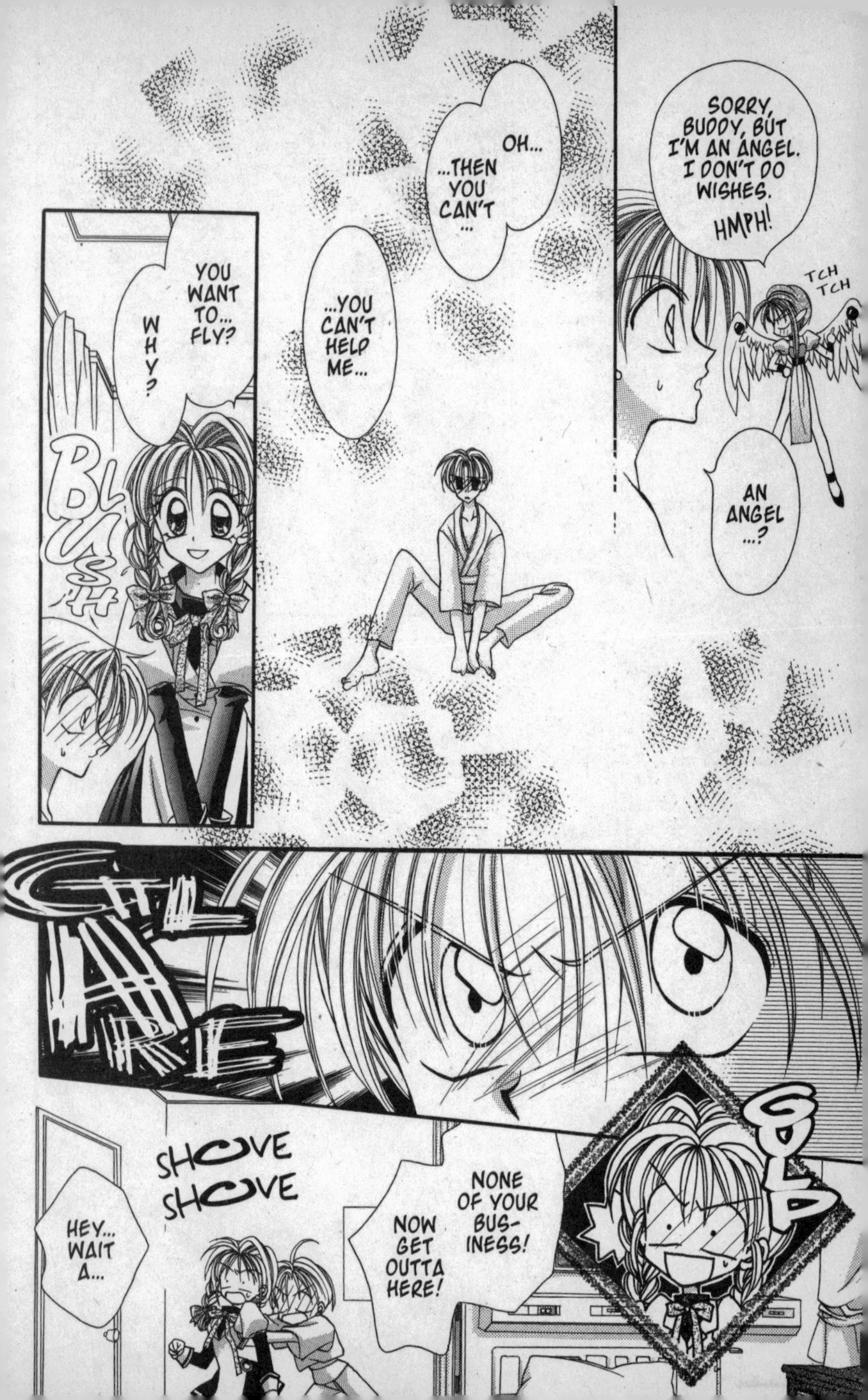
SORRY, BUDDY, BUT I'M AN ANGEL. I DON'T DO WISHES.
HMPH!
TCH TCH
AN ANGEL ...?
OH...
...THEN YOU CAN'T ...
...YOU CAN'T HELP ME...
YOU WANT TO... FLY?
WHY?
BLUSH
GLARE
GULP
NONE OF YOUR BUSINESS!
NOW GET OUTTA HERE!
SHOVE SHOVE
HEY... WAIT A...

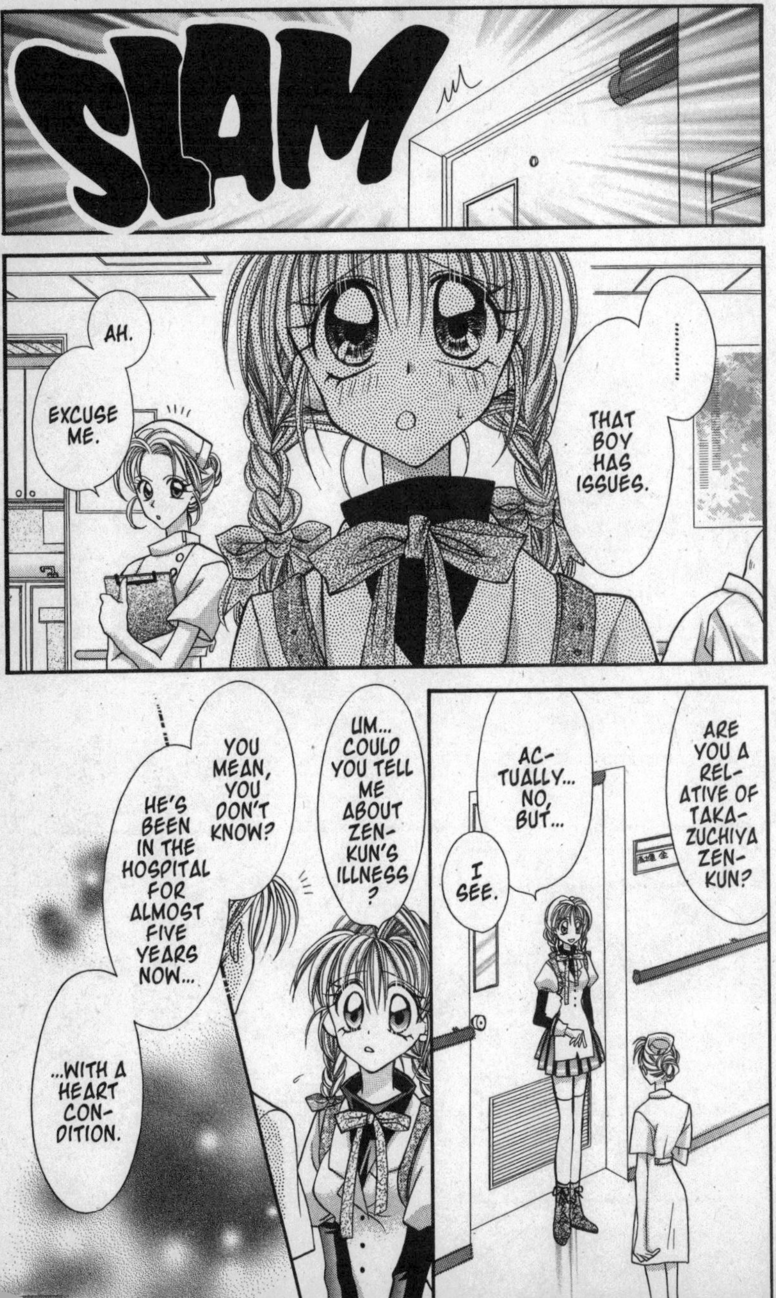
SLAM
......
THAT BOY HAS ISSUES.
AH.
EXCUSE ME.
ARE YOU A RELATIVE OF TAKAZUCHIYA ZEN-KUN?
ACTUALLY... NO, BUT...
I SEE.
UM... COULD YOU TELL ME ABOUT ZEN-KUN'S ILLNESS?
YOU MEAN, YOU DON'T KNOW?
HE'S BEEN IN THE HOSPITAL FOR ALMOST FIVE YEARS NOW...
...WITH A HEART CONDITION.

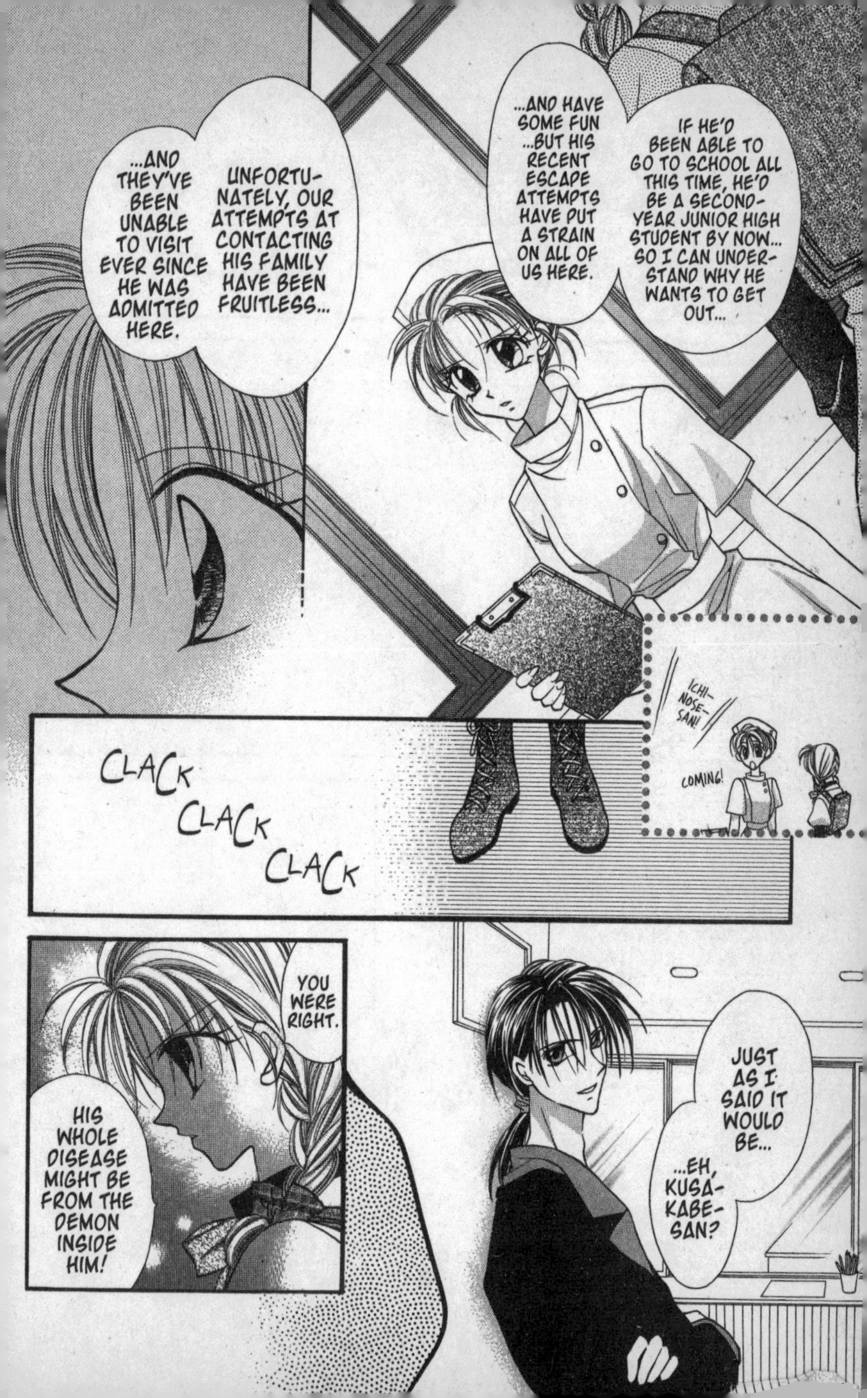
IF HE'D BEEN ABLE TO GO TO SCHOOL ALL THIS TIME, HE'D BE A SECOND-YEAR JUNIOR HIGH STUDENT BY NOW... SO I CAN UNDERSTAND WHY HE WANTS TO GET OUT...
...AND HAVE SOME FUN ...BUT HIS RECENT ESCAPE ATTEMPTS HAVE PUT A STRAIN ON ALL OF US HERE.
UNFORTUNATELY, OUR ATTEMPTS AT CONTACTING HIS FAMILY HAVE BEEN FRUITLESS...
...AND THEY'VE BEEN UNABLE TO VISIT EVER SINCE HE WAS ADMITTED HERE.
ICHINOSE-SAN!
COMING!
CLACK CLACK CLACK
JUST AS I SAID IT WOULD BE...
...EH, KUSAKABE-SAN?
YOU WERE RIGHT.
HIS WHOLE DISEASE MIGHT BE FROM THE DEMON INSIDE HIM!

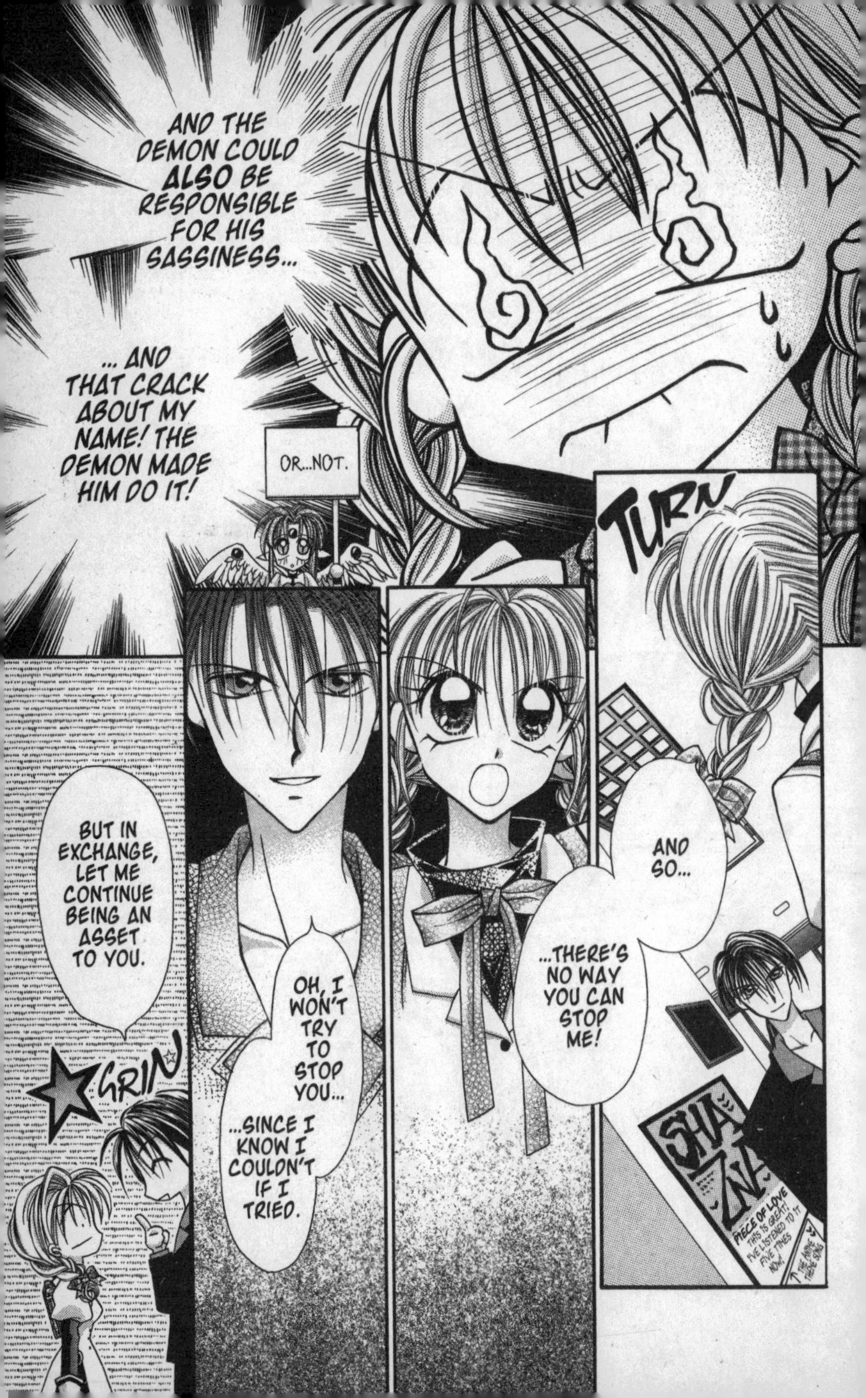
AND THE DEMON COULD ALSO BE RESPONSIBLE FOR HIS SASSINESS...
... AND THAT CRACK ABOUT MY NAME! THE DEMON MADE HIM DO IT!
OR...NOT.
TURN
AND SO...
...THERE'S NO WAY YOU CAN STOP ME!
PIECE OF LOVE
THIS IS GREAT! I'VE LISTENED TO IT FIVE TIMES NOW!
THE ANIME THEME SONG
OH, I WON'T TRY TO STOP YOU...
...SINCE I KNOW I COULDN'T IF I TRIED.
BUT IN EXCHANGE, LET ME CONTINUE BEING AN ASSET TO YOU.
GRIN

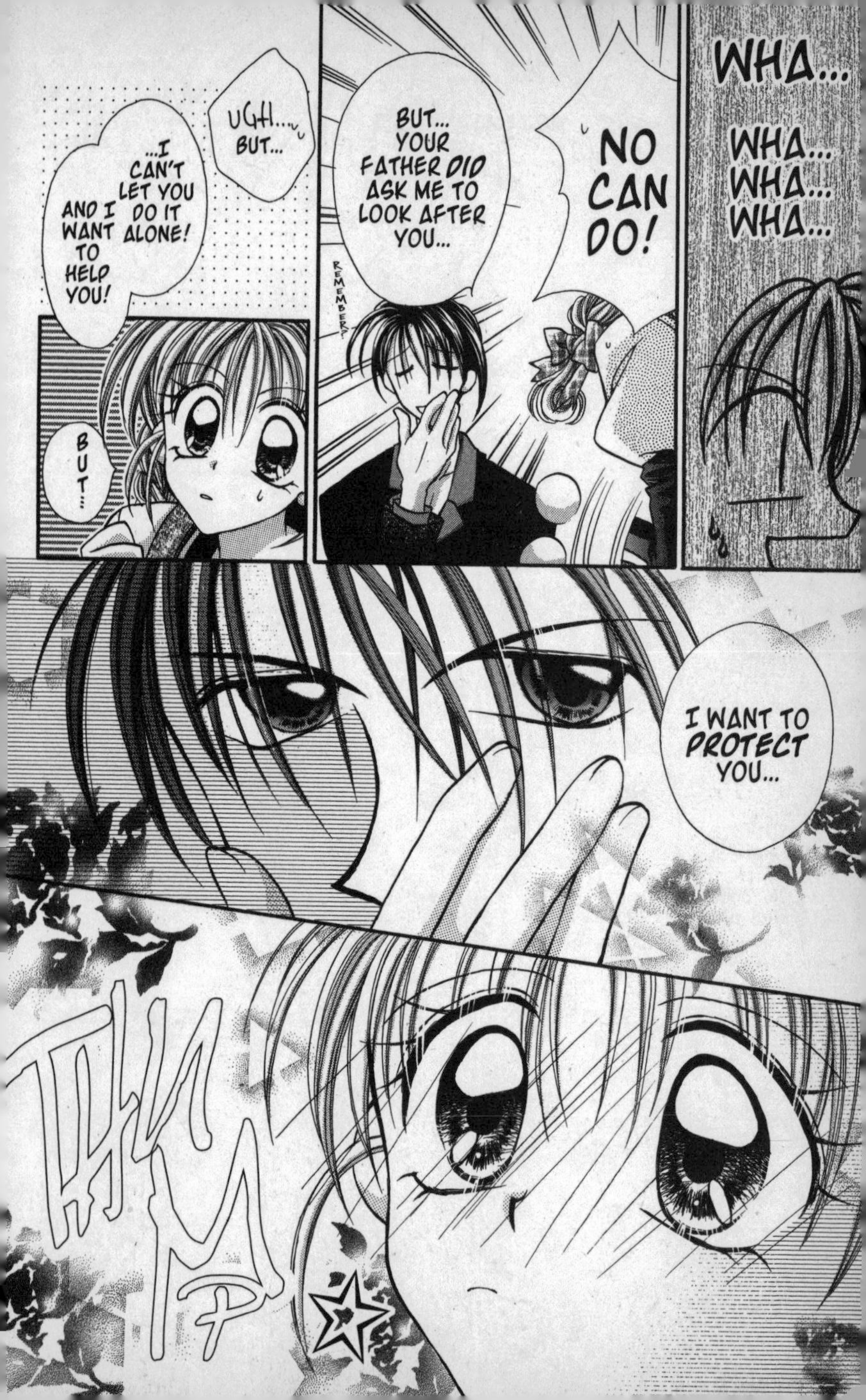
WHA...
WHA... WHA... WHA...
NO CAN DO!
BUT... YOUR FATHER DID ASK ME TO LOOK AFTER YOU...
REMEMBER?
UGH... BUT...
...I CAN'T LET YOU DO IT ALONE!
AND I WANT TO HELP YOU!
BUT...
I WANT TO PROTECT YOU...
THUMP

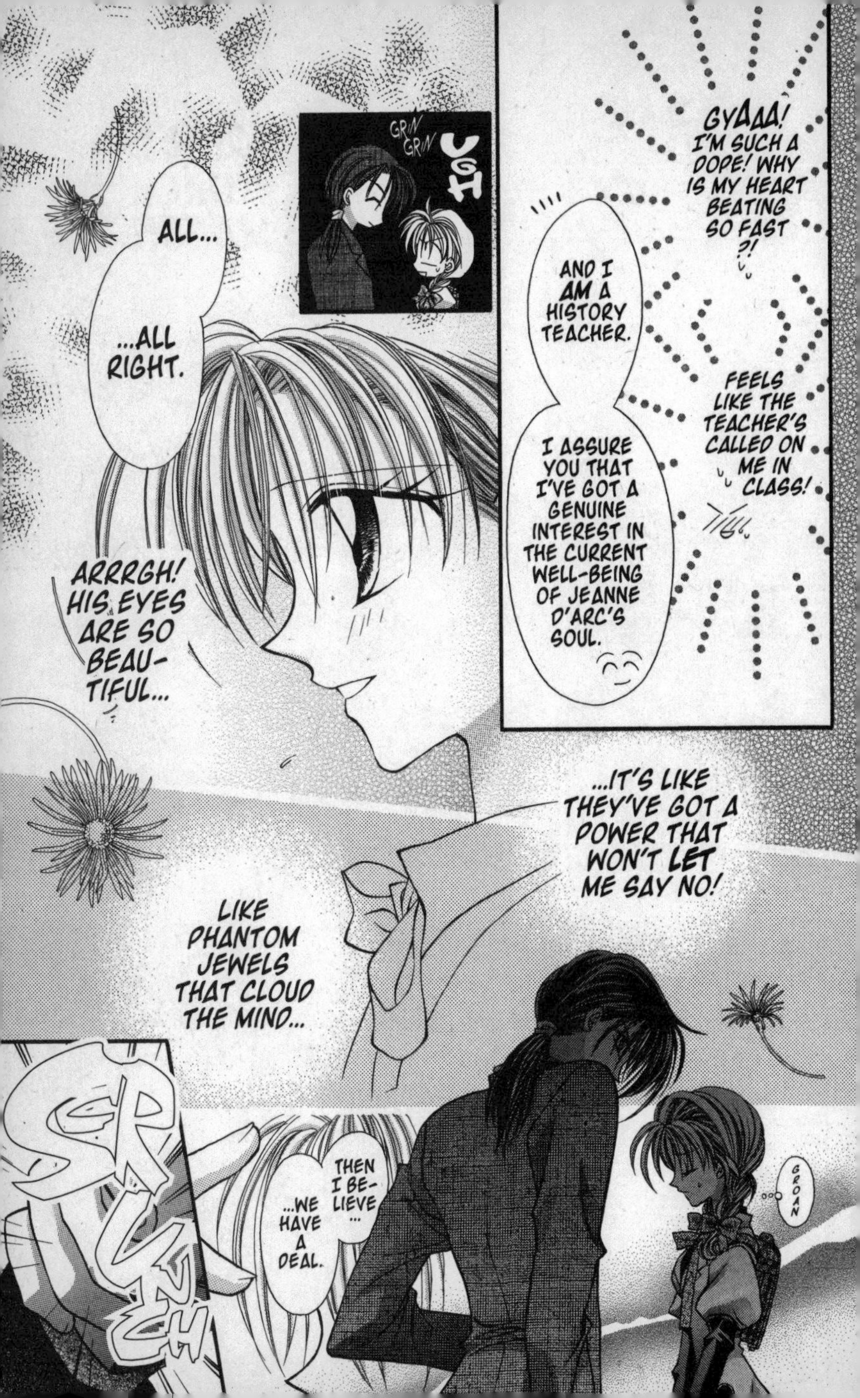
AND I AM A HISTORY TEACHER.
I ASSURE YOU THAT I'VE GOT A GENUINE INTEREST IN THE CURRENT WELL-BEING OF JEANNE D'ARC'S SOUL.
GYAAA! I'M SUCH A DOPE! WHY IS MY HEART BEATING SO FAST ?!
FEELS LIKE THE TEACHER'S CALLED ON ME IN CLASS!
GRIN GRIN
UGH
ALL...
...ALL RIGHT.
ARRRGH! HIS EYES ARE SO BEAU-TIFUL...
...IT'S LIKE THEY'VE GOT A POWER THAT WON'T LET ME SAY NO!
LIKE PHANTOM JEWELS THAT CLOUD THE MIND...
THEN I BE-LIEVE...
...WE HAVE A DEAL.
GROAN
SCRUNCH

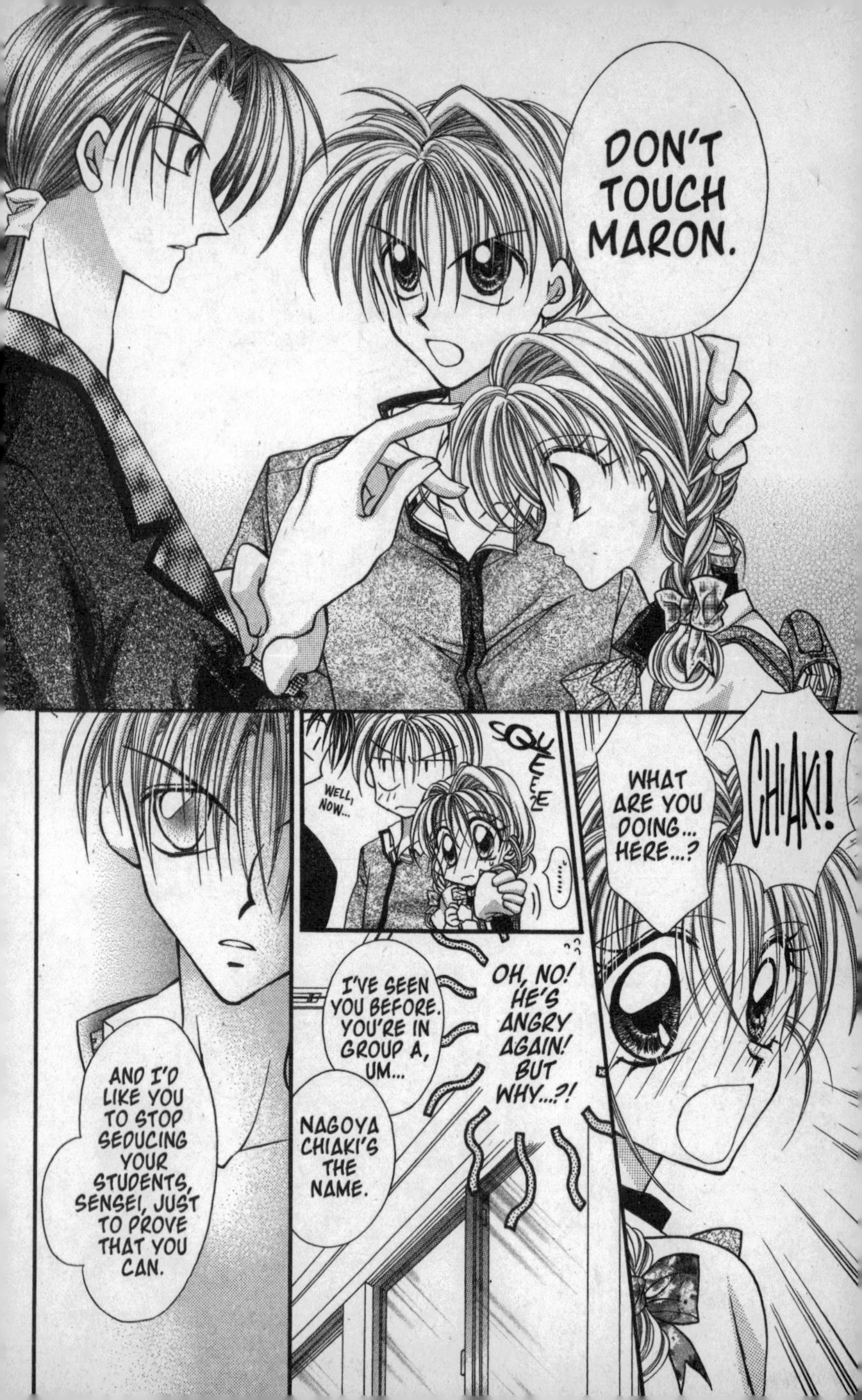
DON'T TOUCH MARON.
CHIAKI!
WHAT ARE YOU DOING... HERE...?
SQUEEZE
WELL, NOW...
......
OH, NO! HE'S ANGRY AGAIN! BUT WHY...?!
I'VE SEEN YOU BEFORE. YOU'RE IN GROUP A, UM...
NAGOYA CHIAKI'S THE NAME.
AND I'D LIKE YOU TO STOP SEDUCING YOUR STUDENTS, SENSEI, JUST TO PROVE THAT YOU CAN.

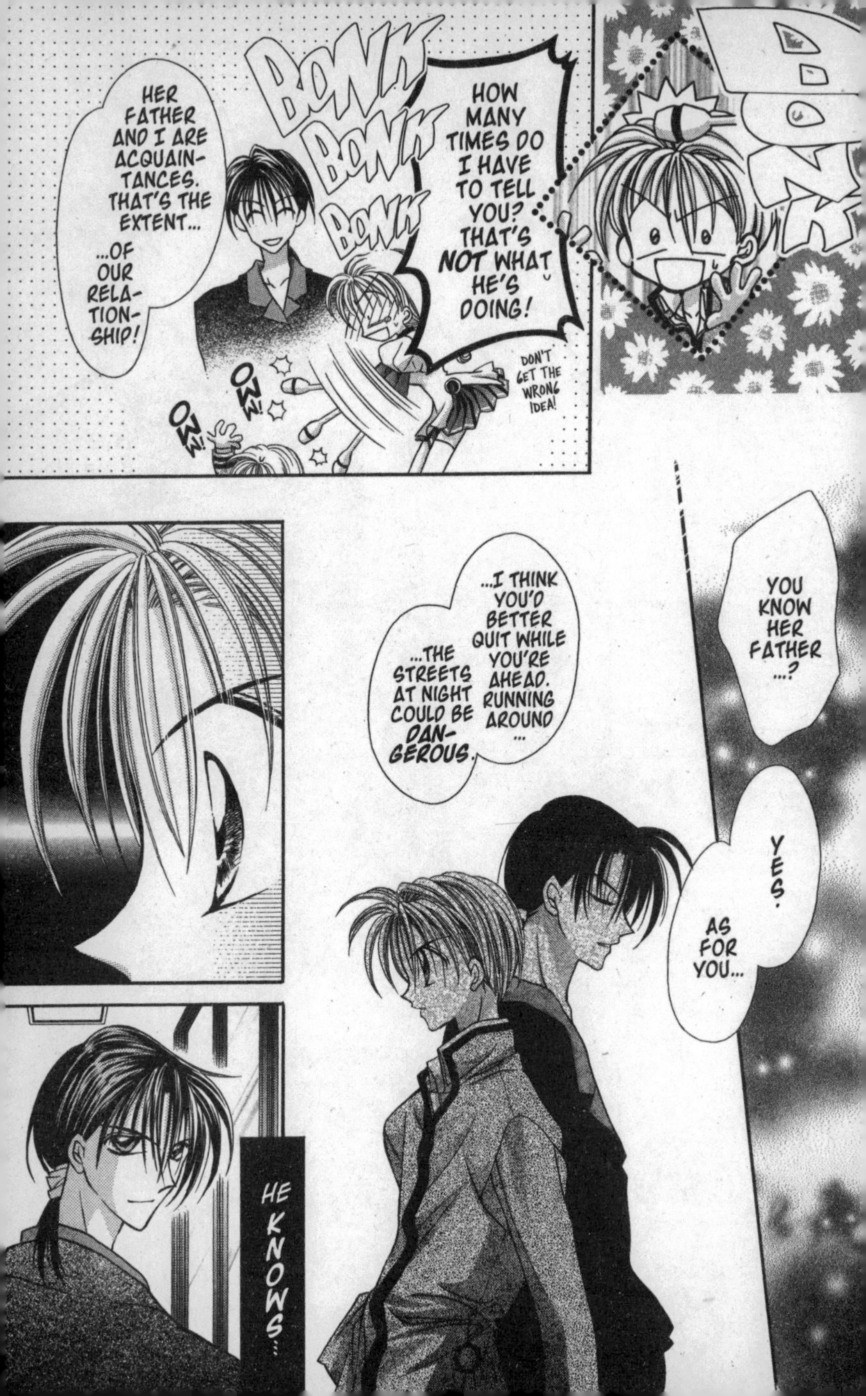
BONK
HOW MANY TIMES DO I HAVE TO TELL YOU? THAT'S **NOT** WHAT HE'S DOING!
BONK BONK BONK
HER FATHER AND I ARE ACQUAINTANCES. THAT'S THE EXTENT...
...OF OUR RELATIONSHIP!
DON'T GET THE WRONG IDEA!
OWW! OWW!
YOU KNOW HER FATHER ...?
YES.
AS FOR YOU...
...I THINK YOU'D BETTER QUIT WHILE YOU'RE AHEAD. RUNNING AROUND ...
...THE STREETS AT NIGHT COULD BE **DANGEROUS**.
HE KNOWS...

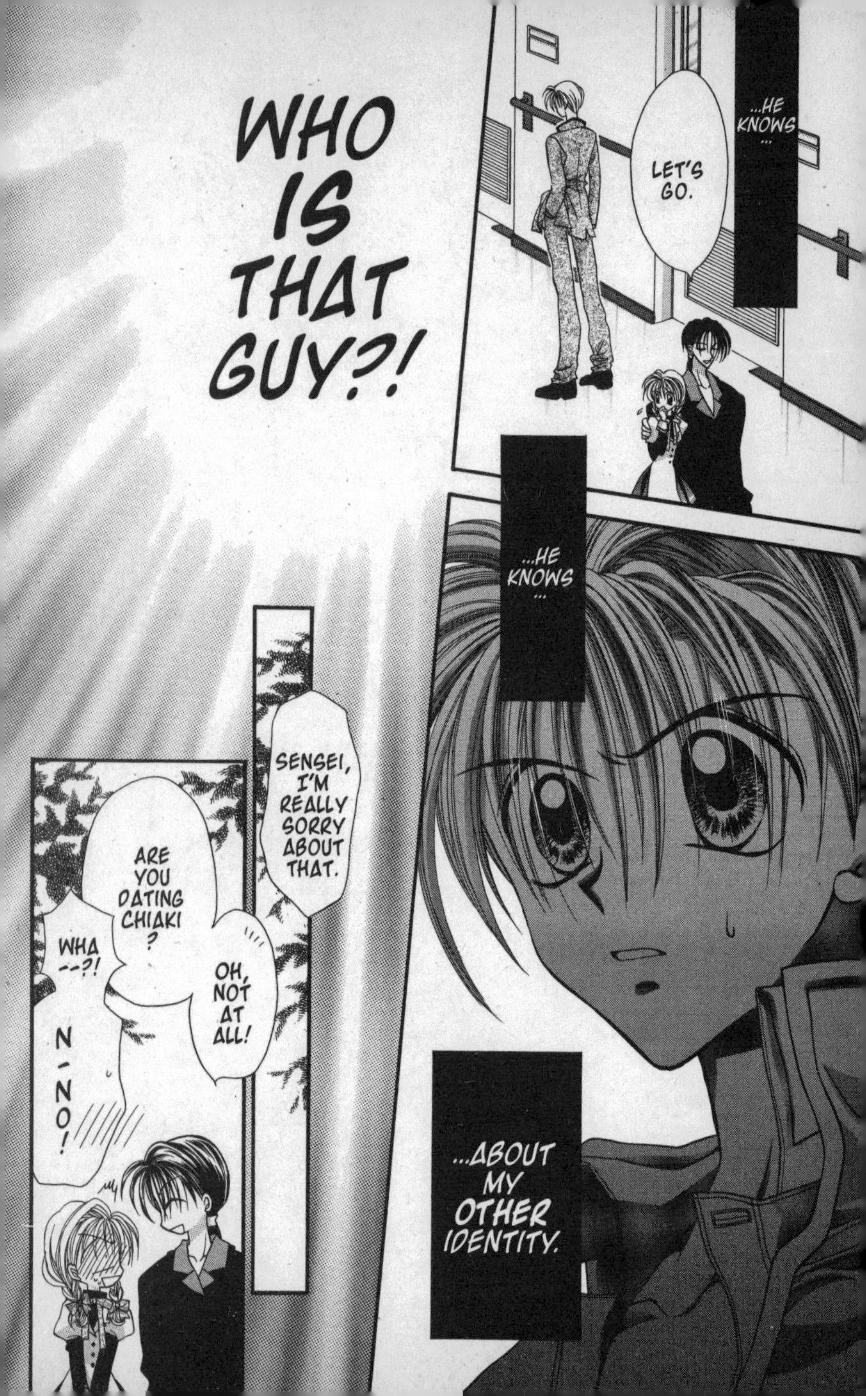
...HE KNOWS...
LET'S GO.
...HE KNOWS...
...ABOUT MY OTHER IDENTITY.
WHO IS THAT GUY?!
SENSEI, I'M REALLY SORRY ABOUT THAT.
OH, NOT AT ALL!
ARE YOU DATING CHIAKI?
WHA--?!
N-NO!

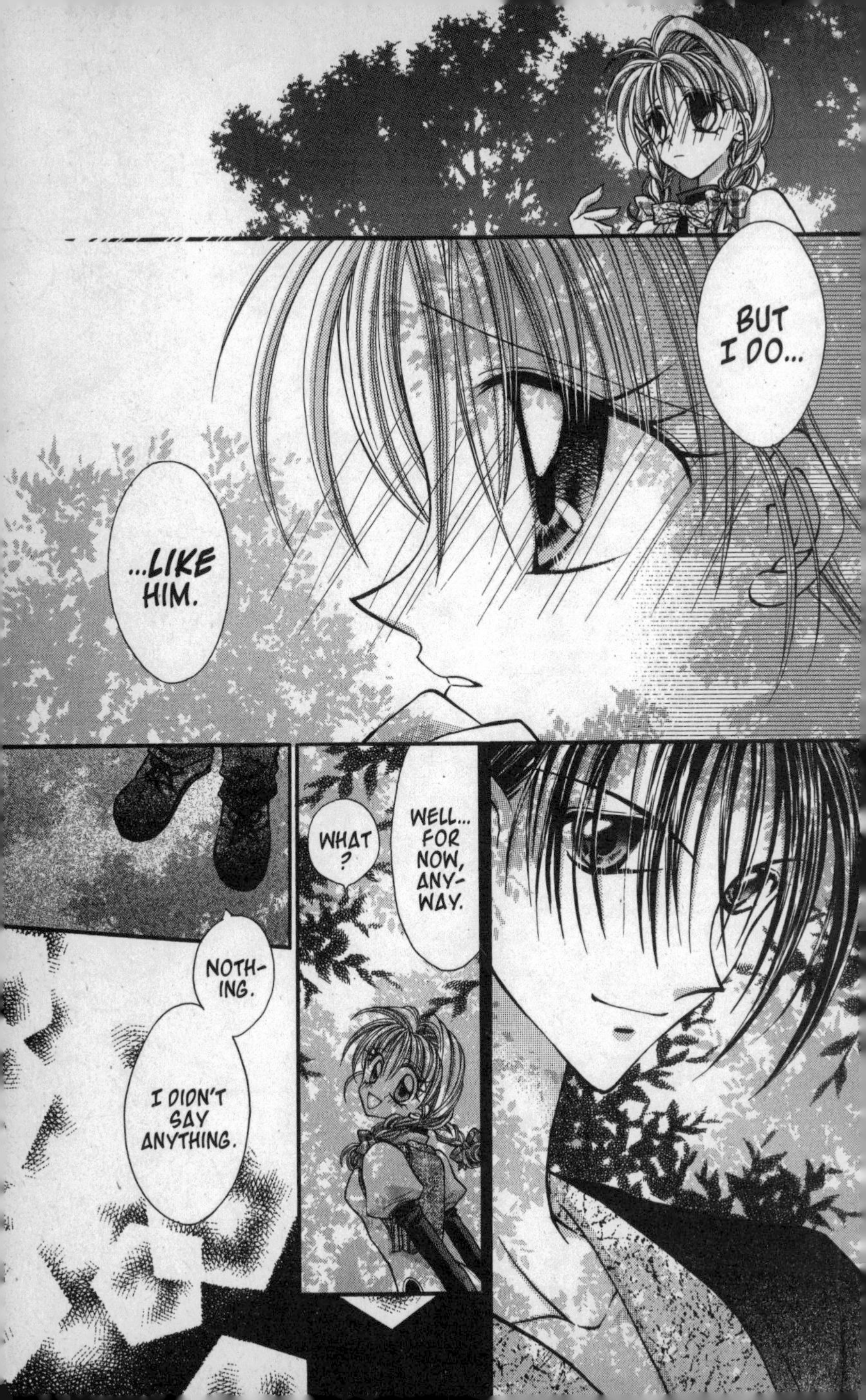
BUT I DO...
...LIKE HIM.
WELL... FOR NOW, ANY-WAY.
WHAT?
NOTH-ING.
I DIDN'T SAY ANYTHING.

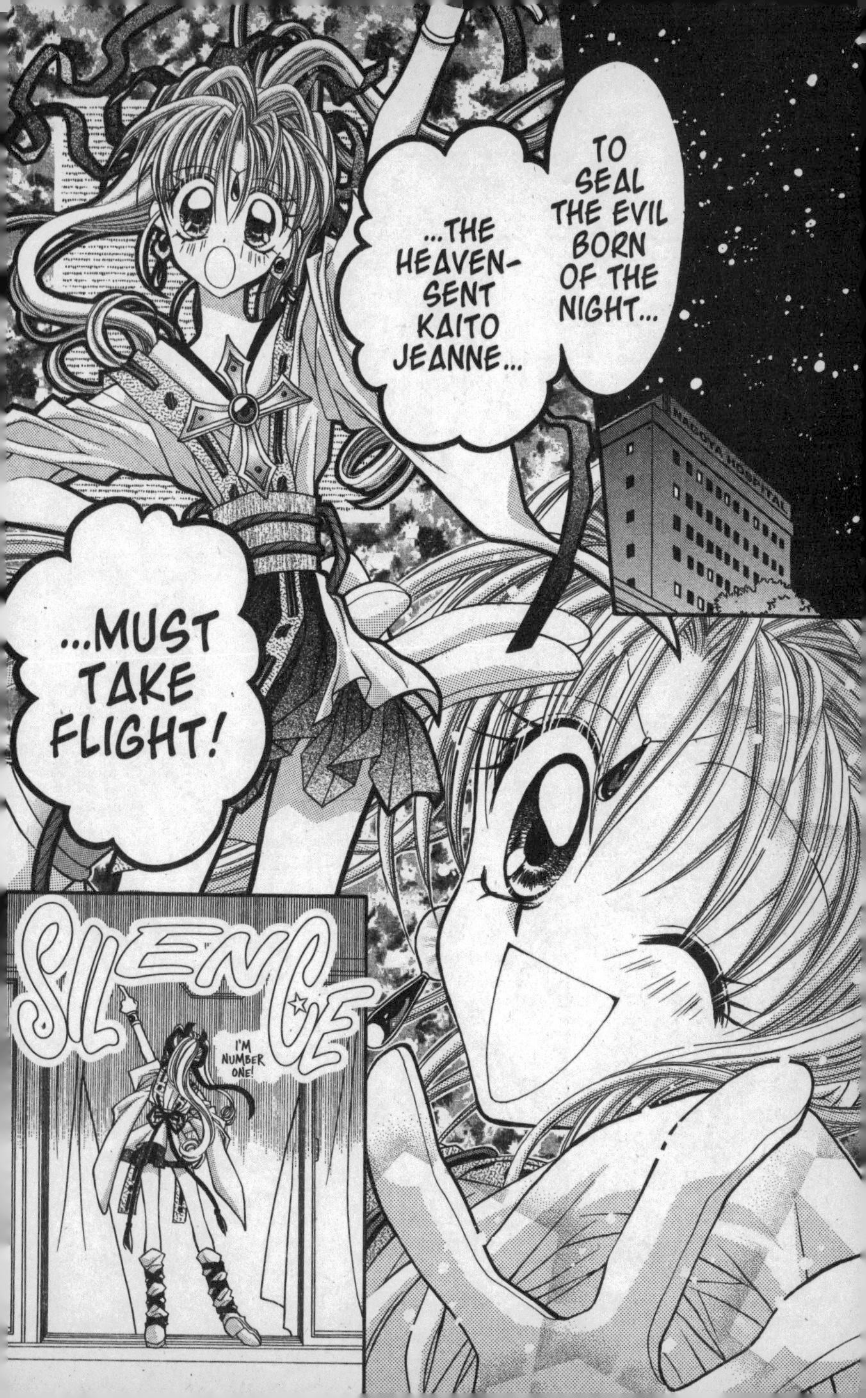
TO SEAL THE EVIL BORN OF THE NIGHT...
...THE HEAVEN-SENT KAITO JEANNE...
NAGOYA HOSPITAL
...MUST TAKE FLIGHT!
SILENCE
I'M NUMBER ONE!

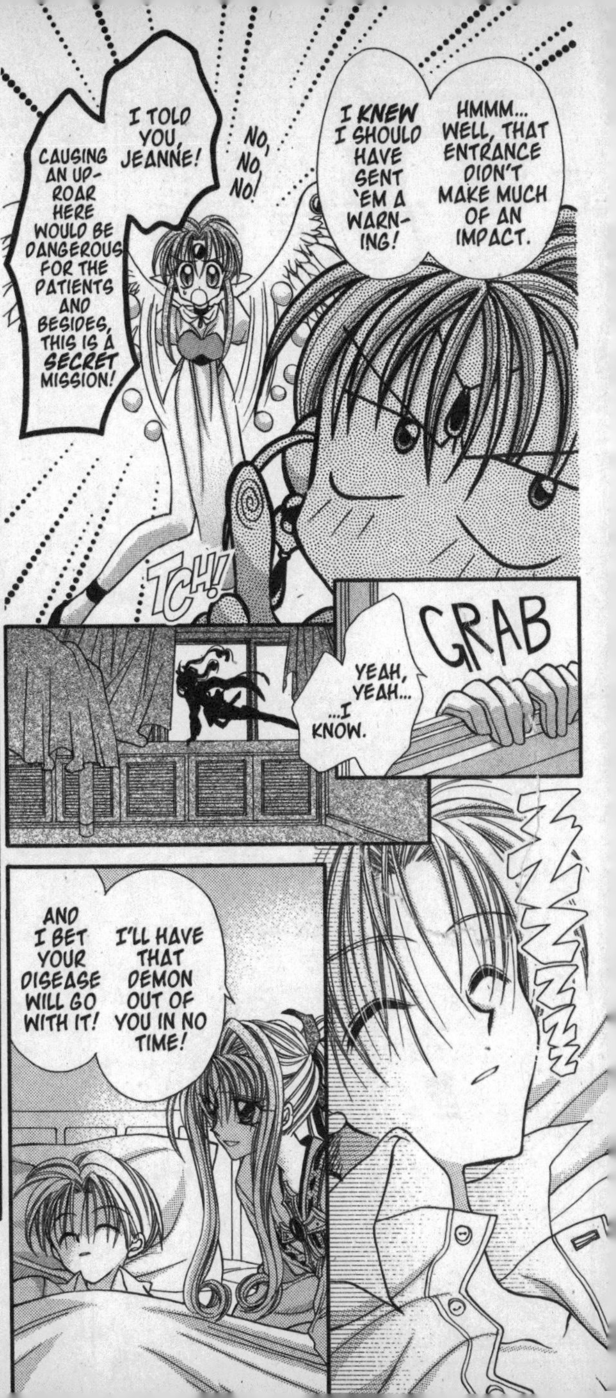
HMMM... WELL, THAT ENTRANCE DIDN'T MAKE MUCH OF AN IMPACT.
I KNEW I SHOULD HAVE SENT 'EM A WARNING!
NO, NO, NO!
I TOLD YOU, JEANNE!
CAUSING AN UP-ROAR HERE WOULD BE DANGEROUS FOR THE PATIENTS AND BESIDES, THIS IS A SECRET MISSION!
TCH!
GRAB
YEAH, YEAH... ...I KNOW.
I'LL HAVE THAT DEMON OUT OF YOU IN NO TIME!
AND I BET YOUR DISEASE WILL GO WITH IT!

ARINA TANEMURA'S "LIKE PULLING TEETH WITH PLIERS" ☆

FALLING IN LOVE WITH LOVE #17.

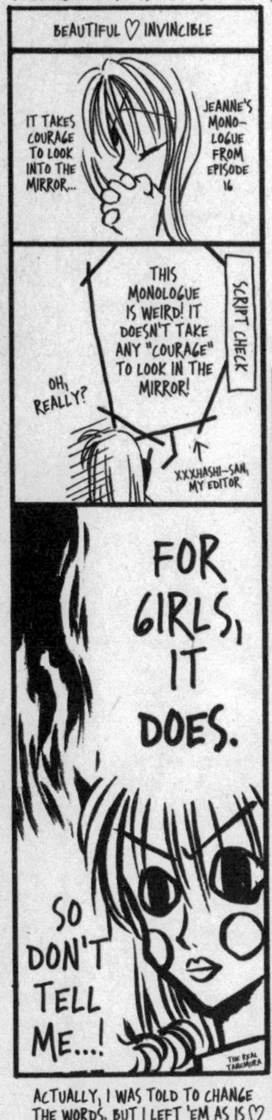
BEAUTIFUL ♡ INVINCIBLE
IT TAKES COURAGE TO LOOK INTO THE MIRROR...
JEANNE'S MONOLOGUE FROM EPISODE 16
SCRIPT CHECK
THIS MONOLOGUE IS WEIRD! IT DOESN'T TAKE ANY "COURAGE" TO LOOK IN THE MIRROR!
OH, REALLY?
XXXHASHI-SAN, MY EDITOR
FOR GIRLS, IT DOES.
SO DON'T TELL ME...!
THE REAL TANEMURA

ACTUALLY, I WAS TOLD TO CHANGE THE WORDS, BUT I LEFT 'EM AS IS ♡ I DO LOOK IN THE MIRROR BUT IT TAKES ME ABOUT TEN SECONDS TO WORK UP THE COURAGE (SINCE I THINK I'M THE UGLIEST GIRL IN THE WORLD)...

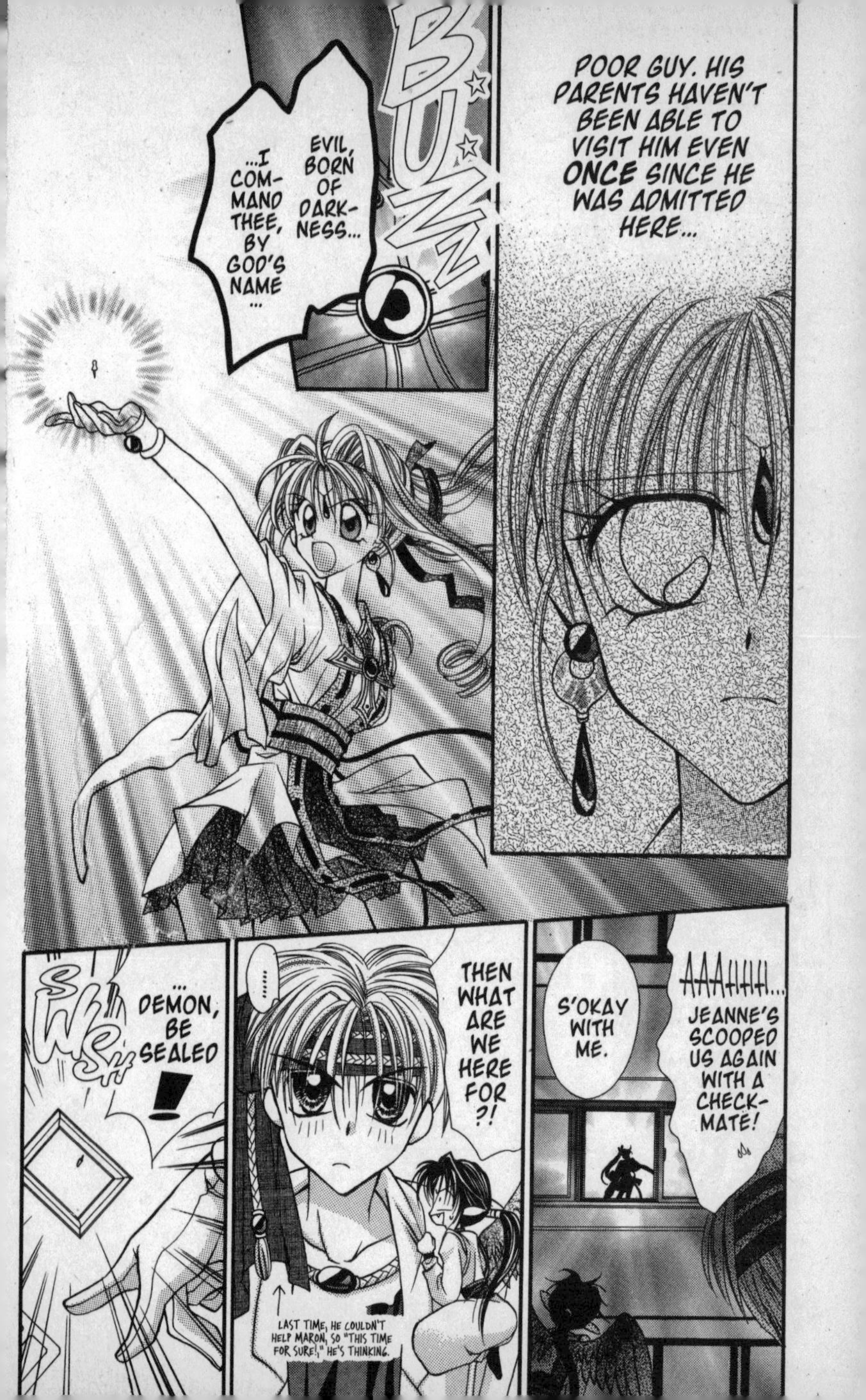
POOR GUY. HIS PARENTS HAVEN'T BEEN ABLE TO VISIT HIM EVEN ONCE SINCE HE WAS ADMITTED HERE...
BUMN
EVIL, BORN OF DARKNESS...
...I COMMAND THEE, BY GOD'S NAME...
AAAHHH...
JEANNE'S SCOOPED US AGAIN WITH A CHECKMATE!
S'OKAY WITH ME.
THEN WHAT ARE WE HERE FOR?!
......
LAST TIME, HE COULDN'T HELP MARON, SO "THIS TIME FOR SURE!," HE'S THINKING.
...DEMON, BE SEALED!
SWSH

GREETINGS

Hello ♡ I'm Arina Tanemura. Peace! Well, "Kamikaze Kaito Jeanne 4" is here. Now fans of the anime and tankobons will get to know Takazuchi Zen-kun, who's already ultra-popular with fans who read the stories in the magazine. For fans who read the magazine, well, you know what a rough time Jeanne is having at the moment (but isn't she always?). For everyone, whether you're reading or rereading these stories, enjoy! ♡♡♡

Oh boy, you're gonna laugh at this, but my fall schedule aims to kill me! For the August 18, 1999 Ribon magazine, I've got a bonus Access story slated. Plus, I have to finish corrections and all supplementary material for the next collected Jeanne volume to be published. And then there's some anime-related work I have to do! Tremendously busy, folks! So I might not be able to fill up all my column space here...or I'll try, but...if I don't have time to write words, I'll throw in an illo, like:

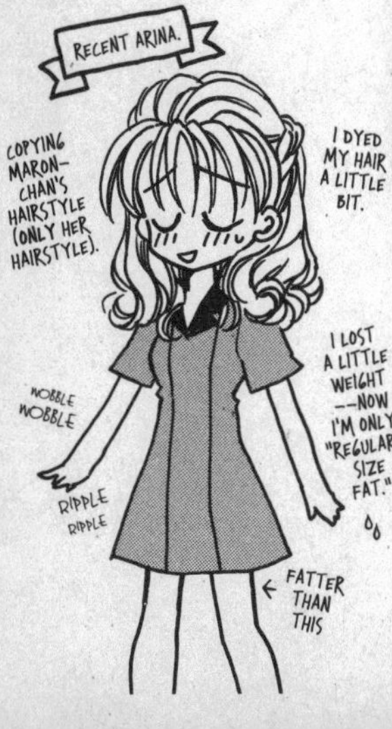
RECENT ARINA.
COPYING MARON-CHAN'S HAIRSTYLE (ONLY HER HAIRSTYLE).
I DYED MY HAIR A LITTLE BIT.
I LOST A LITTLE WEIGHT --NOW I'M ONLY "REGULAR-SIZE FAT."
WOBBLE WOBBLE
RIPPLE RIPPLE
FATTER THAN THIS

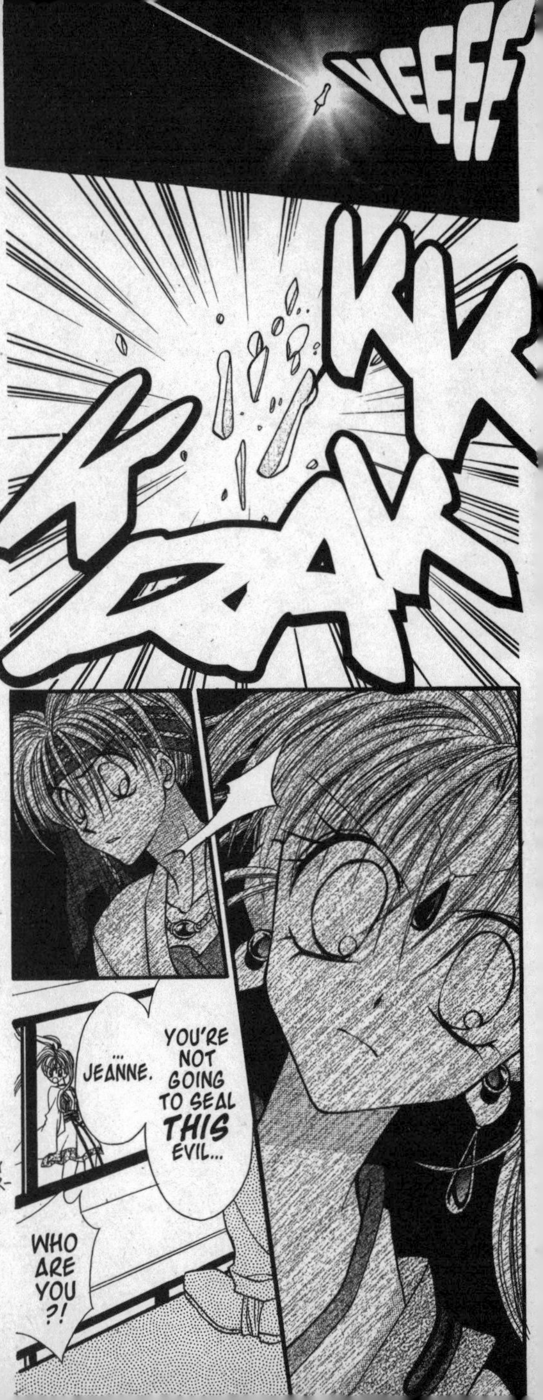
YOU'RE NOT GOING TO SEAL THIS EVIL...
... JEANNE.
WHO ARE YOU?!

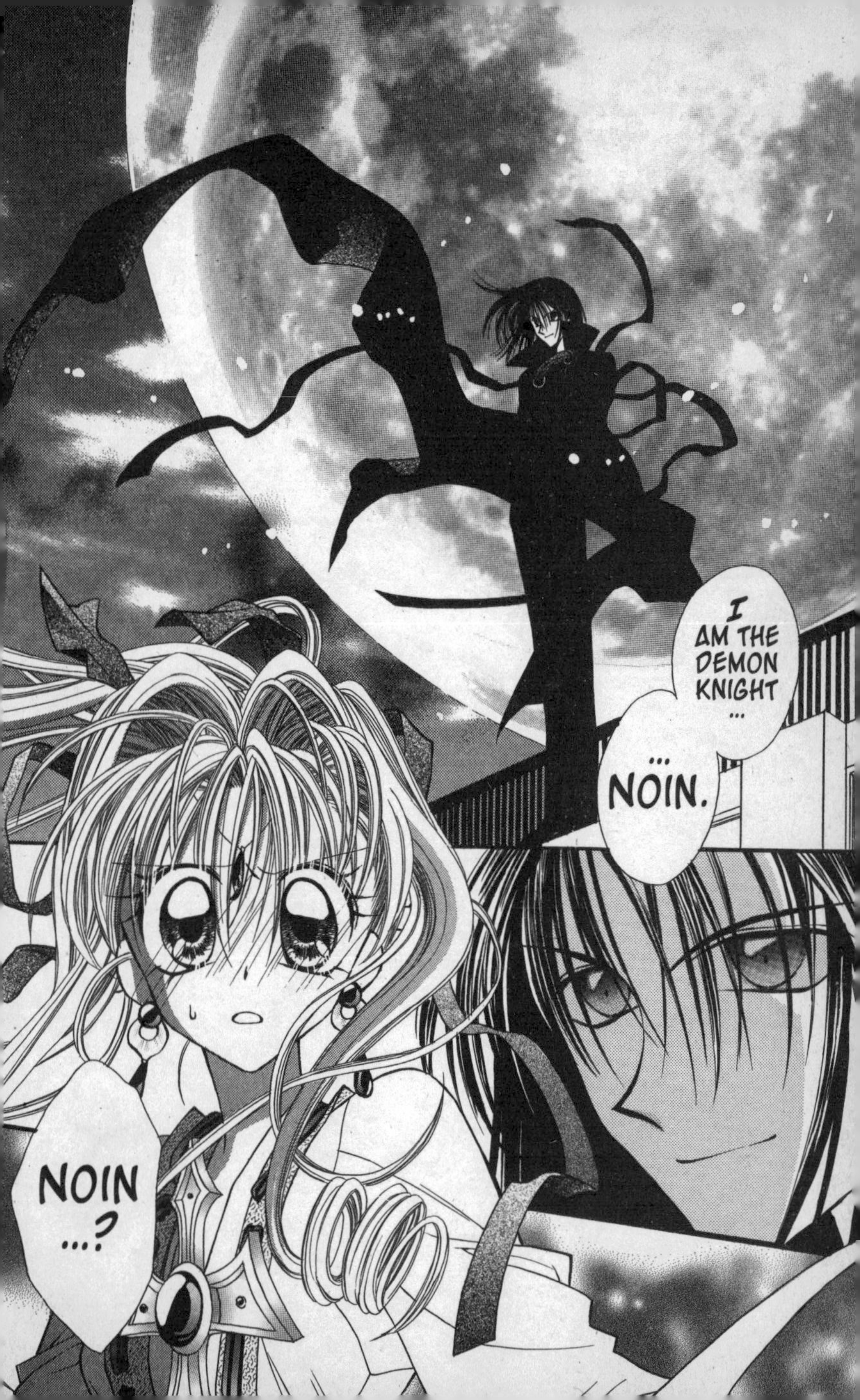
I AM THE DEMON KNIGHT ...
... NOIN.
NOIN ...?

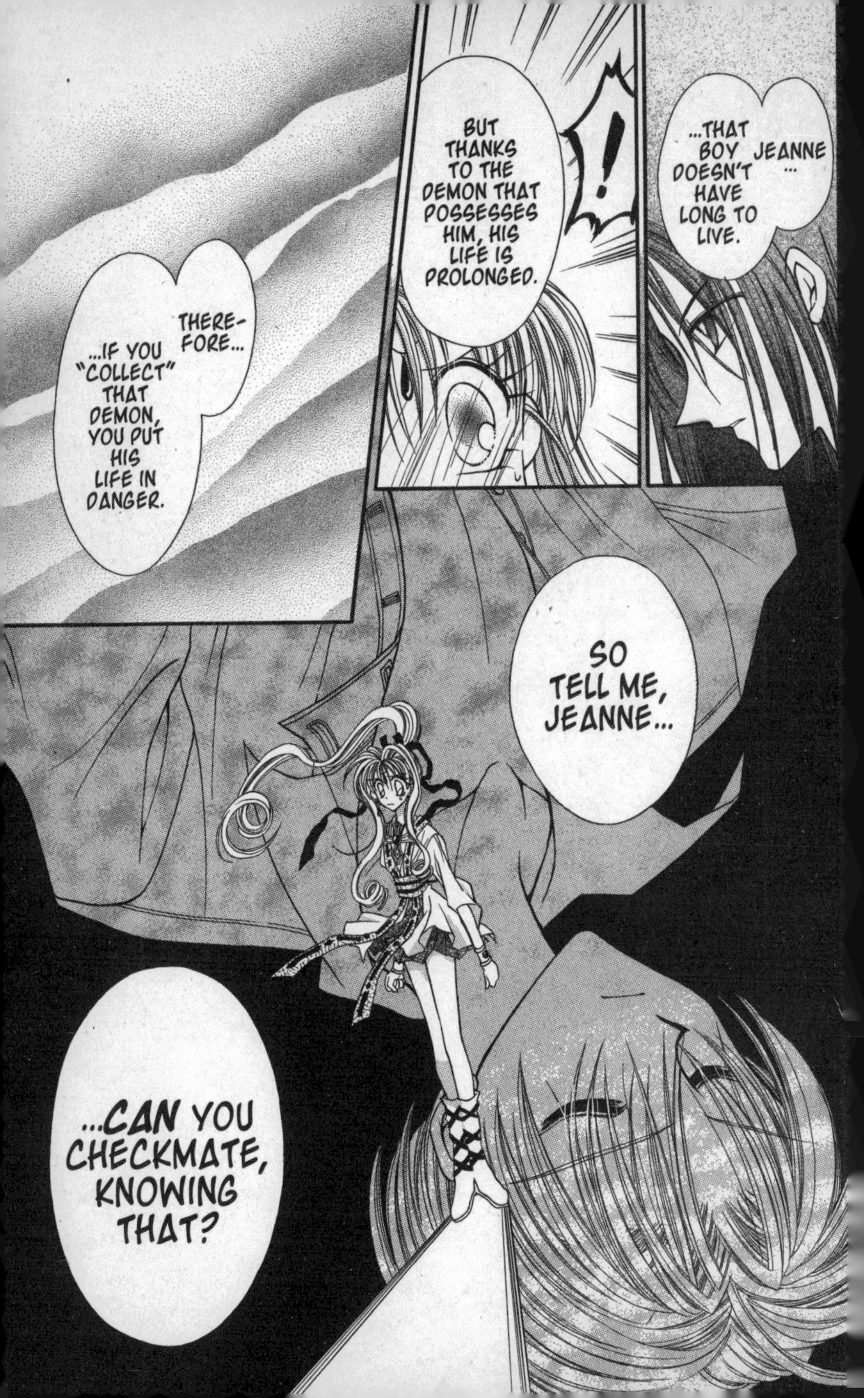

JEANNE ... ...THAT BOY DOESN'T HAVE LONG TO LIVE.
!
BUT THANKS TO THE DEMON THAT POSSESSES HIM, HIS LIFE IS PROLONGED.
THERE-FORE... ...IF YOU "COLLECT" THAT DEMON, YOU PUT HIS LIFE IN DANGER.
SO TELL ME, JEANNE...
...**CAN** YOU CHECKMATE, KNOWING THAT?

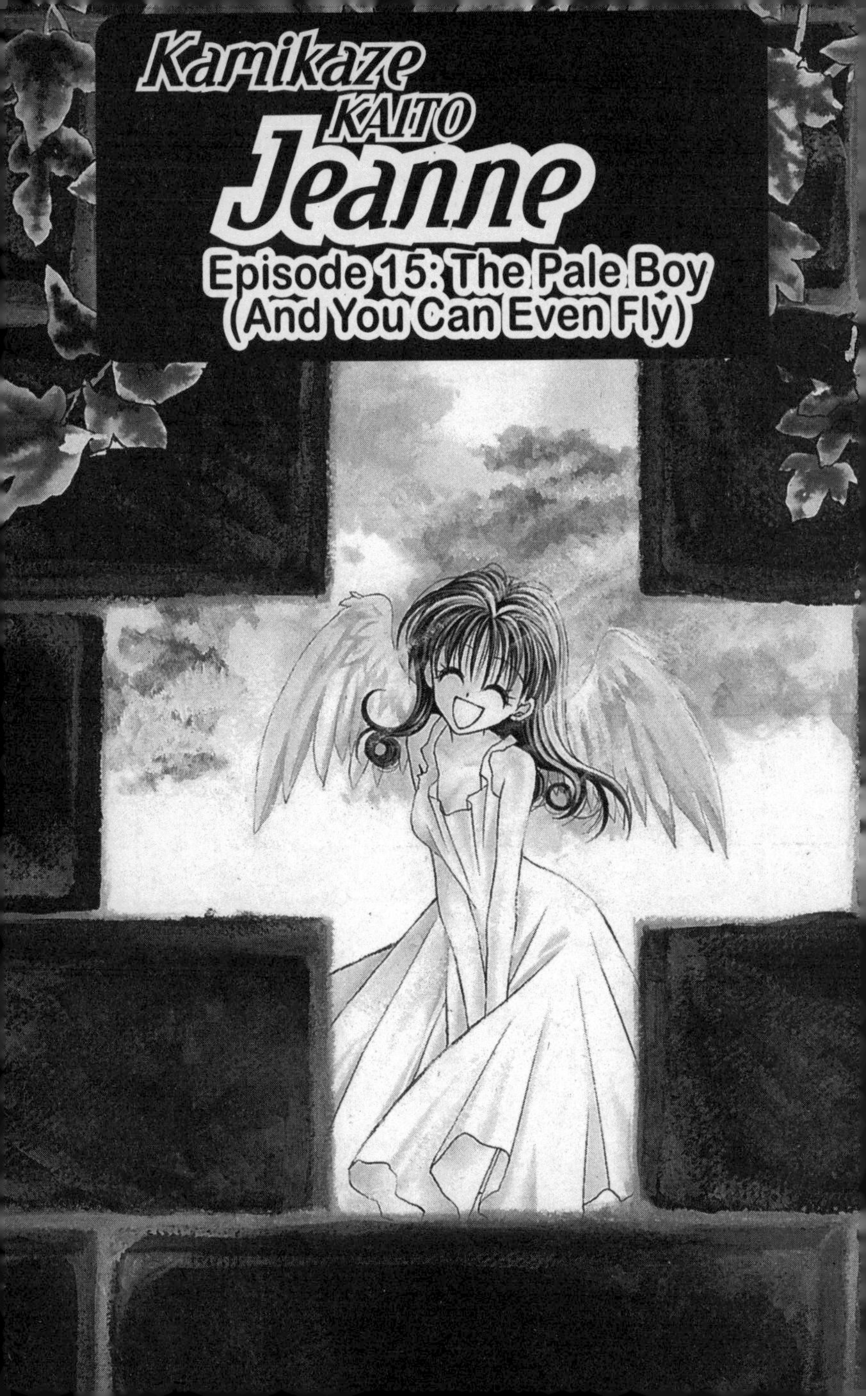
Kamikaze KAITO Jeanne
Episode 15: The Pale Boy (And You Can Even Fly)

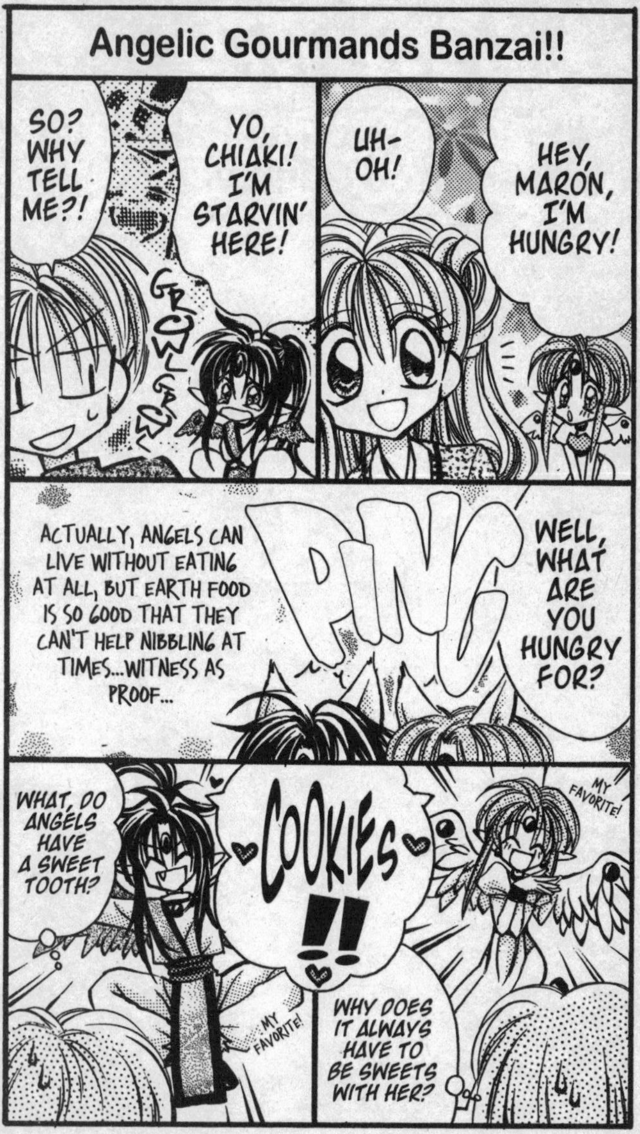
Angelic Gourmands Banzai!!
HEY, MARON, I'M HUNGRY!
UH-OH!
YO, CHIAKI! I'M STARVIN' HERE!
GROWL GROWL
SO? WHY TELL ME?!
WELL, WHAT ARE YOU HUNGRY FOR?
PING
ACTUALLY, ANGELS CAN LIVE WITHOUT EATING AT ALL, BUT EARTH FOOD IS SO GOOD THAT THEY CAN'T HELP NIBBLING AT TIMES...WITNESS AS PROOF...
MY FAVORITE!
COOKIES!!
WHY DOES IT ALWAYS HAVE TO BE SWEETS WITH HER?
MY FAVORITE!
WHAT, DO ANGELS HAVE A SWEET TOOTH?

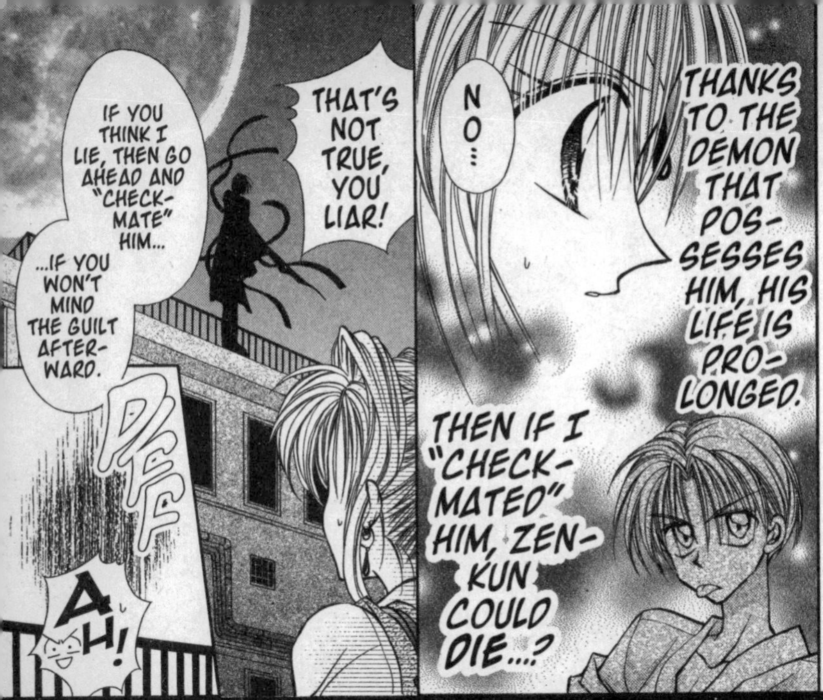
NO...
THANKS TO THE DEMON THAT POS-SESSES HIM, HIS LIFE IS PRO-LONGED.
THEN IF I "CHECK-MATED" HIM, ZEN-KUN COULD DIE...?
THAT'S NOT TRUE, YOU LIAR!
IF YOU THINK I LIE, THEN GO AHEAD AND "CHECK-MATE" HIM...
...IF YOU WON'T MIND THE GUILT AFTER-WARD.
PFF
AH!

Episode 15: "THE PALE BOY (AND YOU CAN EVEN FLY)"

Not too long ago, I used to watch NHK after midnight, when they showed these great documentaries, featuring places in Japan or animals. Sometimes the docs were narrated; sometimes, there was just music playing over the footage. But anyway, I was addicted to 'em and would just stare endlessly in the wee hours of the morning. See, a lot of times they featured oceans and marine life and I just love animals of all stripes! ♡ But this one time, I saw some footage of a brick wall with a cross-like section cut out of it, like a little window, that let you see the landscape beyond (actually, my memory is kinda fuzzy about...no, make that **really fuzzy** about what the original shot looked like). So I thought to myself, y'know, I wanna draw something like that ♡ and that's what inspired this episode's title page art. I like it and yet, it somehow feels incomplete to me. Sometime in the indeterminate future, I'd like to go back and take another crack at that image...

I also kinda like the story this time around. In this episode, I wanted it to feel like Zen-kun was falling in love with Maron-chan. When I read this story now, I'm impressed by Maron-chan's charm and think to myself, "Ahhh...I really love Maron-chan..." She's my character (and indeed, the main character), so the way she thinks is identical to mine, but more than that, she's an idealized version of myself, so I find myself wanting to be more like her. Yeah. I'll do my best! What the heck am I talking about?! I think I just embarrassed myself. Anyway, the truth is, I love my own manga but I don't care too much for myself (only the few parts that I like about myself, I put into Maron-chan.) I mean, I'm slow...I'm clumsy...foolish...stupid...Aaah! This is no good! One thing I'm not is gloomy! Oh yeah! My favorite panel this time around is on page 49, panel 5, the 2-shot ♡ with Maron-chan and Chiaki-kun ("What are you up to?")! Romantic!! Maron-chan doesn't seem embarrassed, does she? She must be used to Chiaki-kun's overtures by now...

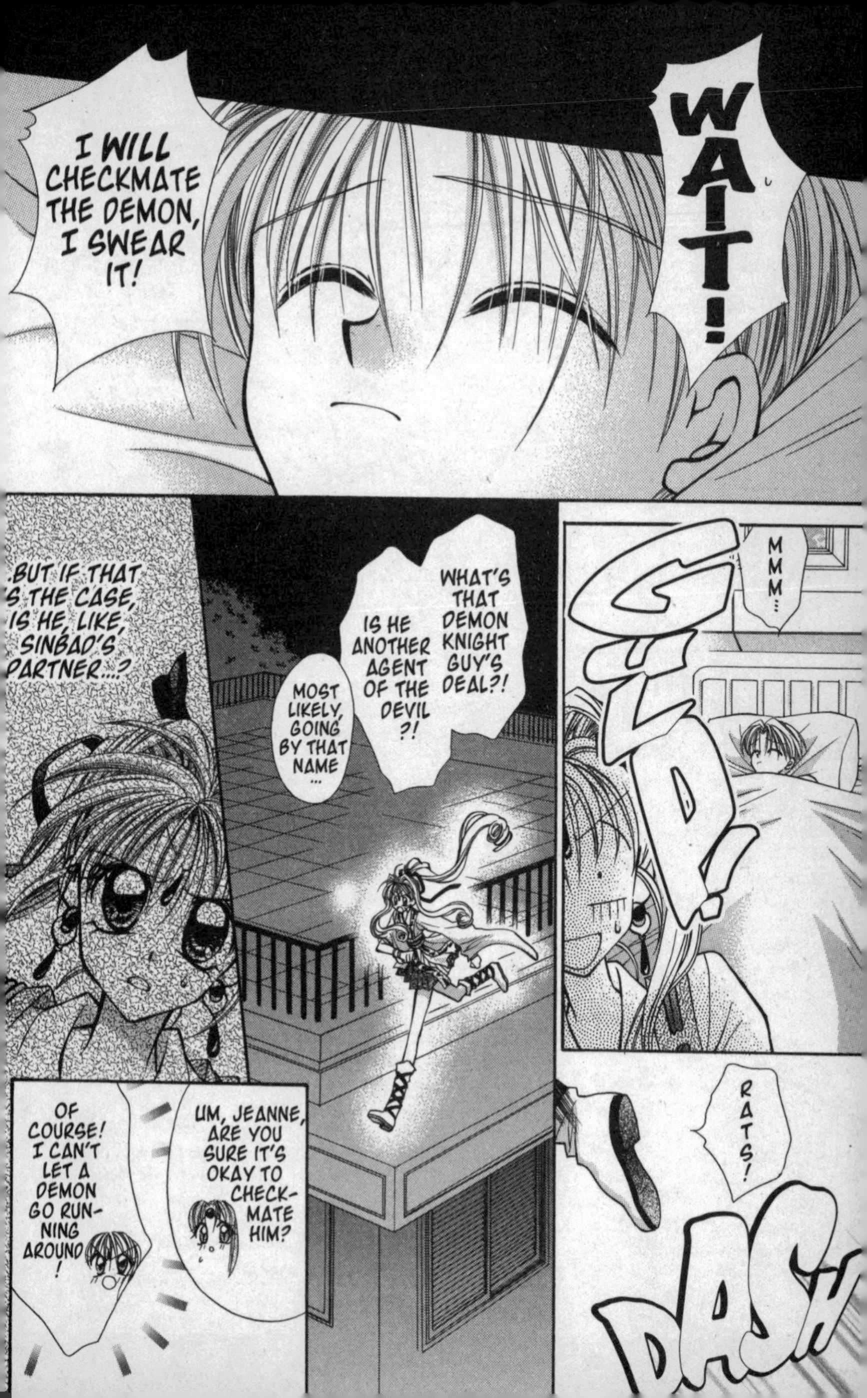
WAIT!
I WILL CHECKMATE THE DEMON, I SWEAR IT!
MMM...
WHAT'S THAT DEMON KNIGHT GUY'S DEAL?!
IS HE ANOTHER AGENT OF THE DEVIL?!
MOST LIKELY, GOING BY THAT NAME...
...BUT IF THAT'S THE CASE, IS HE, LIKE, SINBAD'S PARTNER...?
RATS!
DASH
UM, JEANNE, ARE YOU SURE IT'S OKAY TO CHECKMATE HIM?
OF COURSE! I CAN'T LET A DEMON GO RUNNING AROUND!

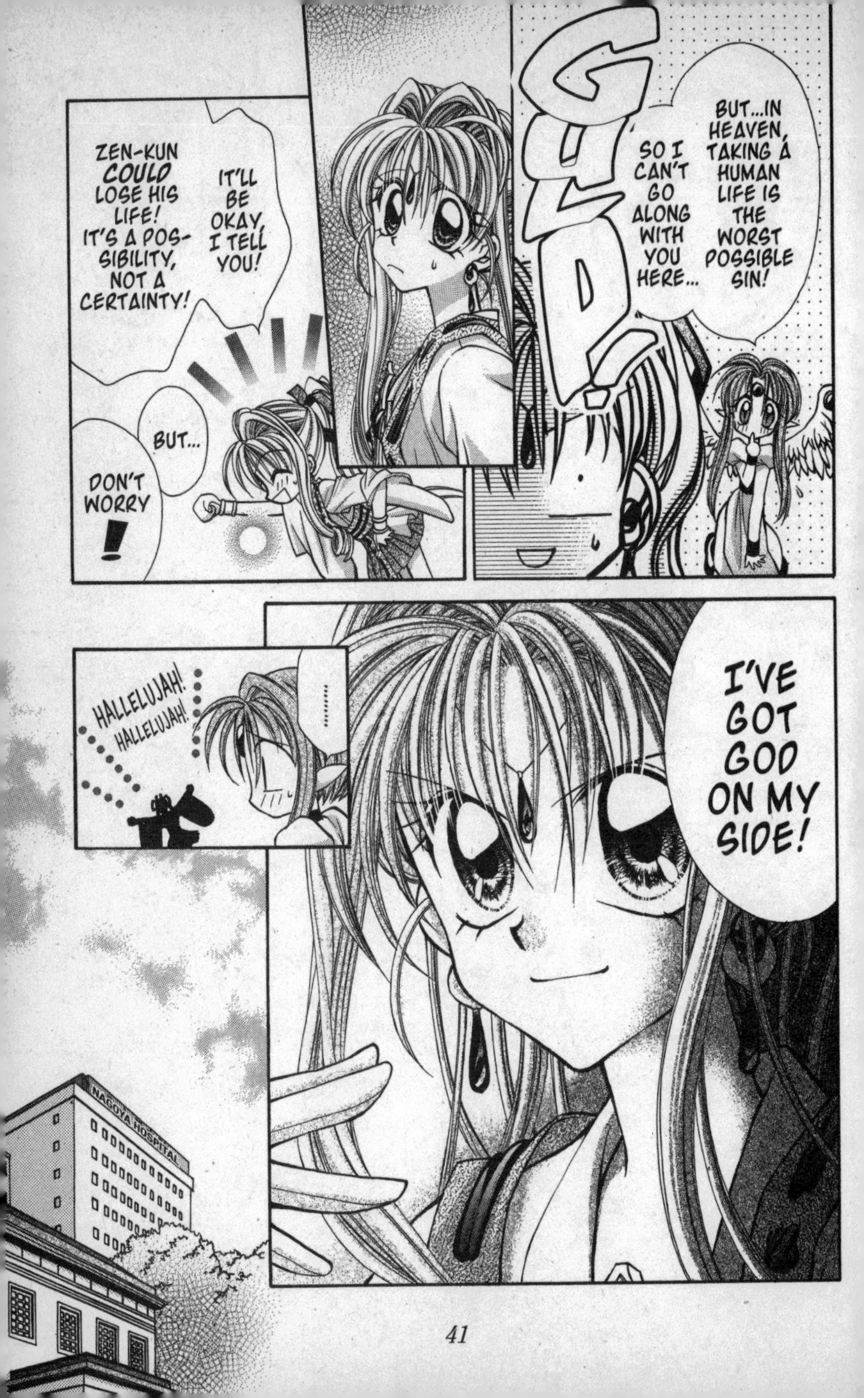
BUT...IN HEAVEN, TAKING A HUMAN LIFE IS THE WORST POSSIBLE SIN!
SO I CAN'T GO ALONG WITH YOU HERE...
IT'LL BE OKAY, I TELL YOU!
ZEN-KUN COULD LOSE HIS LIFE! IT'S A POSSIBILITY, NOT A CERTAINTY!
BUT...
DON'T WORRY!
I'VE GOT GOD ON MY SIDE!
......
HALLELUJAH! HALLELUJAH!
NAGOYA HOSPITAL

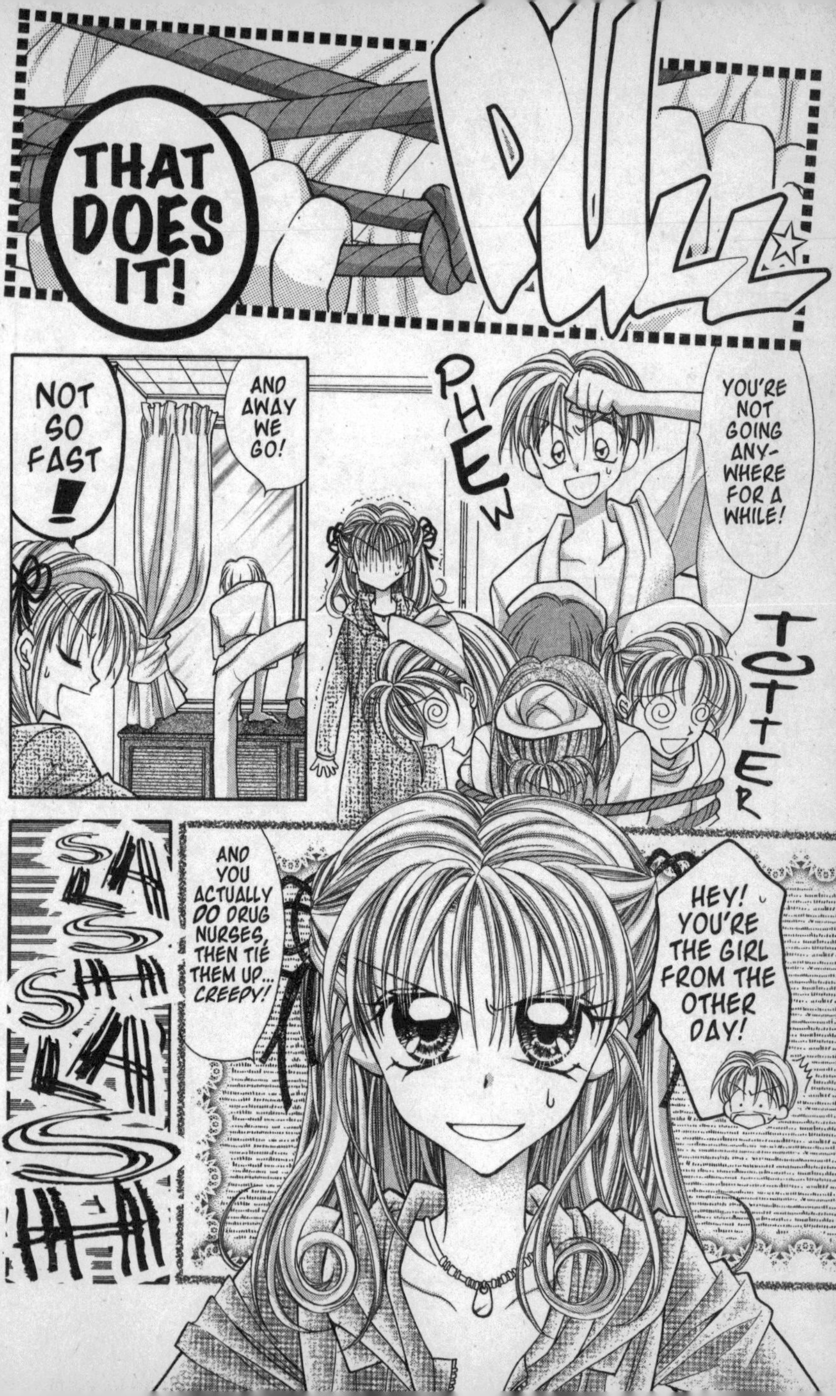
PULL☆
THAT DOES IT!
PHEW
YOU'RE NOT GOING ANYWHERE FOR A WHILE!
TOTTER
AND AWAY WE GO!
NOT SO FAST!
HEY! YOU'RE THE GIRL FROM THE OTHER DAY!
AND YOU ACTUALLY DO DRUG NURSES, THEN TIE THEM UP... CREEPY!

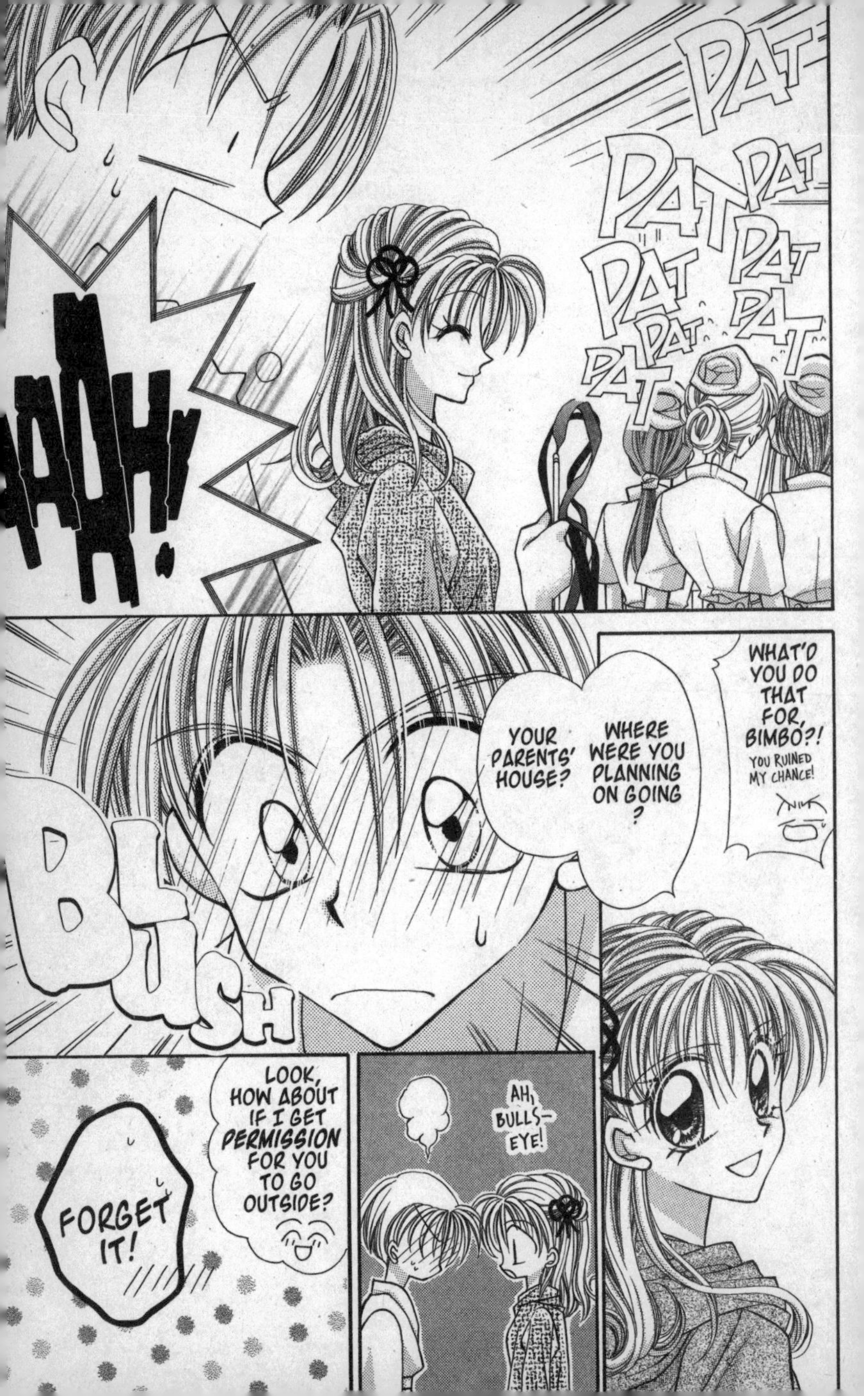
PAT PAT PAT PAT PAT PAT PAT PAT
AAAH!
WHAT'D YOU DO THAT FOR, BIMBO?!
YOU RUINED MY CHANCE!
WHERE WERE YOU PLANNING ON GOING?
YOUR PARENTS' HOUSE?
BLUSH
AH, BULLS-EYE!
LOOK, HOW ABOUT IF I GET PERMISSION FOR YOU TO GO OUTSIDE?
FORGET IT!

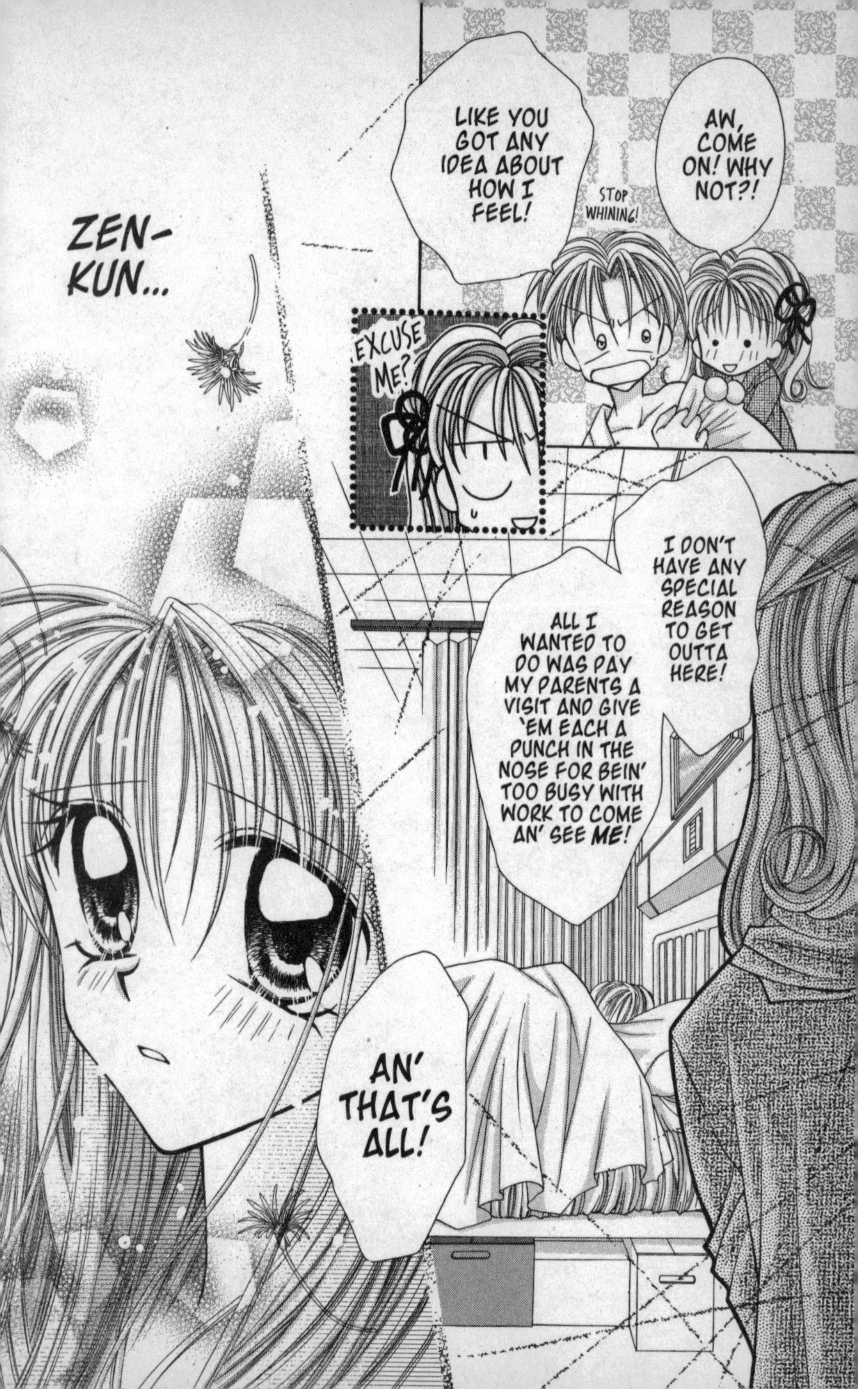
AW, COME ON! WHY NOT?!
STOP WHINING!
LIKE YOU GOT ANY IDEA ABOUT HOW I FEEL!
EXCUSE ME?
I DON'T HAVE ANY SPECIAL REASON TO GET OUTTA HERE!
ALL I WANTED TO DO WAS PAY MY PARENTS A VISIT AND GIVE 'EM EACH A PUNCH IN THE NOSE FOR BEIN' TOO BUSY WITH WORK TO COME AN' SEE **ME**!
AN' THAT'S ALL!
ZEN-KUN...

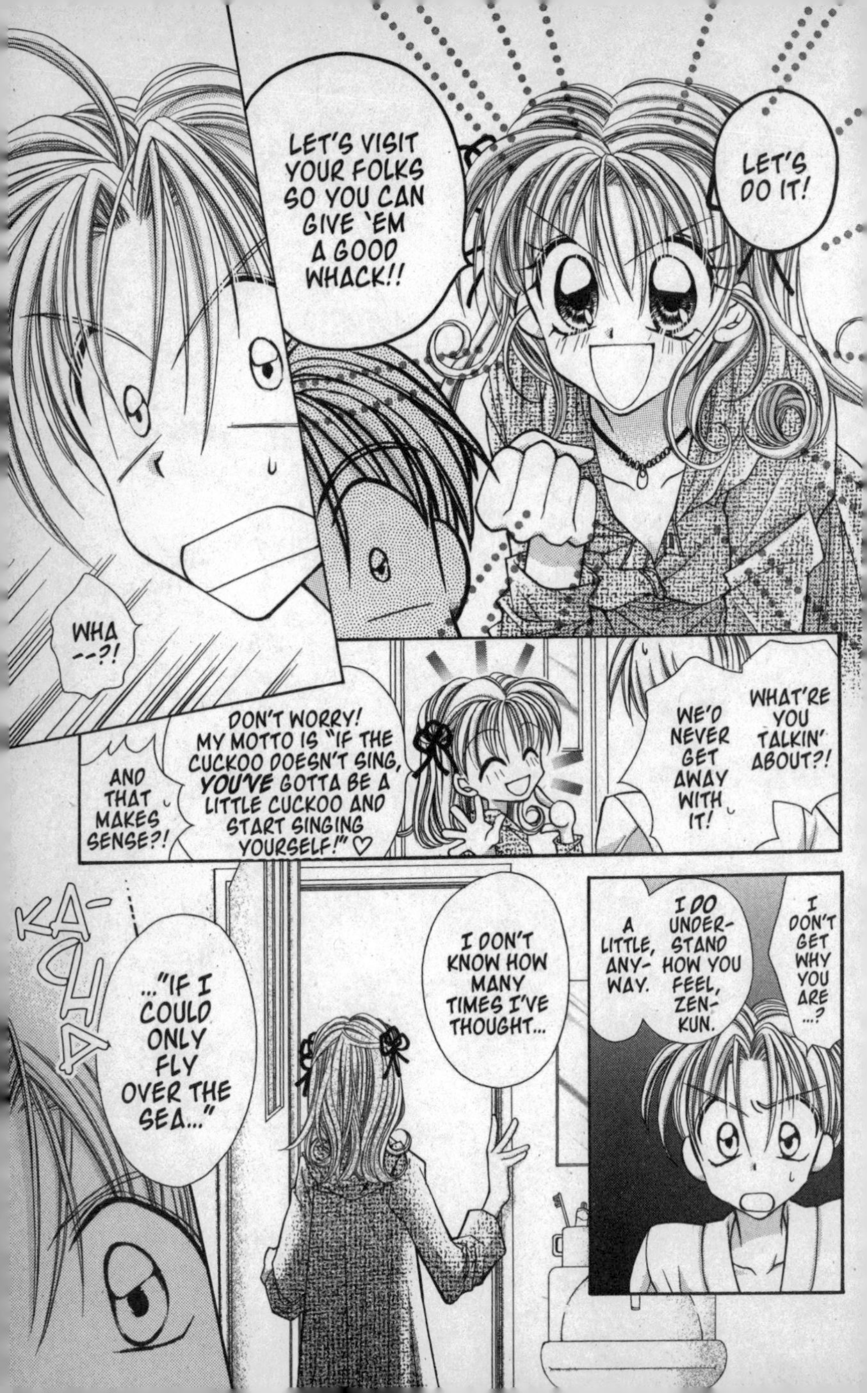
LET'S VISIT YOUR FOLKS SO YOU CAN GIVE 'EM A GOOD WHACK!!
LET'S DO IT!
WHA--?!
WHAT'RE YOU TALKIN' ABOUT?!
WE'D NEVER GET AWAY WITH IT!
DON'T WORRY! MY MOTTO IS "IF THE CUCKOO DOESN'T SING, *YOU'VE* GOTTA BE A LITTLE CUCKOO AND START SINGING YOURSELF!" ♡
AND THAT MAKES SENSE?!
I DON'T GET WHY YOU ARE ...?
I *DO* UNDERSTAND HOW YOU FEEL, ZEN-KUN.
A LITTLE, ANY-WAY.
I DON'T KNOW HOW MANY TIMES I'VE THOUGHT...
KA-CHA
..."IF I COULD ONLY FLY OVER THE SEA..."

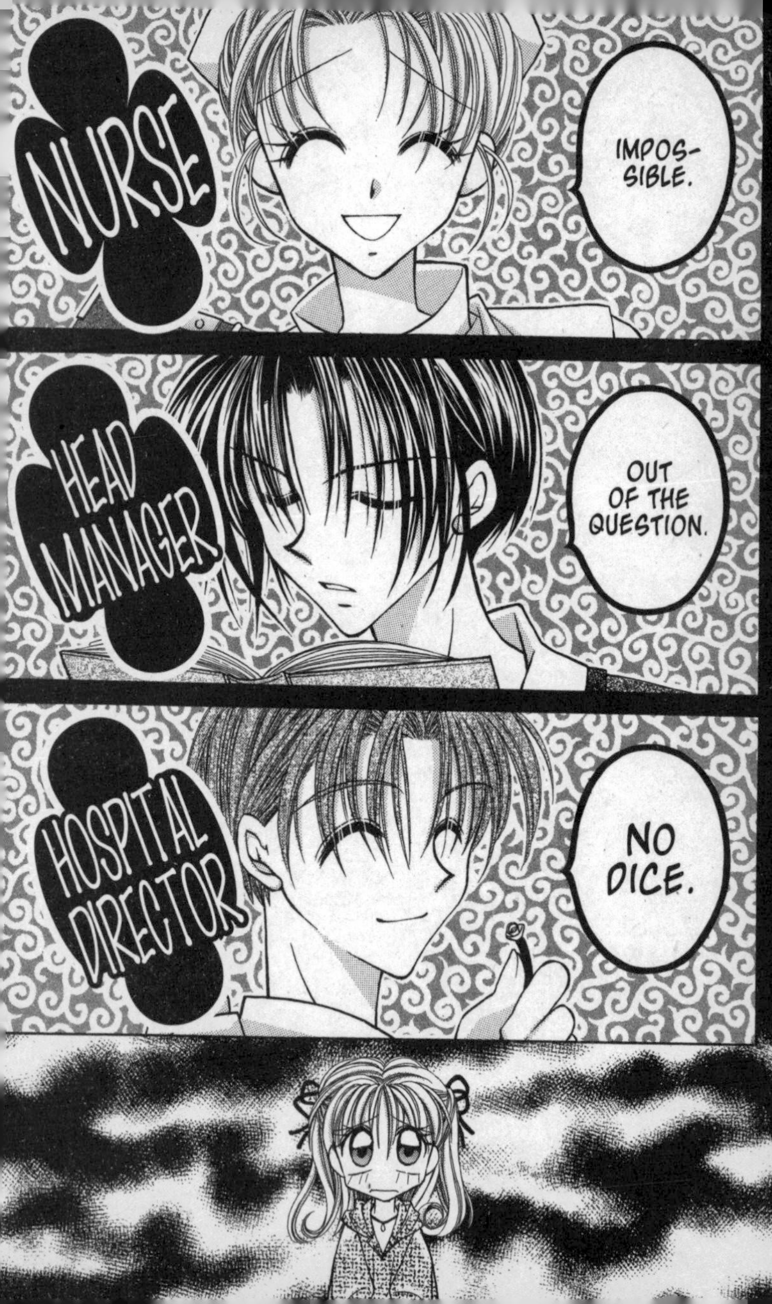
NURSE
IMPOSSIBLE.
HEAD MANAGER
OUT OF THE QUESTION.
HOSPITAL DIRECTOR
NO DICE.

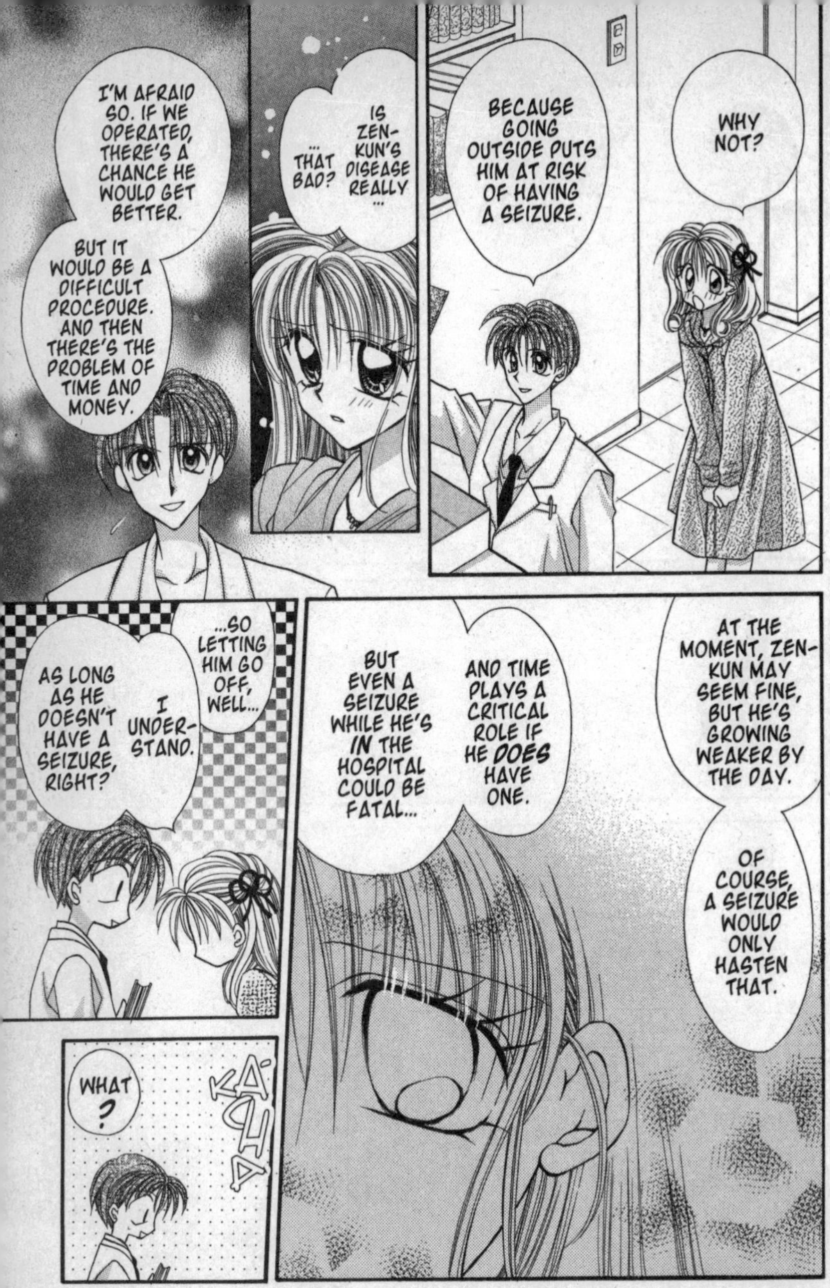
WHY NOT?
BECAUSE GOING OUTSIDE PUTS HIM AT RISK OF HAVING A SEIZURE.
IS ZEN-KUN'S DISEASE REALLY ... THAT BAD?
I'M AFRAID SO. IF WE OPERATED, THERE'S A CHANCE HE WOULD GET BETTER.
BUT IT WOULD BE A DIFFICULT PROCEDURE. AND THEN THERE'S THE PROBLEM OF TIME AND MONEY.
AT THE MOMENT, ZEN-KUN MAY SEEM FINE, BUT HE'S GROWING WEAKER BY THE DAY.
OF COURSE, A SEIZURE WOULD ONLY HASTEN THAT.
BUT EVEN A SEIZURE WHILE HE'S *IN* THE HOSPITAL COULD BE FATAL...
AND TIME PLAYS A CRITICAL ROLE IF HE *DOES* HAVE ONE.
...SO LETTING HIM GO OFF, WELL...
I UNDER-STAND.
AS LONG AS HE DOESN'T HAVE A SEIZURE, RIGHT?
KACHA
WHAT?

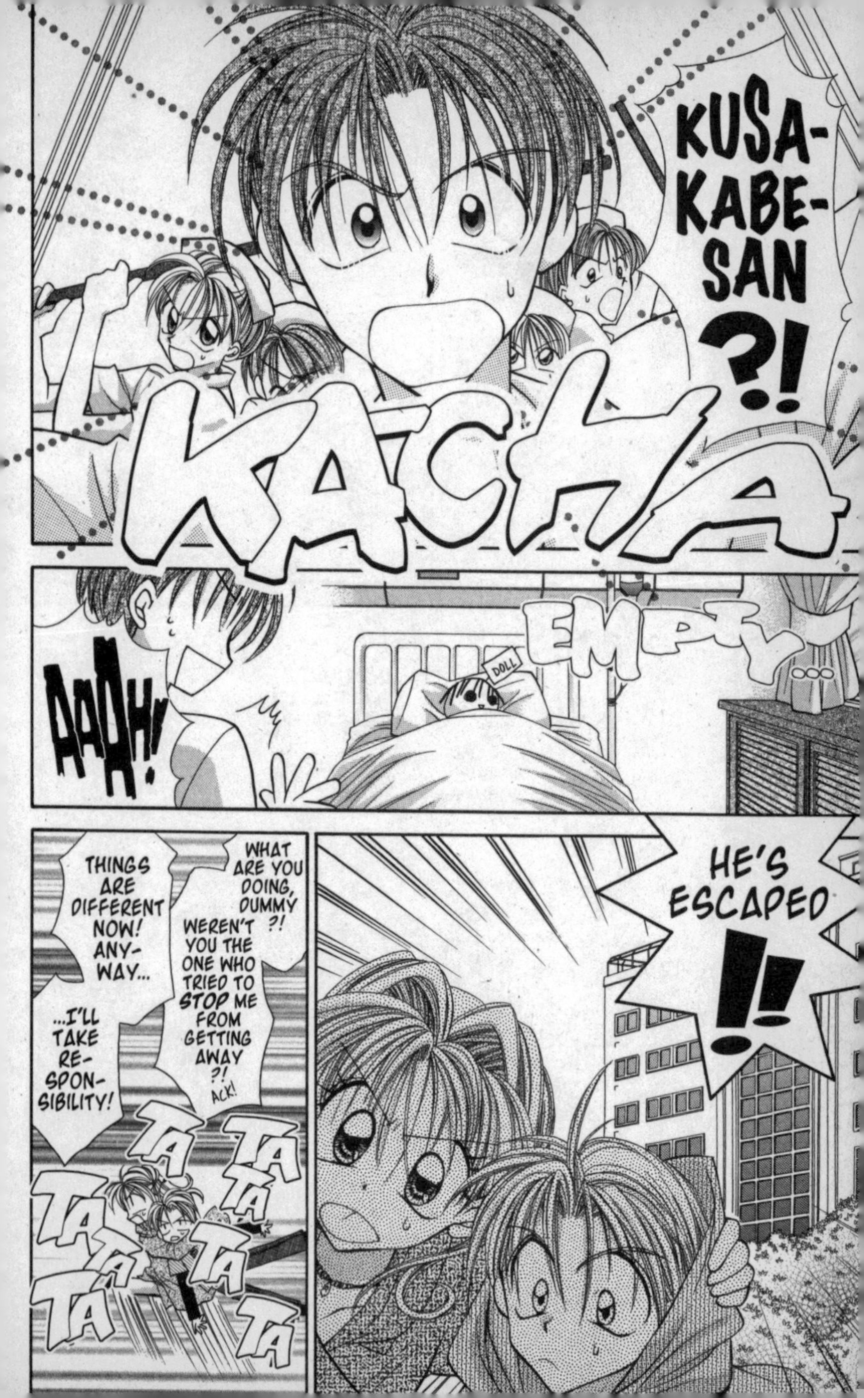
KUSA-KABE-SAN?!
KACHA
EMPTY...
DOLL
AAAH!
HE'S ESCAPED!!
WHAT ARE YOU DOING, DUMMY?!
WEREN'T YOU THE ONE WHO TRIED TO STOP ME FROM GETTING AWAY?!
ACK!
THINGS ARE DIFFERENT NOW! ANYWAY...
...I'LL TAKE RESPONSIBILITY!
TA TA TA TA TA
TA TA TA TA TA

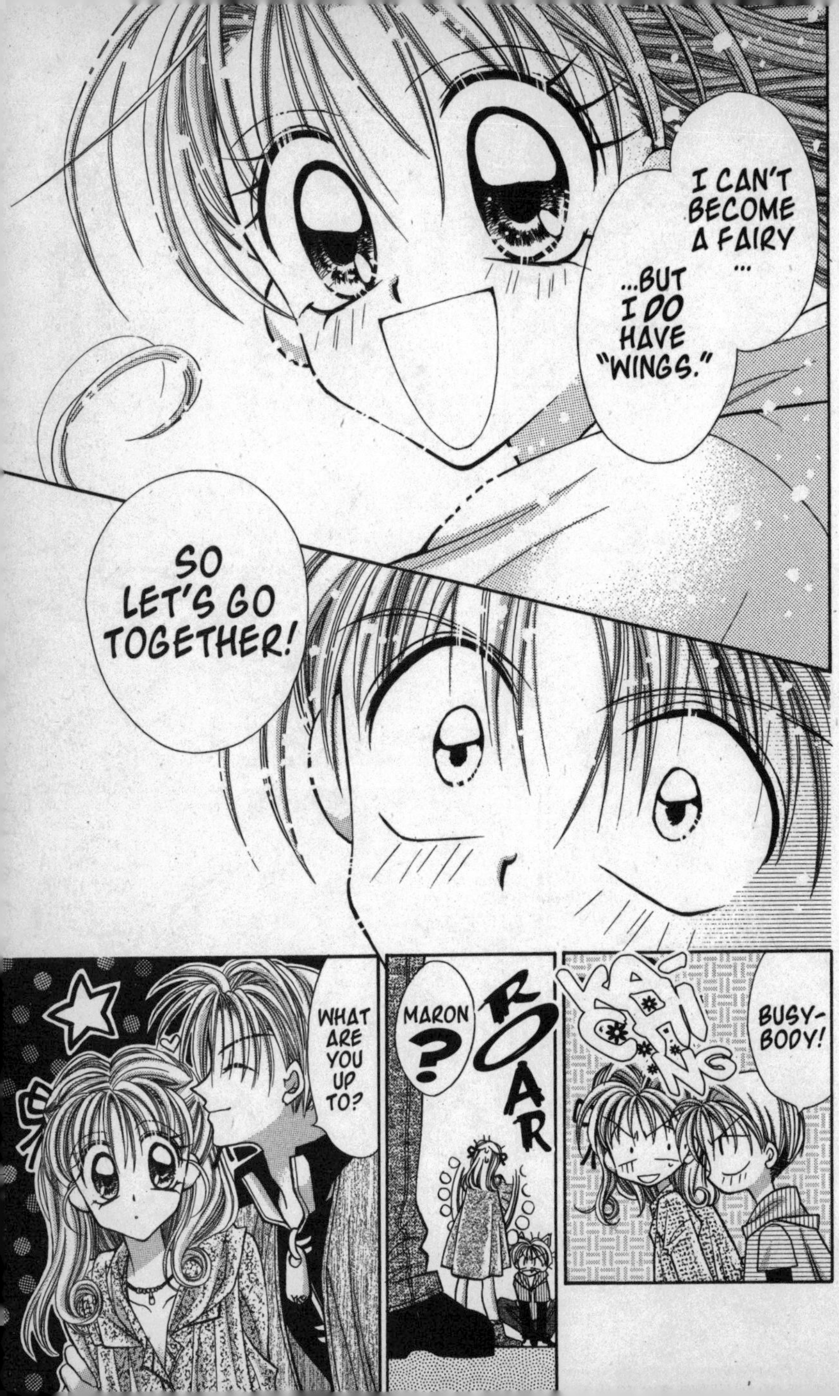
I CAN'T BECOME A FAIRY ...
...BUT I DO HAVE "WINGS."
SO LET'S GO TOGETHER!
YA!
CLING
BUSY-BODY!
ROAR
MARON ?
WHAT ARE YOU UP TO?

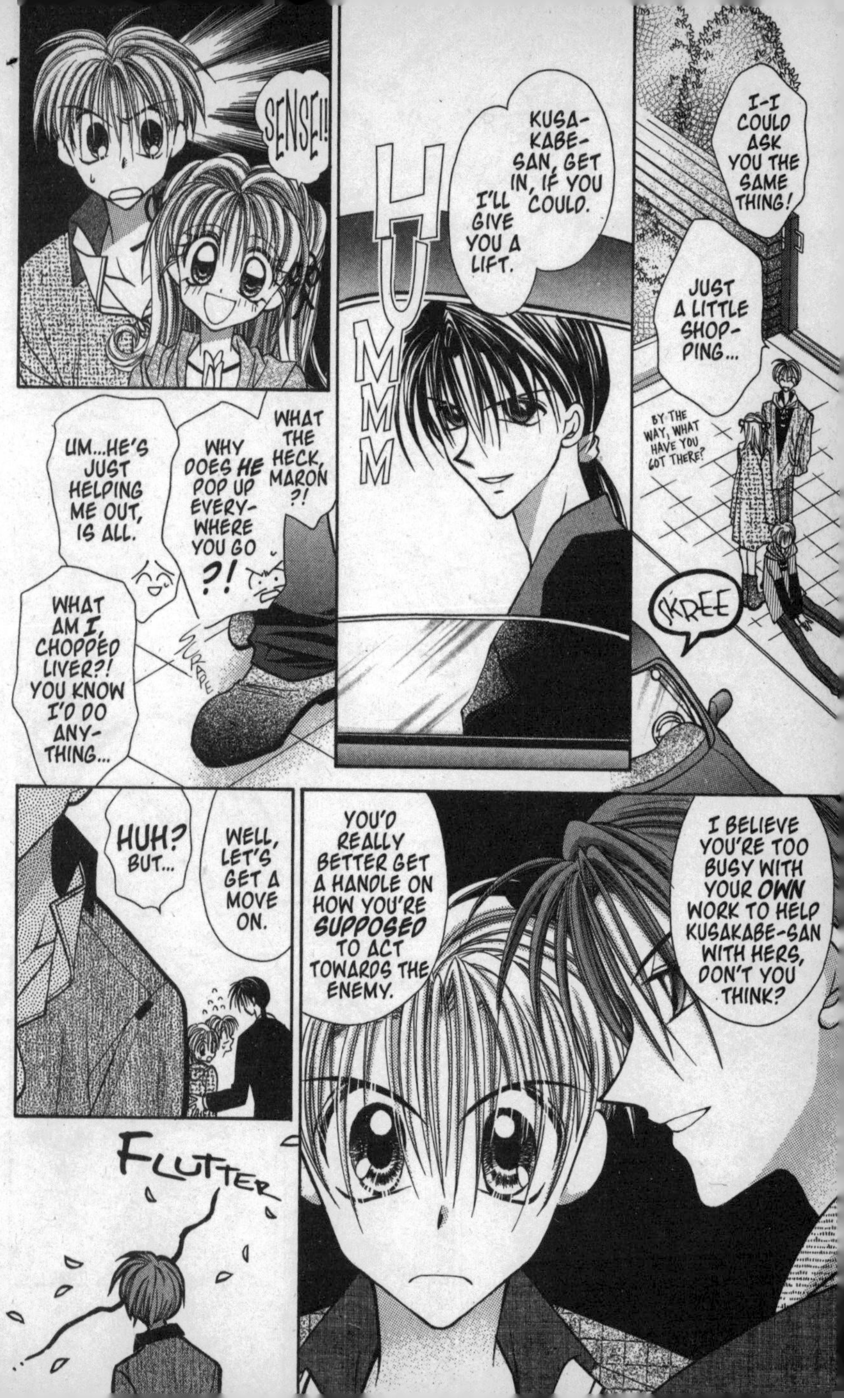
I-I COULD ASK YOU THE SAME THING!
JUST A LITTLE SHOPPING...
BY THE WAY, WHAT HAVE YOU GOT THERE?
SKREE
KUSA-KABE-SAN, GET IN, IF YOU COULD.
I'LL GIVE YOU A LIFT.
HUMMMM
SENSEI!!
WHAT THE HECK, MARON?!
WHY DOES HE POP UP EVERY-WHERE YOU GO?!
UM...HE'S JUST HELPING ME OUT, IS ALL.
WHAT AM I, CHOPPED LIVER?! YOU KNOW I'D DO ANY-THING...
SCRAPE
I BELIEVE YOU'RE TOO BUSY WITH YOUR OWN WORK TO HELP KUSAKABE-SAN WITH HERS, DON'T YOU THINK?
YOU'D REALLY BETTER GET A HANDLE ON HOW YOU'RE SUPPOSED TO ACT TOWARDS THE ENEMY.
WELL, LET'S GET A MOVE ON.
HUH? BUT...
FLUTTER

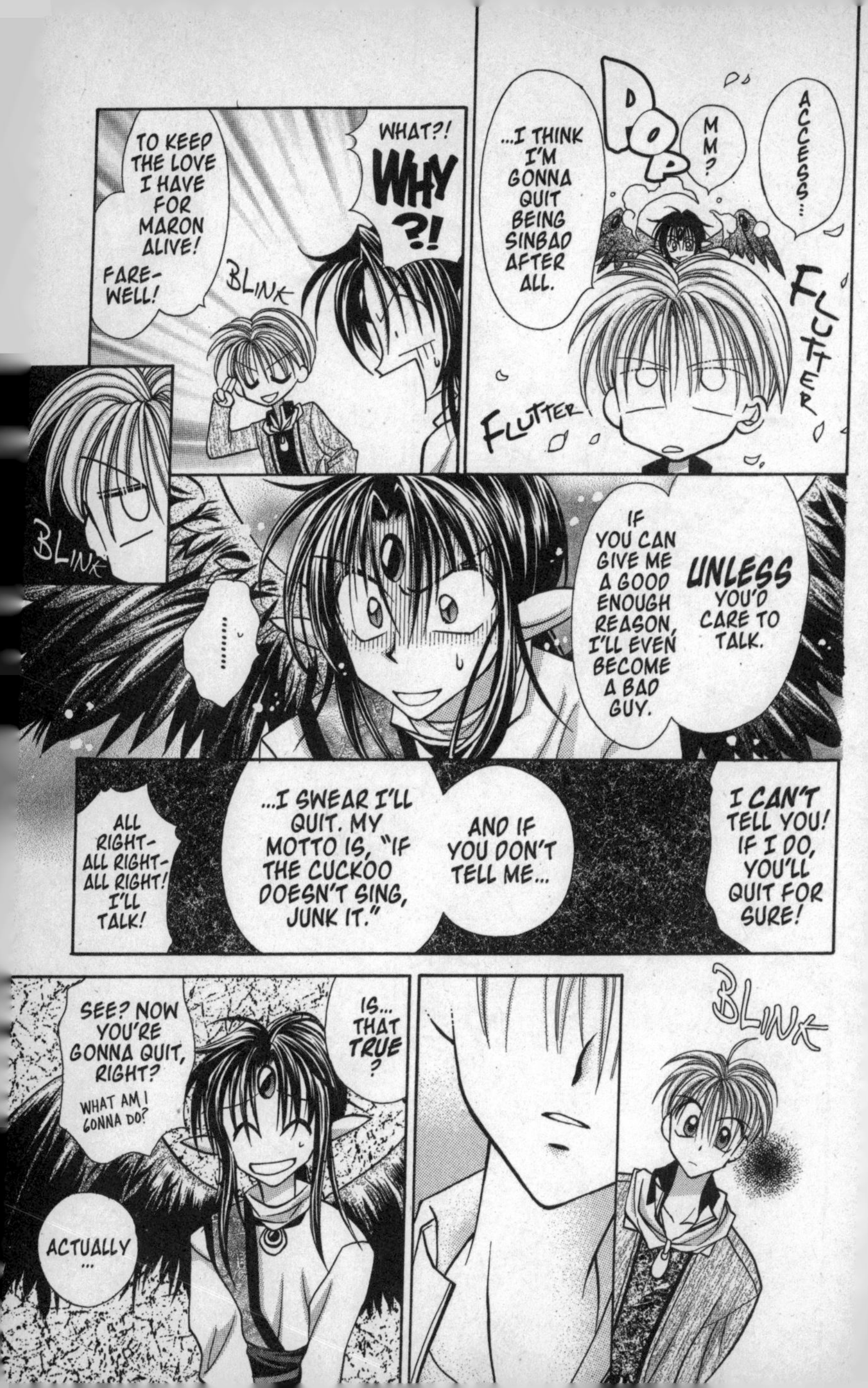
ACCESS...
MM?
POP
...I THINK I'M GONNA QUIT BEING SINBAD AFTER ALL.
FLUTTER
FLUTTER
WHAT?!
WHY ?!
TO KEEP THE LOVE I HAVE FOR MARON ALIVE!
FARE-WELL!
BLINK
UNLESS YOU'D CARE TO TALK.
IF YOU CAN GIVE ME A GOOD ENOUGH REASON, I'LL EVEN BECOME A BAD GUY.
....
BLINK
I CAN'T TELL YOU! IF I DO, YOU'LL QUIT FOR SURE!
AND IF YOU DON'T TELL ME...
...I SWEAR I'LL QUIT. MY MOTTO IS, "IF THE CUCKOO DOESN'T SING, JUNK IT."
ALL RIGHT-ALL RIGHT-ALL RIGHT! I'LL TALK!
BLINK
IS... THAT TRUE?
SEE? NOW YOU'RE GONNA QUIT, RIGHT?
WHAT AM I GONNA DO?
ACTUALLY...

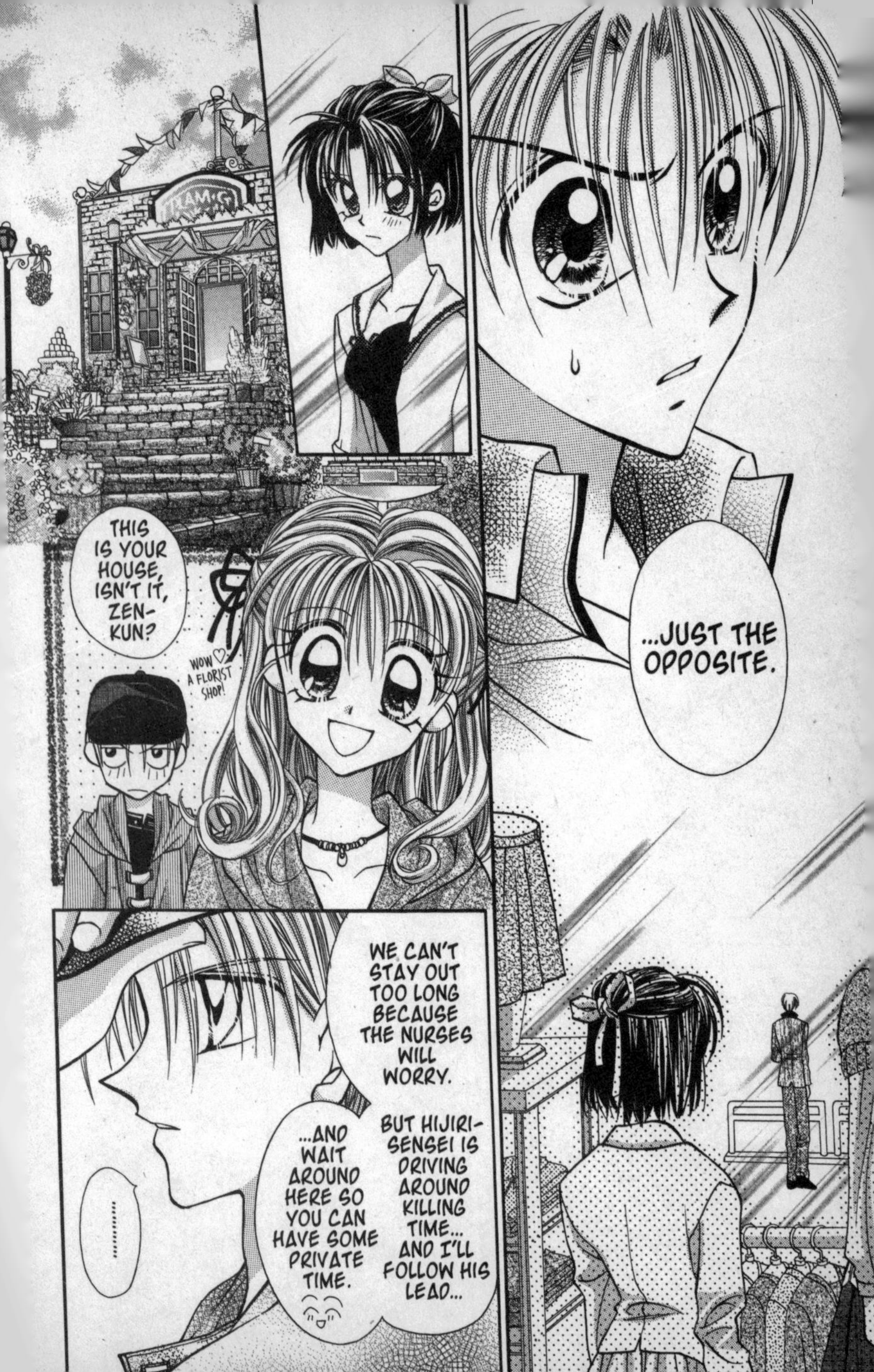
...JUST THE OPPOSITE.
THIS IS YOUR HOUSE, ISN'T IT, ZEN-KUN?
WOW ♡ A FLORIST SHOP!
WE CAN'T STAY OUT TOO LONG BECAUSE THE NURSES WILL WORRY.
BUT HIJIRI-SENSEI IS DRIVING AROUND KILLING TIME... AND I'LL FOLLOW HIS LEAD...
...AND WAIT AROUND HERE SO YOU CAN HAVE SOME PRIVATE TIME.
......

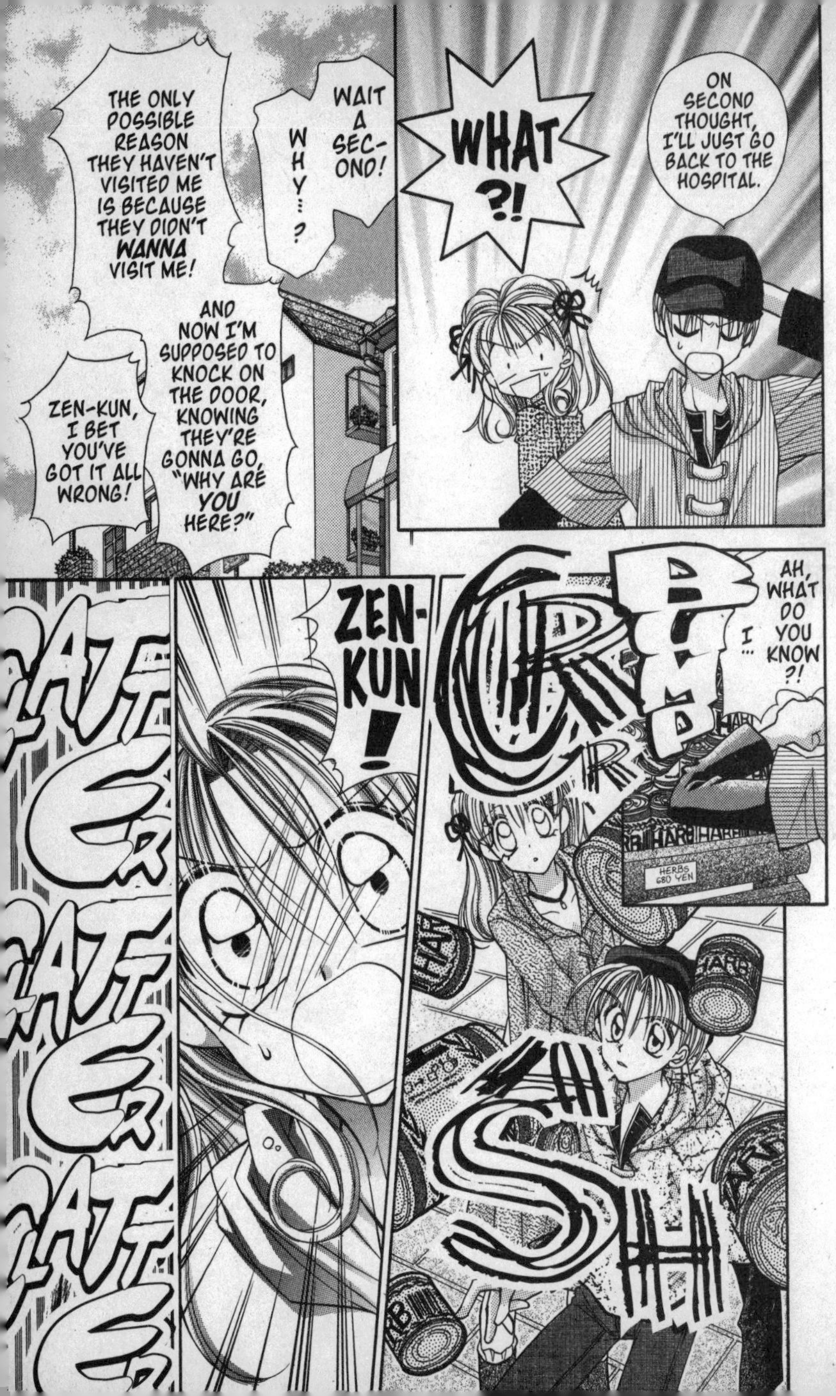
ON SECOND THOUGHT, I'LL JUST GO BACK TO THE HOSPITAL.
WHAT ?!
WAIT A SEC-OND!
WHY...?
THE ONLY POSSIBLE REASON THEY HAVEN'T VISITED ME IS BECAUSE THEY DIDN'T WANNA VISIT ME!
AND NOW I'M SUPPOSED TO KNOCK ON THE DOOR, KNOWING THEY'RE GONNA GO, "WHY ARE YOU HERE?"
ZEN-KUN, I BET YOU'VE GOT IT ALL WRONG!
AH, WHAT DO YOU KNOW?!
I...
HERBS 680 YEN
ZEN-KUN!

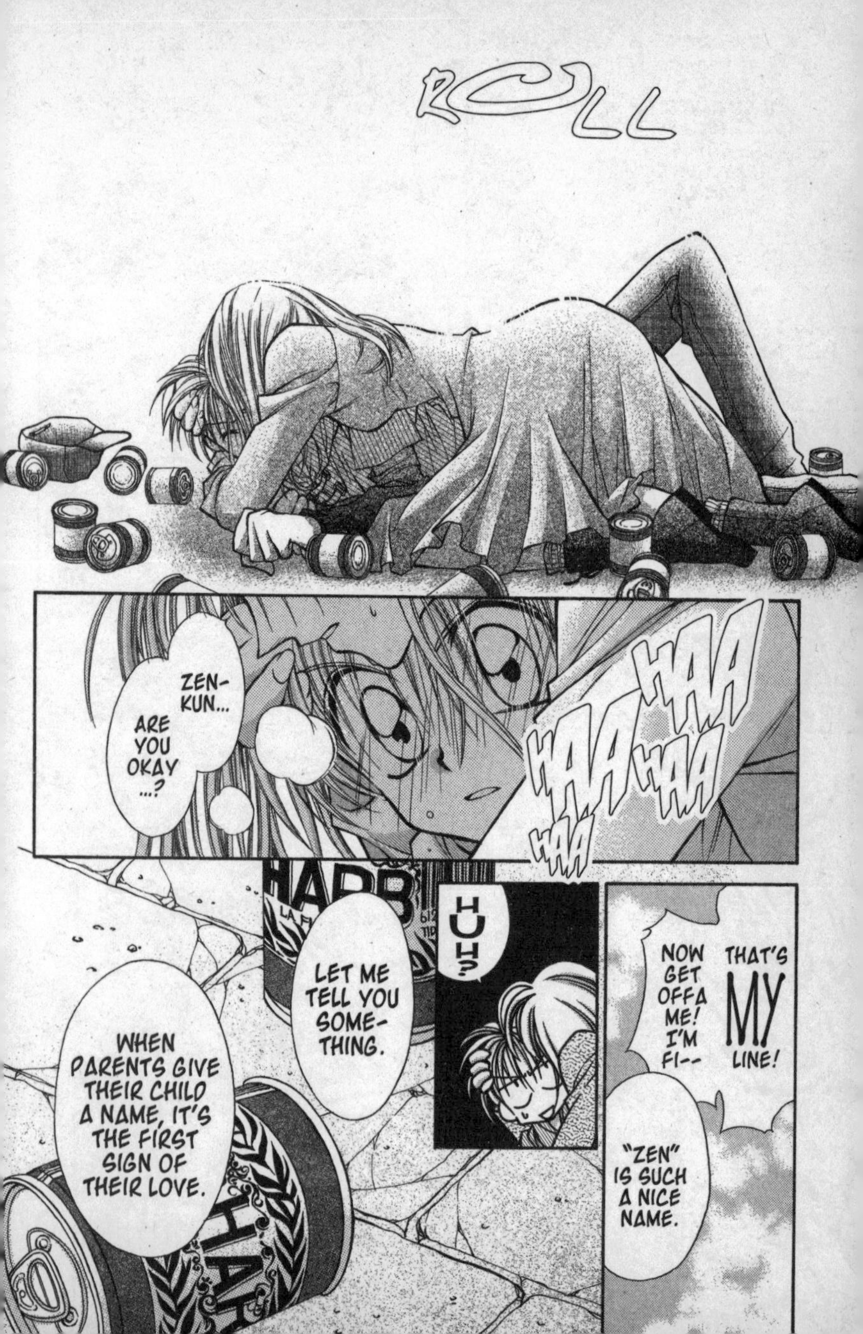
ROLL
HAA HAA HAA HAA
ZEN-KUN... ARE YOU OKAY ...?
THAT'S MY LINE!
NOW GET OFFA ME! I'M FI--
"ZEN" IS SUCH A NICE NAME.
HUH?
LET ME TELL YOU SOMETHING.
WHEN PARENTS GIVE THEIR CHILD A NAME, IT'S THE FIRST SIGN OF THEIR LOVE.

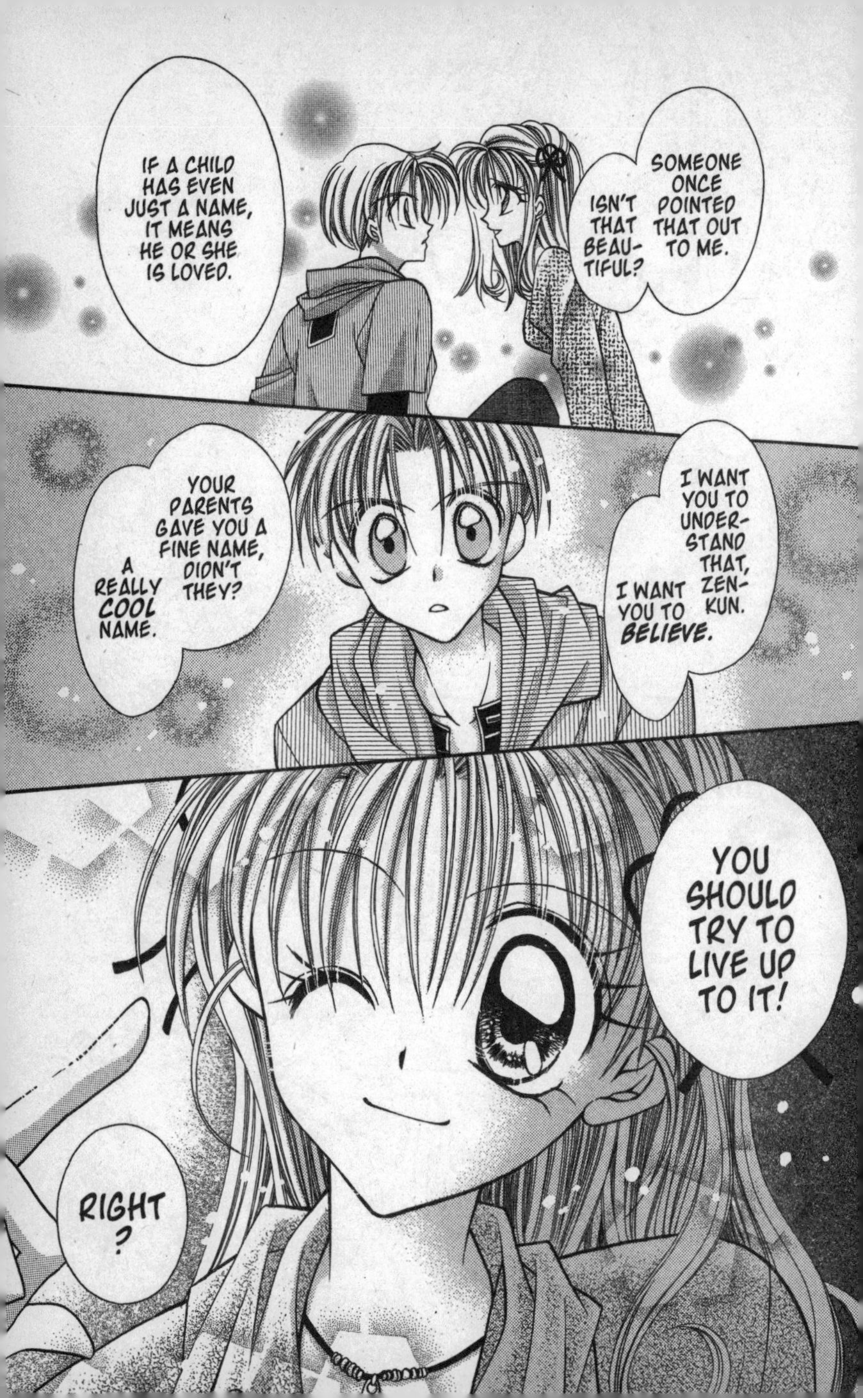
SOMEONE ONCE POINTED THAT OUT TO ME.
ISN'T THAT BEAU-TIFUL?
IF A CHILD HAS EVEN JUST A NAME, IT MEANS HE OR SHE IS LOVED.
I WANT YOU TO UNDER-STAND THAT, ZEN-KUN.
I WANT YOU TO **BELIEVE**.
YOUR PARENTS GAVE YOU A FINE NAME, DIDN'T THEY?
A REALLY **COOL** NAME.
YOU SHOULD TRY TO LIVE UP TO IT!
RIGHT?

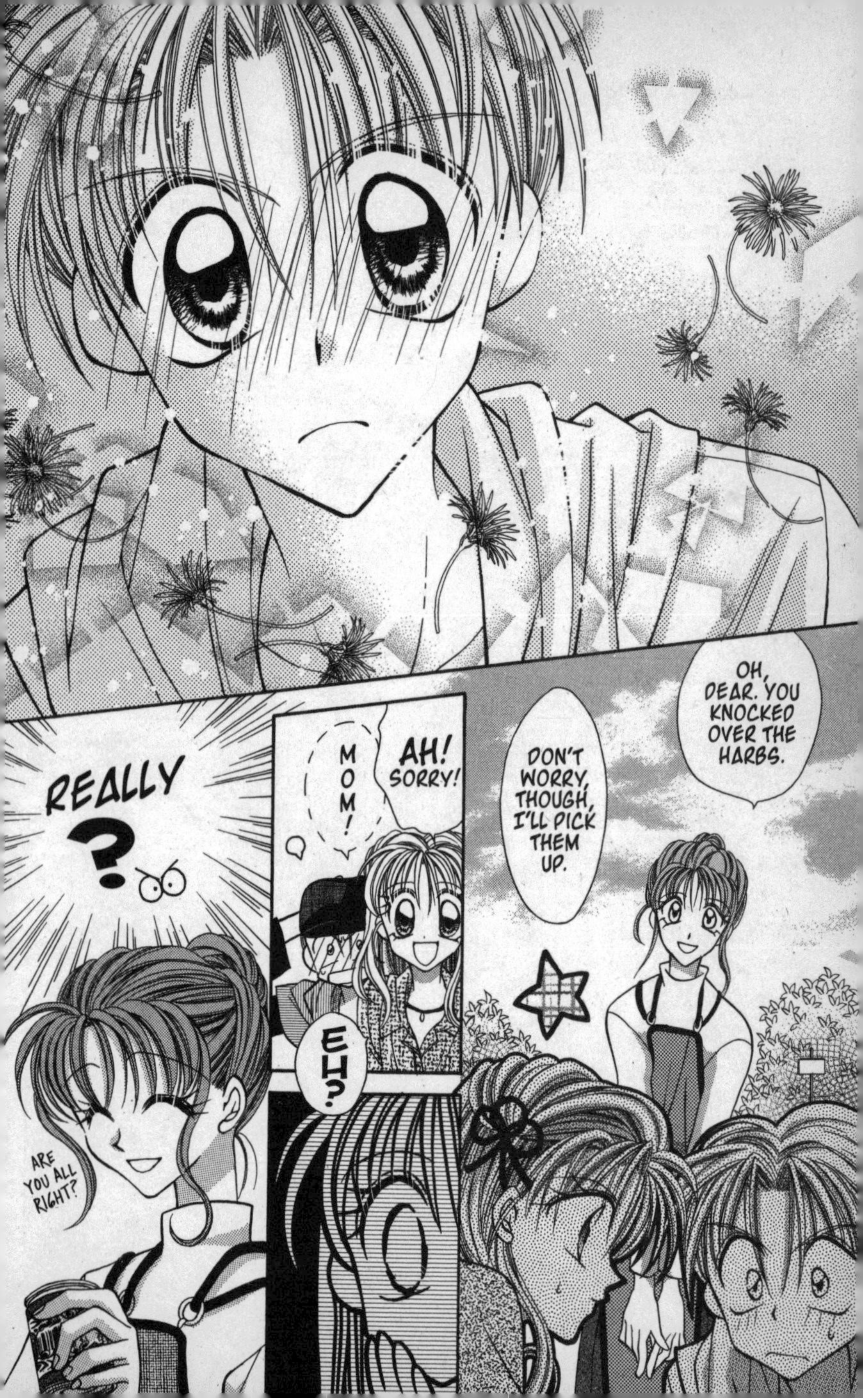
OH, DEAR. YOU KNOCKED OVER THE HARBS.
DON'T WORRY, THOUGH, I'LL PICK THEM UP.
AH! SORRY!
MOM!
EH?
REALLY?
ARE YOU ALL RIGHT?

RADIO

Hi! If you have all my comics, I'm sure you're well aware that I'm a huge fan of Komori Manami-san. Well, just the other day...I had the great fortune to be able to guest on three radio shows! They were "Popun Pajama Revolution," "Mami's Radical Communication" and "Club db," which is hosted by Kuwashima Noriko, the voice actress who plays Maron!♡ It all happened so suddenly that I couldn't get the word out to all you readers beforehand and I'm sorry for that... Anyway, I had so much fun being on the radio and really learned a lot from my appearances. Yep. I had an especially great time on "Pajama Revolution" because Takahashi Naosumi-san (the voice behind Minazuki-kun) and Komori-san were guests along with me and all three of us are so alike personality-wise that we just kept cracking each other up! (Chuckle Chuckle) As for "Radical Communication," I'm a regular listener to the show so it was a blast being able to be on the "other side" of the radio for once ♡ (Takahashi-san was on this show with me as well) Minki Yasu-san was just like I imagined he would be(?) and I was really nervous at first, but somehow I was able to pull it off (I hope). Whew!♡ Thank you to the interviewer, Yasu-san!
On "Club db," I got to play one of my recent faves, "Popun Music" (Konami), so that was cool! ♡ Also, I had the rare chance to talk for a long time to Kuwashima-san.

Continued>>> →

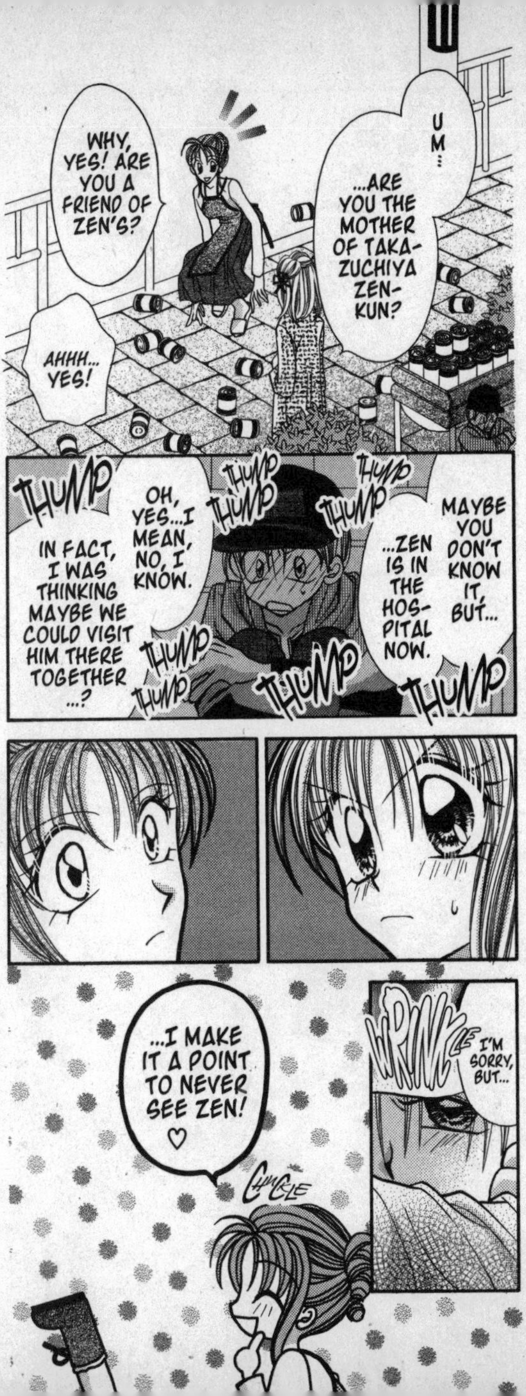
UM...
...ARE YOU THE MOTHER OF TAKA-ZUCHIYA ZEN-KUN?
WHY, YES! ARE YOU A FRIEND OF ZEN'S?
AHHH... YES!
THUMP
MAYBE YOU DON'T KNOW IT, BUT...
...ZEN IS IN THE HOS-PITAL NOW.
THUMP THUMP
THUMP THUMP
OH, YES...I MEAN, NO, I KNOW.
THUMP
IN FACT, I WAS THINKING MAYBE WE COULD VISIT HIM THERE TOGETHER ...?
THUMP
THUMP
THUMP THUMP
WRINKLE
I'M SORRY, BUT...
...I MAKE IT A POINT TO NEVER SEE ZEN! ♡
CHUCKLE

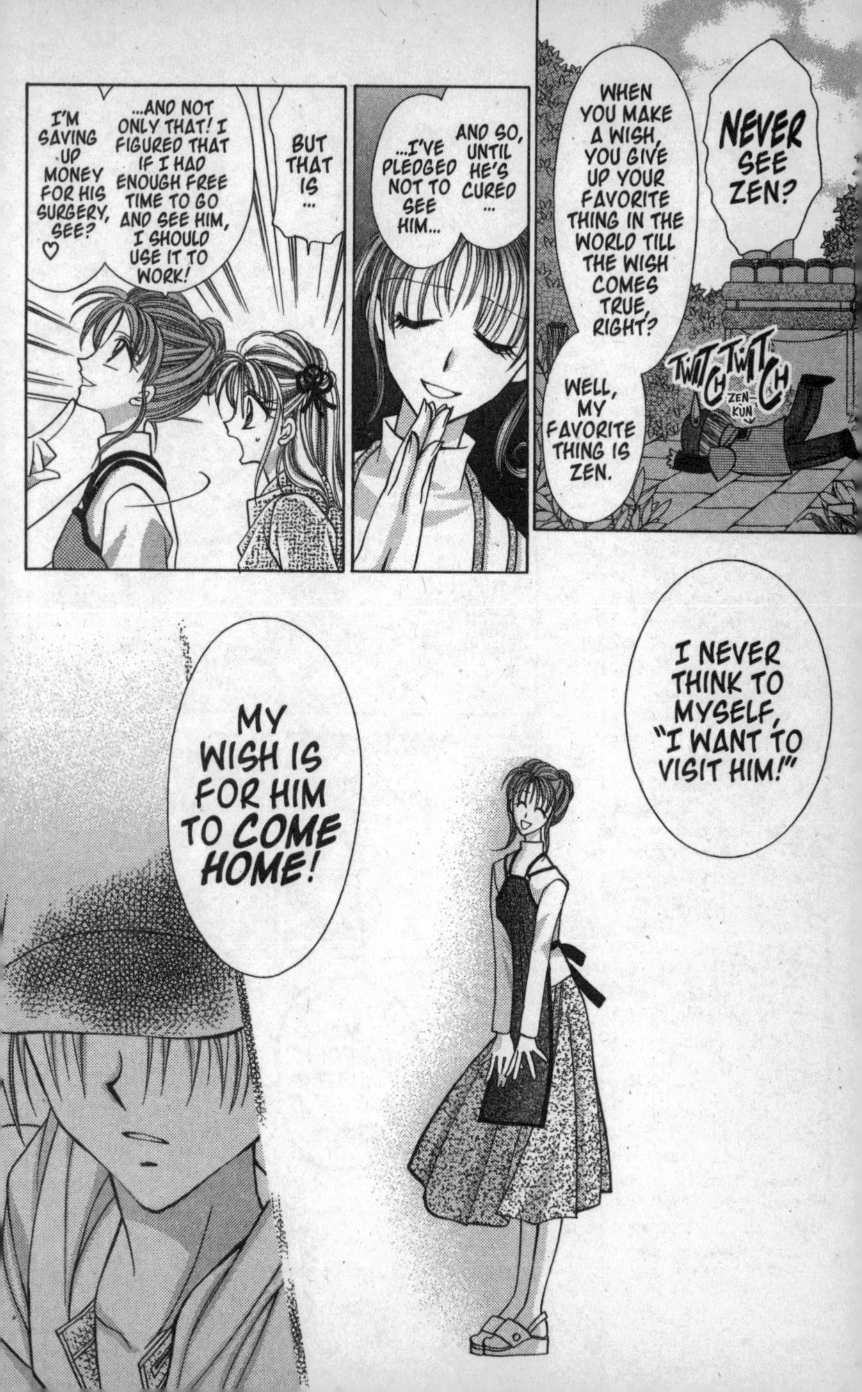
NEVER SEE ZEN?
WHEN YOU MAKE A WISH, YOU GIVE UP YOUR FAVORITE THING IN THE WORLD TILL THE WISH COMES TRUE, RIGHT?
WELL, MY FAVORITE THING IS ZEN.
TWITCH TWITCH
ZEN-KUN
AND SO, UNTIL HE'S CURED...
...I'VE PLEDGED NOT TO SEE HIM...
BUT THAT IS...
...AND NOT ONLY THAT! I FIGURED THAT IF I HAD ENOUGH FREE TIME TO GO AND SEE HIM, I SHOULD USE IT TO WORK!
I'M SAVING UP MONEY FOR HIS SURGERY, SEE? ♡
I NEVER THINK TO MYSELF, "I WANT TO VISIT HIM!"
MY WISH IS FOR HIM TO COME HOME!

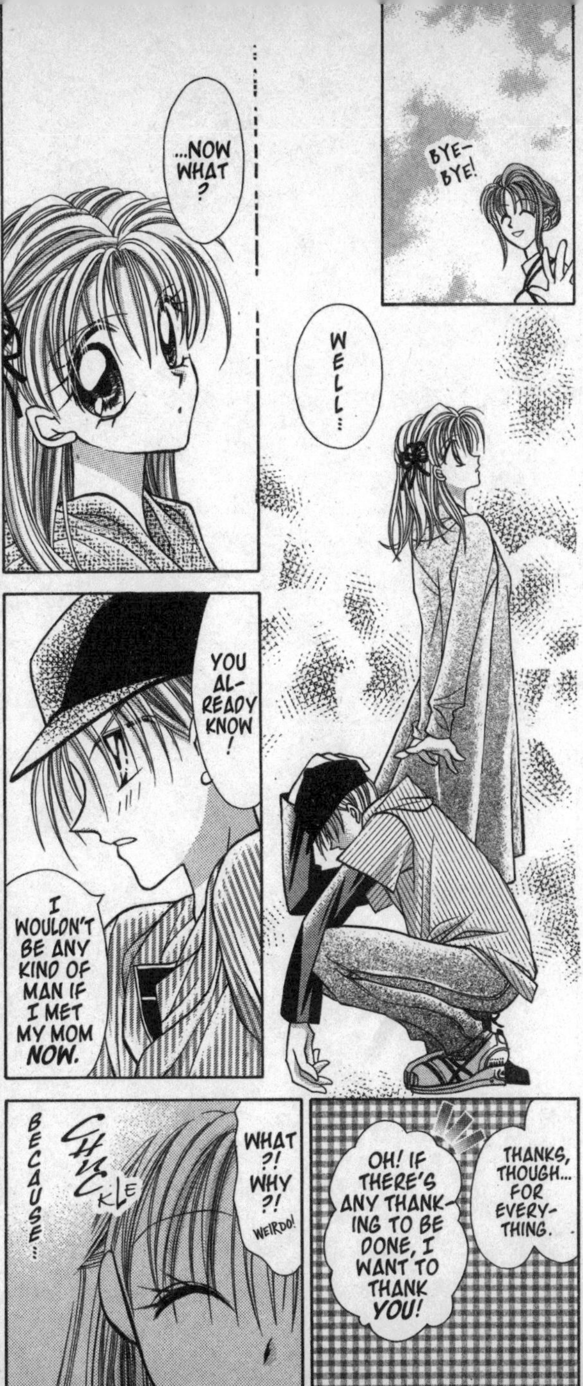
BYE-BYE!
WELL...
...NOW WHAT?
YOU ALREADY KNOW!
I WOULDN'T BE ANY KIND OF MAN IF I MET MY MOM NOW.
THANKS, THOUGH... FOR EVERYTHING.
OH! IF THERE'S ANY THANKING TO BE DONE, I WANT TO THANK YOU!
WHAT?! WHY?!
WEIRDO!
CHUCKLE
BECAUSE...

ARINA TANEMURA'S
"LIKE PULLING TEETH WITH PLIERS"

I STILL HAVEN'T FINISHED "TALES OF XXXANTASIA" #18

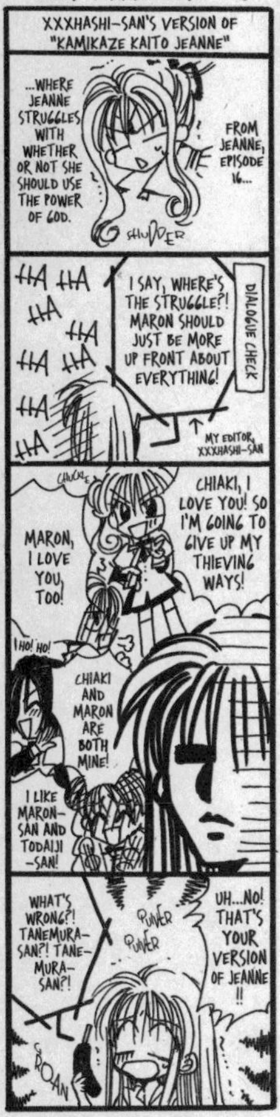
XXXHASHI-SAN'S VERSION OF "KAMIKAZE KAITO JEANNE"
FROM JEANNE, EPISODE 16...
...WHERE JEANNE STRUGGLES WITH WHETHER OR NOT SHE SHOULD USE THE POWER OF GOD.
SHUDDER
DIALOGUE CHECK
I SAY, WHERE'S THE STRUGGLE?! MARON SHOULD JUST BE MORE UP FRONT ABOUT EVERYTHING!
HA HA HA HA HA HA HA HA HA
MY EDITOR, XXXHASHI-SAN
CHIAKI, I LOVE YOU! SO I'M GOING TO GIVE UP MY THIEVING WAYS!
MARON, I LOVE YOU, TOO!
CHUCKLE
HO! HO!
CHIAKI AND MARON ARE BOTH MINE!
I LIKE MARON-SAN AND TODAIJI-SAN!
UH...NO! THAT'S YOUR VERSION OF JEANNE!!
WHAT'S WRONG?! TANEMURA-SAN?! TANE-MURA-SAN?!
PUNER PUNER
GROAN

AH, WELL...THAT VERSION COULD BE INTERESTING...BUT IN FACT, THAT'S THE EXACT OPPOSITE OF MY POINT OF VIEW ON THE SERIES.

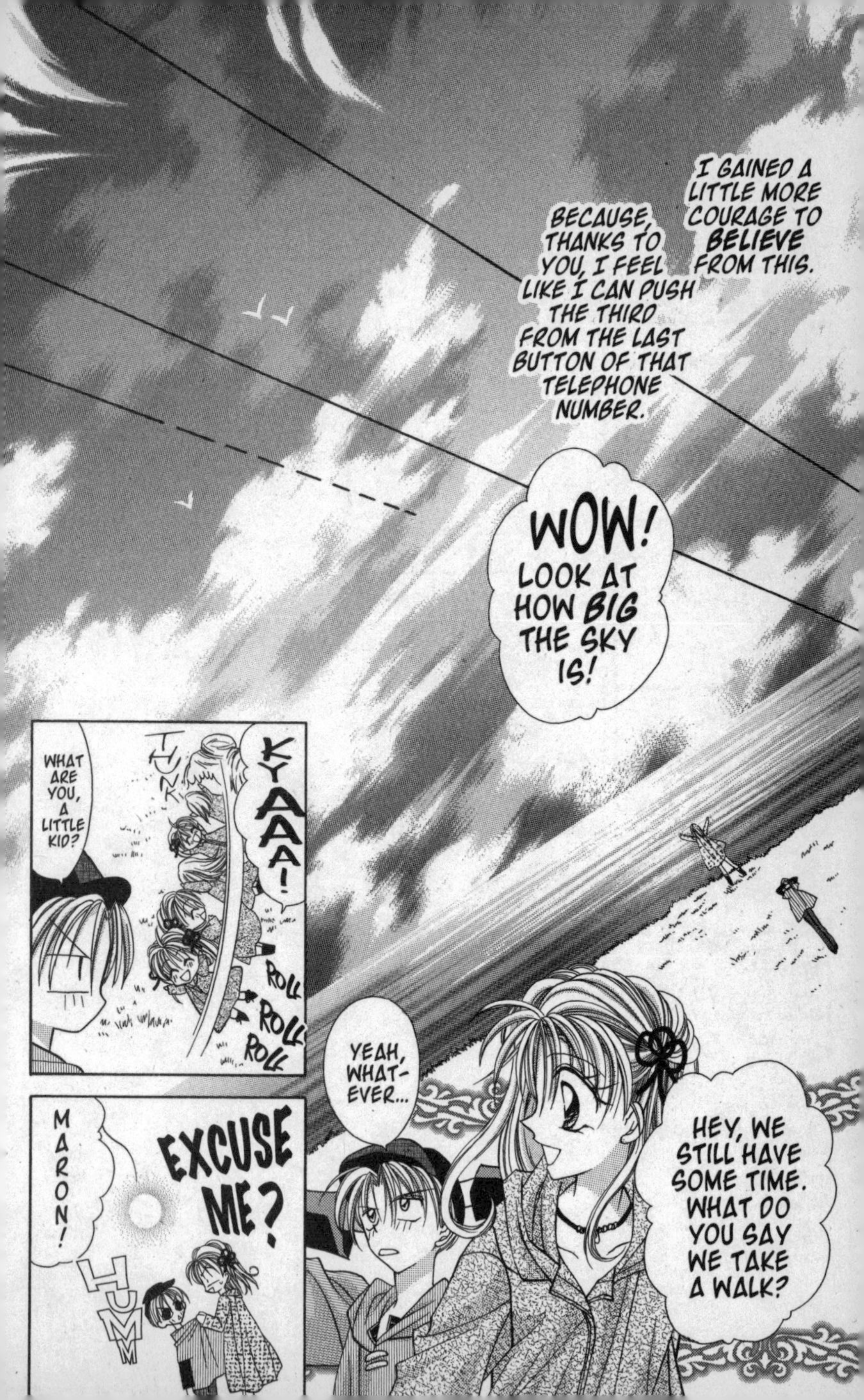
I GAINED A LITTLE MORE COURAGE TO **BELIEVE** FROM THIS.
BECAUSE, THANKS TO YOU, I FEEL LIKE I CAN PUSH THE THIRD FROM THE LAST BUTTON OF THAT TELEPHONE NUMBER.
WOW! LOOK AT HOW **BIG** THE SKY IS!
HEY, WE STILL HAVE SOME TIME. WHAT DO YOU SAY WE TAKE A WALK?
YEAH, WHATEVER...
KYAAAA!
THUNK
WHAT ARE YOU, A LITTLE KID?
ROLL ROLL ROLL
EXCUSE ME?
MARON!
HUMM

RADIO (continued)

I'm stupid, but I did try my best to speak well...so maybe it was okay...Right now, though, I feel so embarrassed that I can't even listen to the taped interviews on the radio. (Really, I am such an idiot. I mean, I knew that, but I didn't know I was this stupid.) But if any of you listened to the shows and recorded them on tape, do me a favor...and seal them away...okay? No? Heh-heh...

Actually, the Komori-san that I met on the radio was exactly the same as in "real life." Being on the air didn't change her a bit; she was super-sweet with a vengeance, like, if there were degrees of being kind, she'd be a black belt. And she's cute to boot...really, the perfect human. I felt so fortunate for getting to meet this person who I have tons of respect for. And even now, I keep those precious memories of talking to Komori-san in my heart. (Really, her "Summer-colored Wings" is a great song. It's a single, available from King Records, out now!!!...)

I love the book "31 Hints Towards Having a Happy Heart" (published in July by Shinseisha). I read it every day. Thank you♡

And to Kuwashima-san, staff member Furutani-san and everyone else, I give a heart-felt thank you. And I'm sorry if I got in anyone's way (especially to Konami's Ikeda-san).

But thanks to you, I'll keep on keeping on, stronger than before, and **definitely** not lose to my own weaknesses...!!!

Sorry for the show of over-confidence. Heh♡

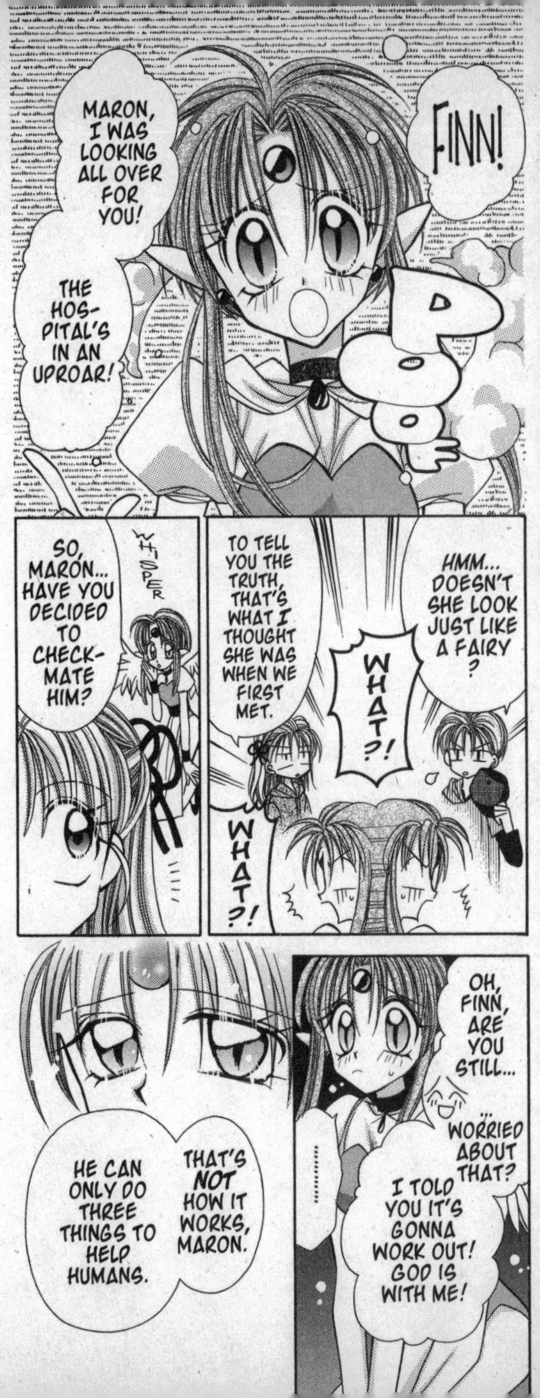
FINN!
POOF
MARON, I WAS LOOKING ALL OVER FOR YOU!
THE HOSPITAL'S IN AN UPROAR!
HMM... DOESN'T SHE LOOK JUST LIKE A FAIRY?
TO TELL YOU THE TRUTH, THAT'S WHAT I THOUGHT SHE WAS WHEN WE FIRST MET.
WHAT?!
WHAT?!
WHISPER
SO, MARON... HAVE YOU DECIDED TO CHECKMATE HIM?
OH, FINN, ARE YOU STILL...
...WORRIED ABOUT THAT?
I TOLD YOU IT'S GONNA WORK OUT! GOD IS WITH ME!
THAT'S NOT HOW IT WORKS, MARON.
HE CAN ONLY DO THREE THINGS TO HELP HUMANS.

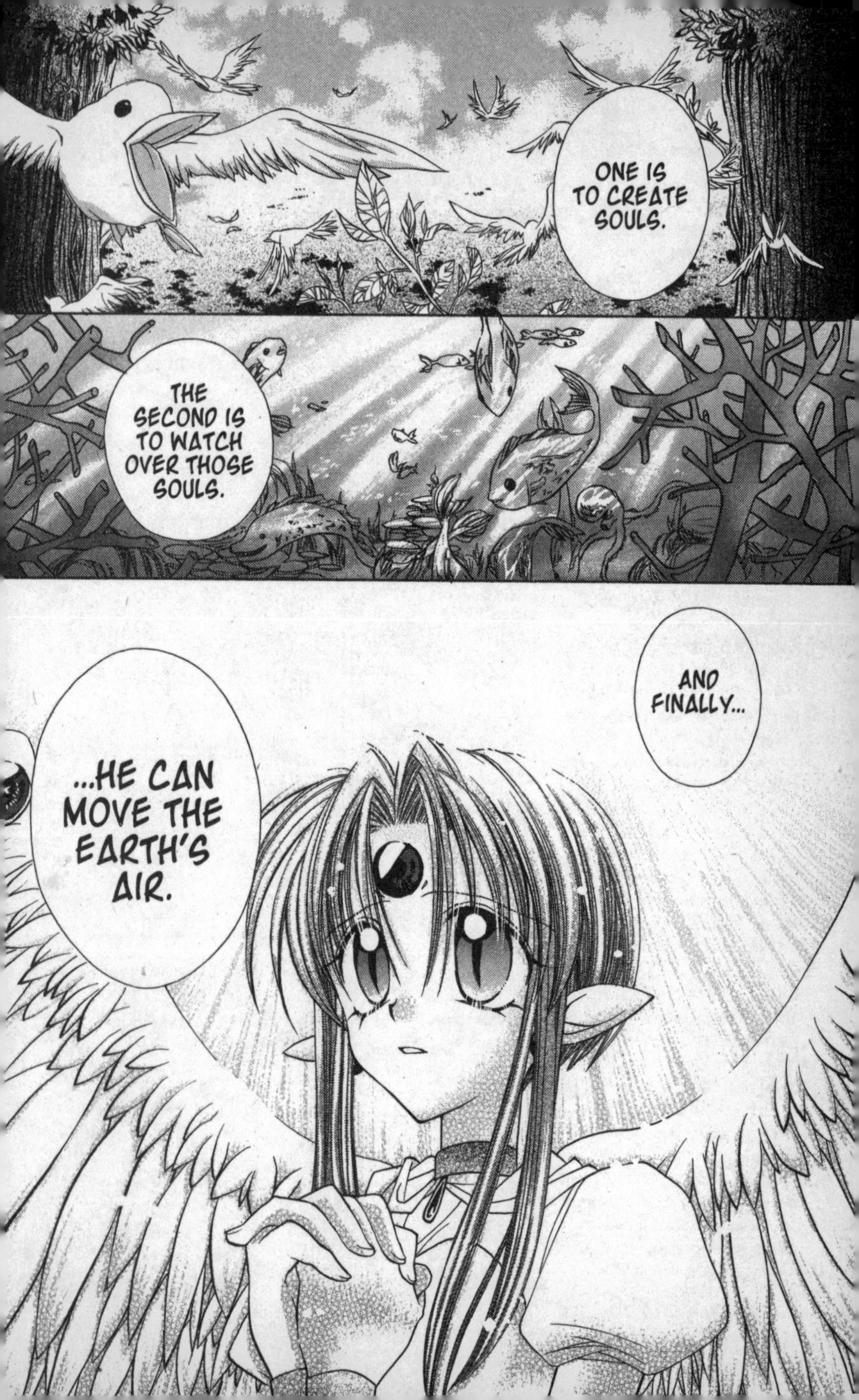
ONE IS TO CREATE SOULS.
THE SECOND IS TO WATCH OVER THOSE SOULS.
AND FINALLY...
...HE CAN MOVE THE EARTH'S AIR.

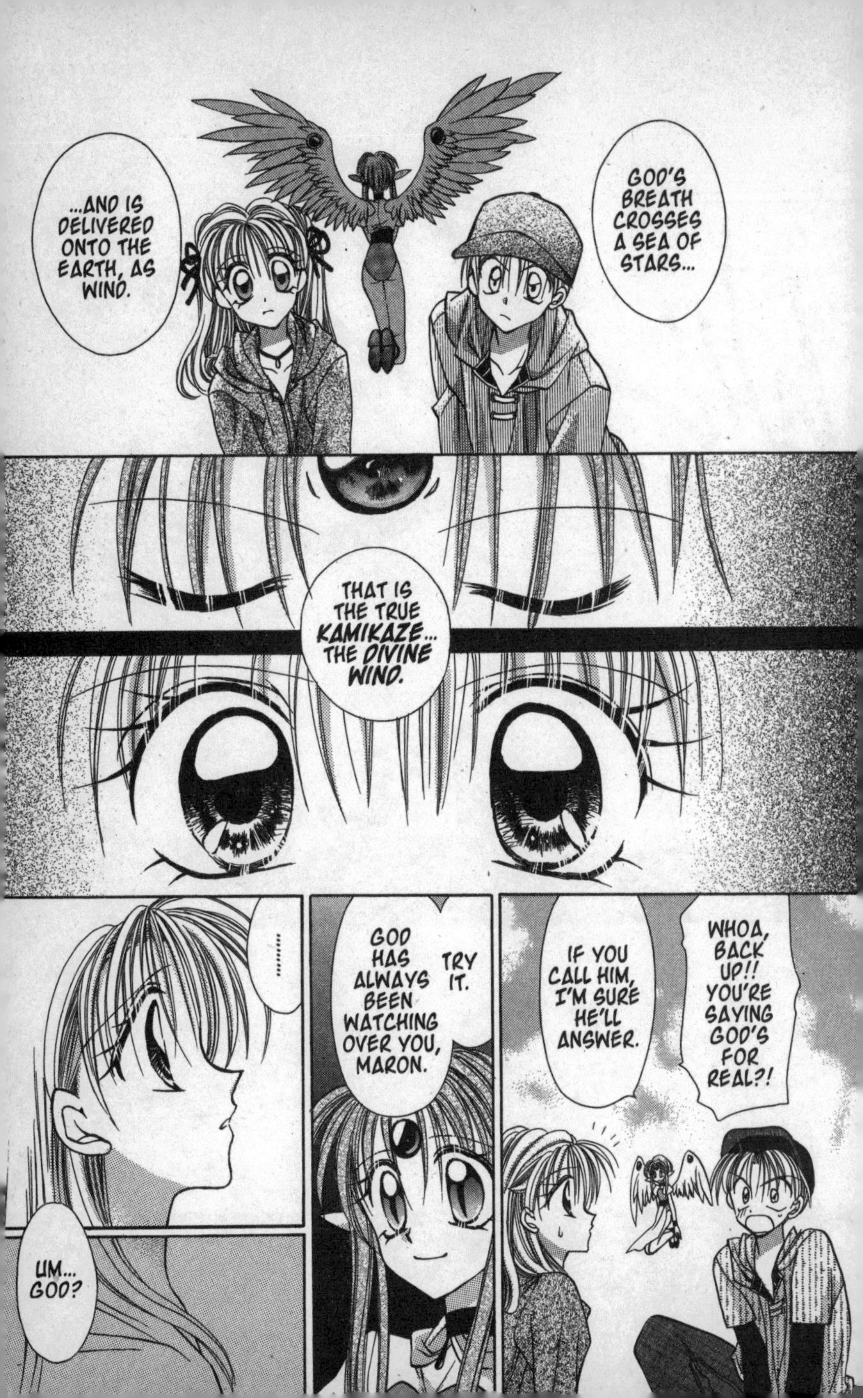
GOD'S BREATH CROSSES A SEA OF STARS...
...AND IS DELIVERED ONTO THE EARTH, AS WIND.
THAT IS THE TRUE *KAMIKAZE*... THE *DIVINE* WIND.
WHOA, BACK UP!! YOU'RE SAYING GOD'S FOR REAL?!
IF YOU CALL HIM, I'M SURE HE'LL ANSWER.
TRY IT.
GOD HAS ALWAYS BEEN WATCHING OVER YOU, MARON.
......
UM... GOD?

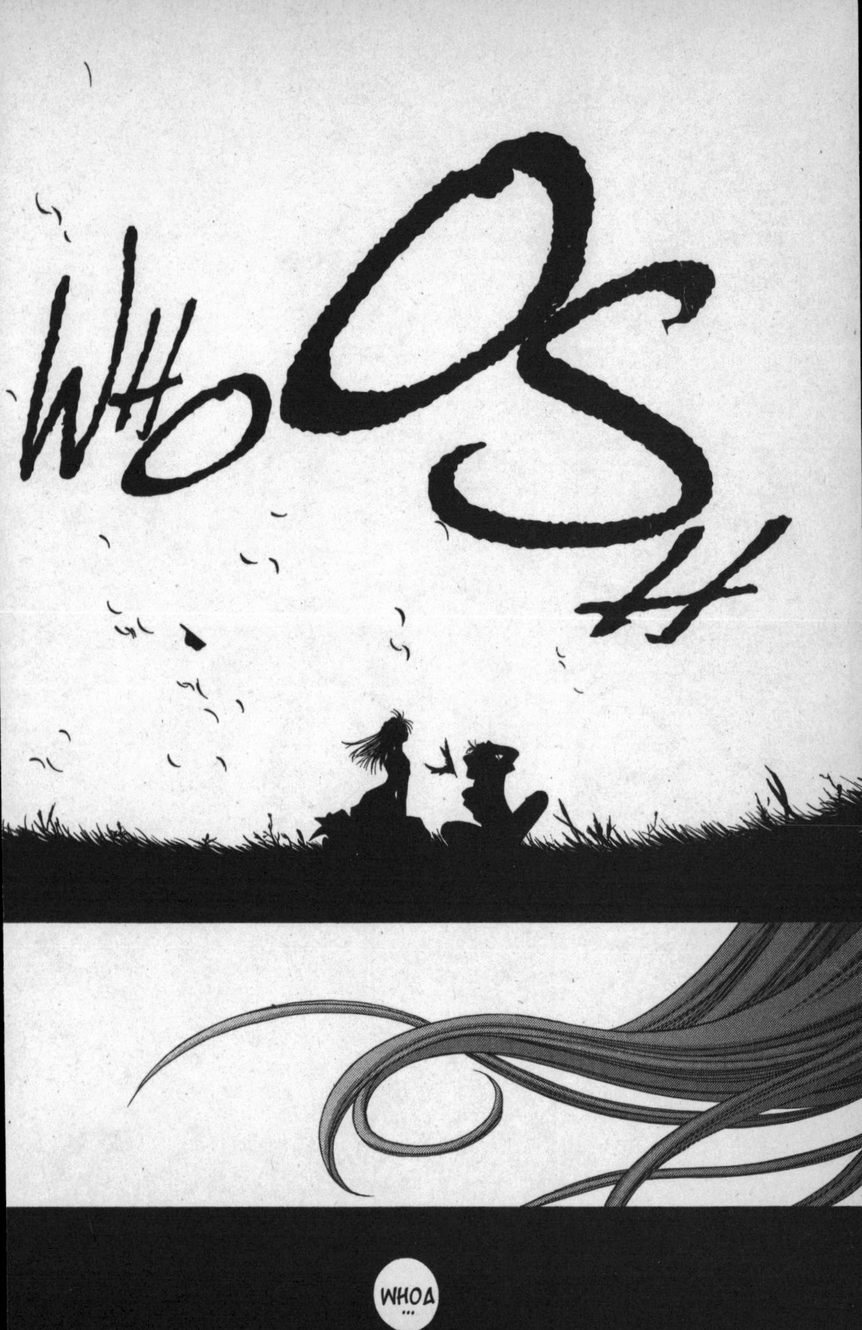
WHOOSH
WHOA...

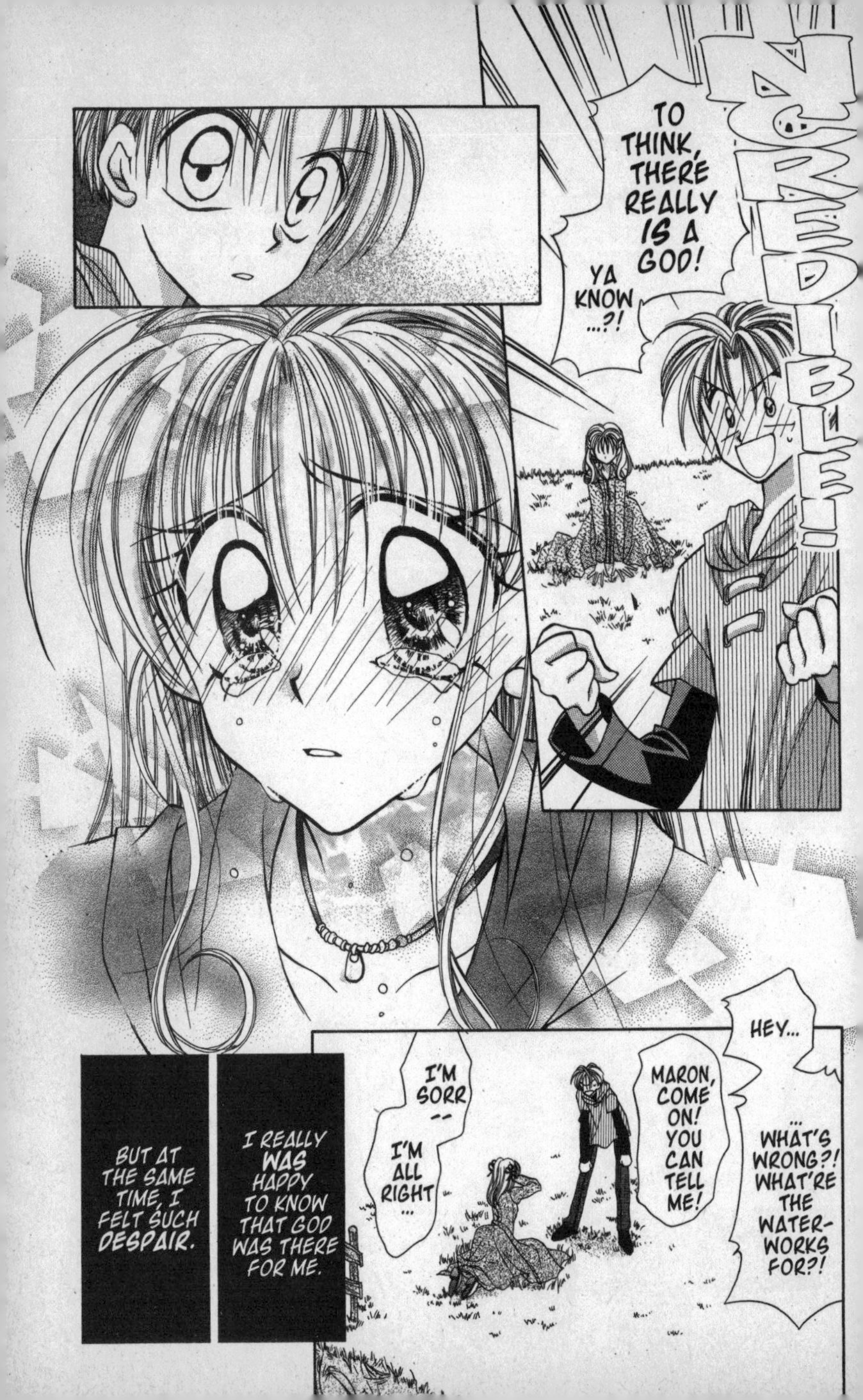

INCREDIBLE!!
TO THINK, THERE REALLY IS A GOD!
YA KNOW...?!
HEY...
...WHAT'S WRONG?! WHAT'RE THE WATER-WORKS FOR?!
MARON, COME ON! YOU CAN TELL ME!
I'M SORR--
I'M ALL RIGHT...
I REALLY WAS HAPPY TO KNOW THAT GOD WAS THERE FOR ME.
BUT AT THE SAME TIME, I FELT SUCH DESPAIR.

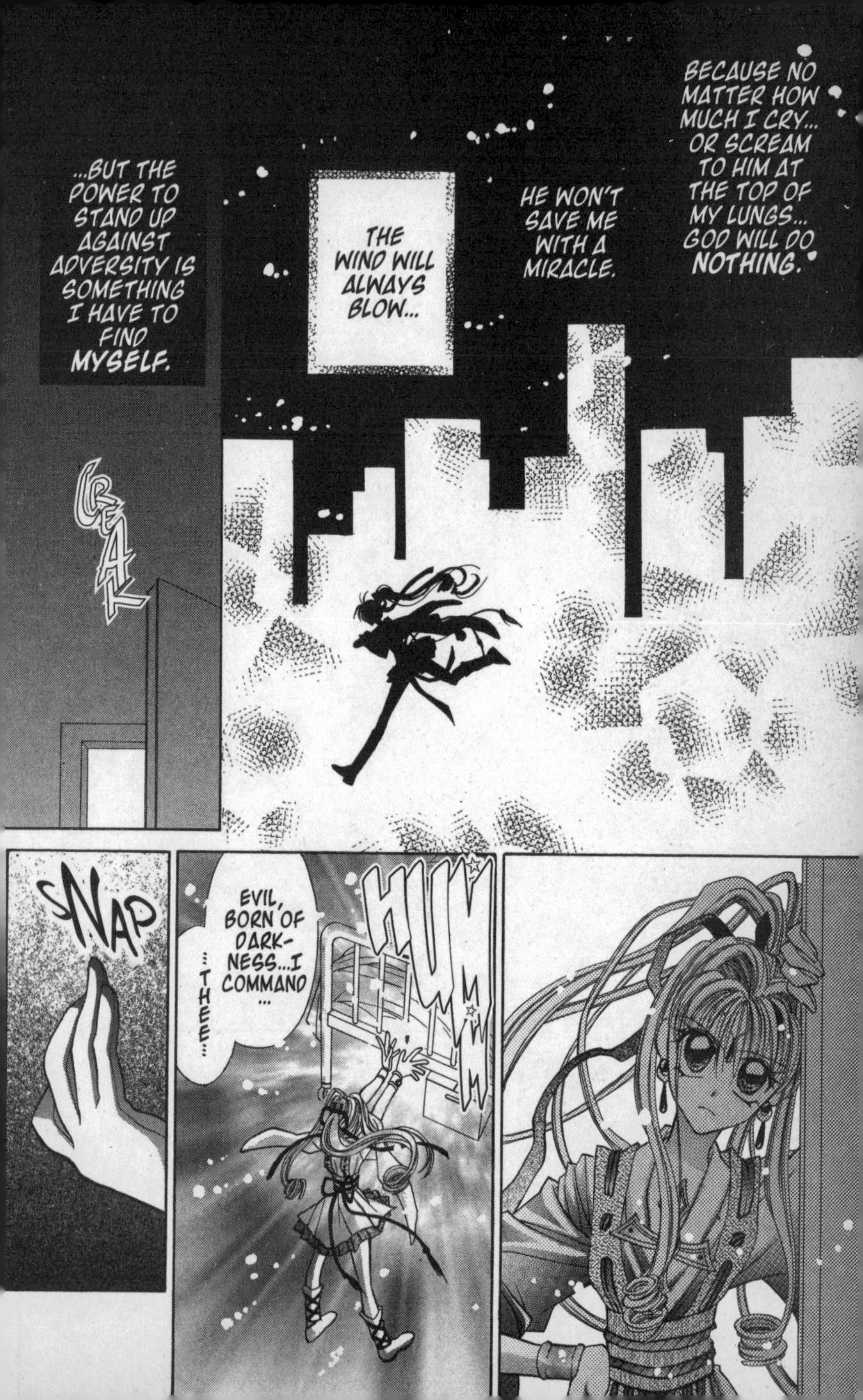
BECAUSE NO MATTER HOW MUCH I CRY... OR SCREAM TO HIM AT THE TOP OF MY LUNGS... GOD WILL DO NOTHING.
HE WON'T SAVE ME WITH A MIRACLE.
THE WIND WILL ALWAYS BLOW...
...BUT THE POWER TO STAND UP AGAINST ADVERSITY IS SOMETHING I HAVE TO FIND MYSELF.
CREAK
EVIL, BORN OF DARKNESS...I COMMAND ...
...THEE...
HUM
SNAP

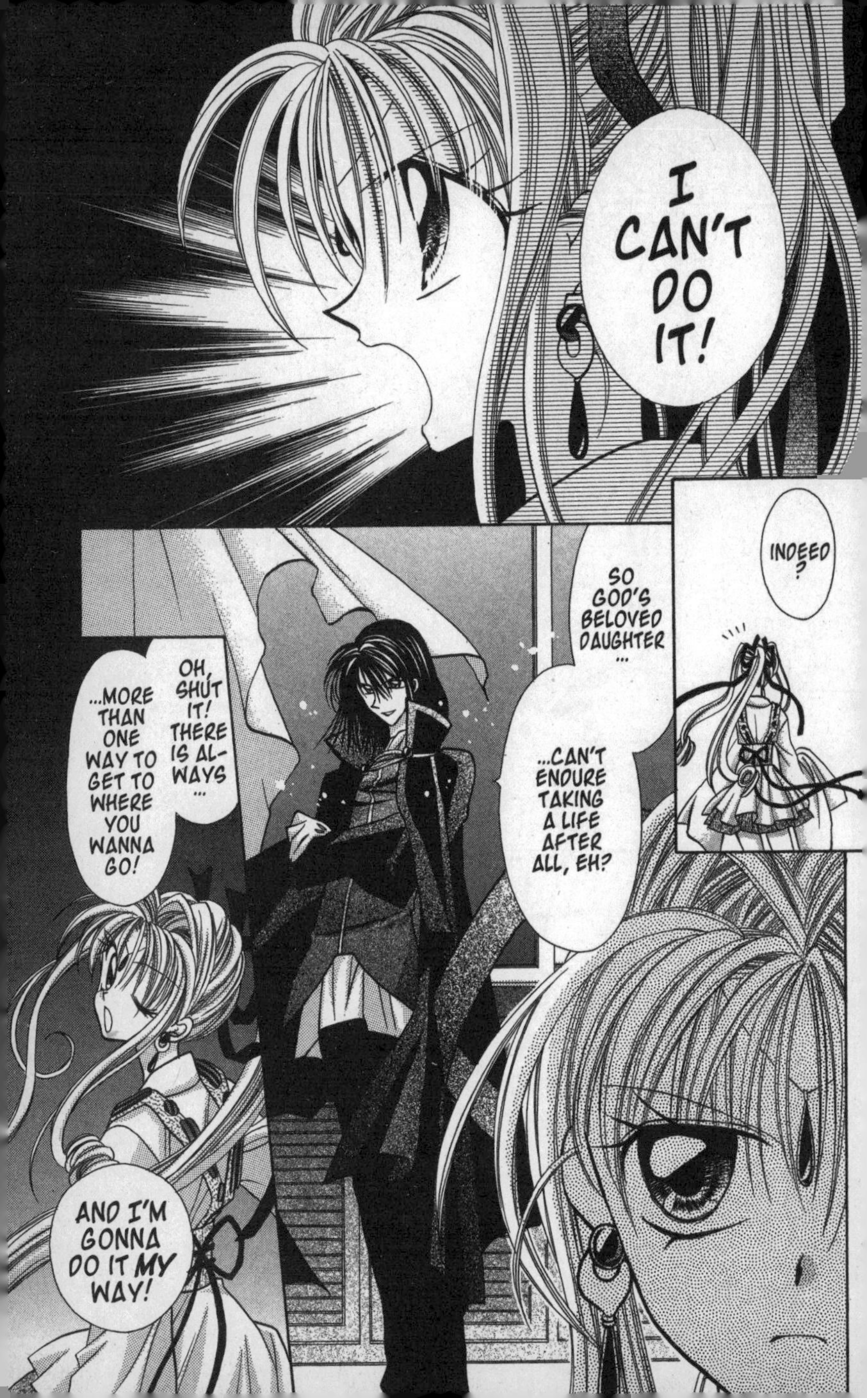
I CAN'T DO IT!
INDEED?
SO GOD'S BELOVED DAUGHTER ...
...CAN'T ENDURE TAKING A LIFE AFTER ALL, EH?
OH, SHUT IT! THERE IS AL-WAYS ...
...MORE THAN ONE WAY TO GET TO WHERE YOU WANNA GO!
AND I'M GONNA DO IT MY WAY!

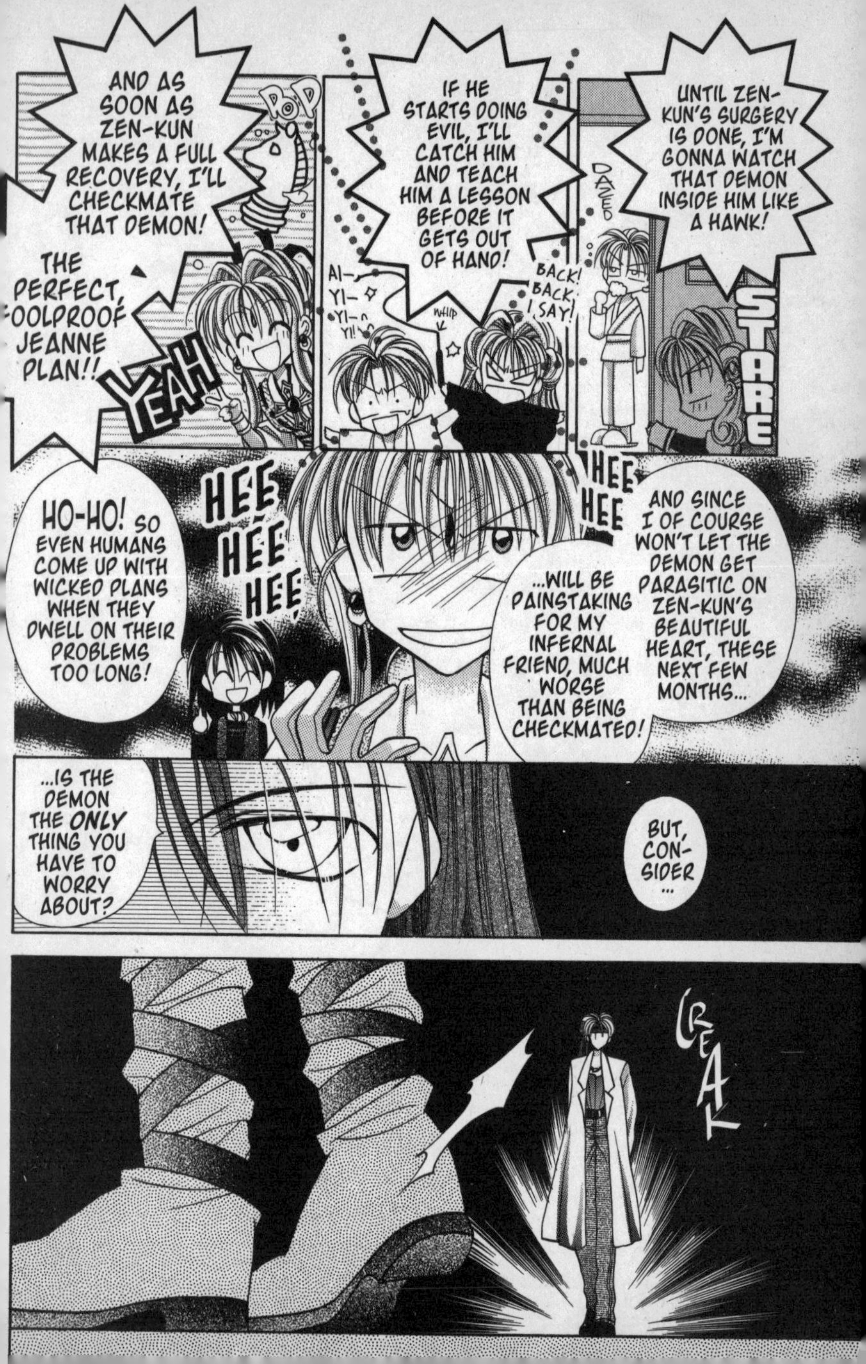
UNTIL ZEN-KUN'S SURGERY IS DONE, I'M GONNA WATCH THAT DEMON INSIDE HIM LIKE A HAWK!
DAZED
STARE
IF HE STARTS DOING EVIL, I'LL CATCH HIM AND TEACH HIM A LESSON BEFORE IT GETS OUT OF HAND!
BACK! BACK! I SAY!
WHIP
AI-YI-YI-YI!
AND AS SOON AS ZEN-KUN MAKES A FULL RECOVERY, I'LL CHECKMATE THAT DEMON!
POP
THE PERFECT, FOOLPROOF JEANNE PLAN!!
YEAH
HEE HEE
AND SINCE I OF COURSE WON'T LET THE DEMON GET PARASITIC ON ZEN-KUN'S BEAUTIFUL HEART, THESE NEXT FEW MONTHS...
...WILL BE PAINSTAKING FOR MY INFERNAL FRIEND, MUCH WORSE THAN BEING CHECKMATED!
HEE HEE HEE
HO-HO! SO EVEN HUMANS COME UP WITH WICKED PLANS WHEN THEY DWELL ON THEIR PROBLEMS TOO LONG!
BUT, CON-SIDER...
...IS THE DEMON THE *ONLY* THING YOU HAVE TO WORRY ABOUT?
CREAK

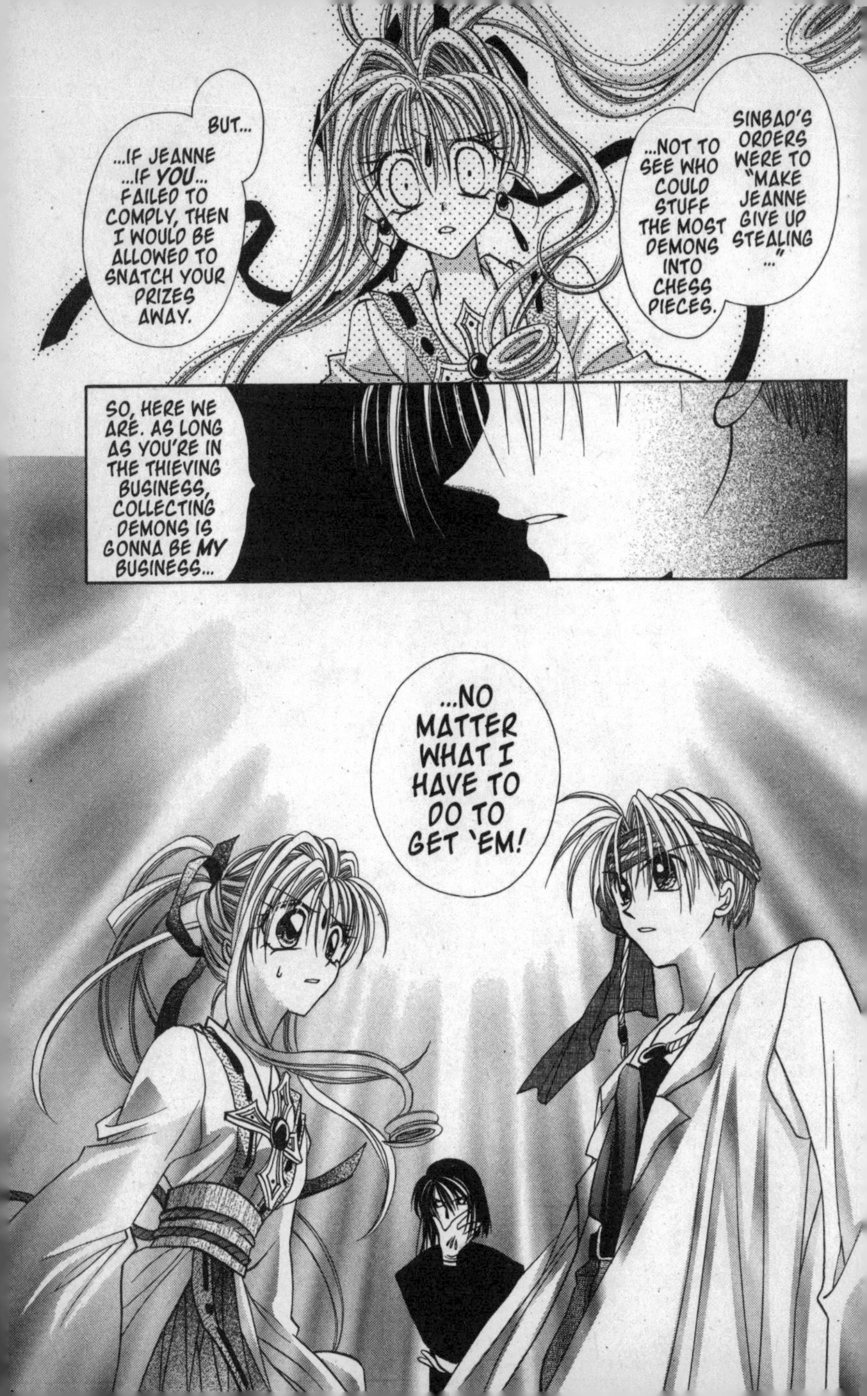
SINBAD'S ORDERS WERE TO "MAKE JEANNE GIVE UP STEALING"... ...NOT TO SEE WHO COULD STUFF THE MOST DEMONS INTO CHESS PIECES.
BUT... ...IF JEANNE ...IF YOU... FAILED TO COMPLY, THEN I WOULD BE ALLOWED TO SNATCH YOUR PRIZES AWAY.
SO, HERE WE ARE. AS LONG AS YOU'RE IN THE THIEVING BUSINESS, COLLECTING DEMONS IS GONNA BE MY BUSINESS...
...NO MATTER WHAT I HAVE TO DO TO GET 'EM!

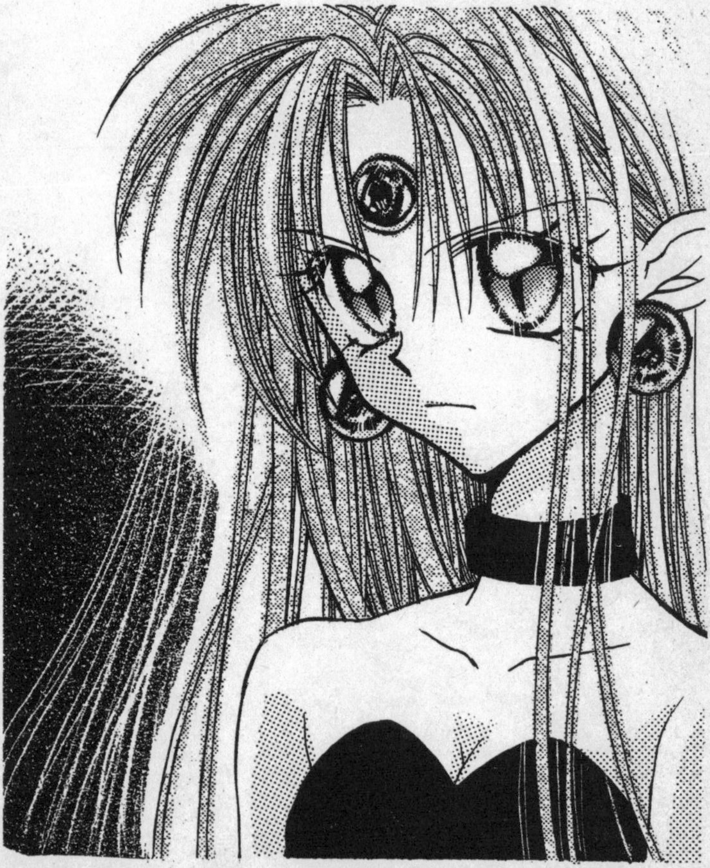

God's breath becomes the wind...
...blowing through the hearts of all creatures, great and small.

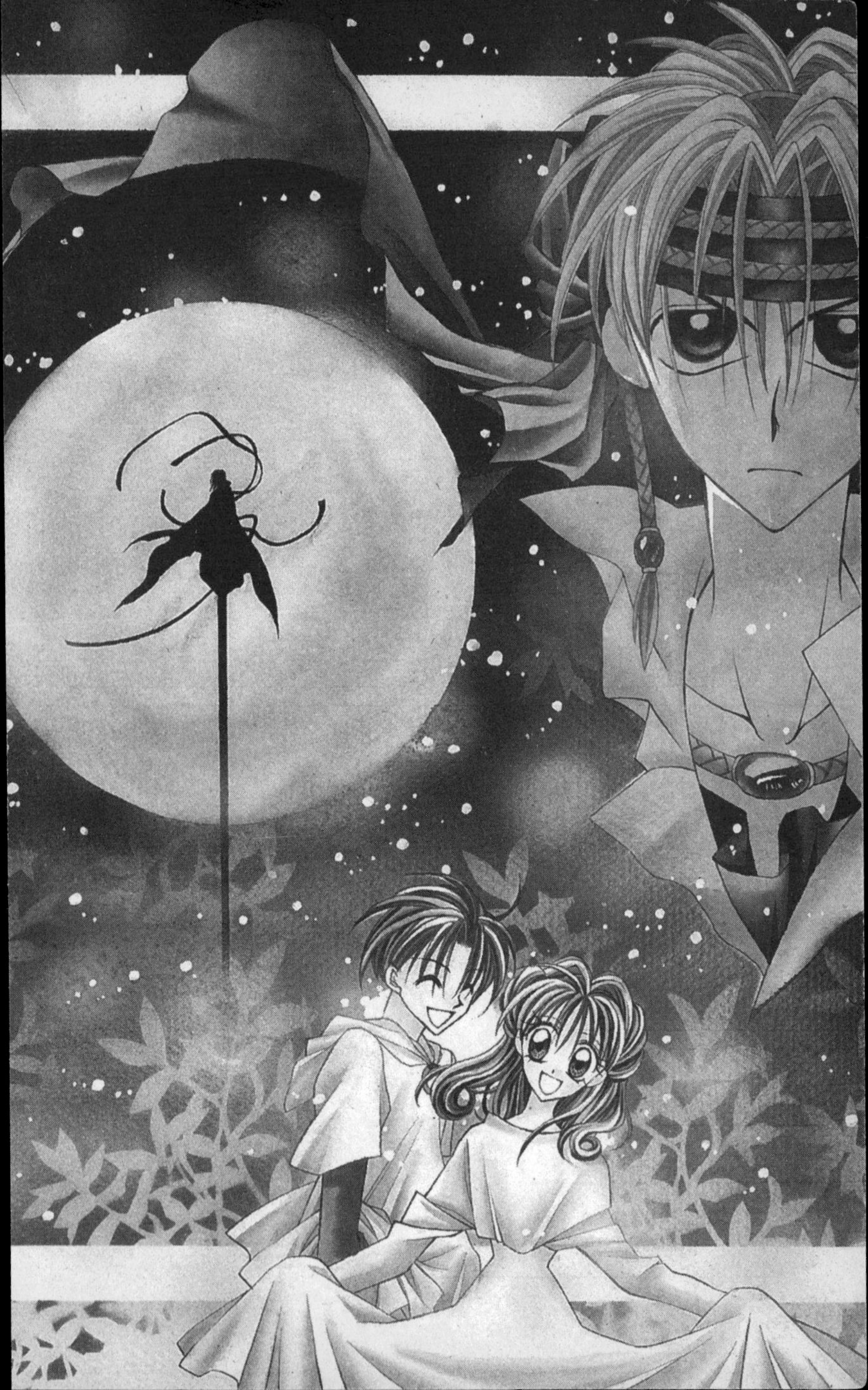

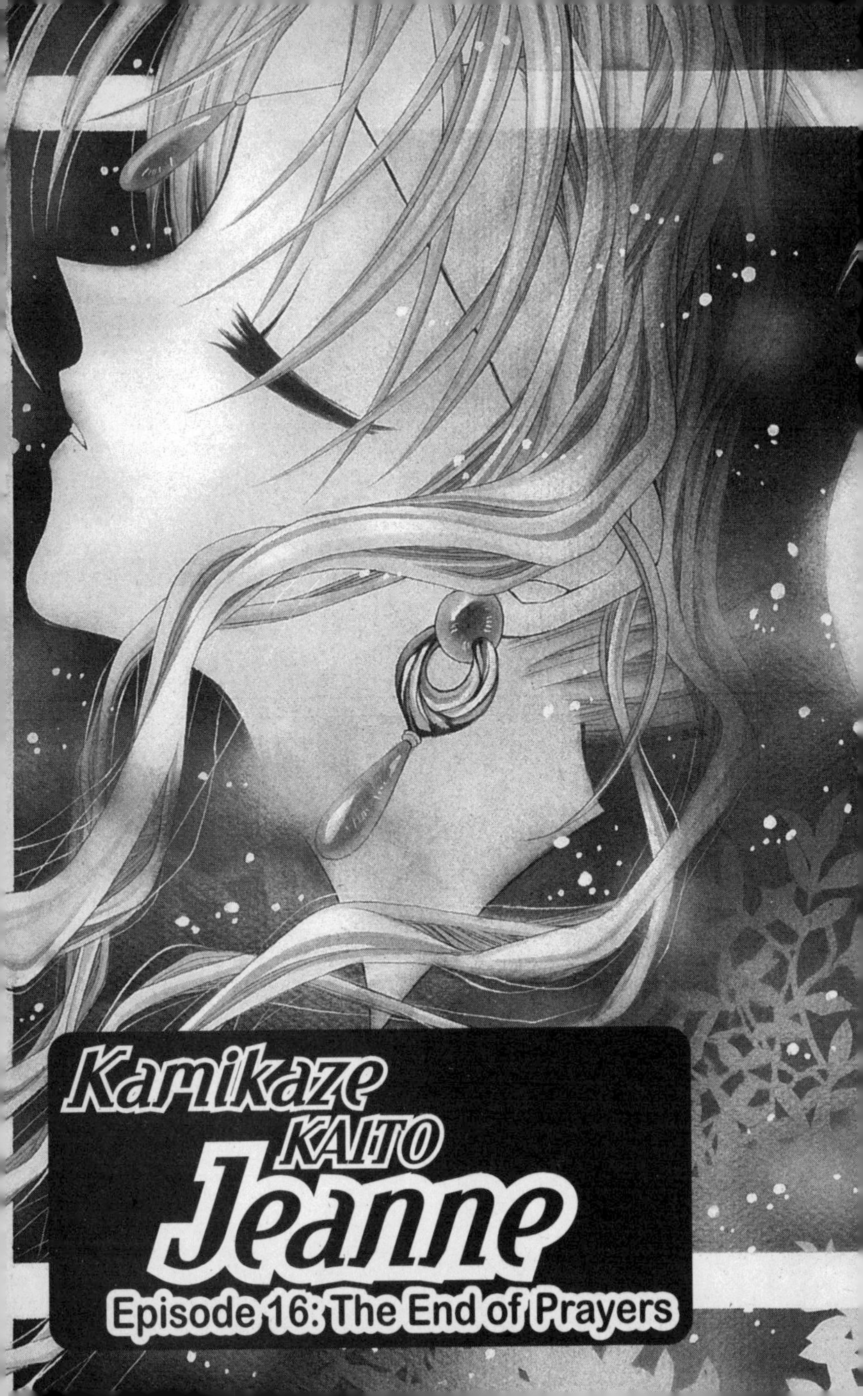
Kamikaze KAITO Jeanne
Episode 16: The End of Prayers

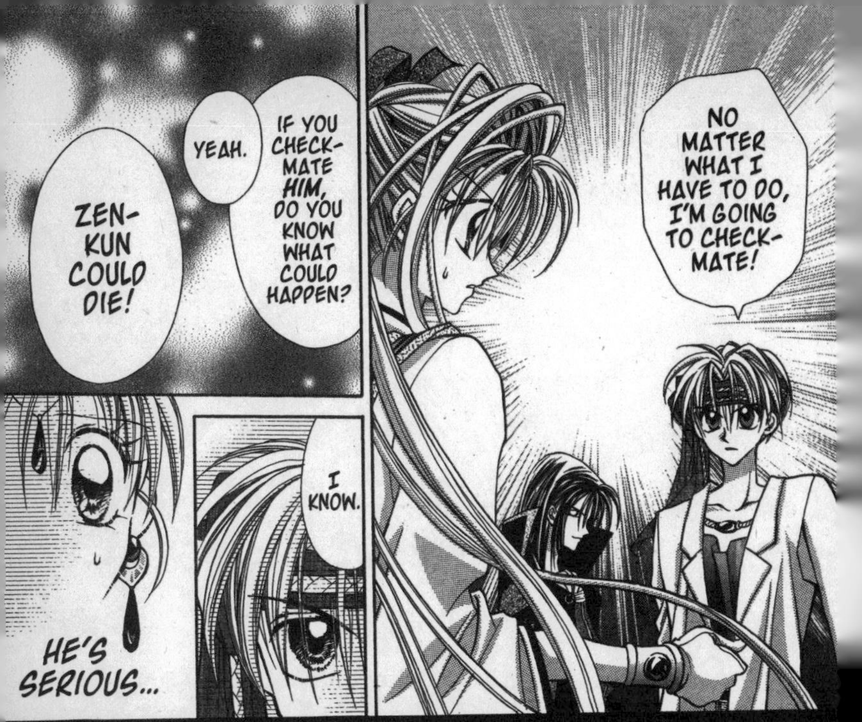
NO MATTER WHAT I HAVE TO DO, I'M GOING TO CHECKMATE!
IF YOU CHECKMATE HIM, DO YOU KNOW WHAT COULD HAPPEN?
YEAH.
ZEN-KUN COULD DIE!
I KNOW.
HE'S SERIOUS...

Episode 16: "THE END OF PRAYERS"

(WARNING: DO NOT READ THE BELOW UNTIL YOU'VE READ THE STORY!!)

The title page artwork reflects the events of episode 16.

The last time I got such a big response to an episode was for episode 8 (published in volume 2), in which we got word that Maron-chan's parents were getting a divorce...or maybe the reaction to this episode was even bigger than that. Not only was there a tremendous amount of fan letters, but also tons of feedback on the magazine's webpage (not to be confused with the webpage for the collected volumes, which doesn't get nearly that much love...) A sampling of reader responses: "It feels like a real friend of mine has died..."; "Zen-kun"; and "I cried all night in my futon."

There were a lot of points I wanted to communicate in episode 16 and I worry about whether I got them across effectively (I'm still a greenhorn regarding this aspect, too, as you can tell with Zen-kun's mother, for example...), but I'm blessed with smart and compassionate readers. Actually, fan letters were the spark for this storyline, as I get hundreds, sometimes thousands a day, with the lion's share coming from puberty-age girls, who often have heavy problems weighing on their minds. I've gotten letters from readers who've said "I want to die" and from one reader: "Even though XXX-chan loved Jeanne, she died in a car accident." I've given a lot of thought about "life" and "death" and to the girls who've said they "want to die" because "nobody wants or needs them" or because they're being bullied. (**Everyone's** been bullied at least once, including me. Everyone gets it sooner or later.) For the girls who say they're not needed by **anyone**, I say "You're **wrong**!!!" I need you, for one. I would get majorly depressed if I lost even one fan because I adore all of you! I mean, I would be extremely sad (and I know I would cry). (You would never be able to send me another fan letter...or read the last episode of Jeanne...Of course, there's a little bit of my own ego mixed in there). But there are a lot of kids in the world like Zen-kun who have a fierce desire to live but **can't** for a long time. So to everyone out there with problems, don't try to escape by choosing death, but instead try dealing with your problems one more time. (I mean, at least **10** more times, because that's how precious life is.) It's worth fighting for! I love life!! It's tough a lot of times, but it's also a lot fun!!!

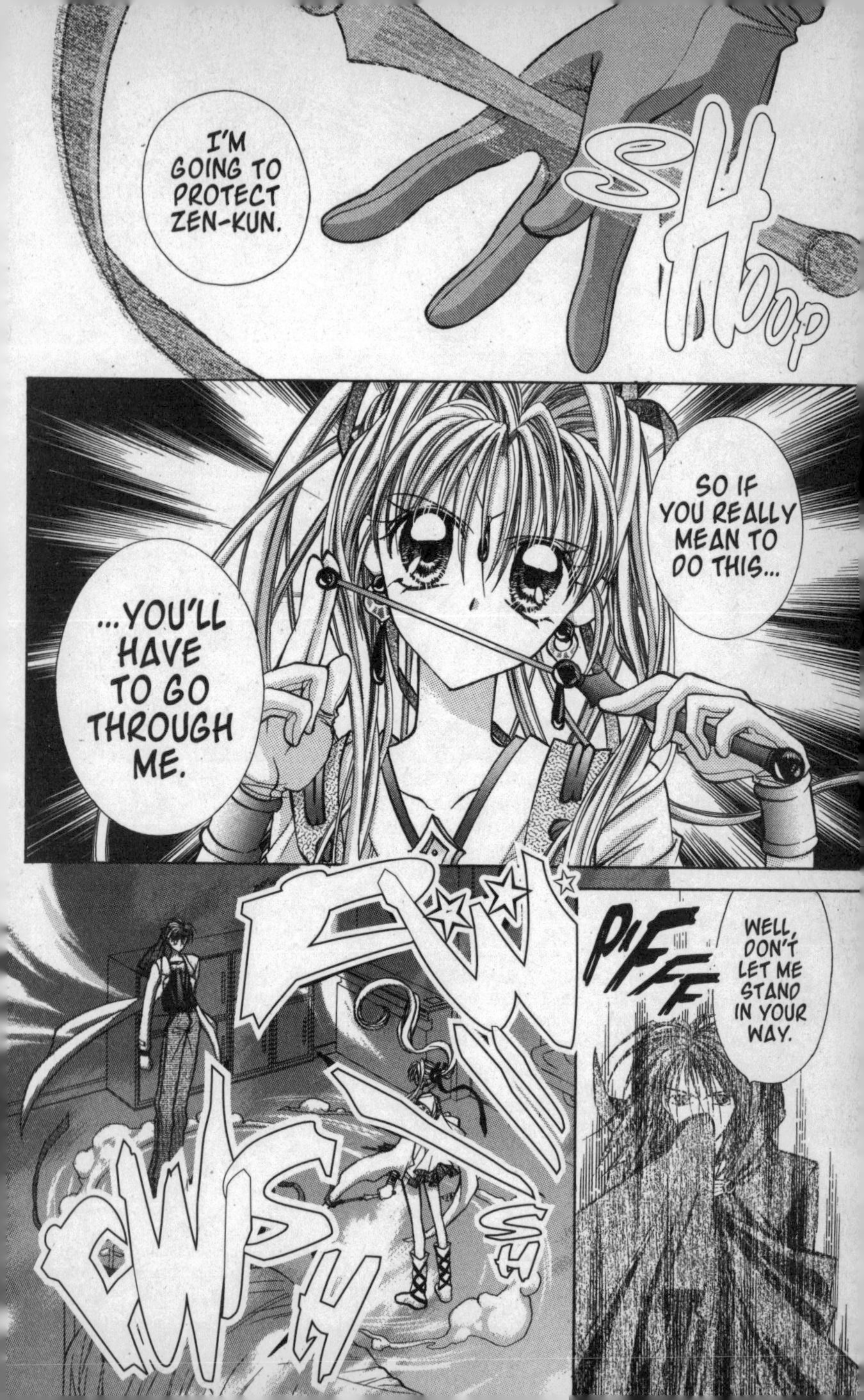
I'M GOING TO PROTECT ZEN-KUN.
SHOOP
SO IF YOU REALLY MEAN TO DO THIS...
...YOU'LL HAVE TO GO THROUGH ME.
WELL, DON'T LET ME STAND IN YOUR WAY.

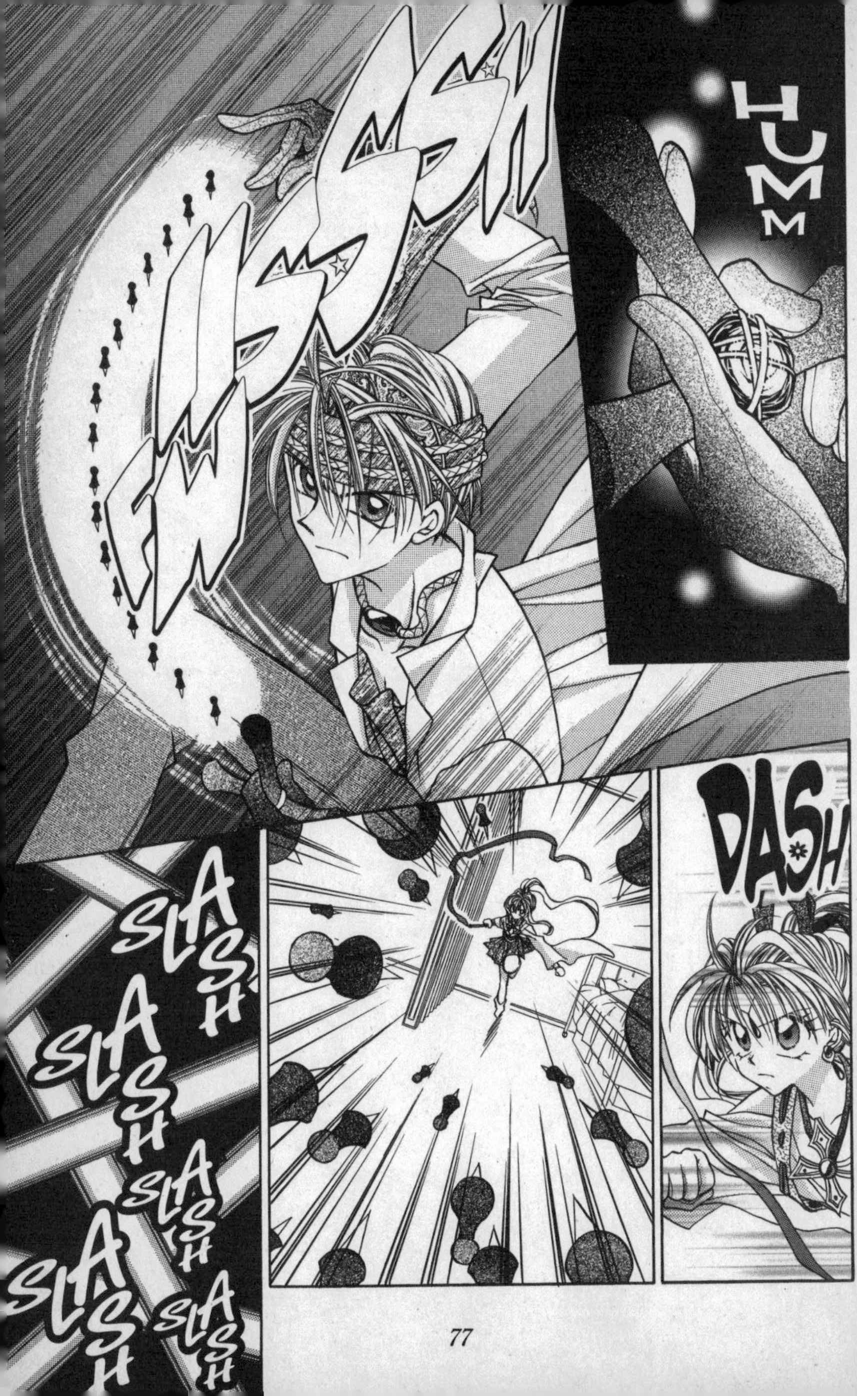
HUMM
SWISH
DASH
SLASH
SLASH
SLASH
SLASH
SLASH

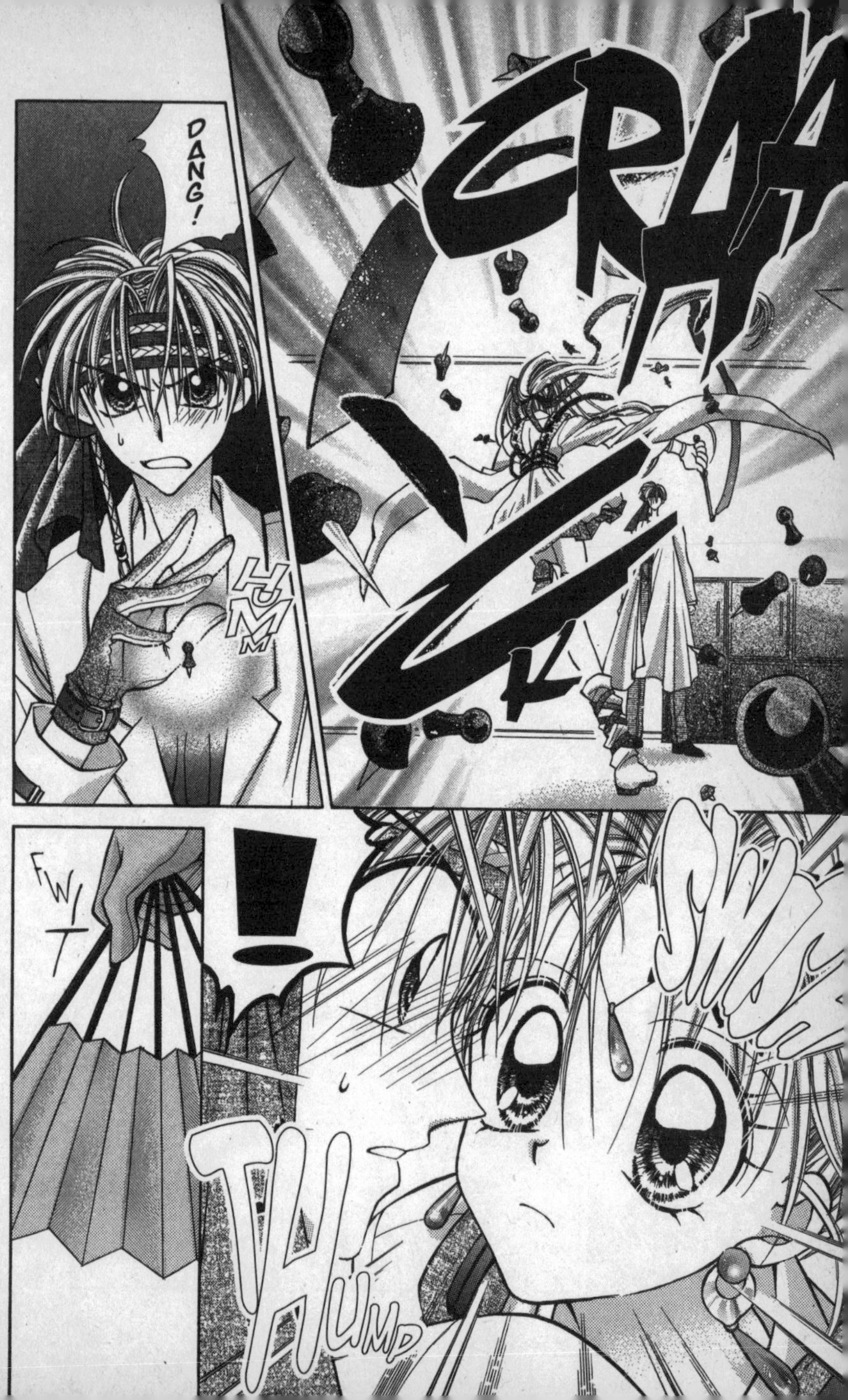
CRACK
DANG!
HUMM
THUMP
FWIT
!

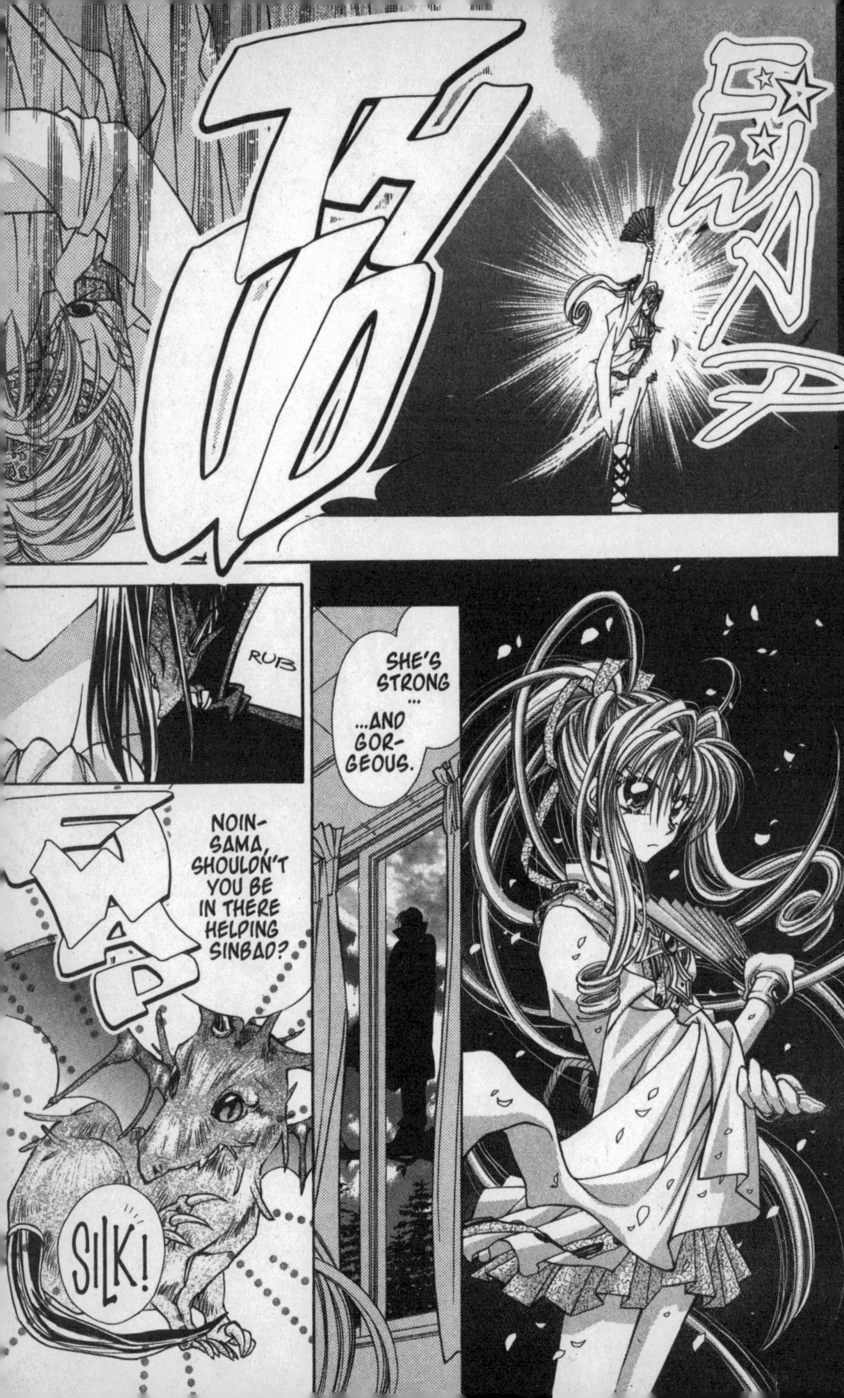
FWAP
SHE'S STRONG ...
...AND GORGEOUS.
RUB
NOIN-SAMA, SHOULDN'T YOU BE IN THERE HELPING SINBAD?
SILK!

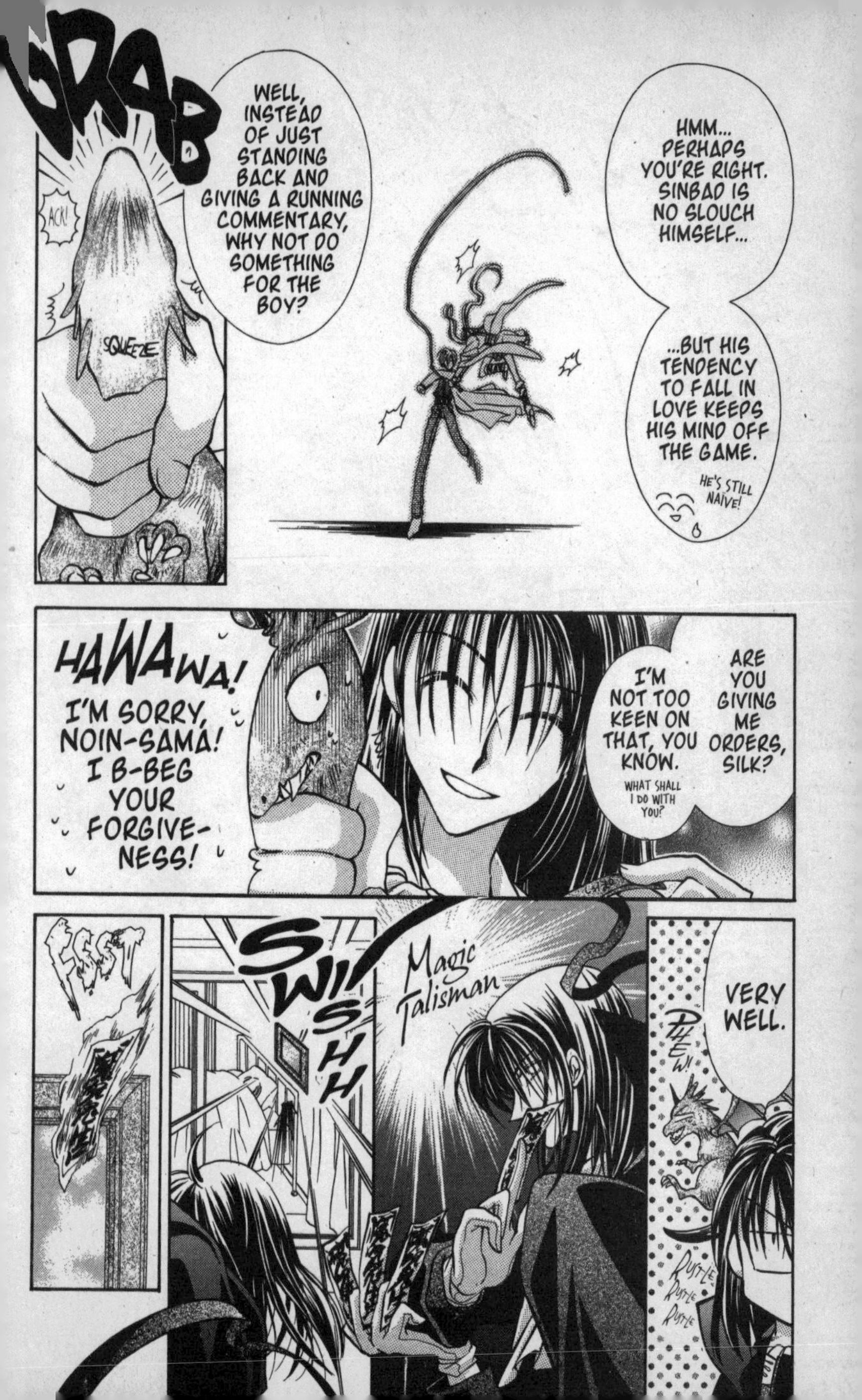
HMM... PERHAPS YOU'RE RIGHT. SINBAD IS NO SLOUCH HIMSELF...
...BUT HIS TENDENCY TO FALL IN LOVE KEEPS HIS MIND OFF THE GAME.
HE'S STILL NAÏVE!
WELL, INSTEAD OF JUST STANDING BACK AND GIVING A RUNNING COMMENTARY, WHY NOT DO SOMETHING FOR THE BOY?
GRAB
ACK!
SQUEEZE
ARE YOU GIVING ME ORDERS, SILK?
I'M NOT TOO KEEN ON THAT, YOU KNOW.
WHAT SHALL I DO WITH YOU?
HAWAWA! I'M SORRY, NOIN-SAMA! I B-BEG YOUR FORGIVE-NESS!
VERY WELL.
PHEW!
RUSTLE RUSTLE RUSTLE
SWISHH
Magic Talisman
SSST

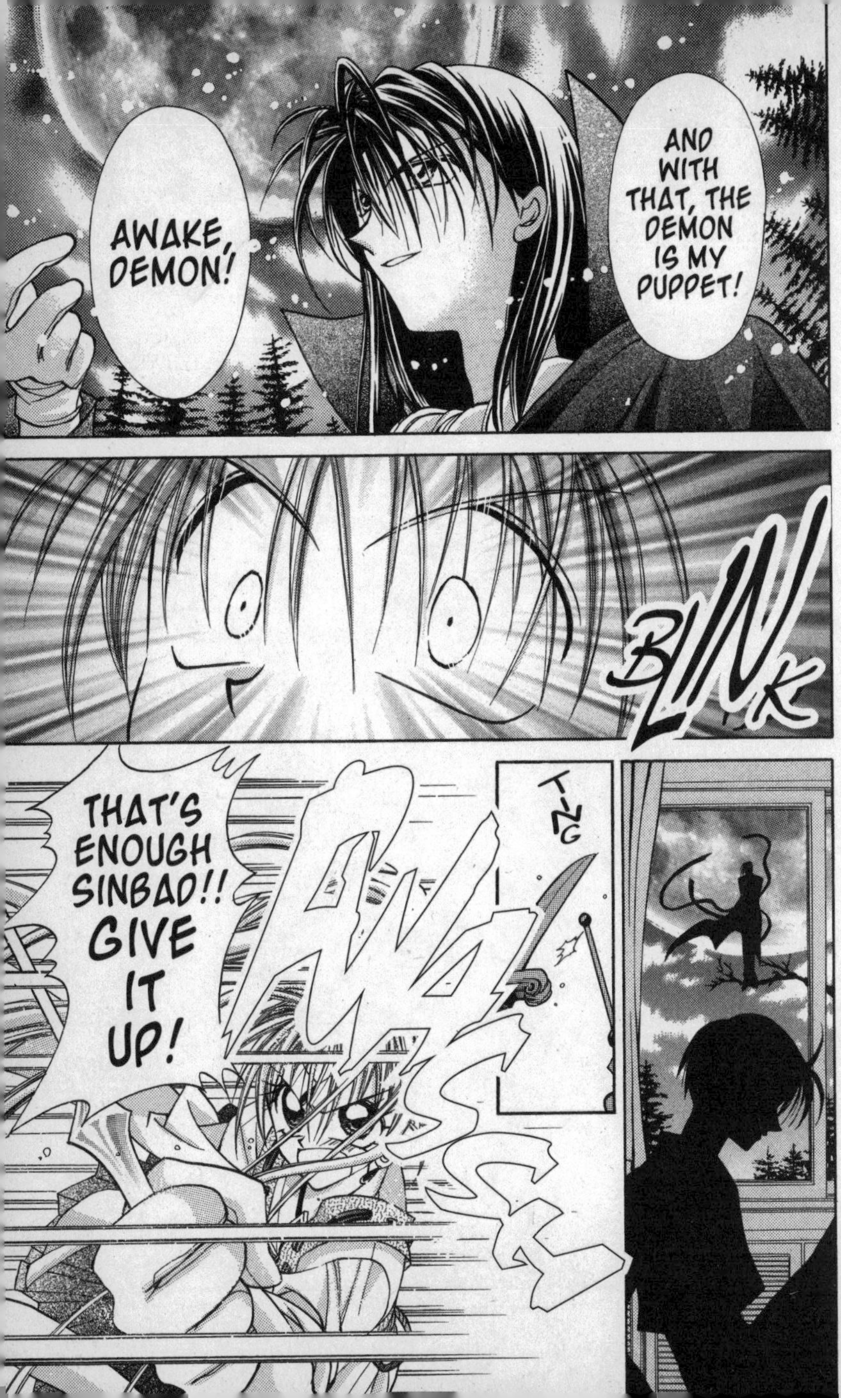
AND WITH THAT, THE DEMON IS MY PUPPET!
AWAKE, DEMON!
BLINK
TING
THAT'S ENOUGH SINBAD!! GIVE IT UP!

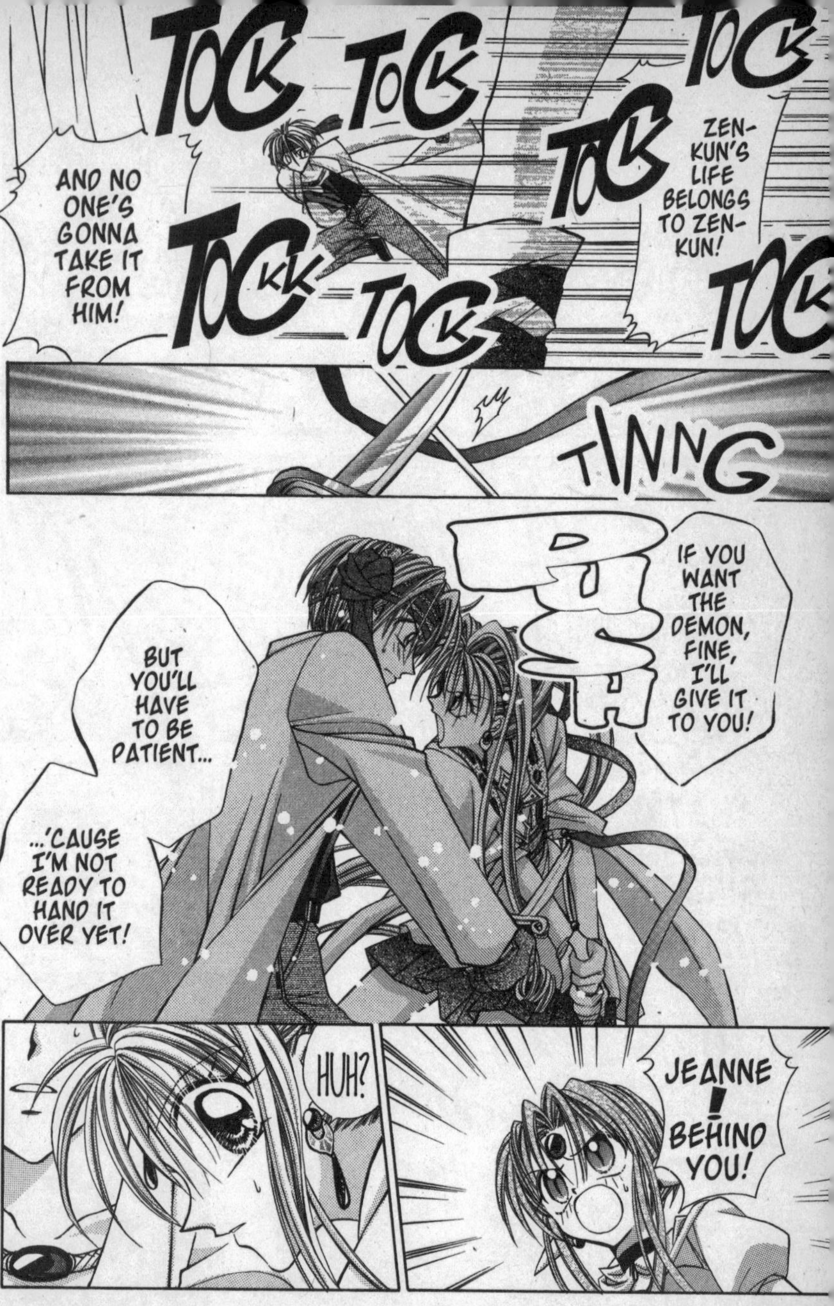
TOCK
TOCK
TOCK
ZEN-KUN'S LIFE BELONGS TO ZEN-KUN!
TOCK
TOCK
TOCKKK
TOCK
AND NO ONE'S GONNA TAKE IT FROM HIM!
TINNG
PUSH
IF YOU WANT THE DEMON, FINE, I'LL GIVE IT TO YOU!
BUT YOU'LL HAVE TO BE PATIENT...
...'CAUSE I'M NOT READY TO HAND IT OVER YET!
JEANNE! BEHIND YOU!
HUH?

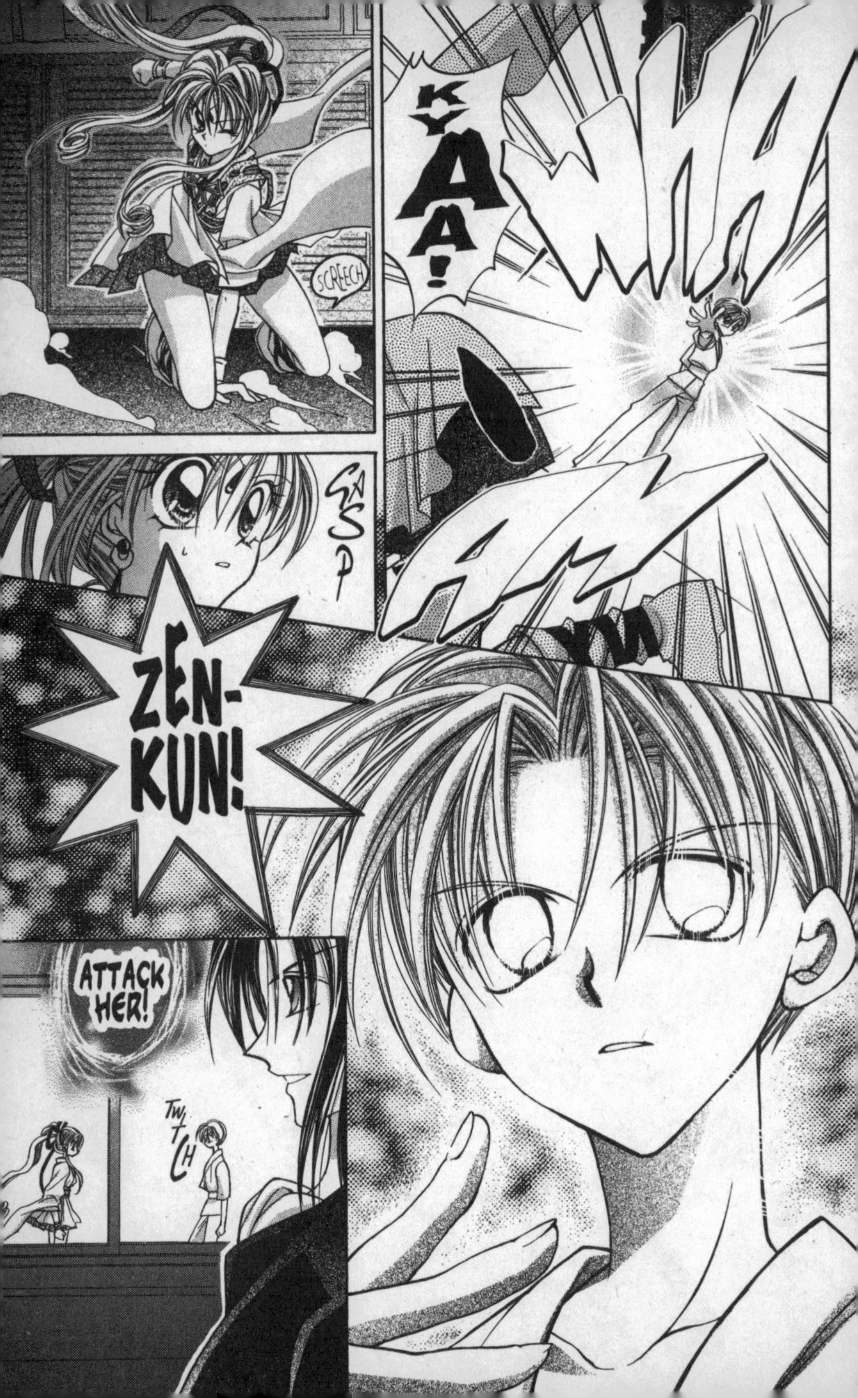
KYAA!
SCREECH
GASP
ZEN-KUN!
ATTACK HER!
TWITCH

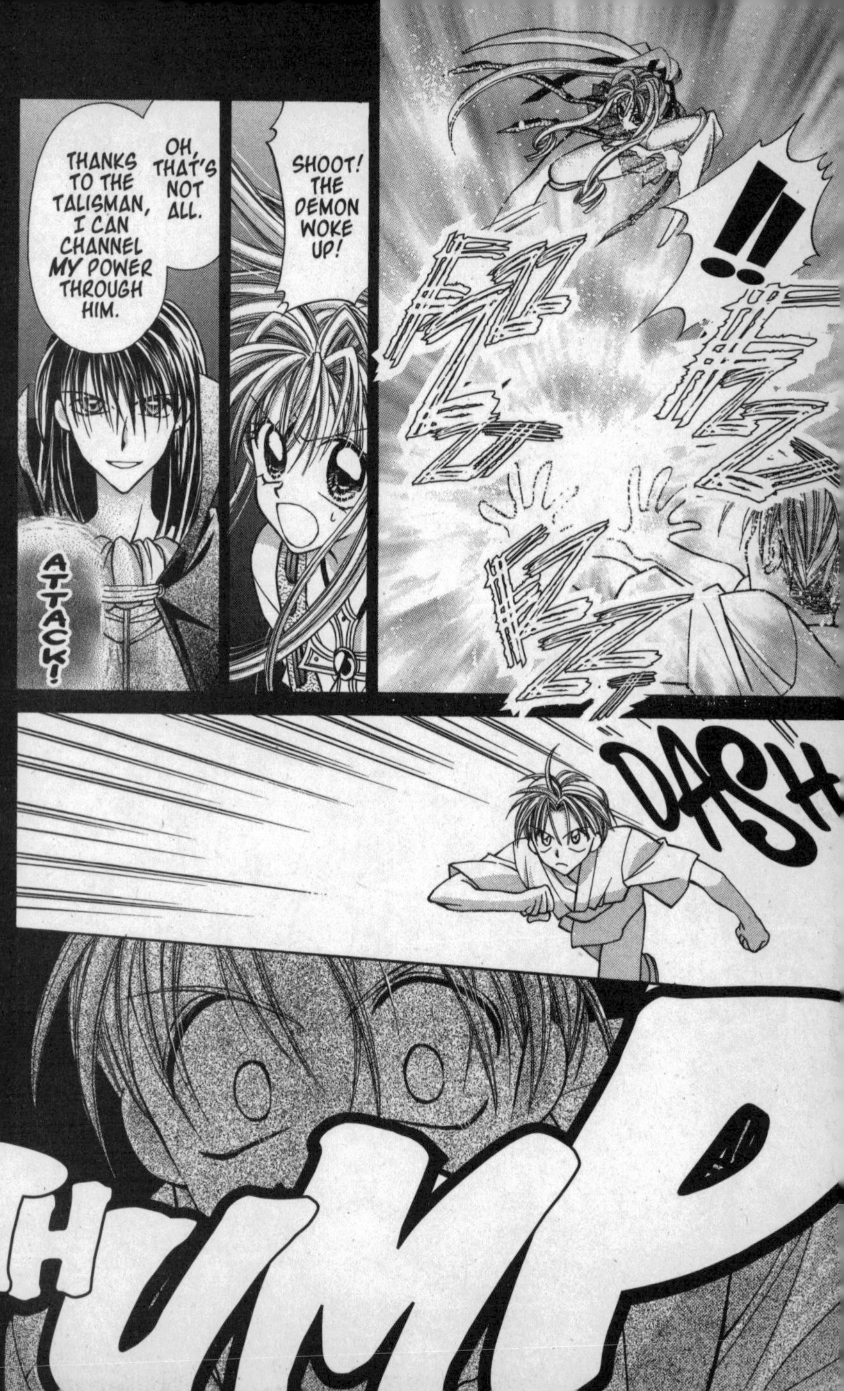
!!
SHOOT! THE DEMON WOKE UP!
OH, THAT'S NOT ALL.
THANKS TO THE TALISMAN, I CAN CHANNEL MY POWER THROUGH HIM.
ATTACK!
DASH
HUMP

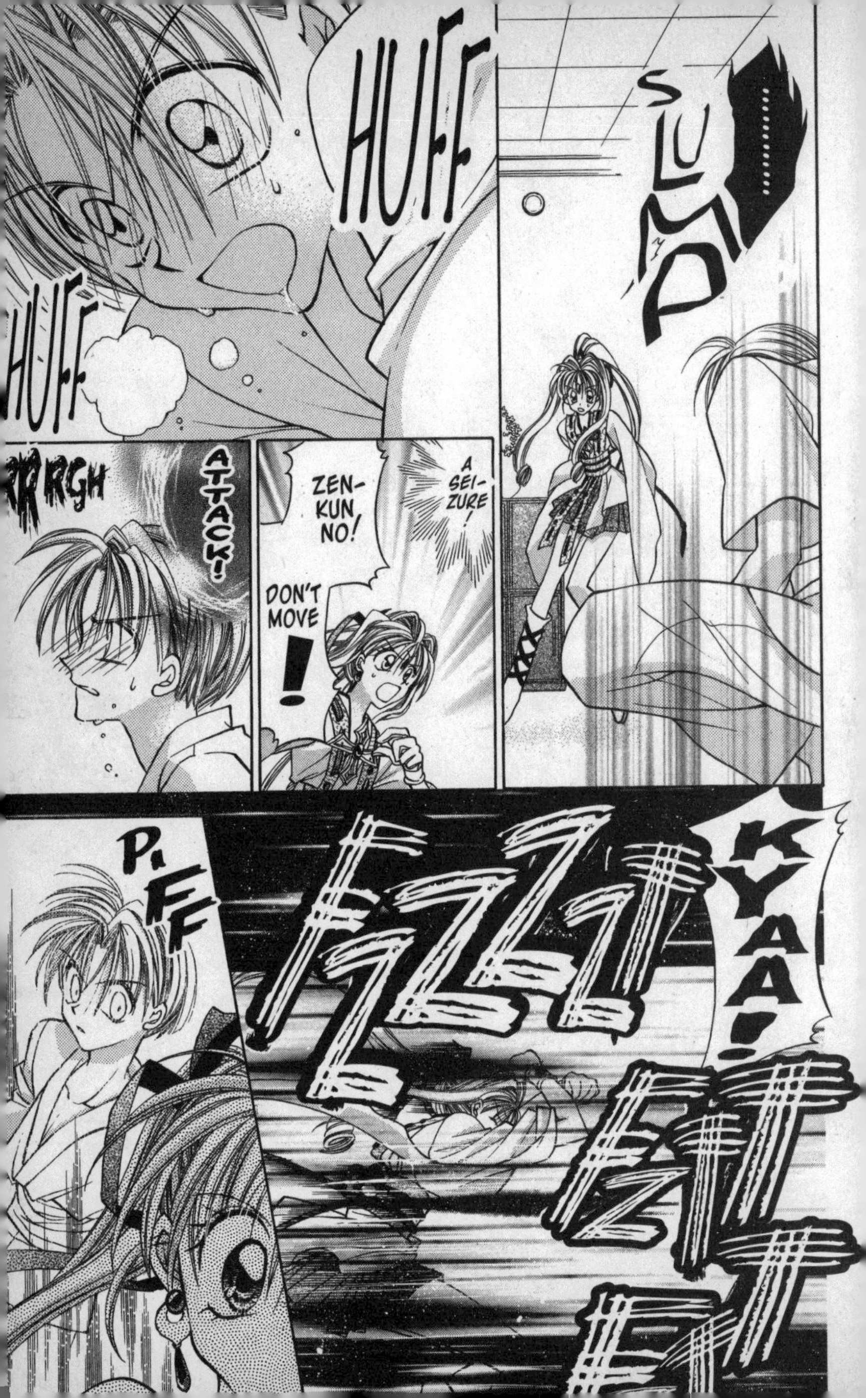
SLUMP
......
HUFF
HUFF
A SEIZURE!
ZEN-KUN NO!
DON'T MOVE!
RRRGH
ATTACK!
KYAA!
FZZT
PiFF

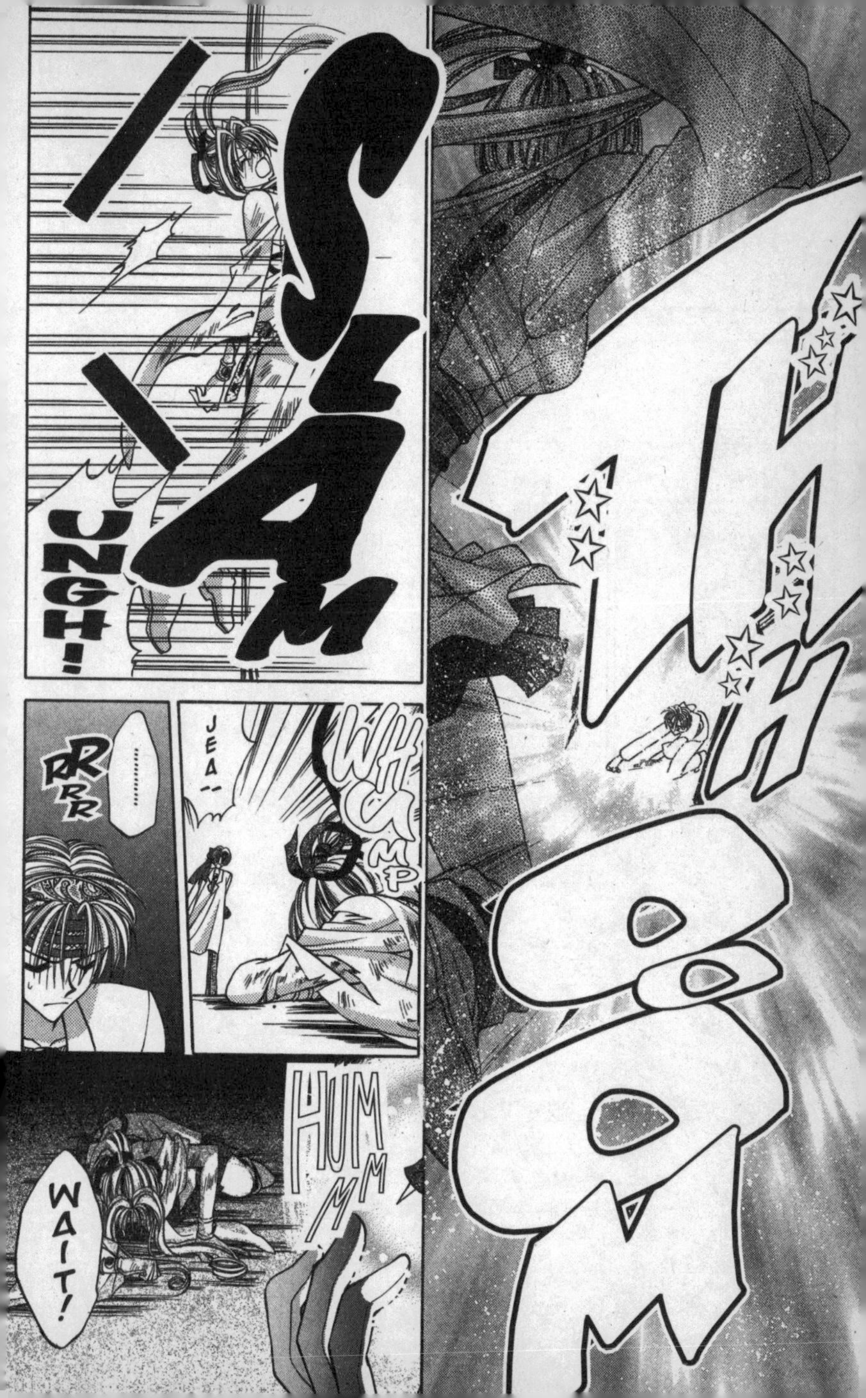
WHOOM
SLAM
UNGH!
WHUMP
JEA-
......
RRRR
HUMMM
WAIT!

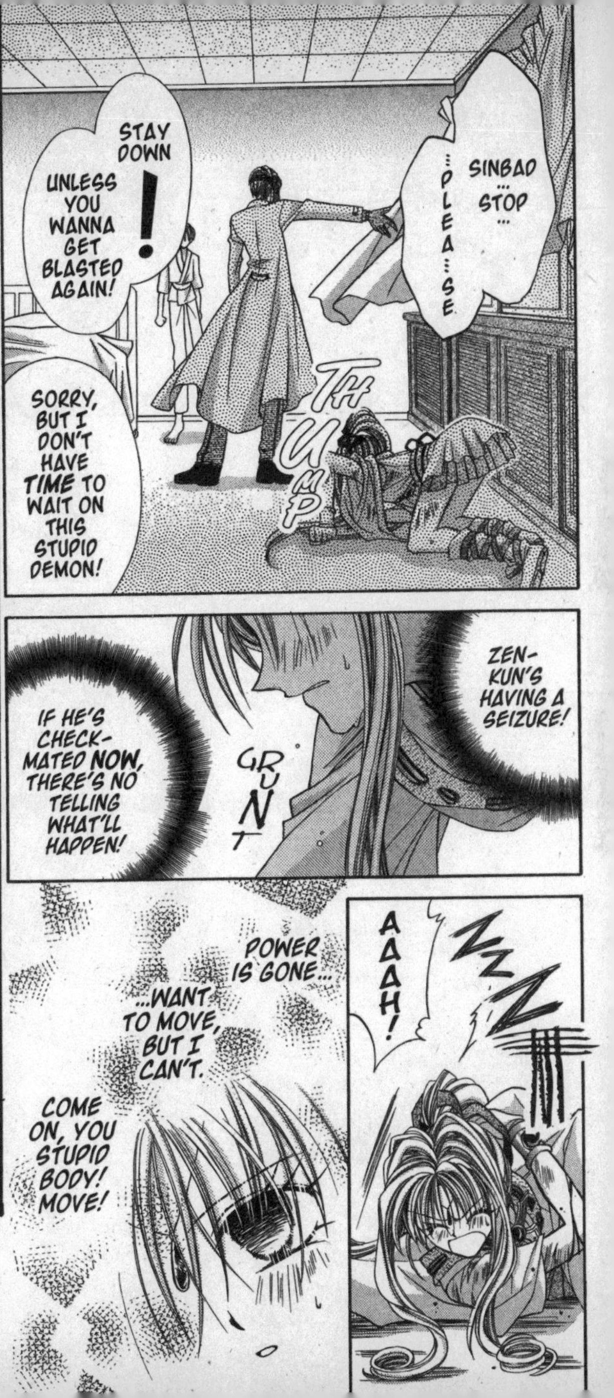
SINBAO... STOP...
...PLEA...SE
STAY DOWN UNLESS YOU WANNA GET BLASTED AGAIN!
SORRY, BUT I DON'T HAVE TIME TO WAIT ON THIS STUPID DEMON!
THUMP
ZEN-KUN'S HAVING A SEIZURE!
GRUNT
IF HE'S CHECKMATED NOW, THERE'S NO TELLING WHAT'LL HAPPEN!
AAAH!
POWER IS GONE...
...WANT TO MOVE, BUT I CAN'T.
COME ON, YOU STUPID BODY! MOVE!

ARINA TANEMURA'S

"LIKE PULLING TEETH WITH PLIERS"

SOY SAUCE IS BETTER THAN BUTTER. #17

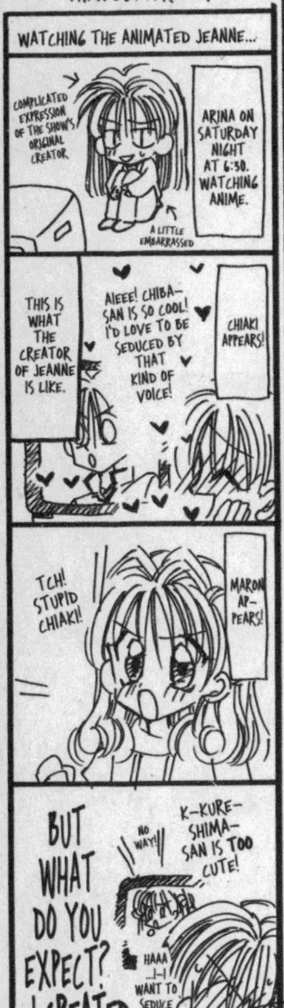
WATCHING THE ANIMATED JEANNE...
ARINA ON SATURDAY NIGHT AT 6:30. WATCHING ANIME.
COMPLICATED EXPRESSION OF THE SHOW'S ORIGINAL CREATOR
A LITTLE EMBARRASSED
CHIAKI APPEARS!
AIEEE! CHIBA-SAN IS SO COOL! I'D LOVE TO BE SEDUCED BY THAT KIND OF VOICE!
THIS IS WHAT THE CREATOR OF JEANNE IS LIKE.
MARON APPEARS!
TCH! STUPID CHIAKI!
K-KURESHIMA-SAN IS TOO CUTE!
NO WAY!
HAAA ...H I WANT TO SEDUCE HER!
BUT WHAT DO YOU EXPECT? I CREATED JEANNE.

I JUST LOVE KURESHIMA-SAN'S VOICE. IN FACT, I'M IN LOVE WITH ALL OF THE VOICE ACTORS AND ACTRESSES THAT MAKE UP THE ANIMATED JEANNE'S CAST. THEY SOUND PERFECT!

THIS IS JUST LIKE THAT OTHER TIME.
I CAN'T PROTECT SOMEONE WHO'S DEAR TO ME.
I'M POWER-LESS!
DRIP
WHY DOES IT ALWAYS HAVE TO BE LIKE THIS?
WHY AM I ALWAYS SO WEAK?
I WANT TO BE STRONG! I WANT TO BE STRONG!

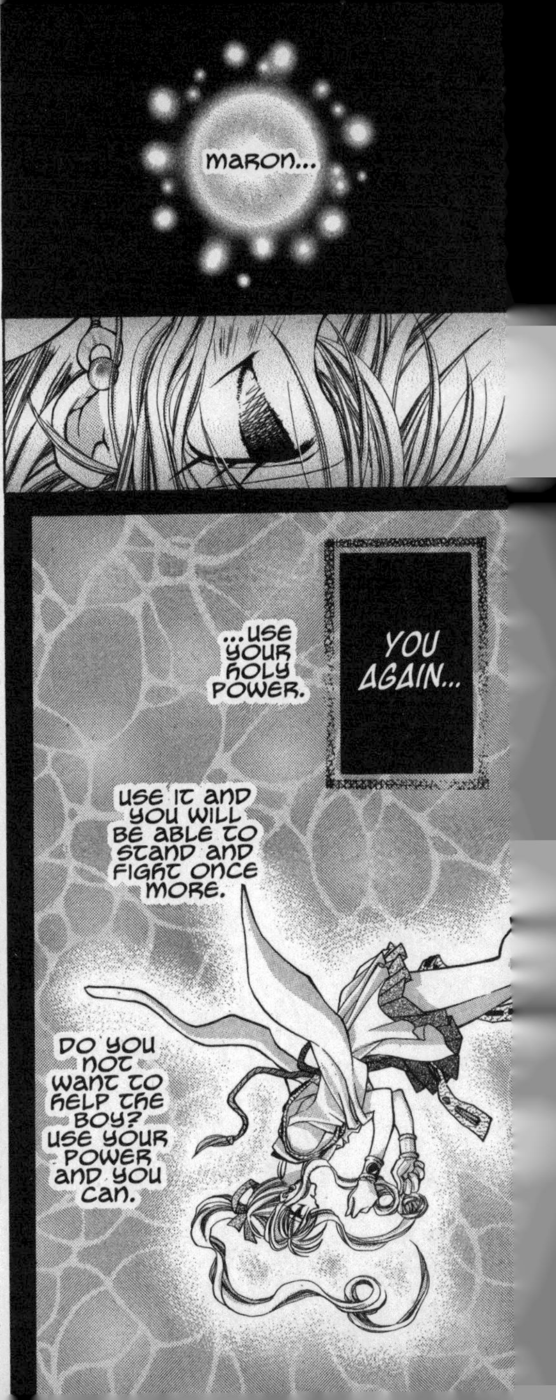
maron...
YOU AGAIN...
...USE YOUR HOLY POWER.
USE IT AND YOU WILL BE ABLE TO STAND AND FIGHT ONCE MORE.
DO YOU NOT WANT TO HELP THE BOY? USE YOUR POWER AND YOU CAN.

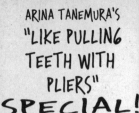

ARINA TANEMURA'S "LIKE PULLING TEETH WITH PLIERS" SPECIAL!

I HAVE NO COLUMNS THIS TIME, SO I'M COVERING IT UP WITH THESE MINI-COMICS #20

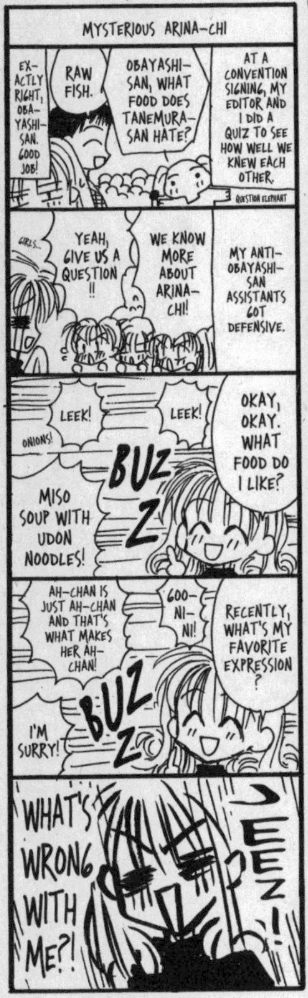
MYSTERIOUS ARINA-CHI
AT A CONVENTION SIGNING, MY EDITOR AND I DID A QUIZ TO SEE HOW WELL WE KNEW EACH OTHER.
QUESTION ELEPHANT
OBAYASHI-SAN, WHAT FOOD DOES TANEMURA-SAN HATE?
RAW FISH.
EXACTLY RIGHT, OBAYASHI-SAN. GOOD JOB!
MY ANTI-OBAYASHI-SAN ASSISTANTS GOT DEFENSIVE.
WE KNOW MORE ABOUT ARINA-CHI!
YEAH, GIVE US A QUESTION!!
GIRLS...
OKAY, OKAY. WHAT FOOD DO I LIKE?
LEEK!
LEEK!
ONIONS!
BUZZ
MISO SOUP WITH UDON NOODLES!
RECENTLY, WHAT'S MY FAVORITE EXPRESSION?
GOO-NI-NI!
AH-CHAN IS JUST AH-CHAN AND THAT'S WHAT MAKES HER AH-CHAN!
BUZZ
I'M SURRY!
JEEZ!
WHAT'S WRONG WITH ME?!

RECENT FAVORITE FOOD: MUSHROOMS FRIED WITH BUTTER
RECENT FAVORITE EXPRESSION: ME NO KNOW. (FOR "I DON'T KNOW").

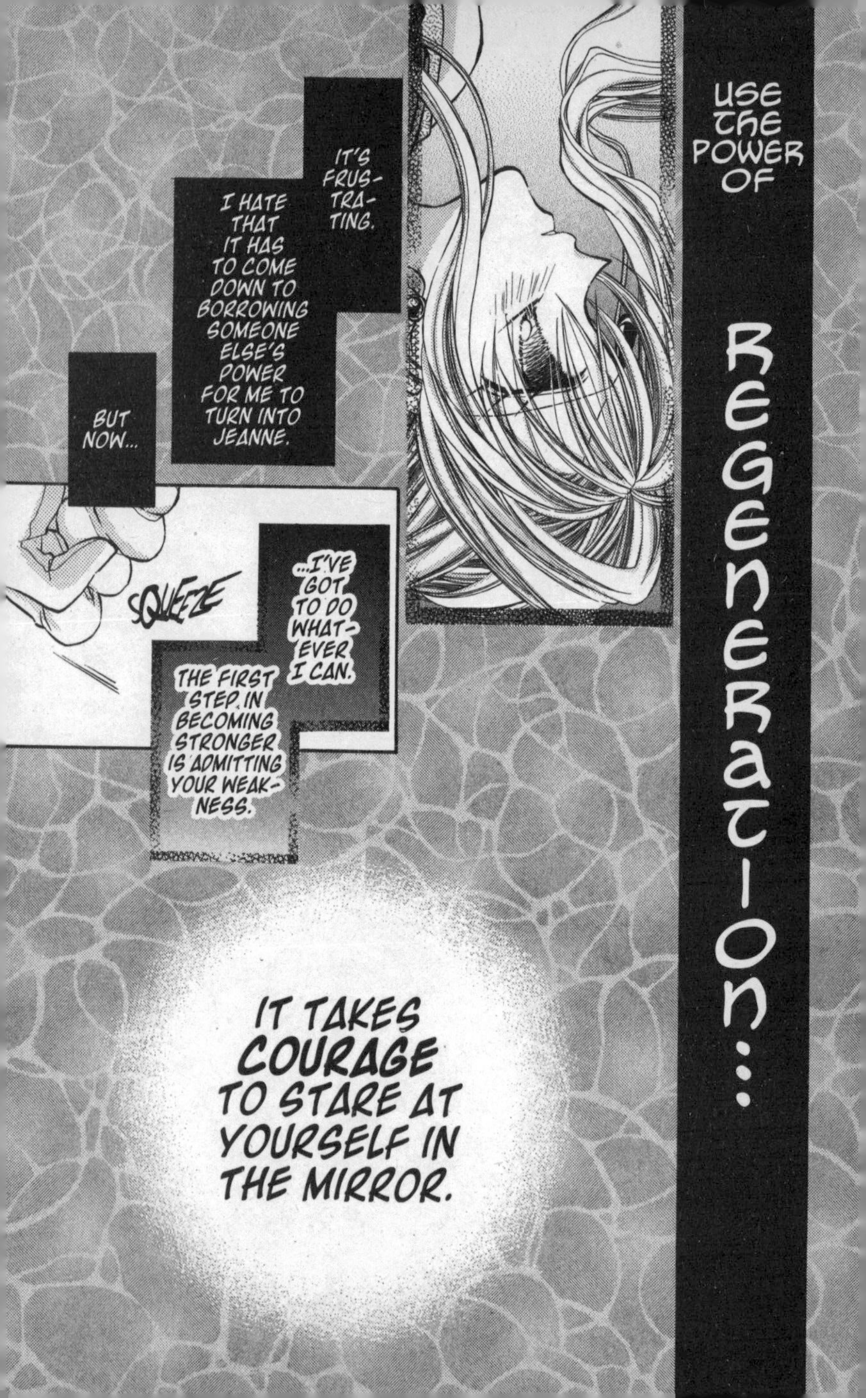
USE THE POWER OF
REGENERATION...
IT'S FRUS-TRA-TING.
I HATE THAT IT HAS TO COME DOWN TO BORROWING SOMEONE ELSE'S POWER FOR ME TO TURN INTO JEANNE.
BUT NOW...
...I'VE GOT TO DO WHAT-EVER I CAN.
SQUEEZE
THE FIRST STEP IN BECOMING STRONGER IS ADMITTING YOUR WEAK-NESS.
IT TAKES COURAGE TO STARE AT YOURSELF IN THE MIRROR.

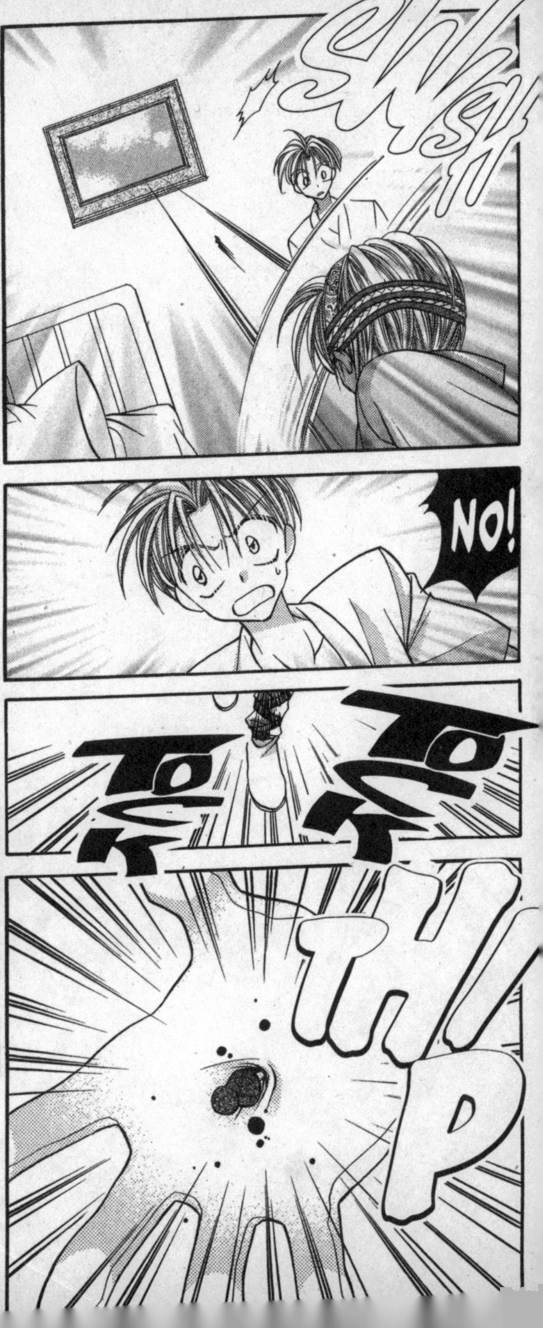

NO!
TOK
TOK

ARINA TANEMURA'S "LIKE PULLING TEETH WITH PLIERS" ☆

A SUPER-POPULAR SERIES EVEN FOR MALE READERS #21

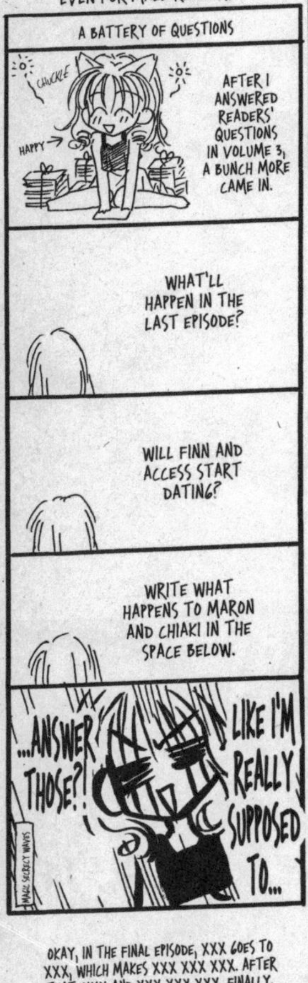

A BATTERY OF QUESTIONS
CHUCKLE
HAPPY
AFTER I ANSWERED READERS' QUESTIONS IN VOLUME 3, A BUNCH MORE CAME IN.
WHAT'LL HAPPEN IN THE LAST EPISODE?
WILL FINN AND ACCESS START DATING?
WRITE WHAT HAPPENS TO MARON AND CHIAKI IN THE SPACE BELOW.
...ANSWER THOSE?
LIKE I'M REALLY SUPPOSED TO...
MAGIC SECRECY WAVES

OKAY, IN THE FINAL EPISODE, XXX GOES TO XXX, WHICH MAKES XXX XXX XXX. AFTER THAT, XXX AND XXX XXX XXX. FINALLY, XXX XXX XXX XXX. GOT IT? (LOL)

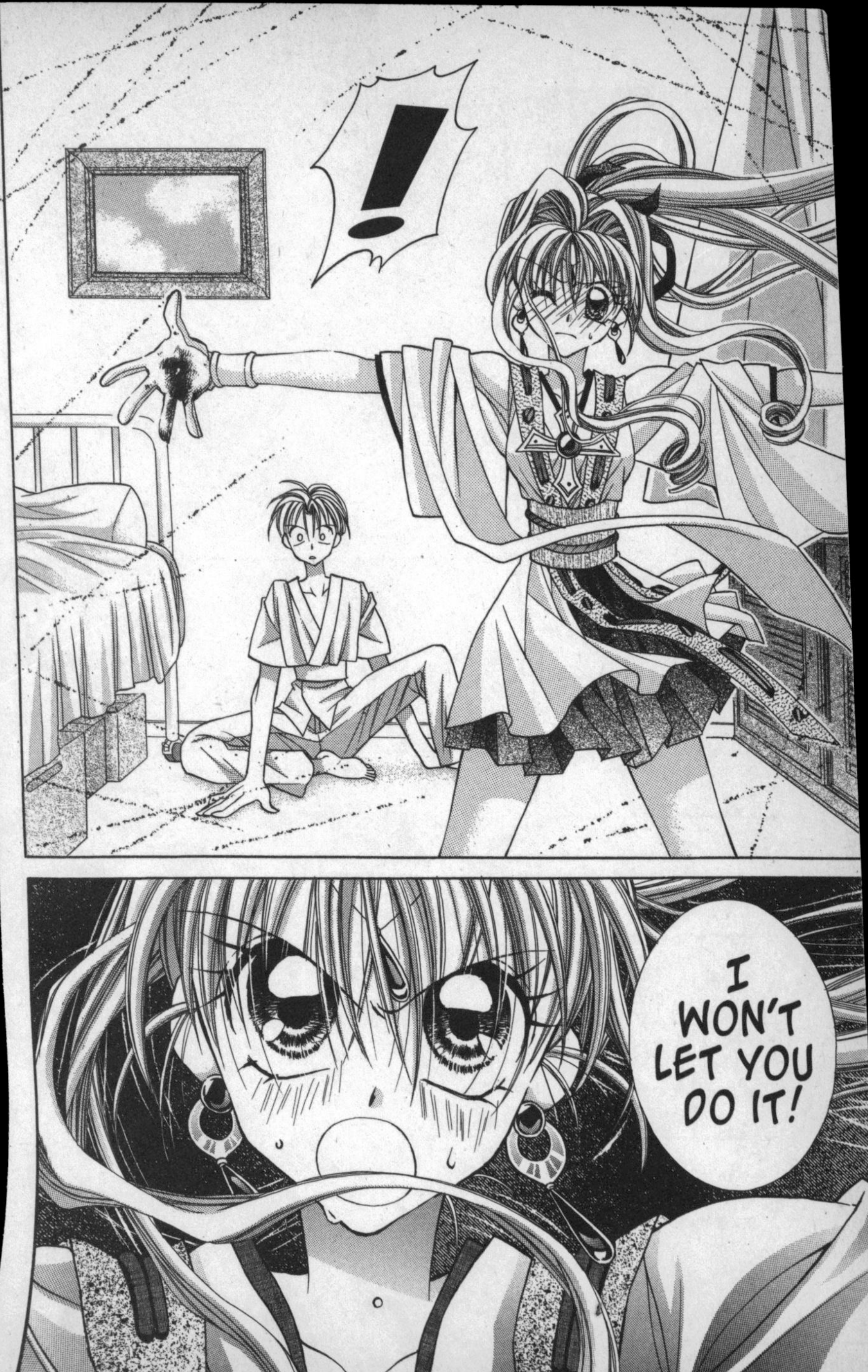
!
I WON'T LET YOU DO IT!

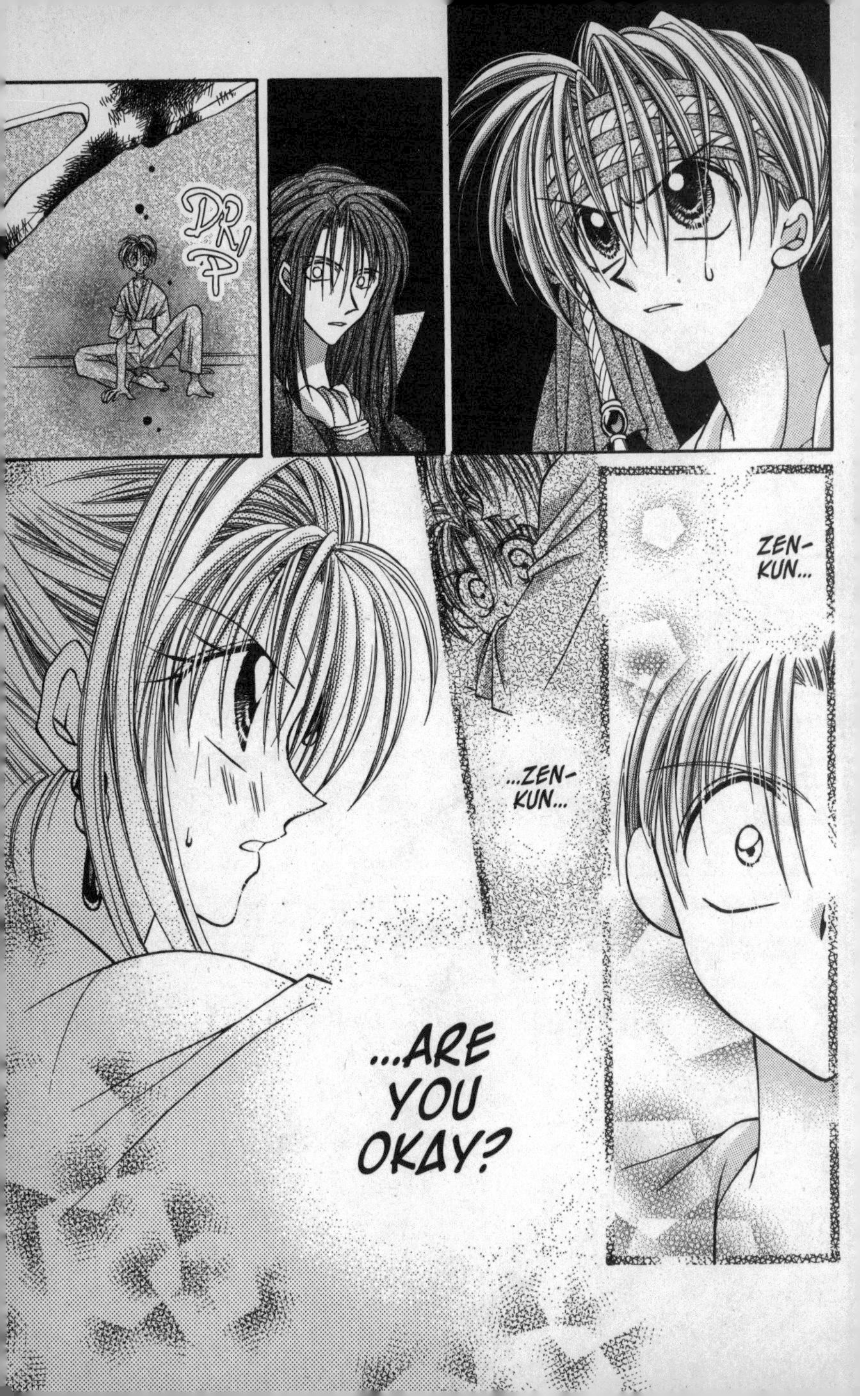
DRIP
ZEN-KUN...
...ZEN-KUN...
...ARE YOU OKAY?

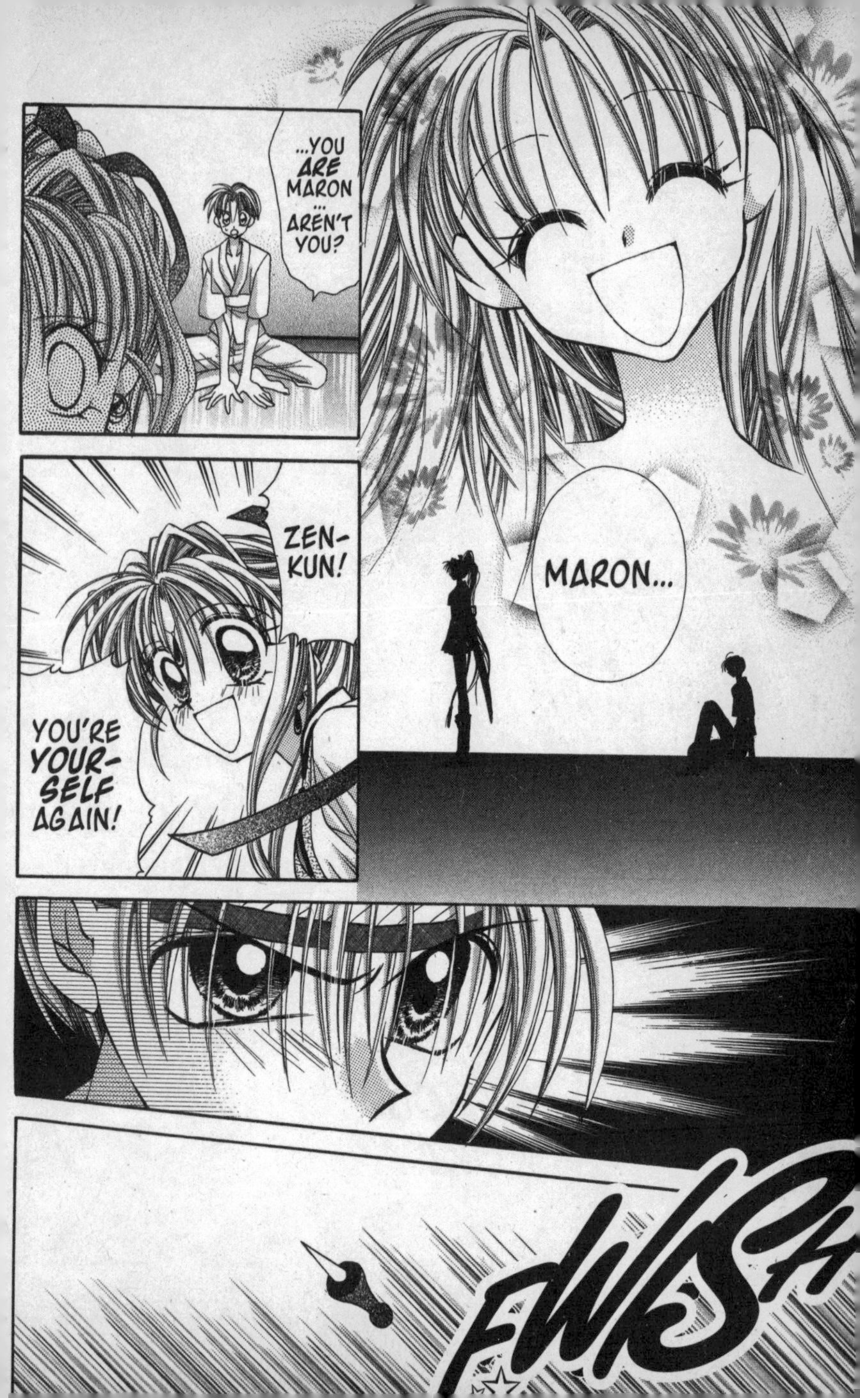
MARON...
...YOU ARE MARON ... AREN'T YOU?
ZEN-KUN!
YOU'RE YOURSELF AGAIN!
FWISH

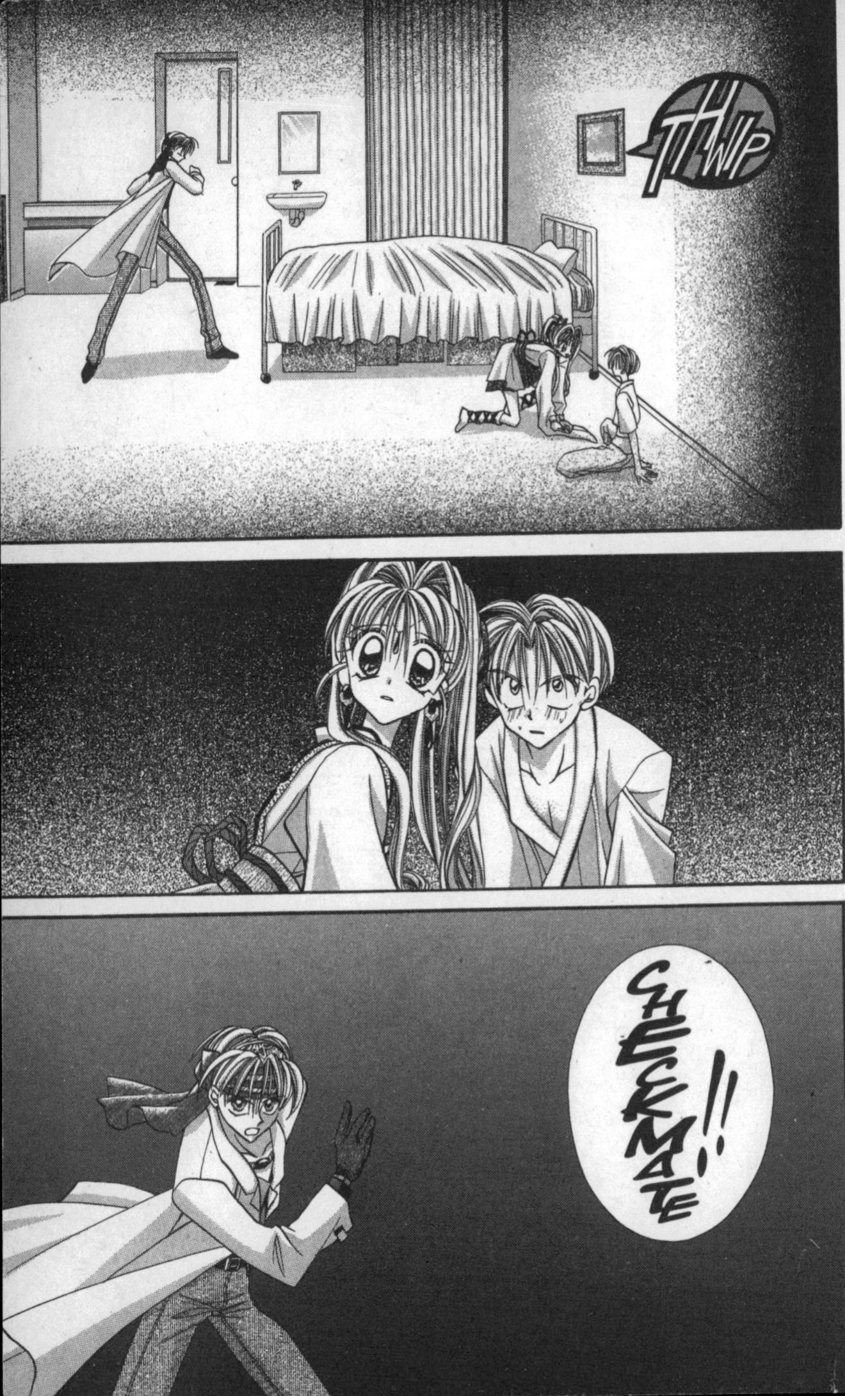
THWIP
CHECKMATE!!

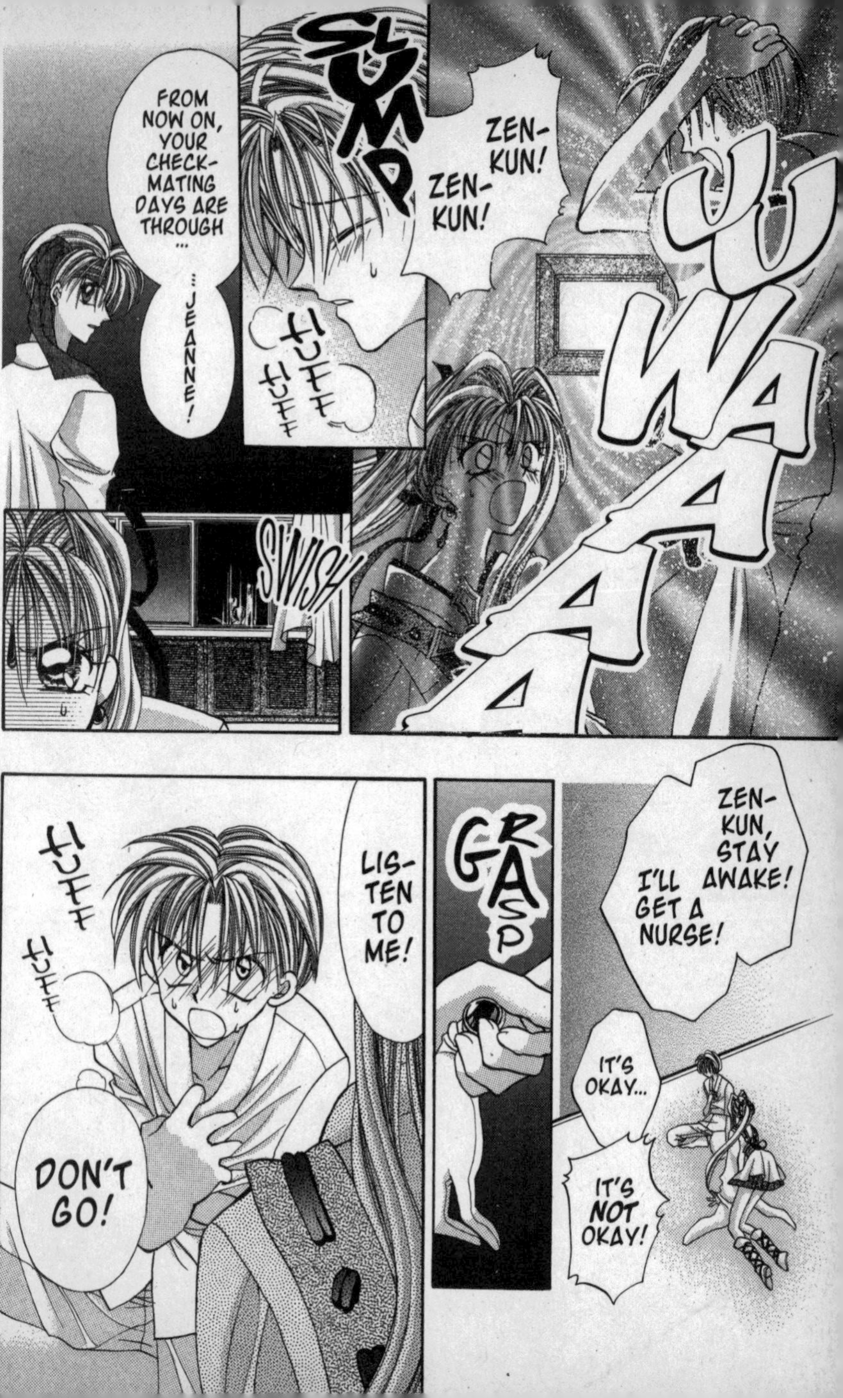
ZEN-KUN!
ZEN-KUN!
UWAAAA
SLUMP
HUFF HUFF
FROM NOW ON, YOUR CHECK-MATING DAYS ARE THROUGH...
...JEANNE!
SWISH
ZEN-KUN, STAY AWAKE! I'LL GET A NURSE!
IT'S OKAY...
IT'S NOT OKAY!
GRASP
LIS-TEN TO ME!
HUFF HUFF
DON'T GO!

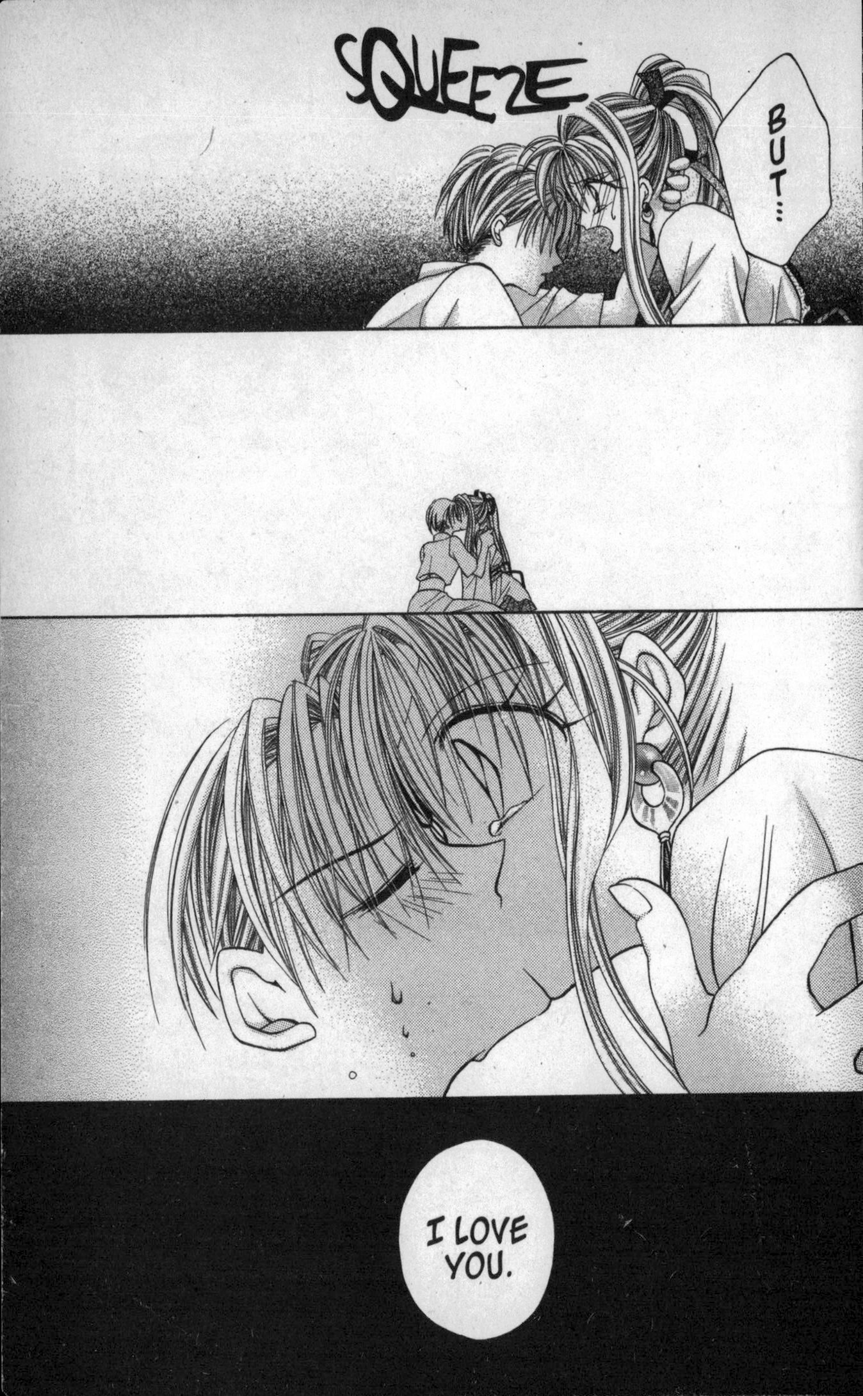
BUT...
SQUEEZE
I LOVE YOU.

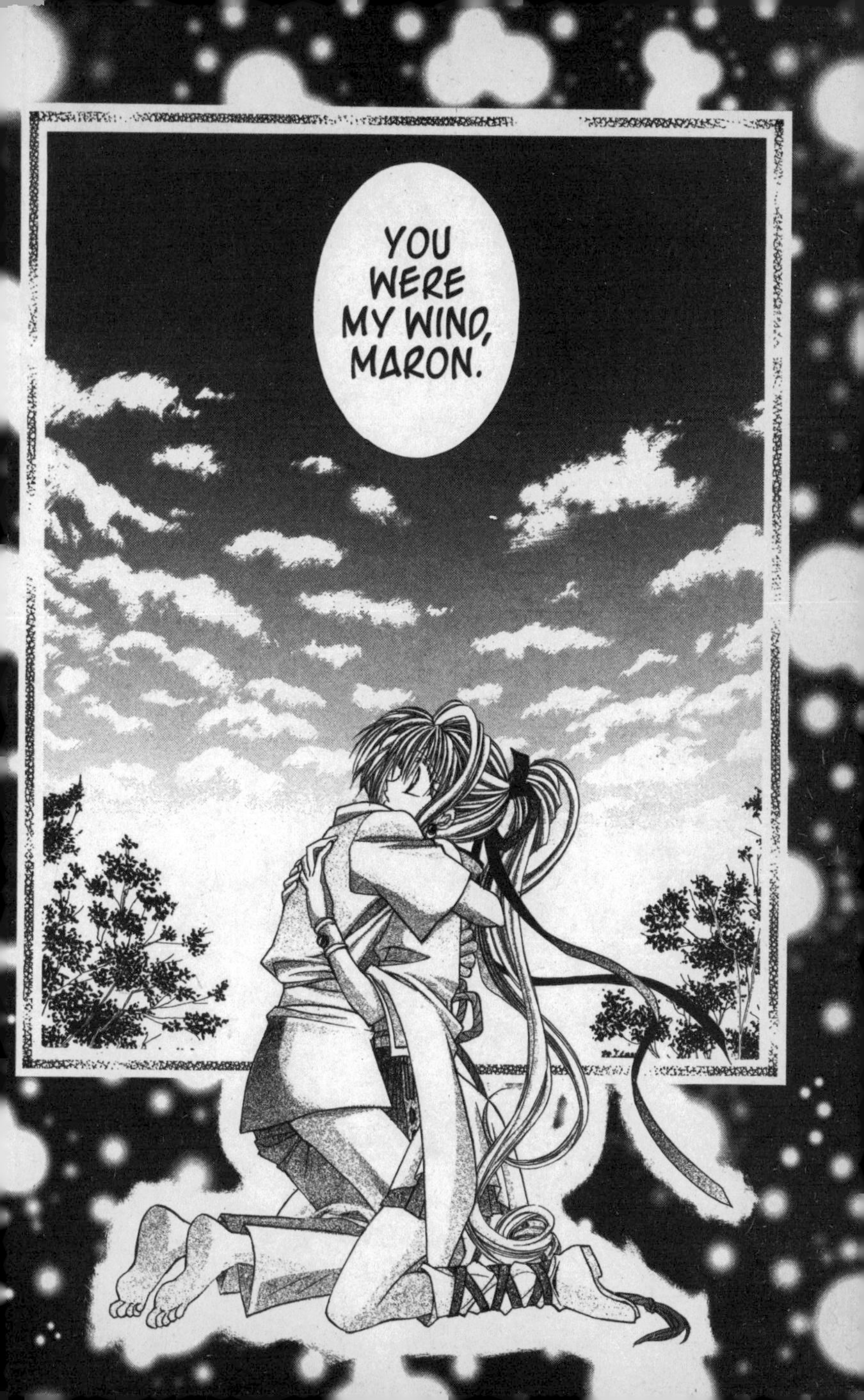
YOU WERE MY WIND, MARON.

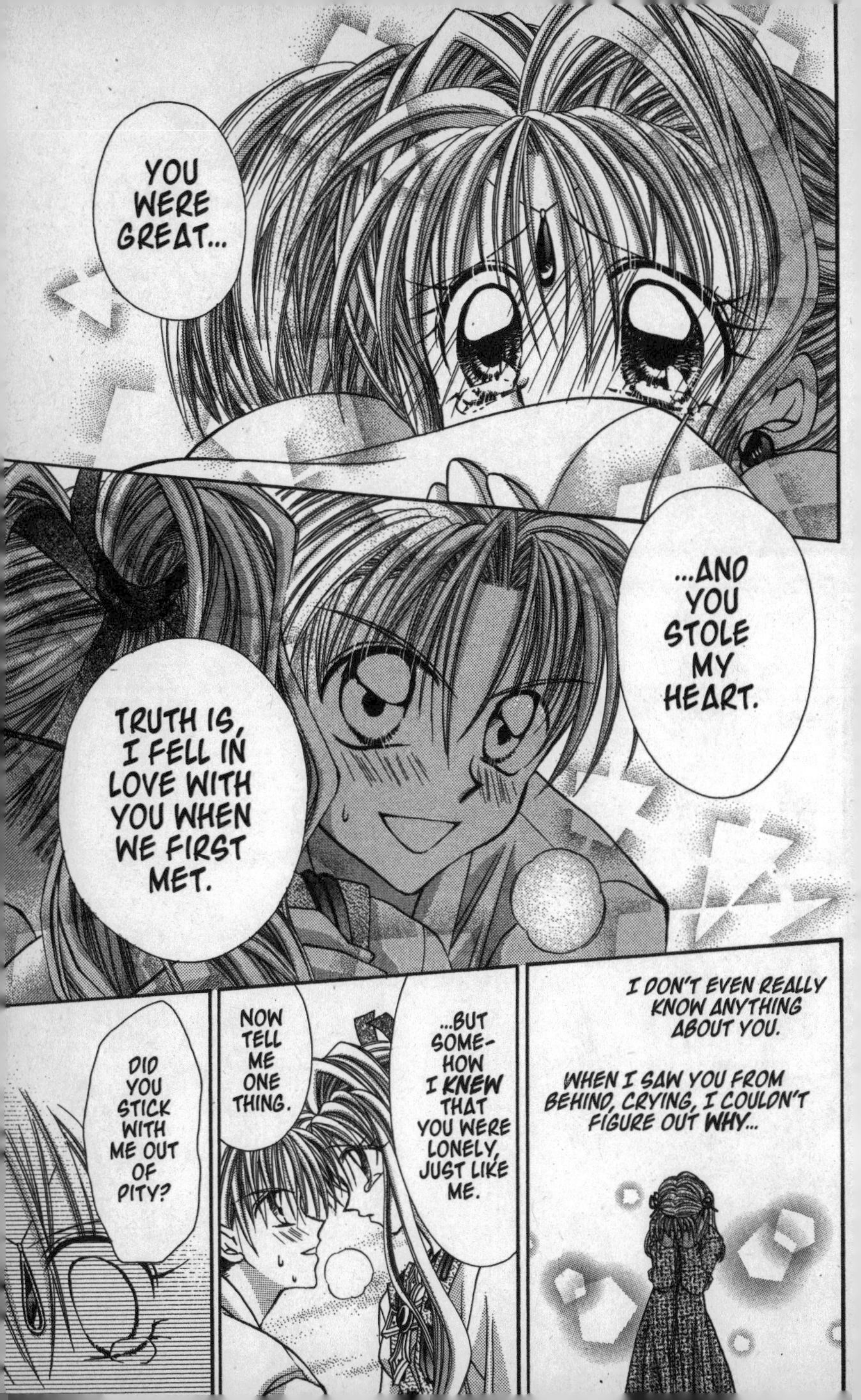
YOU WERE GREAT...
...AND YOU STOLE MY HEART.
TRUTH IS, I FELL IN LOVE WITH YOU WHEN WE FIRST MET.
I DON'T EVEN REALLY KNOW ANYTHING ABOUT YOU.
WHEN I SAW YOU FROM BEHIND, CRYING, I COULDN'T FIGURE OUT WHY...
...BUT SOME-HOW I KNEW THAT YOU WERE LONELY, JUST LIKE ME.
NOW TELL ME ONE THING.
DID YOU STICK WITH ME OUT OF PITY?

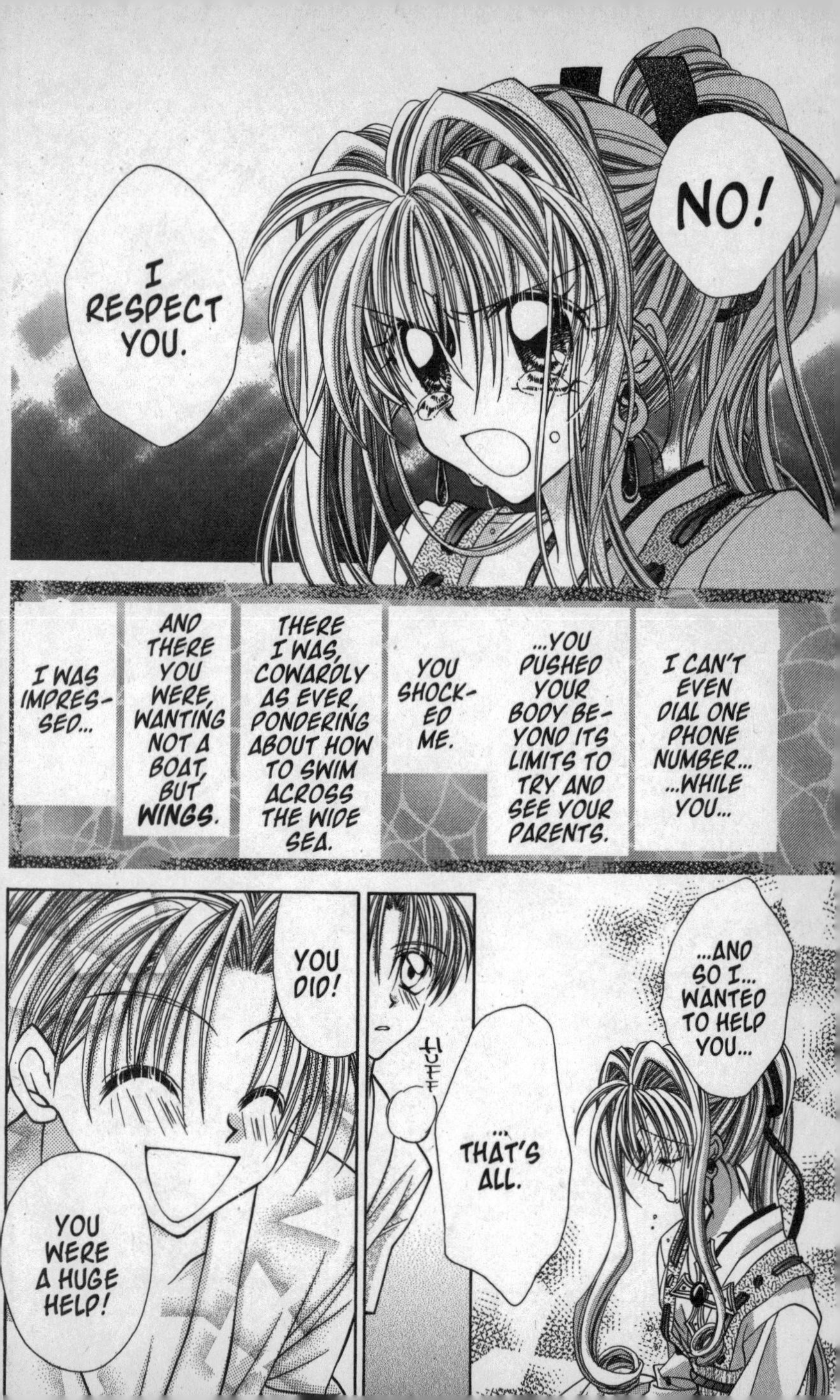
NO!
I RESPECT YOU.
I CAN'T EVEN DIAL ONE PHONE NUMBER... ...WHILE YOU...
...YOU PUSHED YOUR BODY BEYOND ITS LIMITS TO TRY AND SEE YOUR PARENTS.
YOU SHOCKED ME.
THERE I WAS, COWARDLY AS EVER, PONDERING ABOUT HOW TO SWIM ACROSS THE WIDE SEA.
AND THERE YOU WERE, WANTING NOT A BOAT, BUT **WINGS**.
I WAS IMPRESSED...
...AND SO I... WANTED TO HELP YOU...
...THAT'S ALL.
HUFF
YOU DID!
YOU WERE A HUGE HELP!

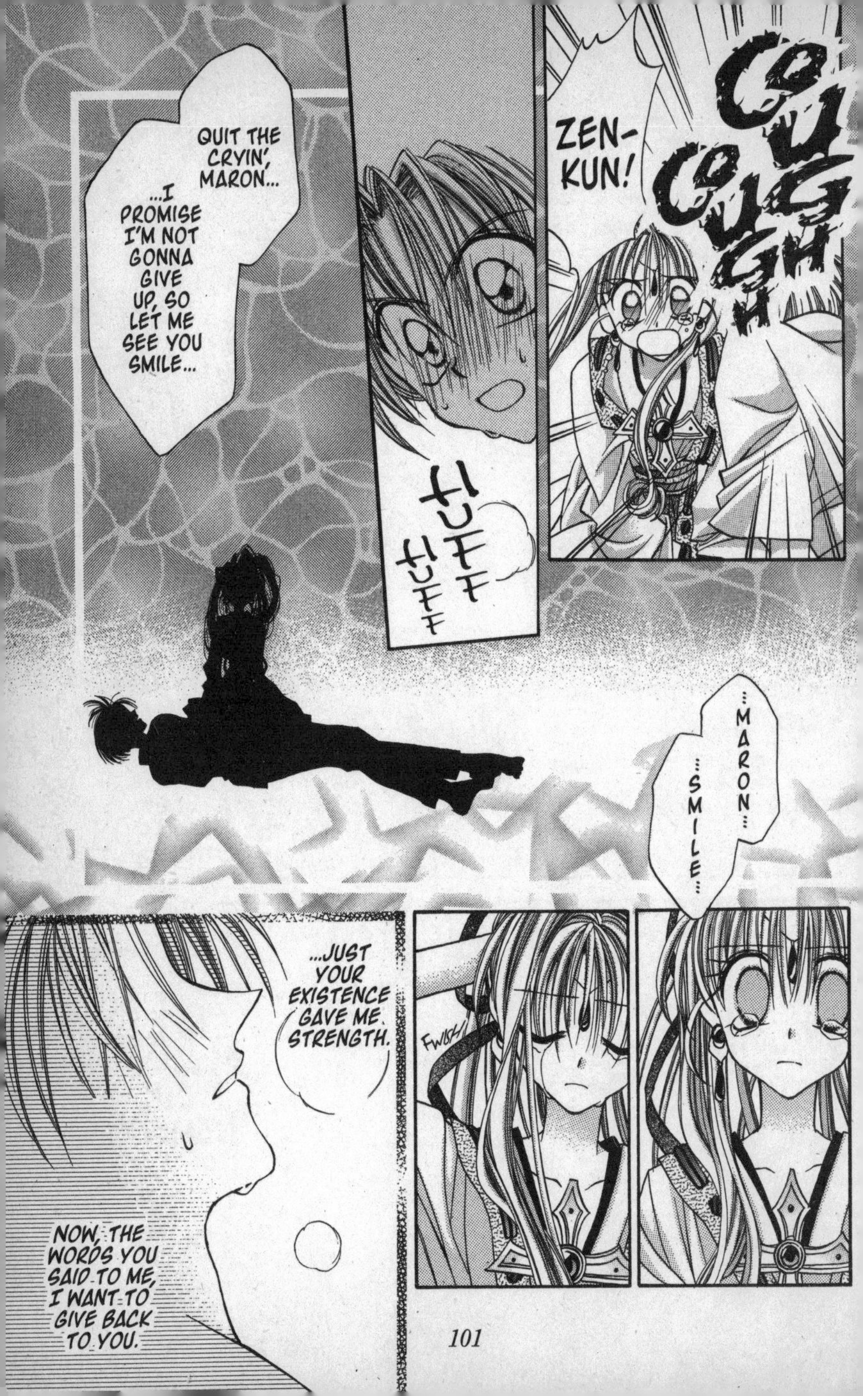
ZEN-KUN!
COUGH COUGH
HUFF HUFF
QUIT THE CRYIN', MARON... ...I PROMISE I'M NOT GONNA GIVE UP, SO LET ME SEE YOU SMILE...
...MARON... ...SMILE...
FWISH
...JUST YOUR EXISTENCE GAVE ME STRENGTH.
NOW, THE WORDS YOU SAID TO ME, I WANT TO GIVE BACK TO YOU.

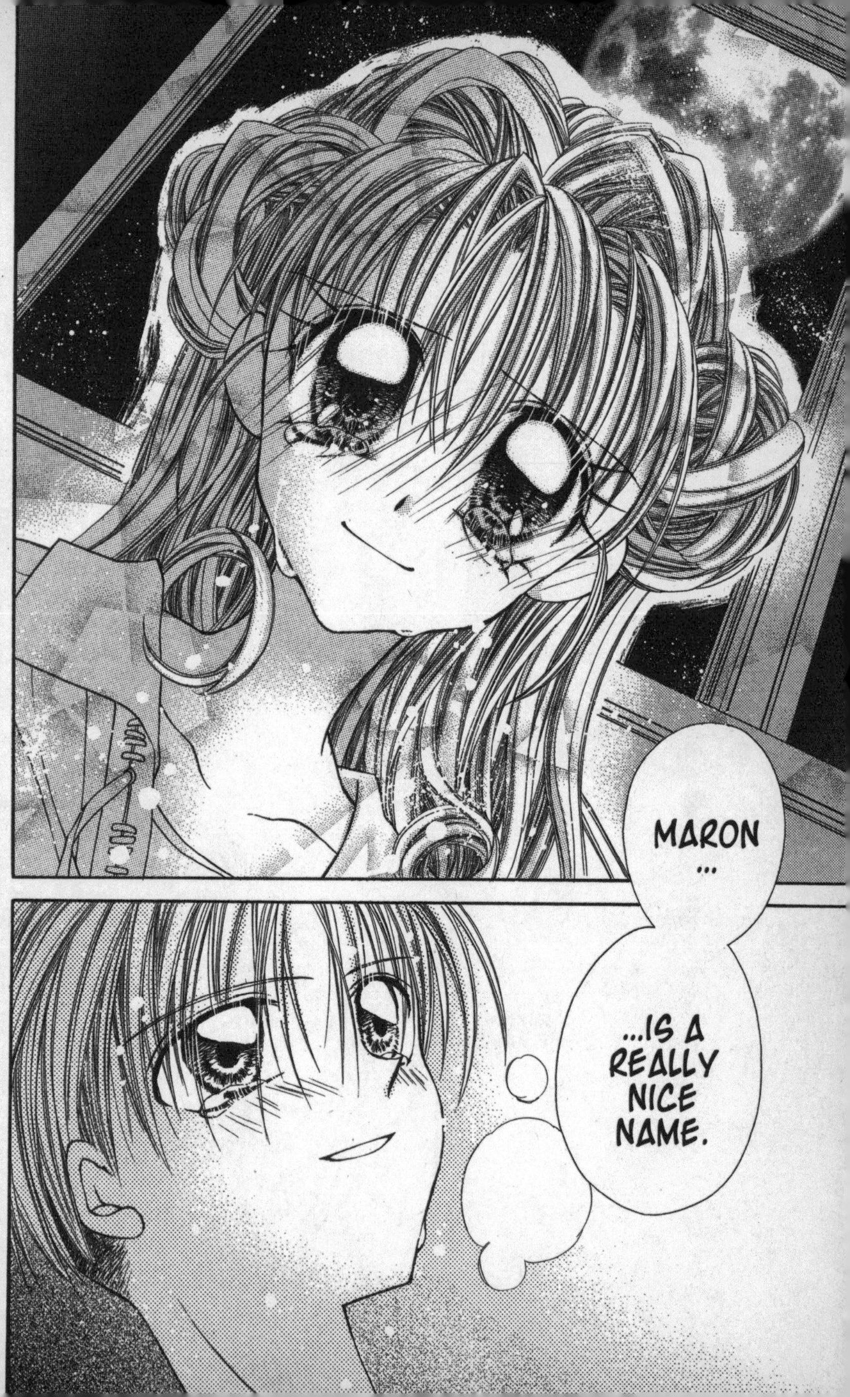
MARON ...
...IS A REALLY NICE NAME.

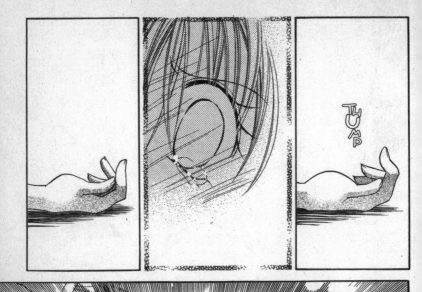

THUMP

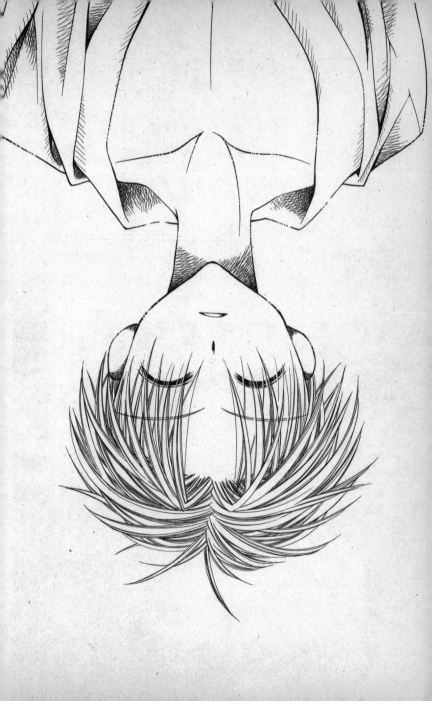

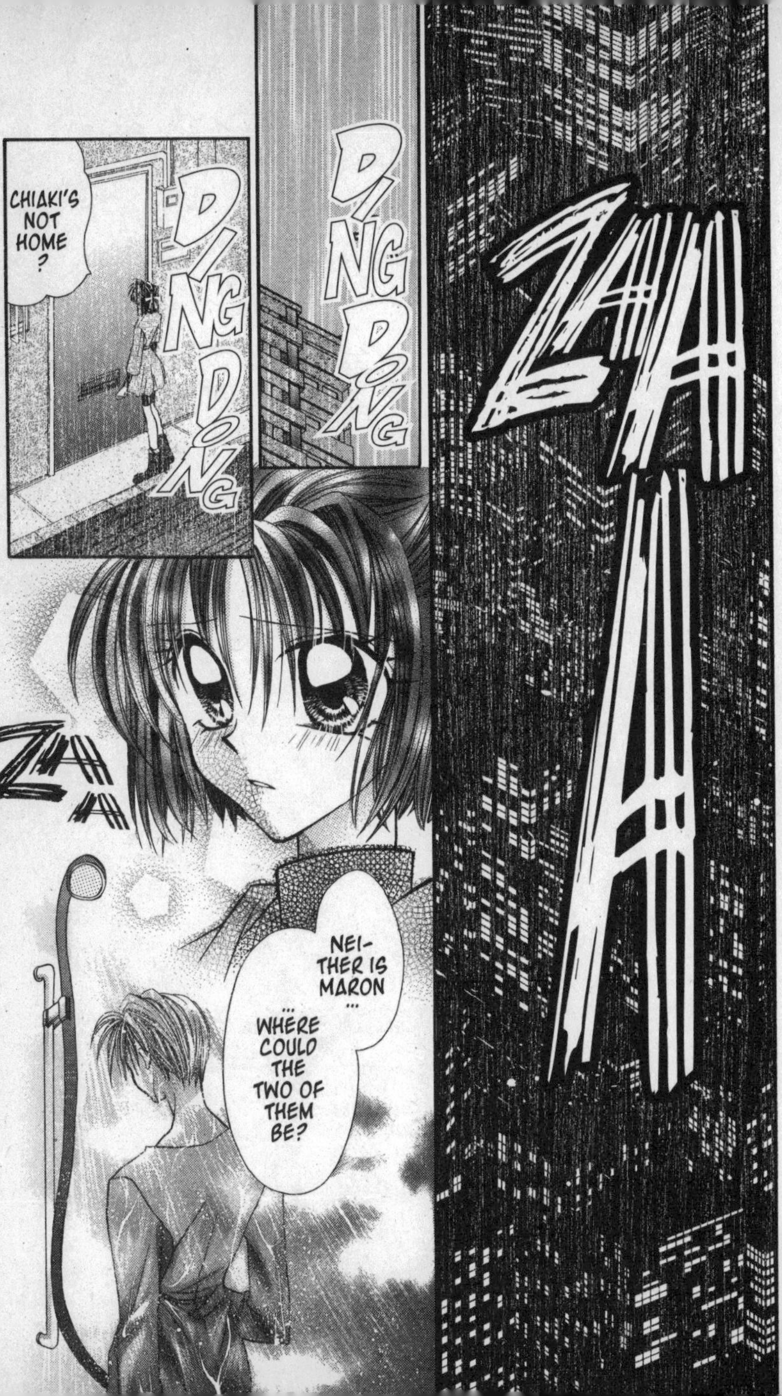
ZAA
DING DONG
CHIAKI'S NOT HOME?
DING DONG
ZAA
NEI-THER IS MARON ... WHERE COULD THE TWO OF THEM BE?

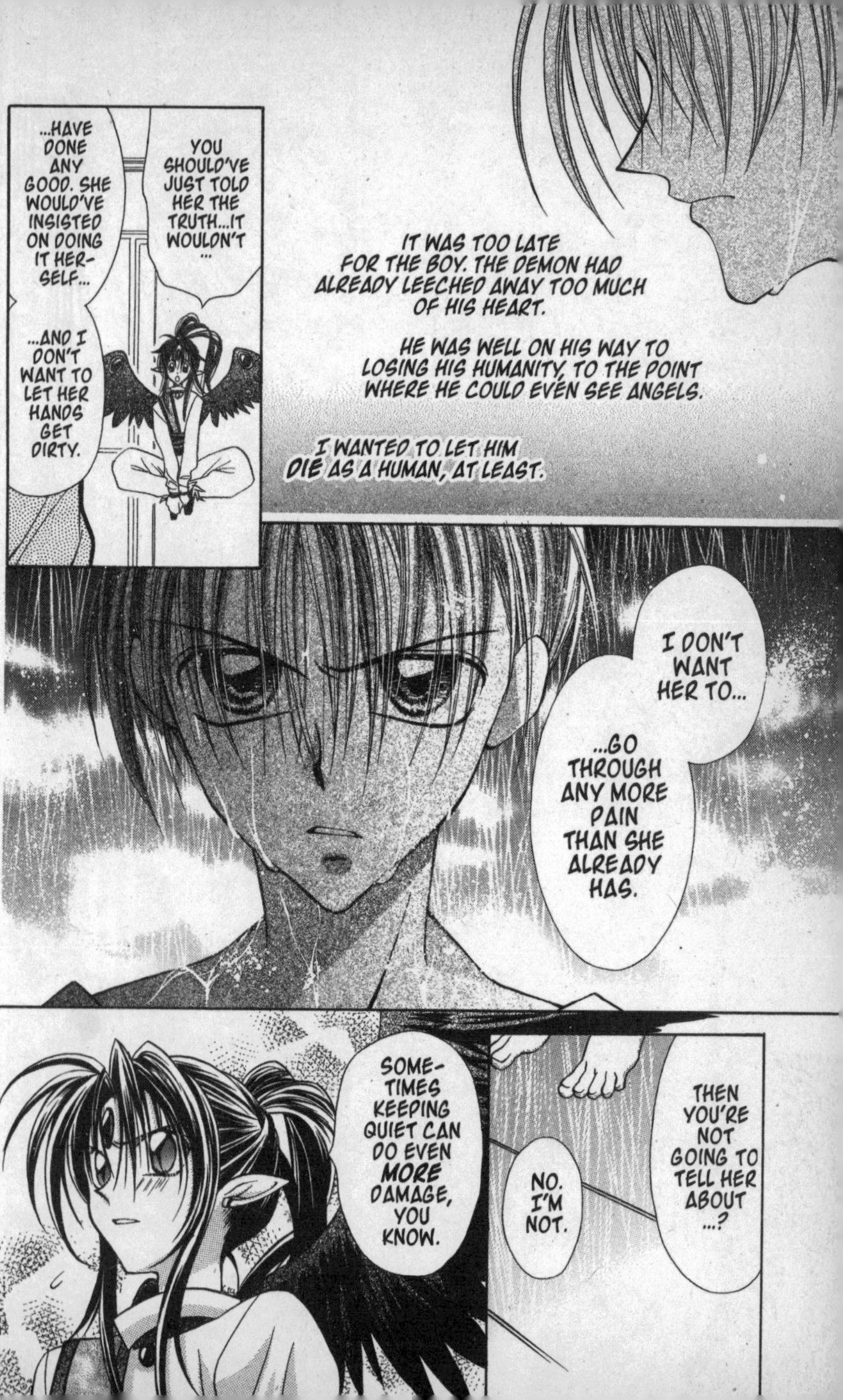
IT WAS TOO LATE FOR THE BOY. THE DEMON HAD ALREADY LEECHED AWAY TOO MUCH OF HIS HEART.
HE WAS WELL ON HIS WAY TO LOSING HIS HUMANITY, TO THE POINT WHERE HE COULD EVEN SEE ANGELS.
I WANTED TO LET HIM **DIE** AS A HUMAN, AT LEAST.
YOU SHOULD'VE JUST TOLD HER THE TRUTH...IT WOULDN'T ...
...HAVE DONE ANY GOOD. SHE WOULD'VE INSISTED ON DOING IT HER-SELF...
...AND I DON'T WANT TO LET HER HANDS GET DIRTY.
I DON'T WANT HER TO...
...GO THROUGH ANY MORE PAIN THAN SHE ALREADY HAS.
THEN YOU'RE NOT GOING TO TELL HER ABOUT ...?
NO. I'M NOT.
SOME-TIMES KEEPING QUIET CAN DO EVEN **MORE** DAMAGE, YOU KNOW.

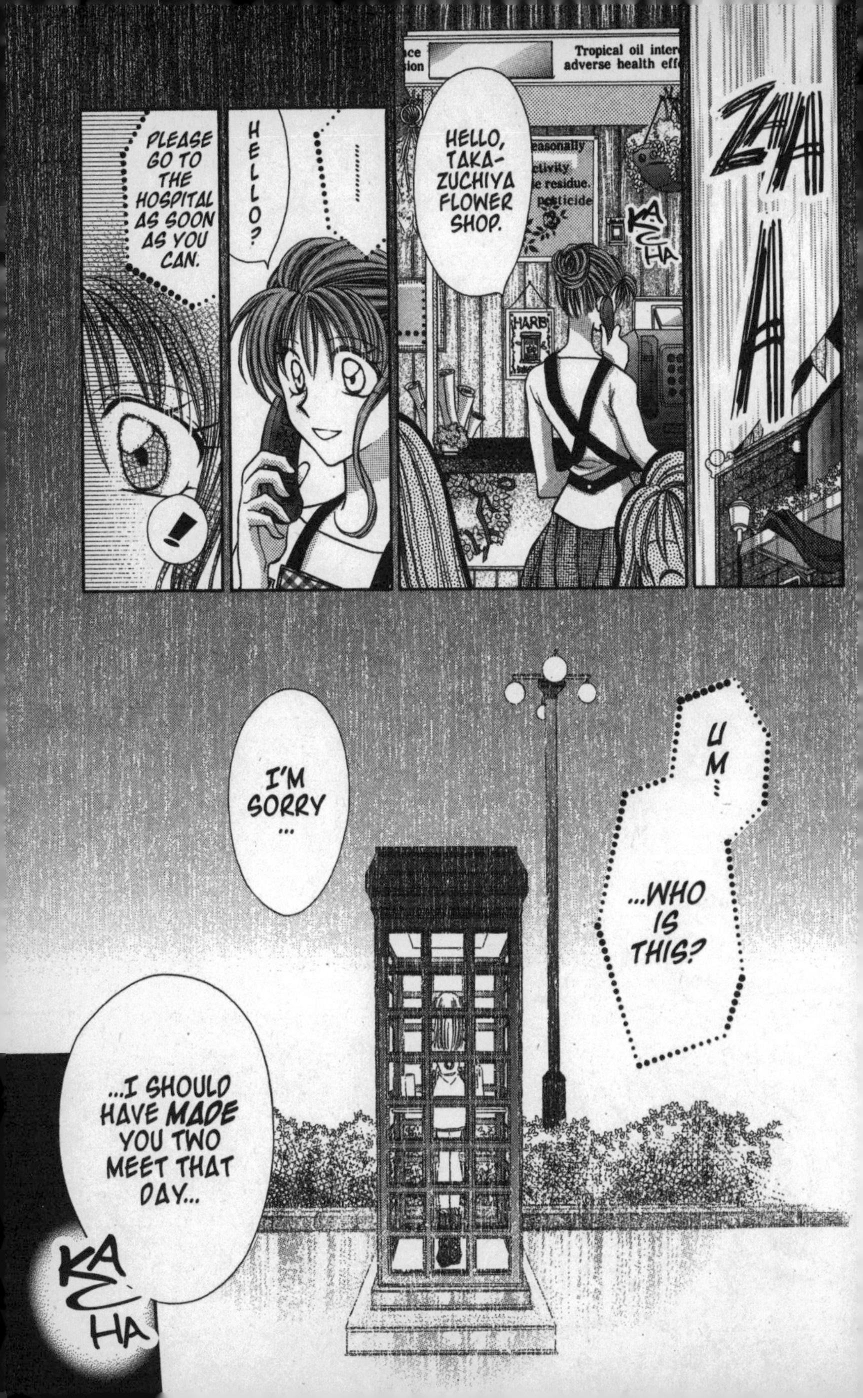
ZAHAA
HELLO, TAKA-ZUCHIYA FLOWER SHOP.
KACHA
HARB
HELLO?
......
PLEASE GO TO THE HOSPITAL AS SOON AS YOU CAN.
!
UM...
...WHO IS THIS?
I'M SORRY...
...I SHOULD HAVE **MADE** YOU TWO MEET THAT DAY...
KACHA

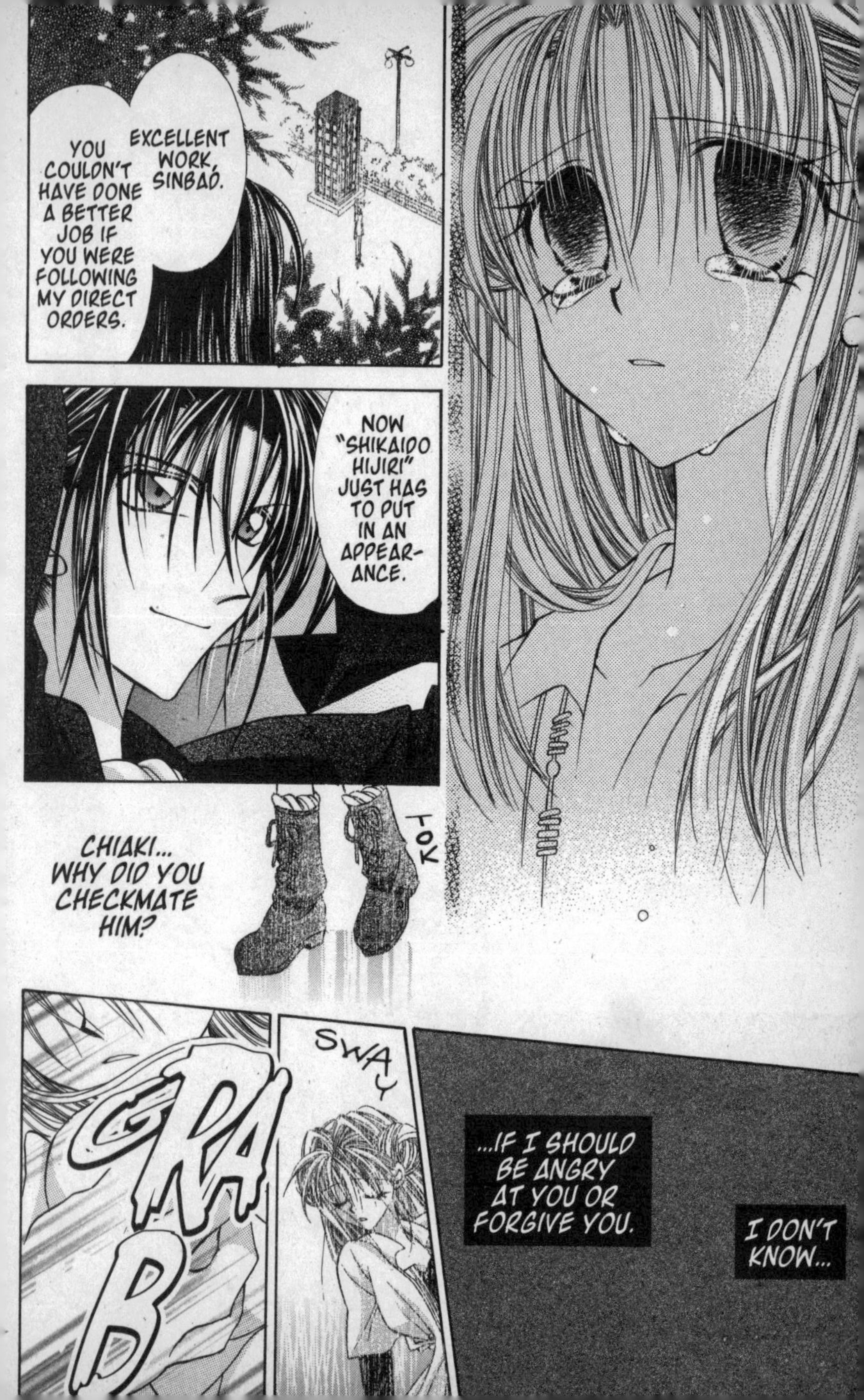

EXCELLENT WORK, SINBAD.
YOU COULDN'T HAVE DONE A BETTER JOB IF YOU WERE FOLLOWING MY DIRECT ORDERS.
NOW "SHIKAIDO HIJIRI" JUST HAS TO PUT IN AN APPEAR-ANCE.
TOK
CHIAKI... WHY DID YOU CHECKMATE HIM?
I DON'T KNOW...
...IF I SHOULD BE ANGRY AT YOU OR FORGIVE YOU.
SWAY
GRAB

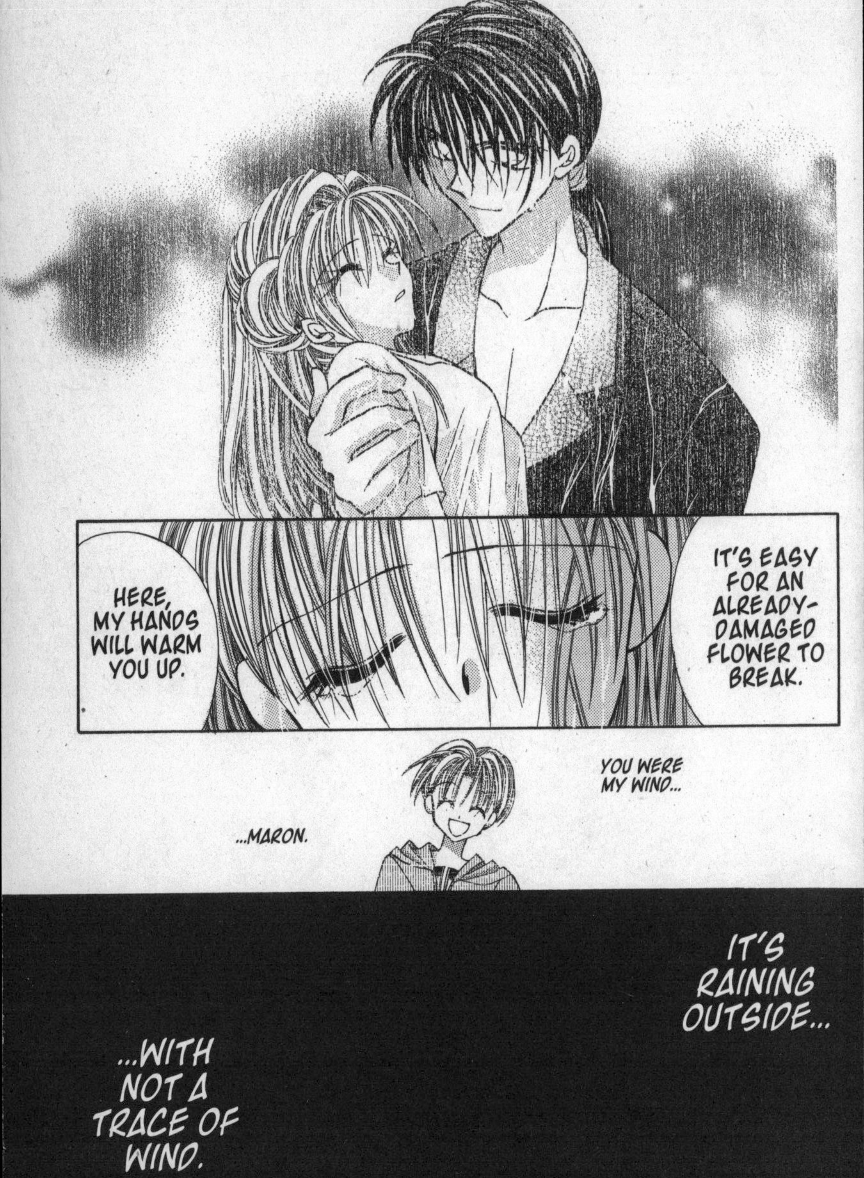
IT'S EASY FOR AN ALREADY-DAMAGED FLOWER TO BREAK.
HERE, MY HANDS WILL WARM YOU UP.
YOU WERE MY WIND...
...MARON.
IT'S RAINING OUTSIDE...
...WITH NOT A TRACE OF WIND.

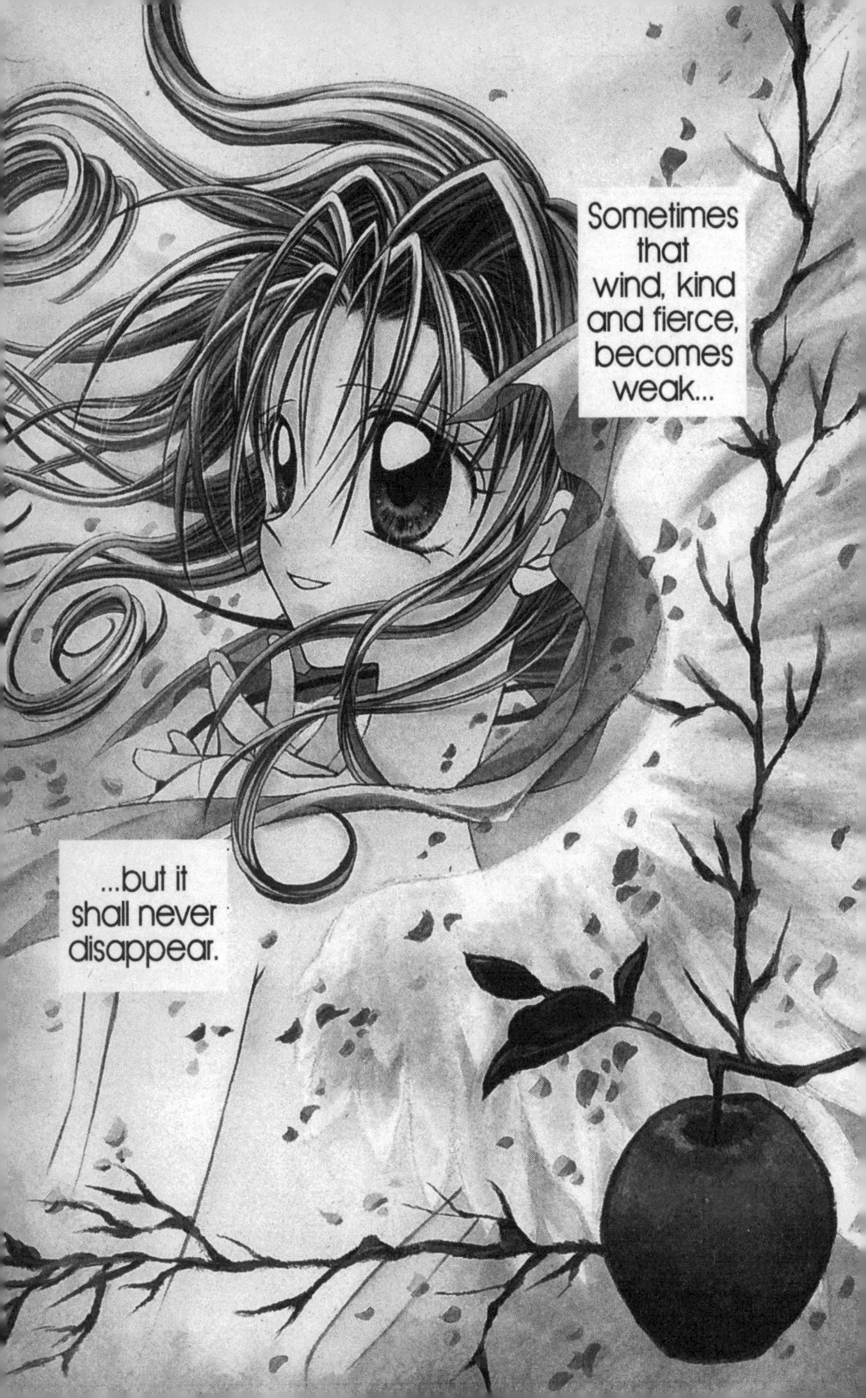
Sometimes that wind, kind and fierce, becomes weak...
...but it shall never disappear.

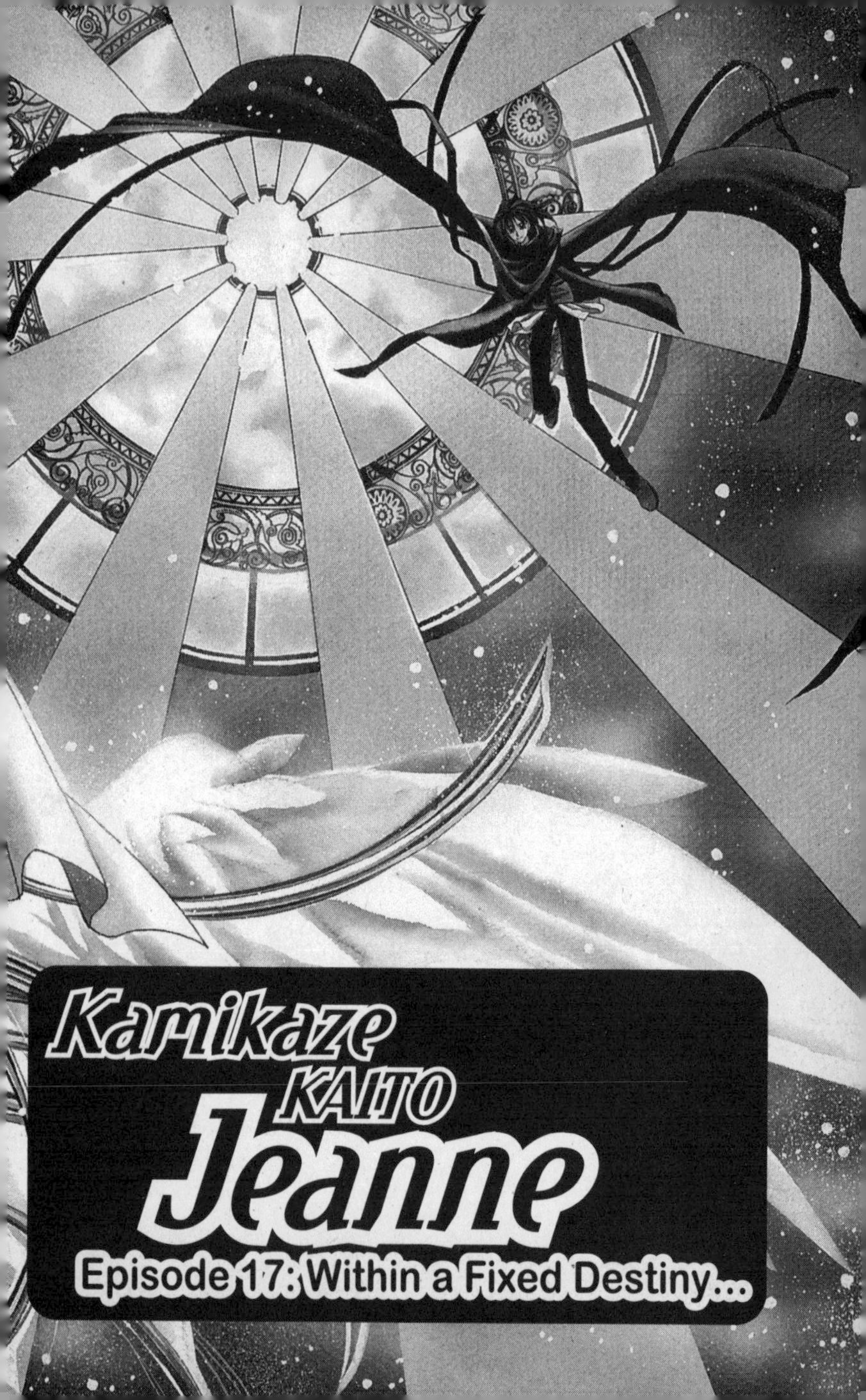
Kamikaze
KAITO
Jeanne
Episode 17: Within a Fixed Destiny...

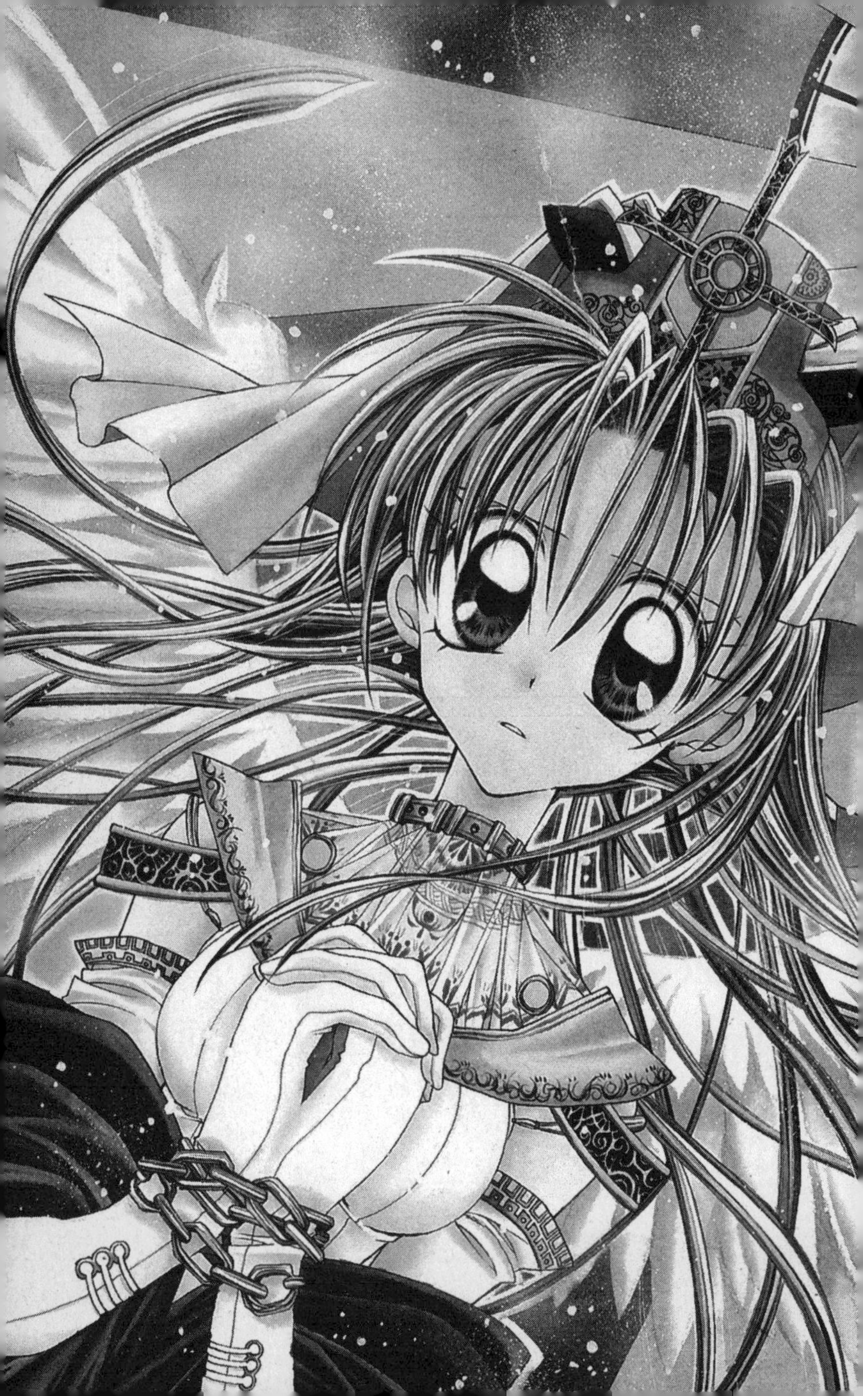

Hijiri-sensei's Lecture on Jeanne D'Arc

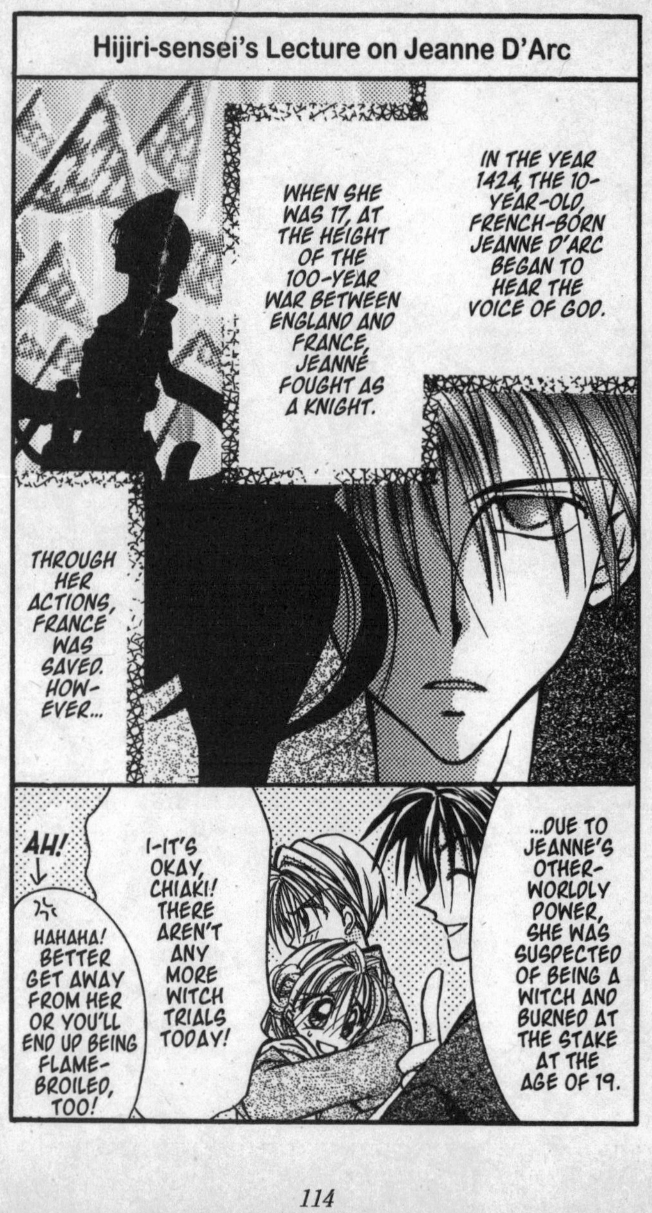
IN THE YEAR 1424, THE 10-YEAR-OLD, FRENCH-BORN JEANNE D'ARC BEGAN TO HEAR THE VOICE OF GOD.
WHEN SHE WAS 17, AT THE HEIGHT OF THE 100-YEAR WAR BETWEEN ENGLAND AND FRANCE, JEANNE FOUGHT AS A KNIGHT.
THROUGH HER ACTIONS, FRANCE WAS SAVED. HOW-EVER...
...DUE TO JEANNE'S OTHER-WORLDLY POWER, SHE WAS SUSPECTED OF BEING A WITCH AND BURNED AT THE STAKE AT THE AGE OF 19.
I-IT'S OKAY, CHIAKI! THERE AREN'T ANY MORE WITCH TRIALS TODAY!
AH!
HAHAHA! BETTER GET AWAY FROM HER OR YOU'LL END UP BEING FLAME-BROILED, TOO!

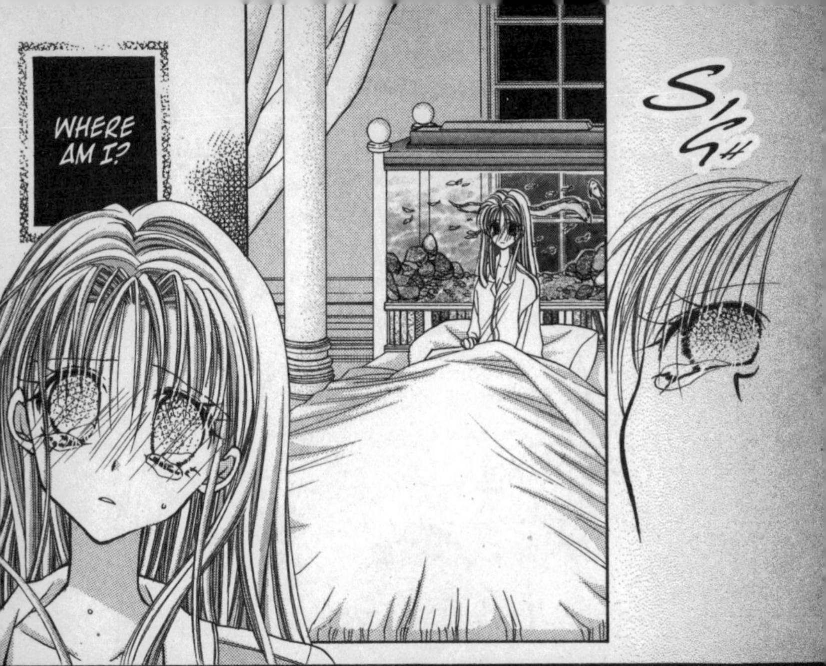
SIGH
WHERE AM I?

Episode 17: "WITHIN A FIXED DESTINY" Tagline: "Will my wish get through...?!"

Hiya! My assistants loved the artwork for this ep's title page!! (Of course, it went over well with all the fans, too...♡) Have you noticed how Noin has become just a little bit bigger since the title page art on episode 16? Hee-hee-hee...Anyway, the idea was to have a princess and the demon who captures her. I liked the art for it, too, and had it turned into a telephone card for Ribon's Fun Festival. Do any of you out there have the card? If you do, I hope you take good care of it. Storywise, I really enjoyed doing the subplot of Kagura and Yashiro-chan's romance, but I ran out of pages, so I have to apologize for delivering a truncated romance! Oww! Quit throwing rocks! Ah! Ah! I'm always aiming to satisfy the first requirement of good manga, which is to make the stories easy to read...but unfortunately, I'm putting out this manga, which is hard to read! Gotta work on that...Eh-heh. Anyway, I like the Nagoya men. I'd love to be their maid! (Ah! I just remembered, Chiaki-sama doesn't live at the family mansion anymore...Shucks!) What else? In this installment, Hijiri-sensei's secret comes to light, a little at a time...Betcha can't wait to see what comes next, huh? Interestingly enough, the Hijiri character isn't popular at all with readers of "Ribon" magazine, but the "Jeanne" trade paperback readers can't get enough of him! Go figure, huh? I think the trader paperback readers are more willing to just kick back and go along with whatever I've got planned. Anyway, I'm looking forward to getting more feedback! Oh yeah, my favorite bits for this ep: I like all of pg. 126 for the words ♡ and for the art, I like pg. 141, panel 5, Yashiro-chan's fed-up look. One more thing! Last time here, I complained about a reader who accused me of having my assistant do all the art and other readers took me to task for it (I apologize for wording my complaint poorly,) but now, I've been accused of having my assistants do all the coloring work (I can't get peeved about this?) I don't know what the deal is with trying to brand me as unprofessional, but just to set the record straight, sometimes my assistants draw the "extras" for a crowd scene...again, I stress the word **sometimes**. But please don't think that they draw the main characters...because that's **my** job!

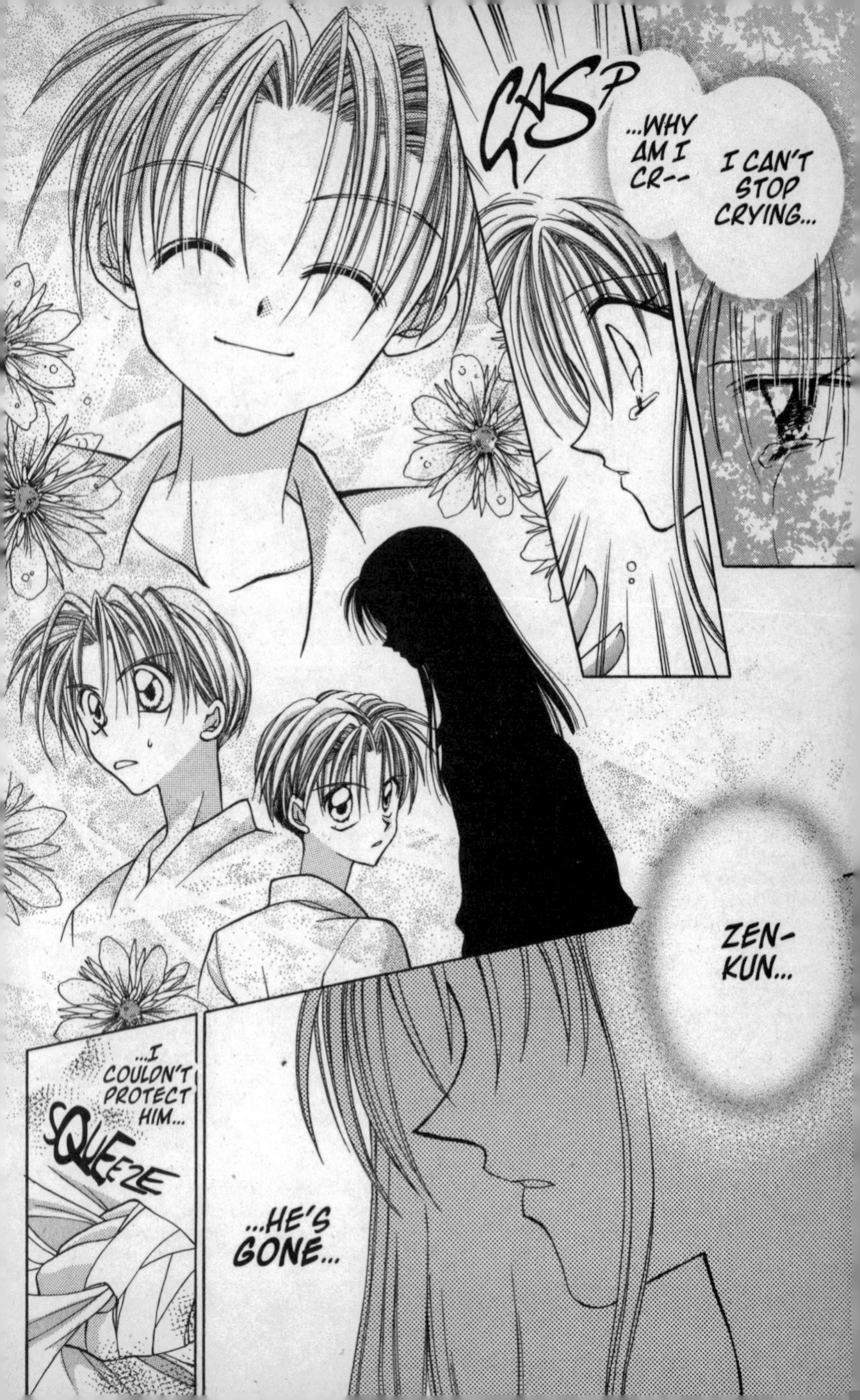
GASP
...WHY AM I CR--
I CAN'T STOP CRYING...
ZEN-KUN...
...HE'S GONE...
...I COULDN'T PROTECT HIM...
SQUEEZE

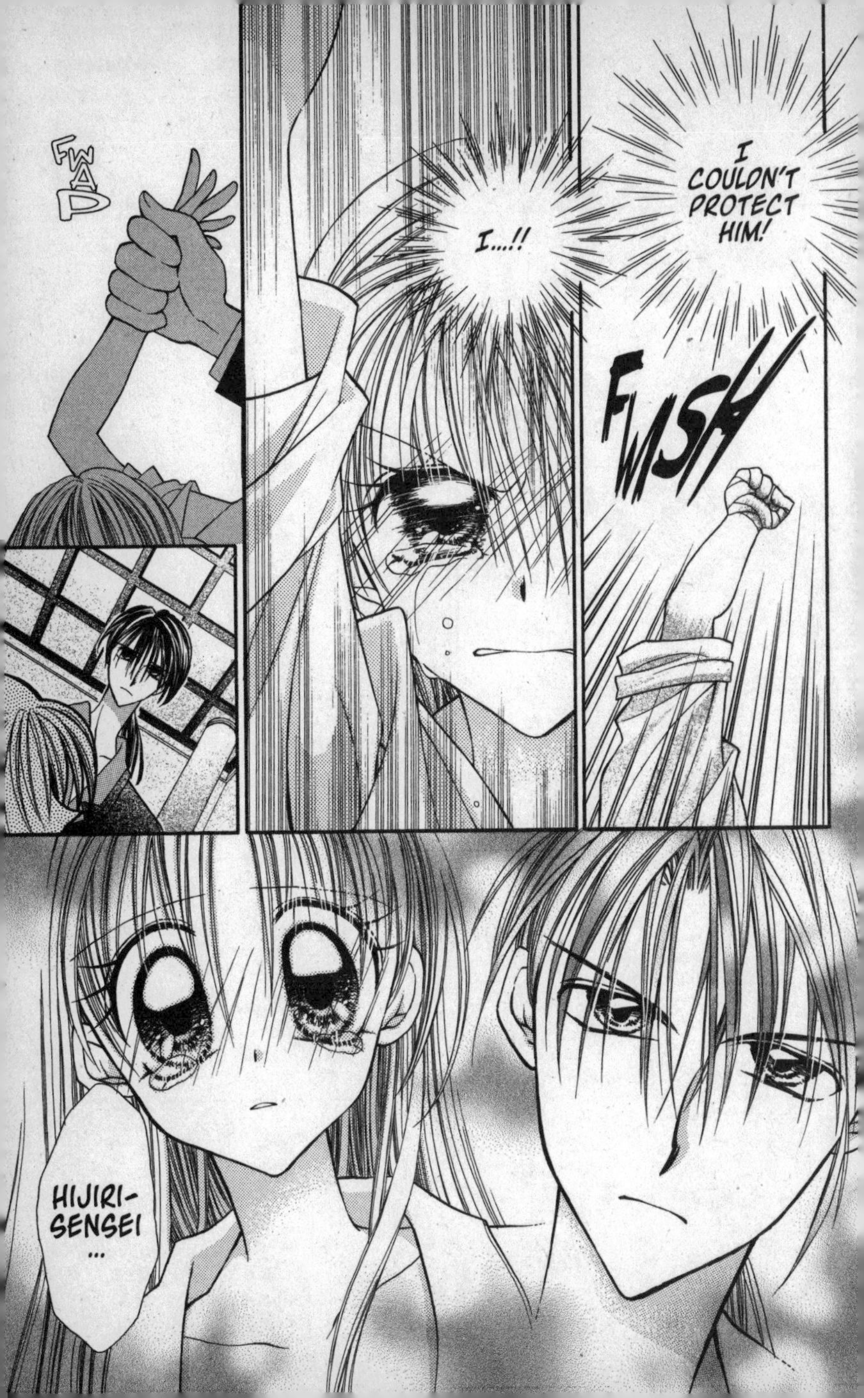
I COULDN'T PROTECT HIM!
FWASH
I...!!
FWAP
HIJIRI-SENSEI ...

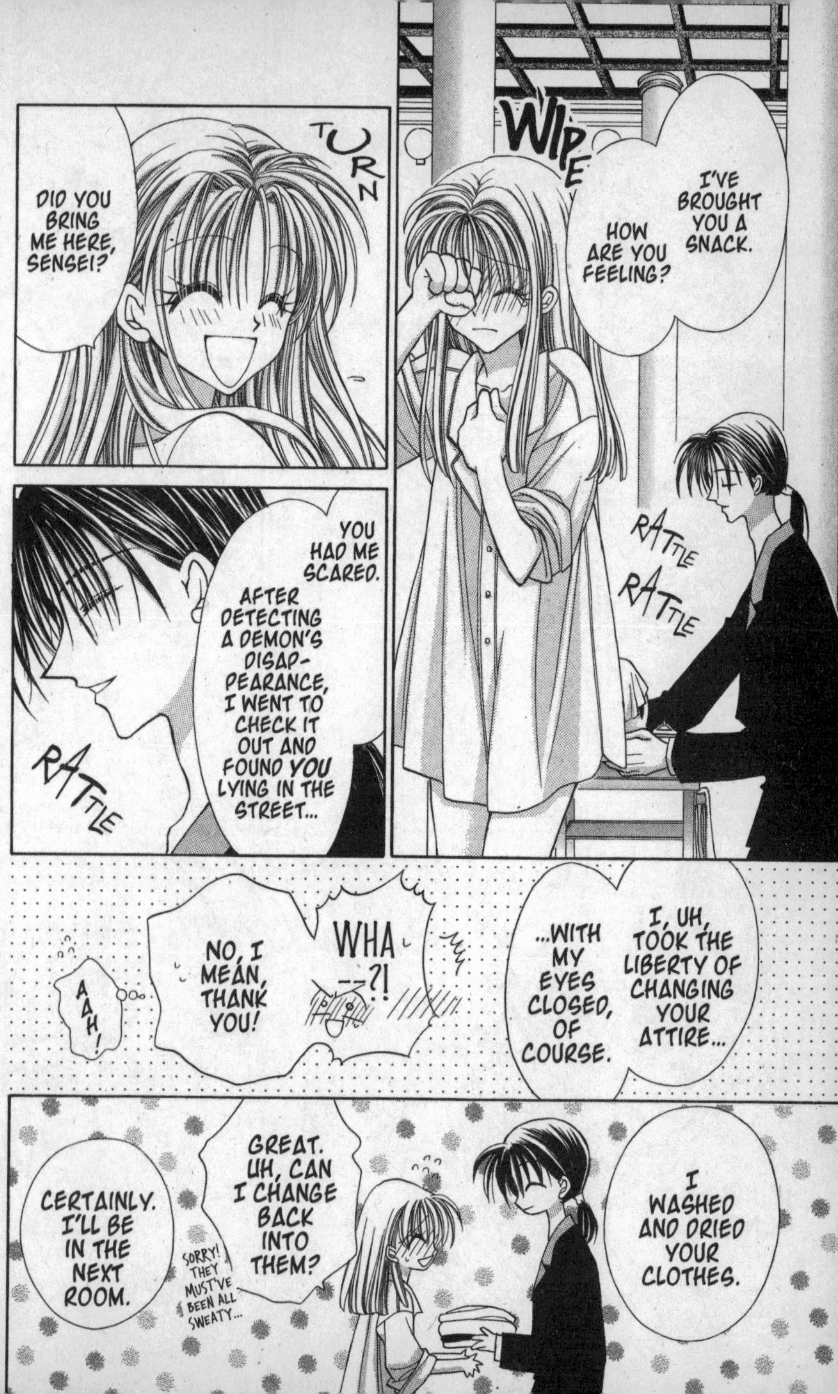
WIPE
I'VE BROUGHT YOU A SNACK.
HOW ARE YOU FEELING?
RATTLE RATTLE
TURN
DID YOU BRING ME HERE, SENSEI?
YOU HAD ME SCARED.
AFTER DETECTING A DEMON'S DISAP-PEARANCE, I WENT TO CHECK IT OUT AND FOUND YOU LYING IN THE STREET...
RATTLE
I, UH, TOOK THE LIBERTY OF CHANGING YOUR ATTIRE...
...WITH MY EYES CLOSED, OF COURSE.
WHA--?!
NO, I MEAN, THANK YOU!
AAH!
I WASHED AND DRIED YOUR CLOTHES.
GREAT. UH, CAN I CHANGE BACK INTO THEM?
SORRY! THEY MUST'VE BEEN ALL SWEATY...
CERTAINLY. I'LL BE IN THE NEXT ROOM.

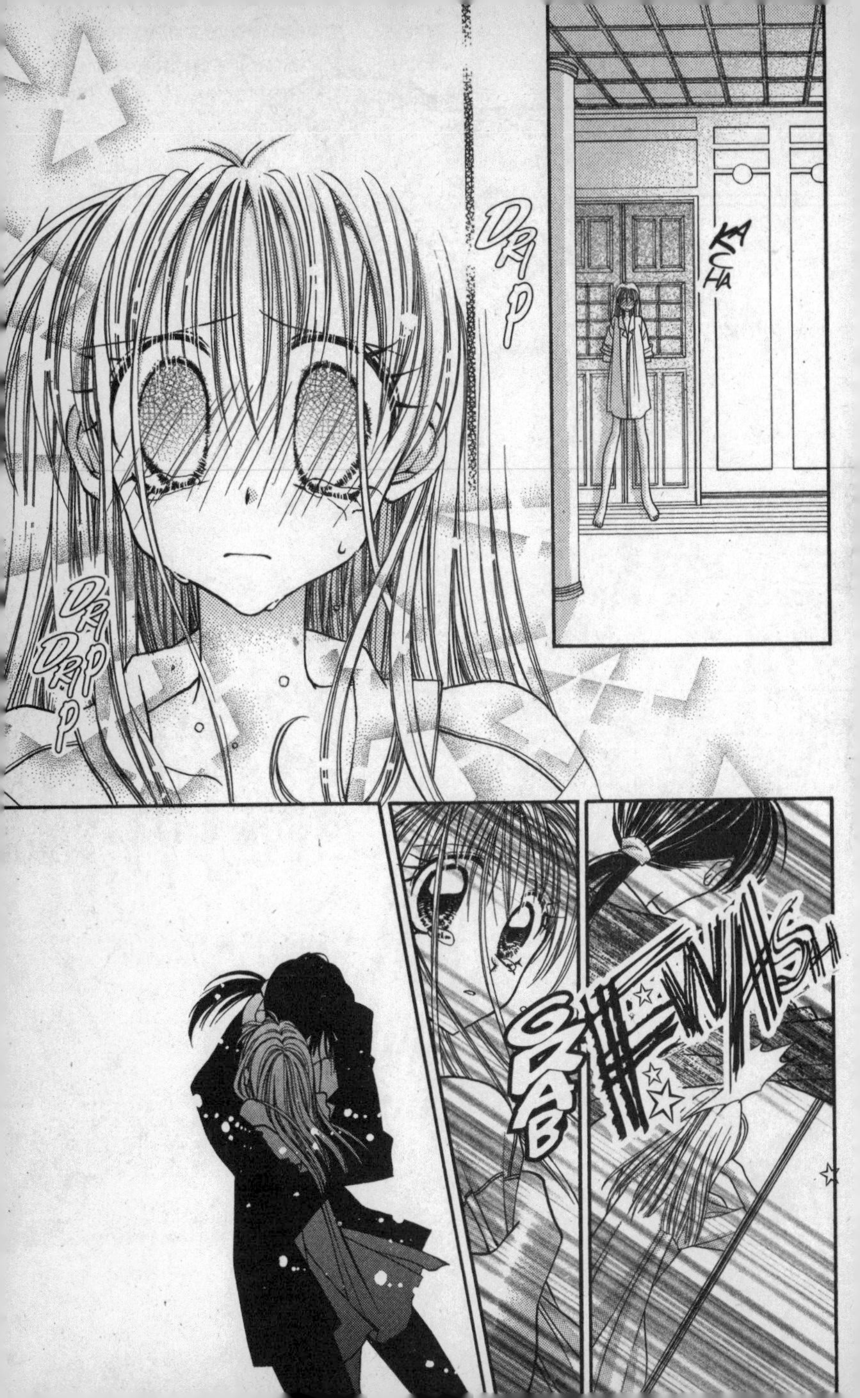
KACHA
DRIP
DRIP DRIP
FWASH
GRAB

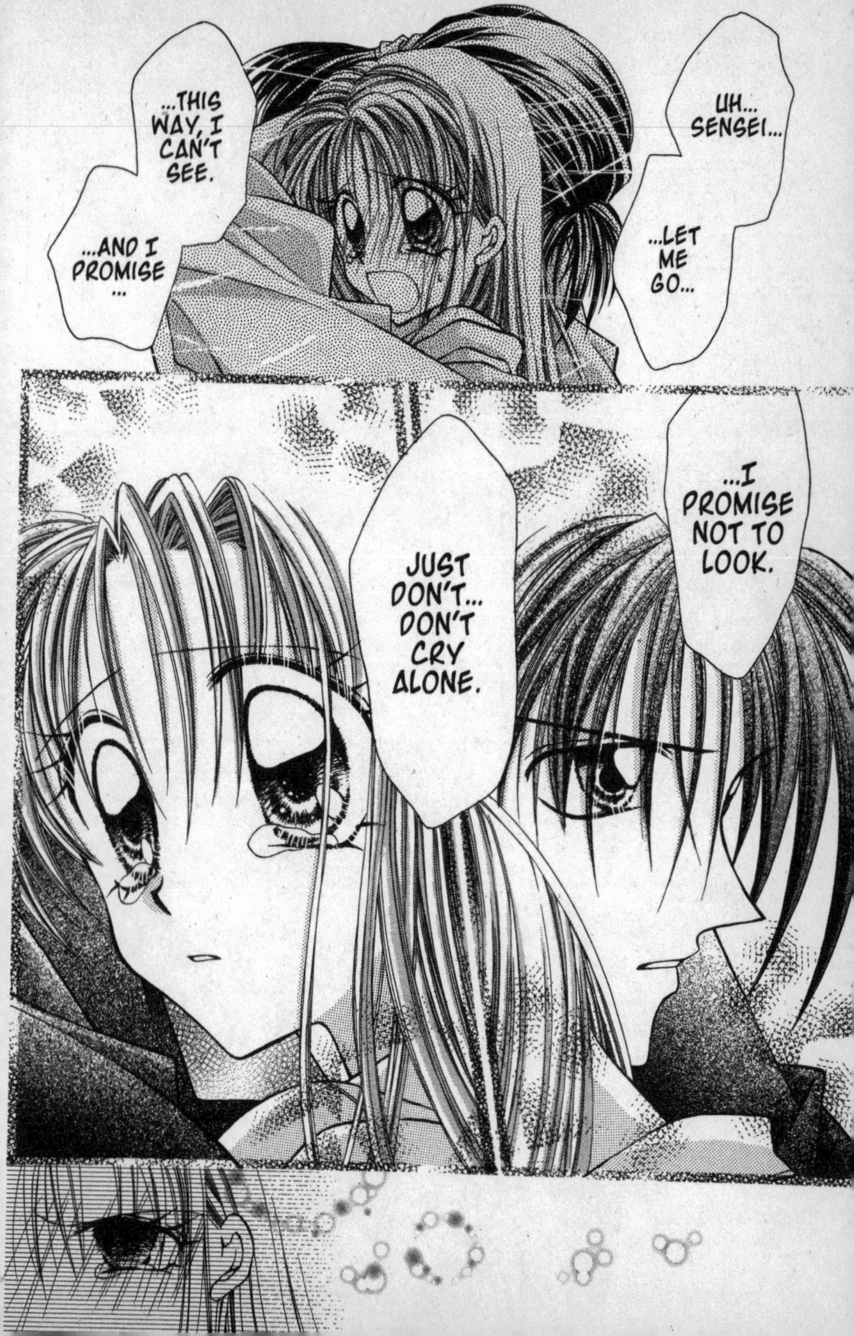
UH... SENSEI...
...LET ME GO...
...THIS WAY, I CAN'T SEE.
...AND I PROMISE ...
...I PROMISE NOT TO LOOK.
JUST DON'T... DON'T CRY ALONE.

HUGE SERVICE FOR JEANNE FANS

In public for the first time! Early sketches from when the series just started to be published!!!

JEANNE

MARON

WELCOME HOME, CHIAKI-KUN!

POP

CLAP
CLAP
CLAP
CLAP

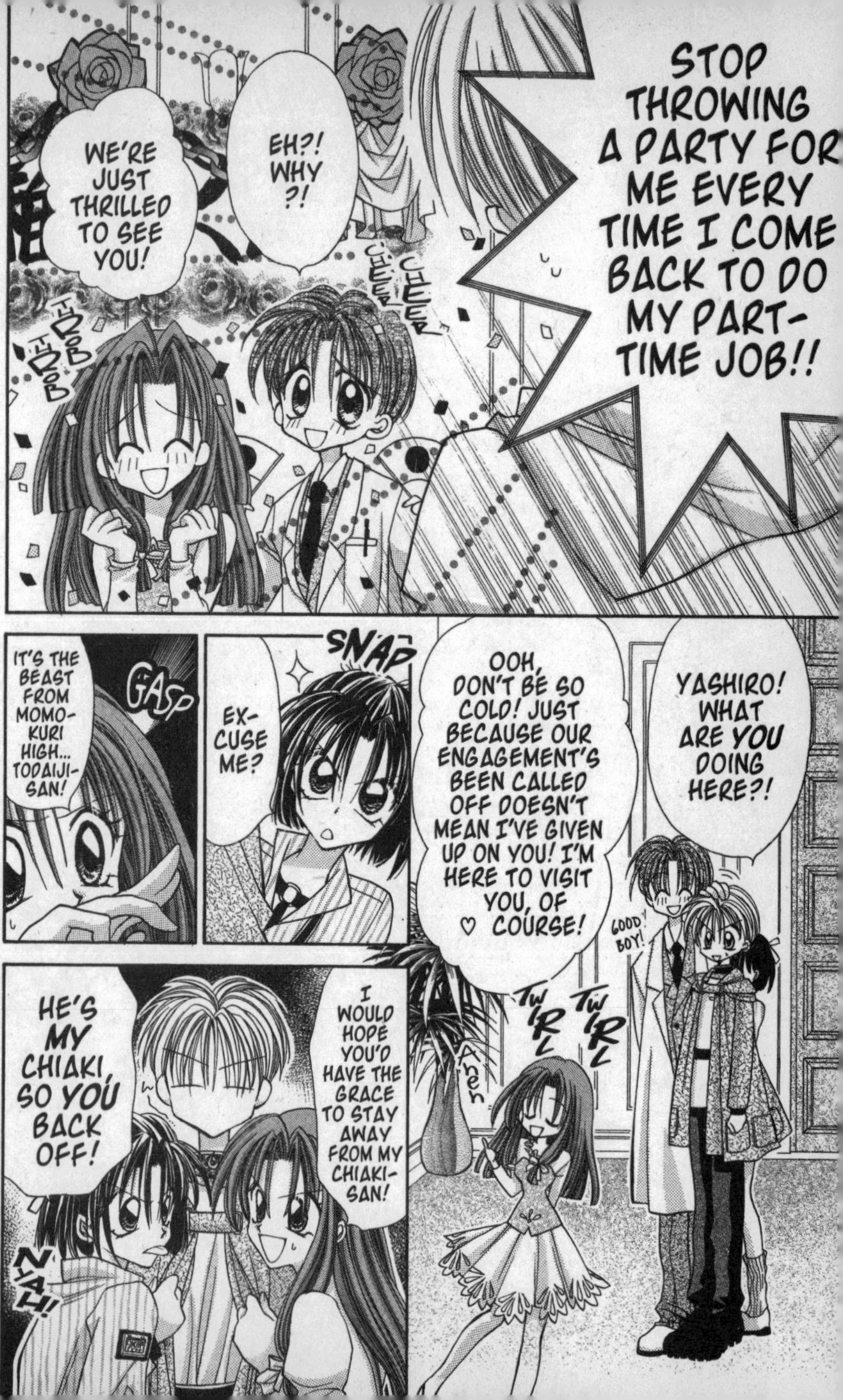
STOP THROWING A PARTY FOR ME EVERY TIME I COME BACK TO DO MY PART-TIME JOB!!
EH?! WHY?!
WE'RE JUST THRILLED TO SEE YOU!
CHEER CHEER
THROB THROB
YASHIRO! WHAT ARE YOU DOING HERE?!
OOH, DON'T BE SO COLD! JUST BECAUSE OUR ENGAGEMENT'S BEEN CALLED OFF DOESN'T MEAN I'VE GIVEN UP ON YOU! I'M HERE TO VISIT YOU, OF COURSE! ♡
GOOD BOY!
TWIRL TWIRL
Ahen
SNAP
EX-CUSE ME?
GASP
IT'S THE BEAST FROM MOMO-KURI HIGH... TODAIJI-SAN!
I WOULD HOPE YOU'D HAVE THE GRACE TO STAY AWAY FROM MY CHIAKI-SAN!
HE'S MY CHIAKI, SO YOU BACK OFF!
NYAH!

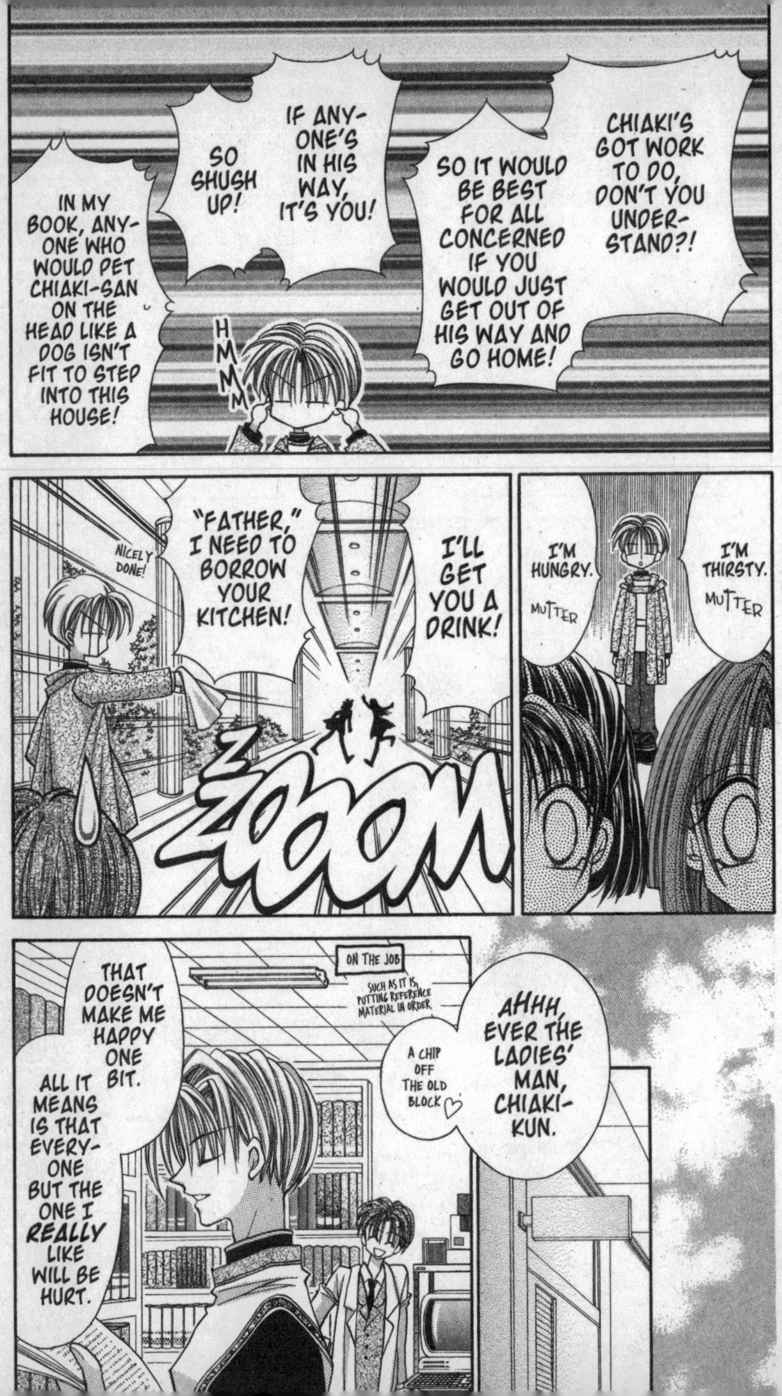

CHIAKI'S GOT WORK TO DO, DON'T YOU UNDERSTAND?!
SO IT WOULD BE BEST FOR ALL CONCERNED IF YOU WOULD JUST GET OUT OF HIS WAY AND GO HOME!
IF ANYONE'S IN HIS WAY, IT'S YOU!
SO SHUSH UP!
IN MY BOOK, ANYONE WHO WOULD PET CHIAKI-SAN ON THE HEAD LIKE A DOG ISN'T FIT TO STEP INTO THIS HOUSE!
HMMMM
I'M THIRSTY.
MUTTER
I'M HUNGRY.
MUTTER
I'LL GET YOU A DRINK!
"FATHER," I NEED TO BORROW YOUR KITCHEN!
NICELY DONE!
ZOOOM
ON THE JOB
SUCH AS IT IS, PUTTING REFERENCE MATERIAL IN ORDER
AHHH, EVER THE LADIES' MAN, CHIAKI-KUN.
A CHIP OFF THE OLD BLOCK ♡
THAT DOESN'T MAKE ME HAPPY ONE BIT.
ALL IT MEANS IS THAT EVERYONE BUT THE ONE I REALLY LIKE WILL BE HURT.

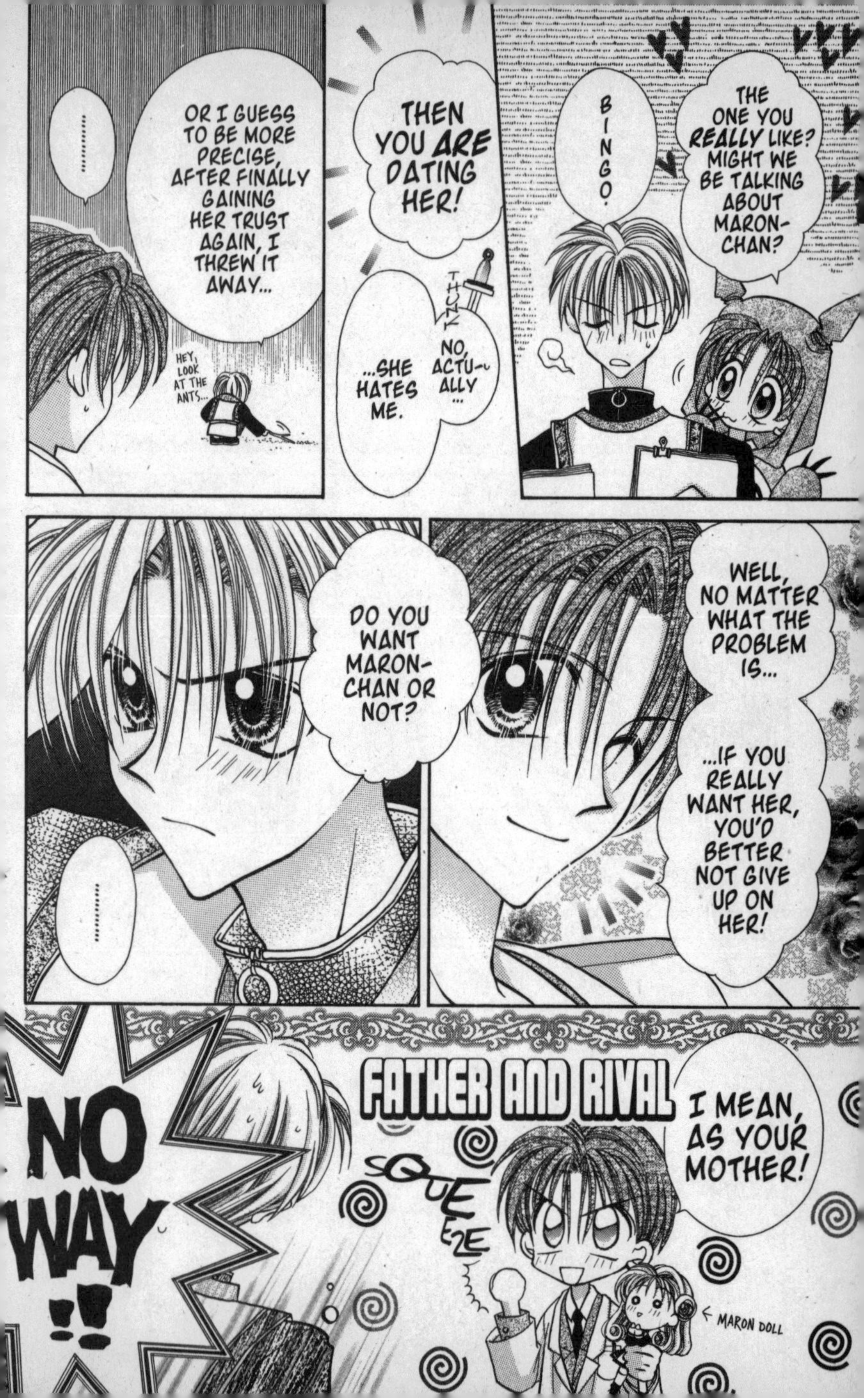
THE ONE YOU REALLY LIKE? MIGHT WE BE TALKING ABOUT MARON-CHAN?
BINGO.
THEN YOU ARE DATING HER!
NO, ACTUALLY...
THUNK
...SHE HATES ME.
OR I GUESS TO BE MORE PRECISE, AFTER FINALLY GAINING HER TRUST AGAIN, I THREW IT AWAY...
HEY, LOOK AT THE ANTS...
....
WELL, NO MATTER WHAT THE PROBLEM IS...
...IF YOU REALLY WANT HER, YOU'D BETTER NOT GIVE UP ON HER!
DO YOU WANT MARON-CHAN OR NOT?
....
FATHER AND RIVAL
I MEAN, AS YOUR MOTHER!
SQUEEZE
MARON DOLL
NO WAY!!

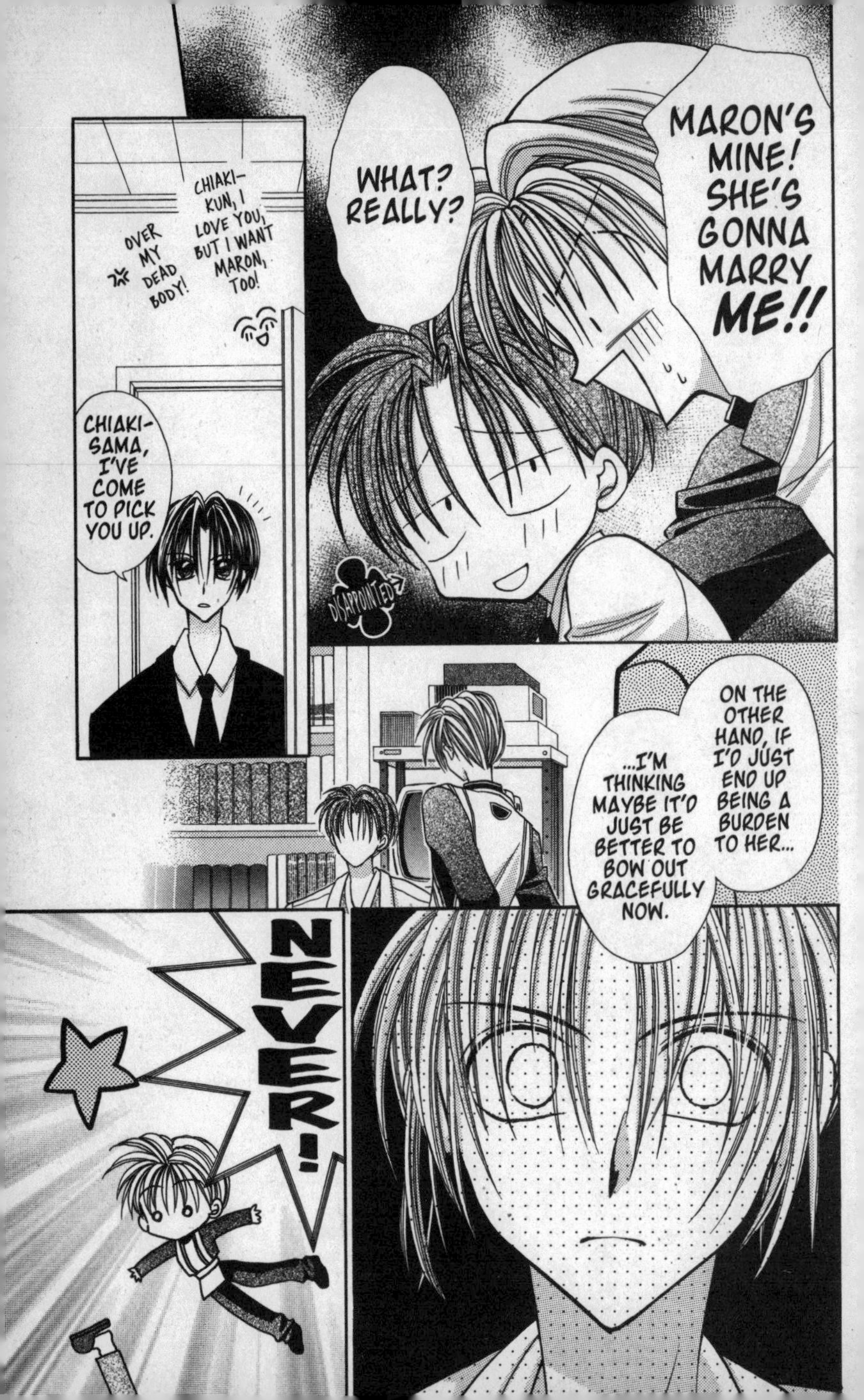
MARON'S MINE! SHE'S GONNA MARRY ME!!
WHAT? REALLY?
DISAPPOINTED
CHIAKI-KUN, I LOVE YOU, BUT I WANT MARON, TOO!
OVER MY DEAD BODY!
CHIAKI-SAMA, I'VE COME TO PICK YOU UP.
ON THE OTHER HAND, IF I'D JUST END UP BEING A BURDEN TO HER...
...I'M THINKING MAYBE IT'D JUST BE BETTER TO BOW OUT GRACEFULLY NOW.
NEVER!

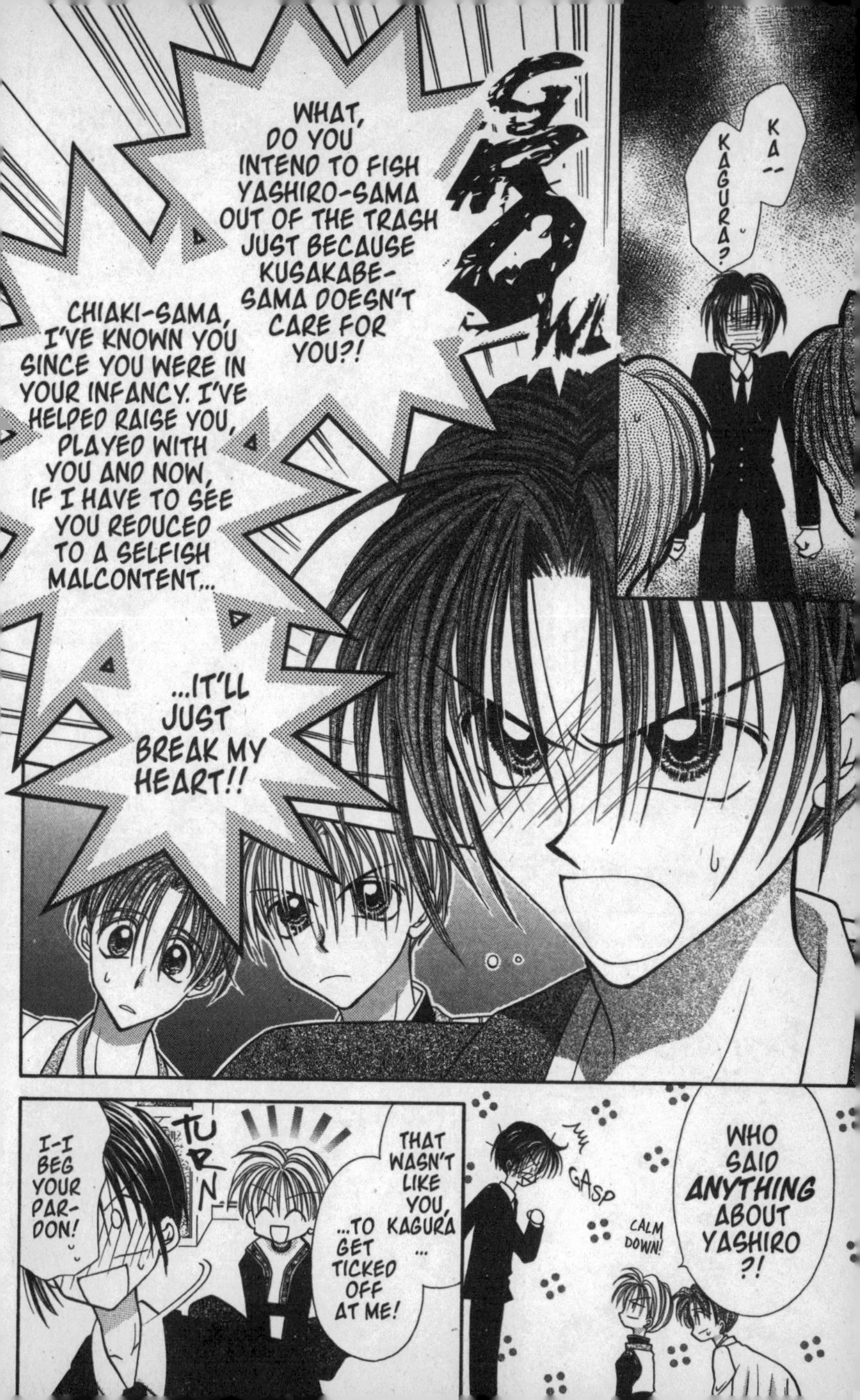
KA-- KAGURA?
WHAT, DO YOU INTEND TO FISH YASHIRO-SAMA OUT OF THE TRASH JUST BECAUSE KUSAKABE-SAMA DOESN'T CARE FOR YOU?!
CHIAKI-SAMA, I'VE KNOWN YOU SINCE YOU WERE IN YOUR INFANCY. I'VE HELPED RAISE YOU, PLAYED WITH YOU AND NOW, IF I HAVE TO SEE YOU REDUCED TO A SELFISH MALCONTENT...
...IT'LL JUST BREAK MY HEART!!
WHO SAID ANYTHING ABOUT YASHIRO?!
CALM DOWN!
GASP
THAT WASN'T LIKE YOU, KAGURA...
...TO GET TICKED OFF AT ME!
TURN
I-I BEG YOUR PARDON!

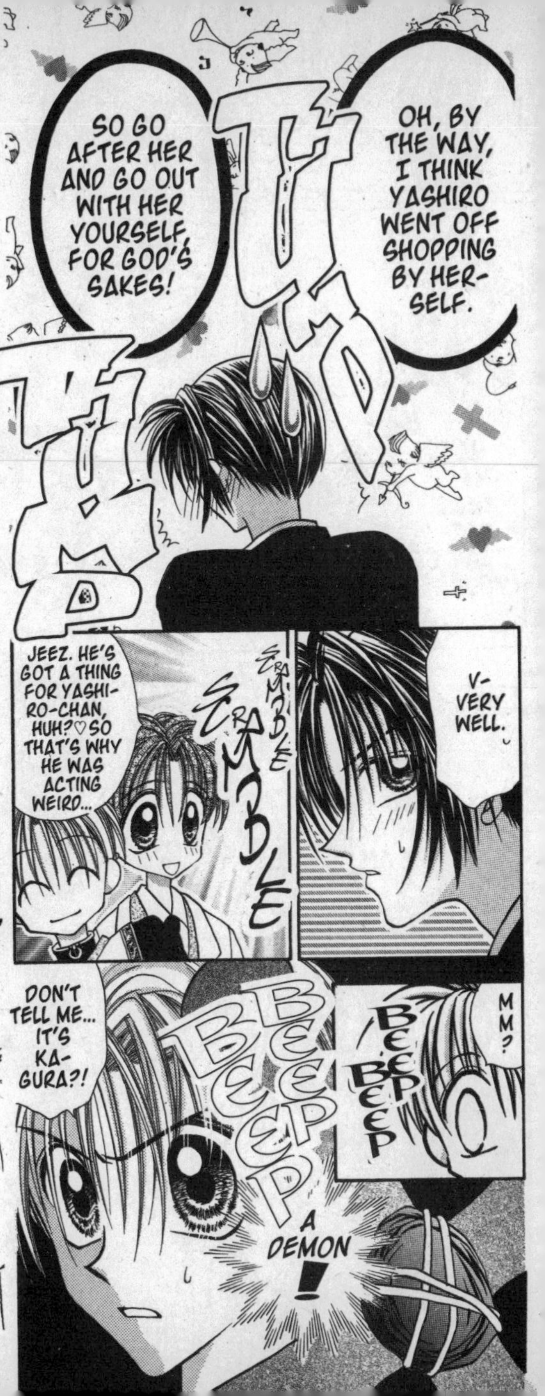
OH, BY THE WAY, I THINK YASHIRO WENT OFF SHOPPING BY HER-SELF.
SO GO AFTER HER AND GO OUT WITH HER YOURSELF, FOR GOD'S SAKES!
V-VERY WELL.
JEEZ. HE'S GOT A THING FOR YASHIRO-CHAN, HUH?♡ SO THAT'S WHY HE WAS ACTING WEIRD...
SCRAMBLE
SCRAMBLE
MM?
BEEP BEEP
BEEP BEEP
DON'T TELL ME... IT'S KA-GURA?!
A DEMON!

A VERY SPECIAL SERVICE FOR "I.O.N." FANS!

Secret, never before seen illos (drawn during the time when I.O.N. was still being serialized)!

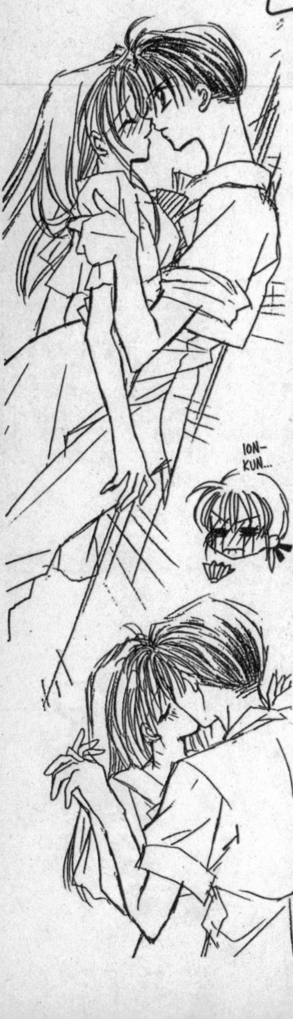
ION-KUN...

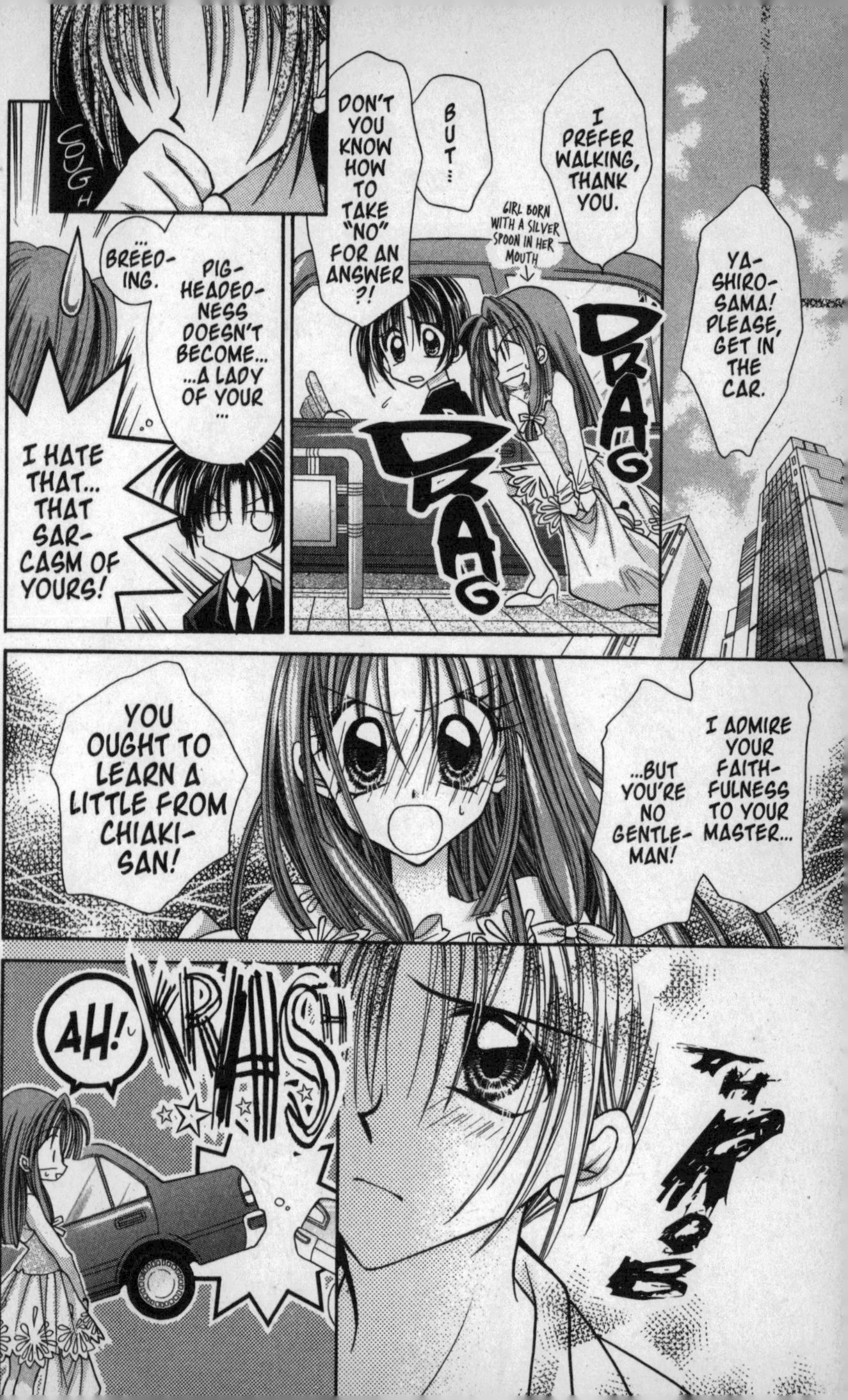
YA-SHIRO-SAMA! PLEASE, GET IN THE CAR.
I PREFER WALKING, THANK YOU.
GIRL BORN WITH A SILVER SPOON IN HER MOUTH
DRAG
DRAG
BUT...
DON'T YOU KNOW HOW TO TAKE "NO" FOR AN ANSWER?!
COUGH
PIG-HEADEDNESS DOESN'T BECOME... ...A LADY OF YOUR ...
... BREEDING.
I HATE THAT... THAT SARCASM OF YOURS!
I ADMIRE YOUR FAITHFULNESS TO YOUR MASTER...
...BUT YOU'RE NO GENTLEMAN!
YOU OUGHT TO LEARN A LITTLE FROM CHIAKI-SAN!
THROB
KRASH
AH!

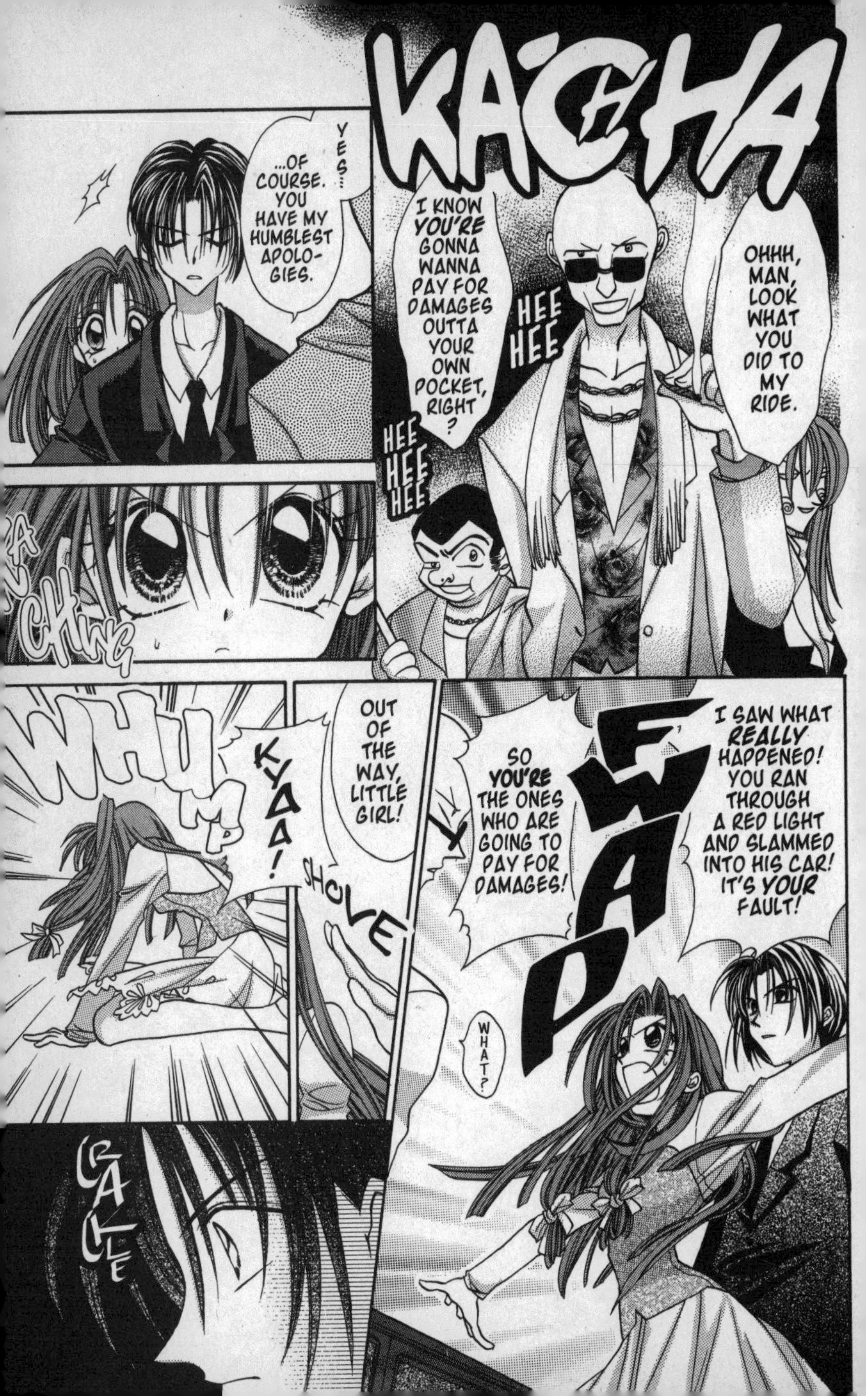
KACHA
OHHH, MAN, LOOK WHAT YOU DID TO MY RIDE.
I KNOW YOU'RE GONNA WANNA PAY FOR DAMAGES OUTTA YOUR OWN POCKET, RIGHT?
HEE HEE
HEE HEE HEE
YES...
...OF COURSE. YOU HAVE MY HUMBLEST APOLOGIES.
CHING
I SAW WHAT REALLY HAPPENED! YOU RAN THROUGH A RED LIGHT AND SLAMMED INTO HIS CAR! IT'S YOUR FAULT!
FWAP
SO YOU'RE THE ONES WHO ARE GOING TO PAY FOR DAMAGES!
WHAT?
OUT OF THE WAY, LITTLE GIRL!
KYAAA!
SHOVE
WHUMP
CRACKLE

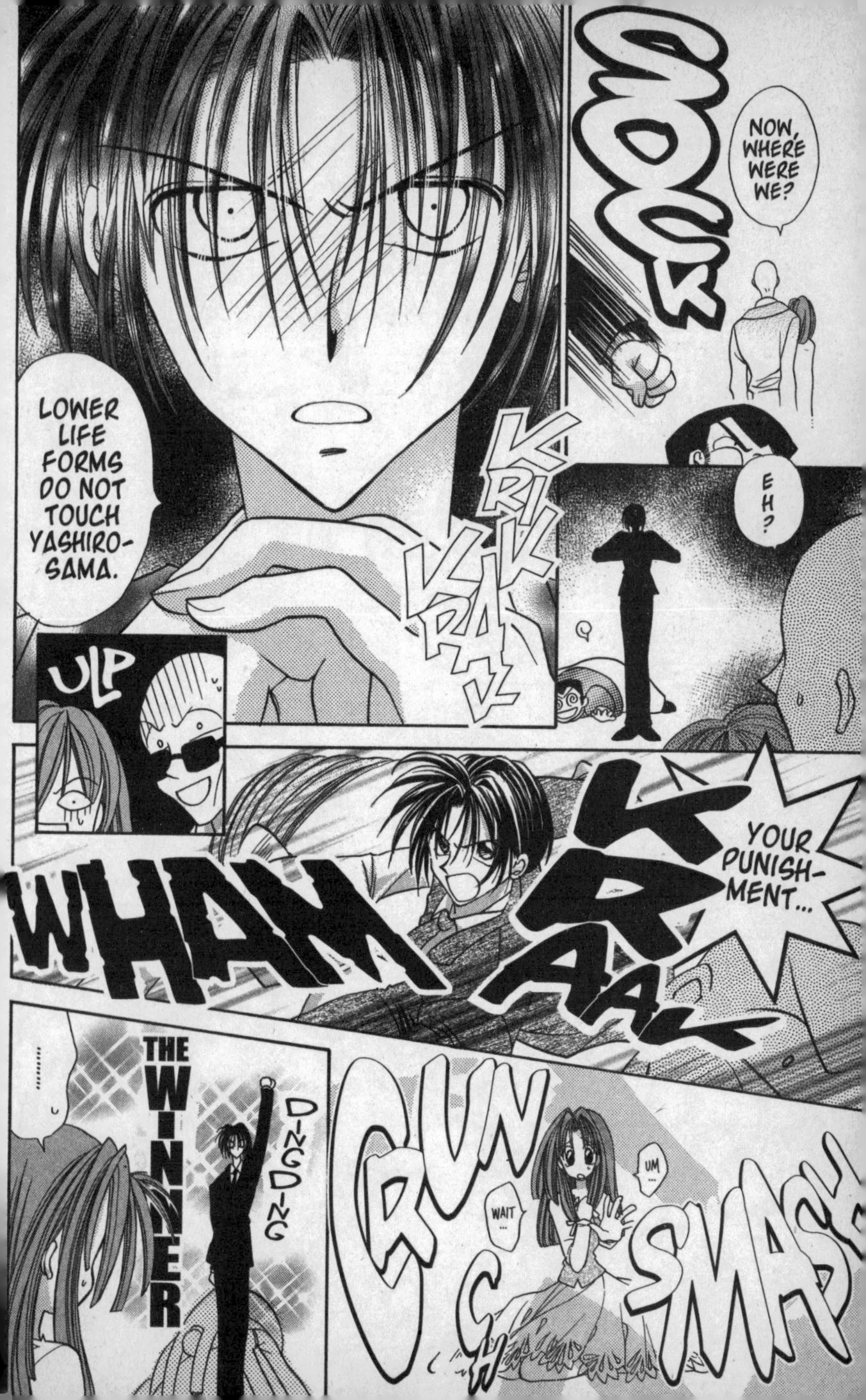
NOW, WHERE WERE WE?
SOCK
LOWER LIFE FORMS DO NOT TOUCH YASHIRO-SAMA.
KRIK
KRAK
EH?
ULP
YOUR PUNISH-MENT...
WHAM
KRAAK
UM...
WAIT...
CRUNCH
SMASH
DING DING
THE WINNER
......

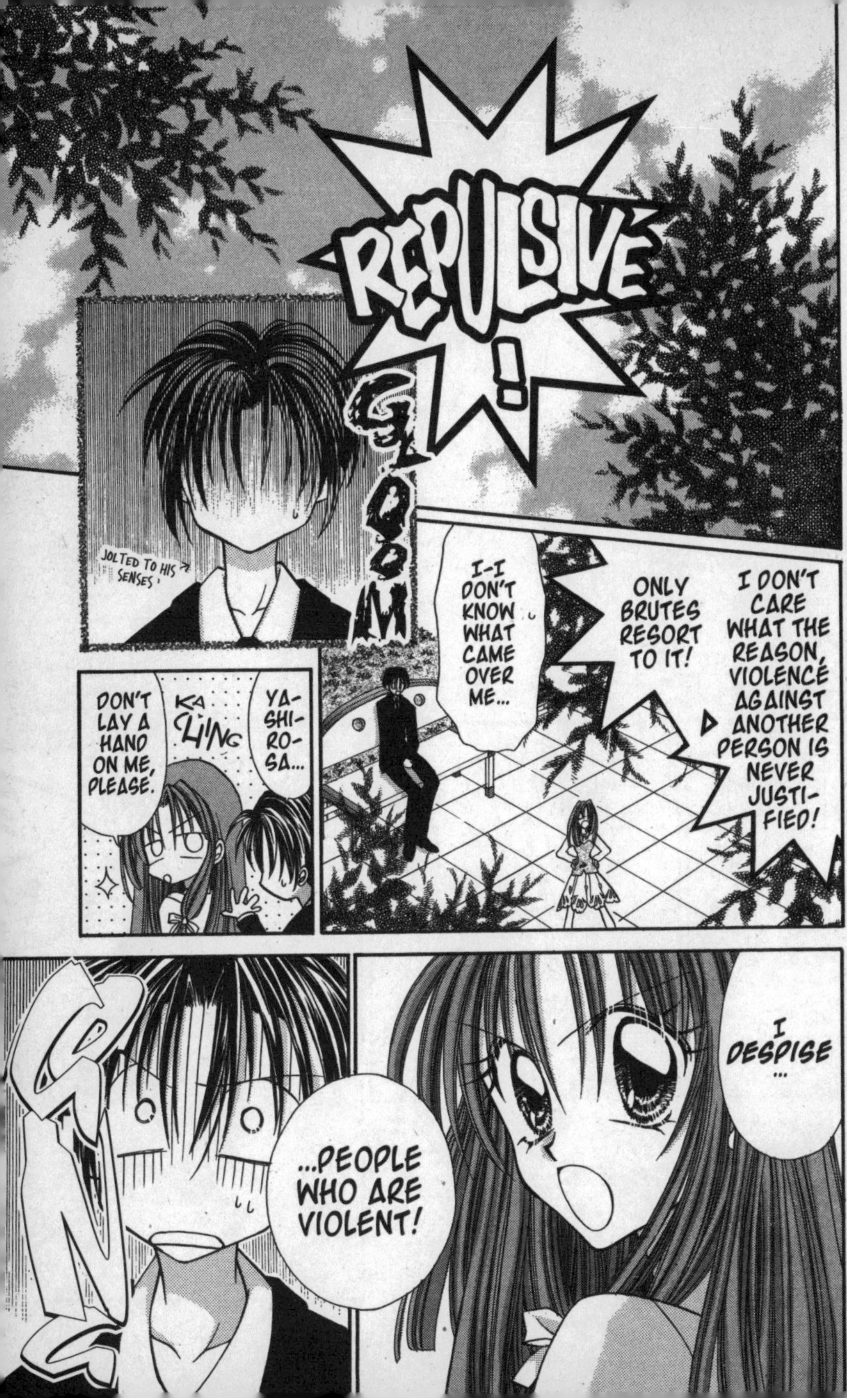
REPULSIVE!
JOLTED TO HIS SENSES
GLOOM
I DON'T CARE WHAT THE REASON, VIOLENCE AGAINST ANOTHER PERSON IS NEVER JUSTIFIED!
ONLY BRUTES RESORT TO IT!
I-I DON'T KNOW WHAT CAME OVER ME...
YASHIROSA...
KA CHING
DON'T LAY A HAND ON ME, PLEASE.
I DESPISE...
...PEOPLE WHO ARE VIOLENT!

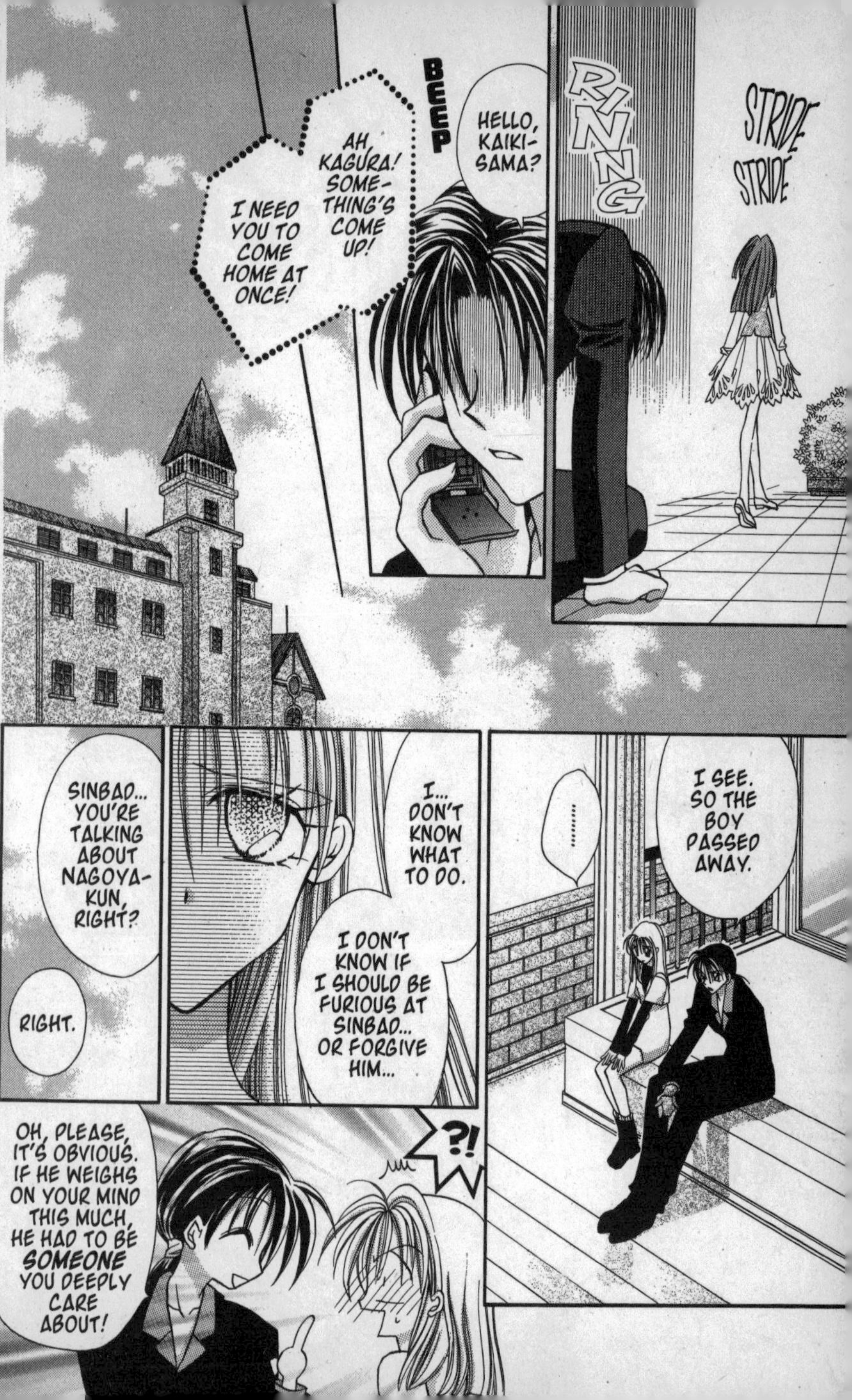
STRIDE STRIDE
RING
BEEP
HELLO, KAIKI-SAMA?
AH, KAGURA! SOME-THING'S COME UP!
I NEED YOU TO COME HOME AT ONCE!
I SEE. SO THE BOY PASSED AWAY.
......
I... DON'T KNOW WHAT TO DO.
I DON'T KNOW IF I SHOULD BE FURIOUS AT SINBAD... OR FORGIVE HIM...
SINBAD... YOU'RE TALKING ABOUT NAGOYA-KUN, RIGHT?
RIGHT.
?!
OH, PLEASE, IT'S OBVIOUS. IF HE WEIGHS ON YOUR MIND THIS MUCH, HE HAD TO BE SOMEONE YOU DEEPLY CARE ABOUT!

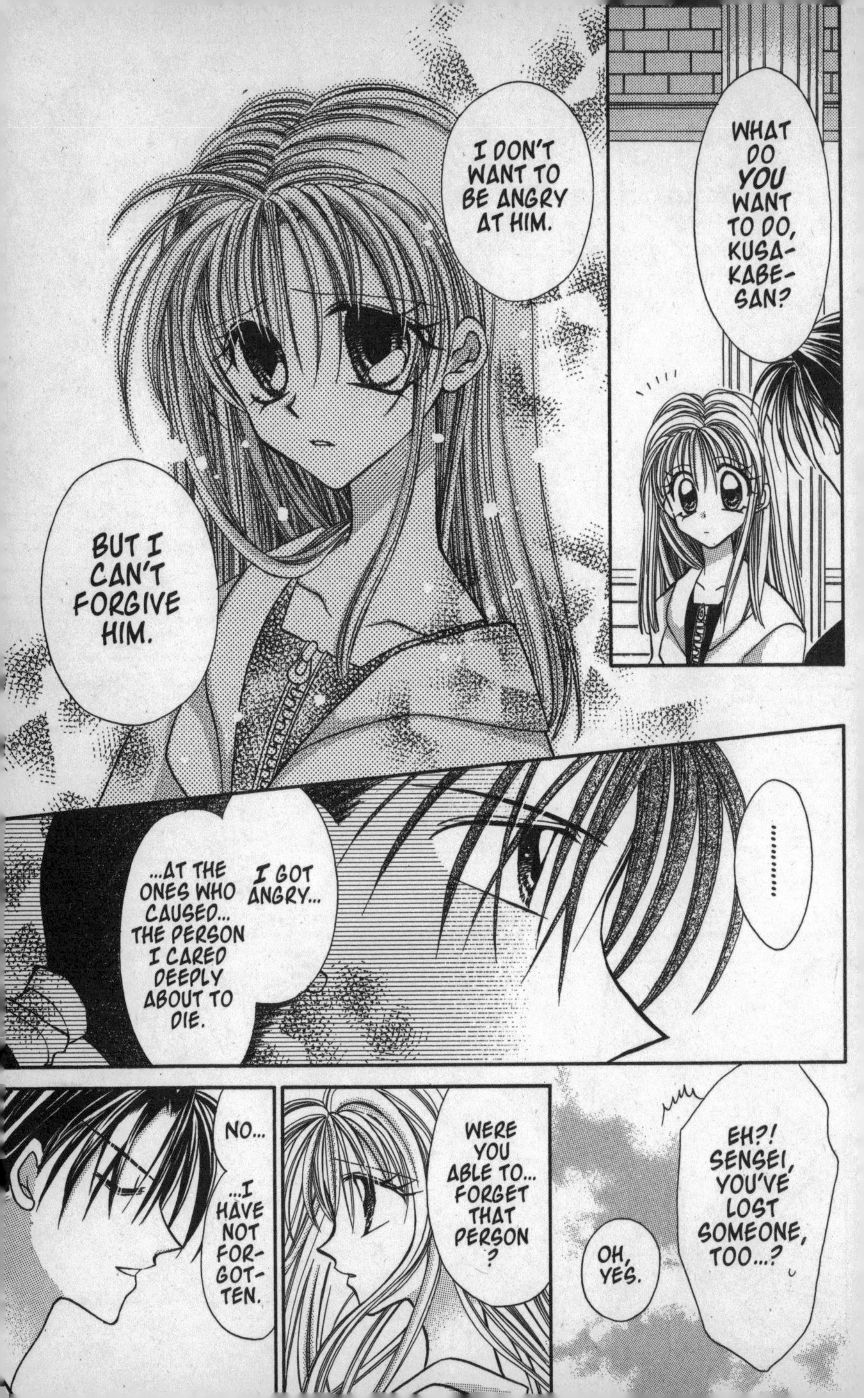
WHAT DO YOU WANT TO DO, KUSAKABE-SAN?
I DON'T WANT TO BE ANGRY AT HIM.
BUT I CAN'T FORGIVE HIM.
......
I GOT ANGRY...
...AT THE ONES WHO CAUSED... THE PERSON I CARED DEEPLY ABOUT TO DIE.
EH?! SENSEI, YOU'VE LOST SOMEONE, TOO...?
OH, YES.
WERE YOU ABLE TO... FORGET THAT PERSON?
NO...
...I HAVE NOT FOR-GOT-TEN.

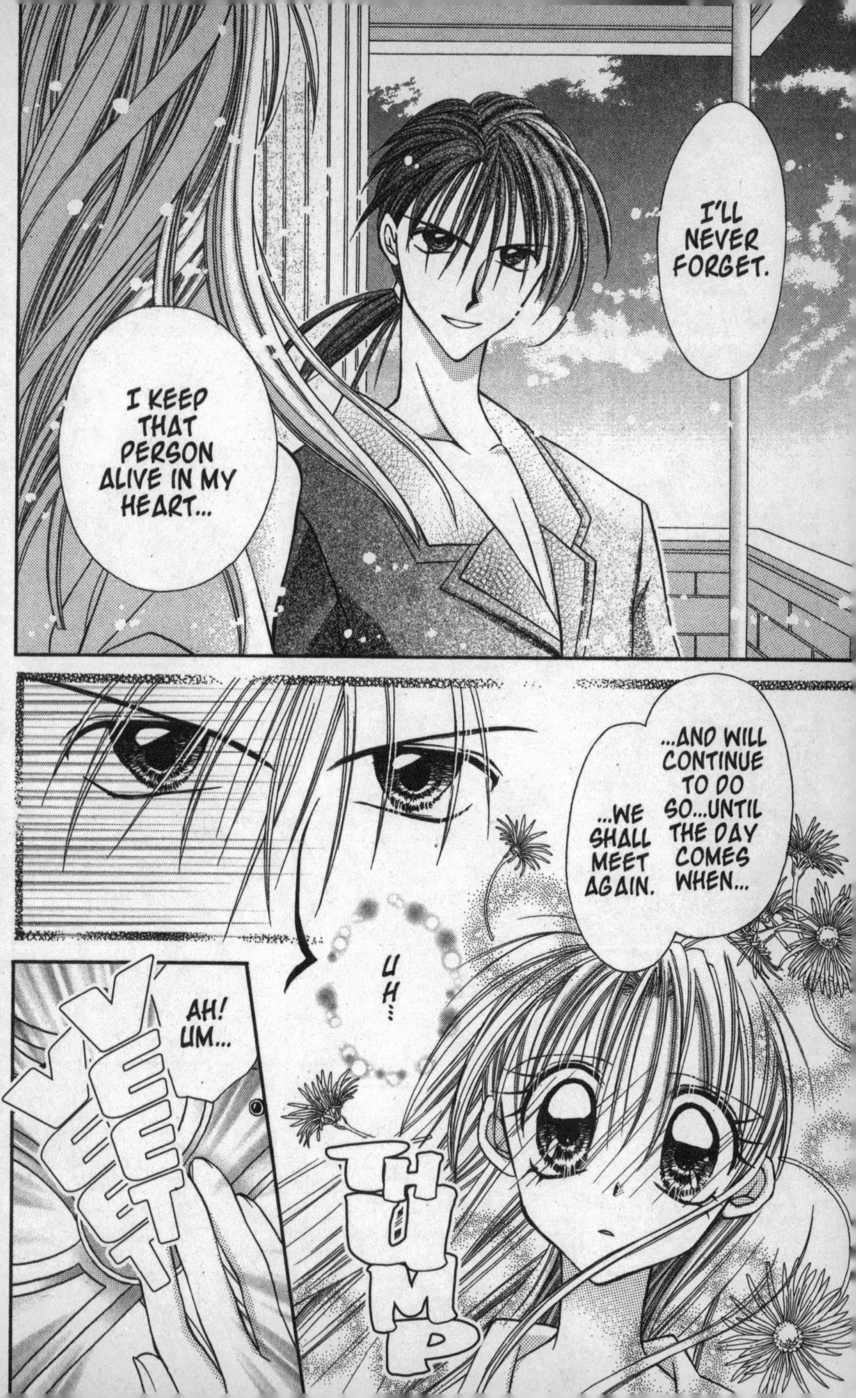

I'LL NEVER FORGET.
I KEEP THAT PERSON ALIVE IN MY HEART...
...AND WILL CONTINUE TO DO SO...UNTIL THE DAY COMES WHEN...
...WE SHALL MEET AGAIN.
UH...
THUMP
AH! UM...
YEET
YEET

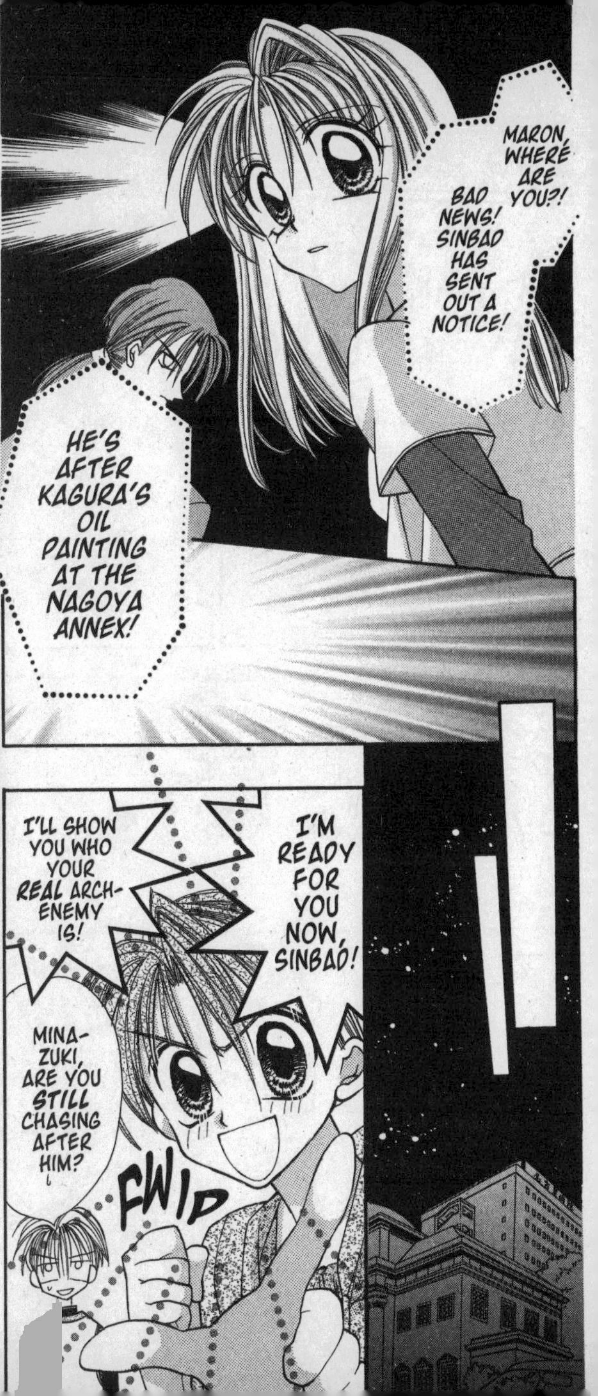
MARON, WHERE ARE YOU?!
BAD NEWS! SINBAD HAS SENT OUT A NOTICE!
HE'S AFTER KAGURA'S OIL PAINTING AT THE NAGOYA ANNEX!
I'M READY FOR YOU NOW, SINBAD!
I'LL SHOW YOU WHO YOUR REAL ARCH-ENEMY IS!
MINA-ZUKI, ARE YOU STILL CHASING AFTER HIM?
FWIP

A-CHAN'S PEN AND SCISSORS

FOR THIS YEAR'S STAR FESTIVAL, I WORE MY FRIEND'S DOLPHIN YUKATA. #22

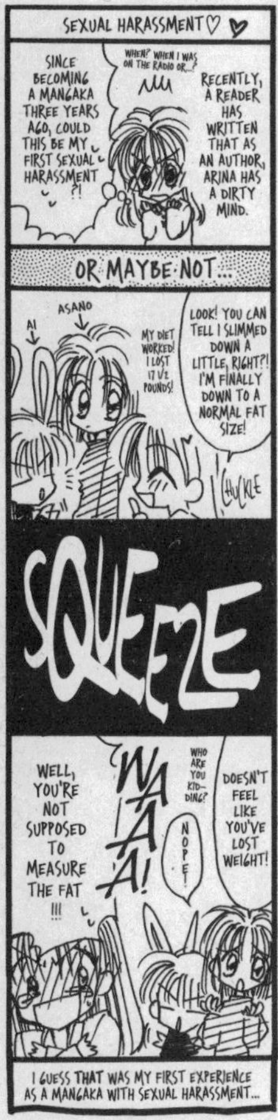
SEXUAL HARASSMENT♡
RECENTLY, A READER HAS WRITTEN THAT AS AN AUTHOR, ARINA HAS A DIRTY MIND.
WHEN? WHEN I WAS ON THE RADIO OR...?
SINCE BECOMING A MANGAKA THREE YEARS AGO, COULD THIS BE MY FIRST SEXUAL HARASSMENT?!
OR MAYBE NOT...
LOOK! YOU CAN TELL I SLIMMED DOWN A LITTLE, RIGHT?! I'M FINALLY DOWN TO A NORMAL FAT SIZE!
MY DIET WORKED! I LOST 17 1/2 POUNDS!
ASANO
AI
CHUCKLE
SQUEEZE
DOESN'T FEEL LIKE YOU'VE LOST WEIGHT!
WHO ARE YOU KIDDING?
NOPE!
WAAA!
WELL, YOU'RE NOT SUPPOSED TO MEASURE THE FAT!!!
I GUESS THAT WAS MY FIRST EXPERIENCE AS A MANGAKA WITH SEXUAL HARASSMENT...

AND IT ALL HAPPENED IN ABOUT TWO SECONDS. THOSE DIRTY RATS! I'LL GET 'EM BACK AND ATTACK WHEN THEY'RE SLEEPING! WAAA!

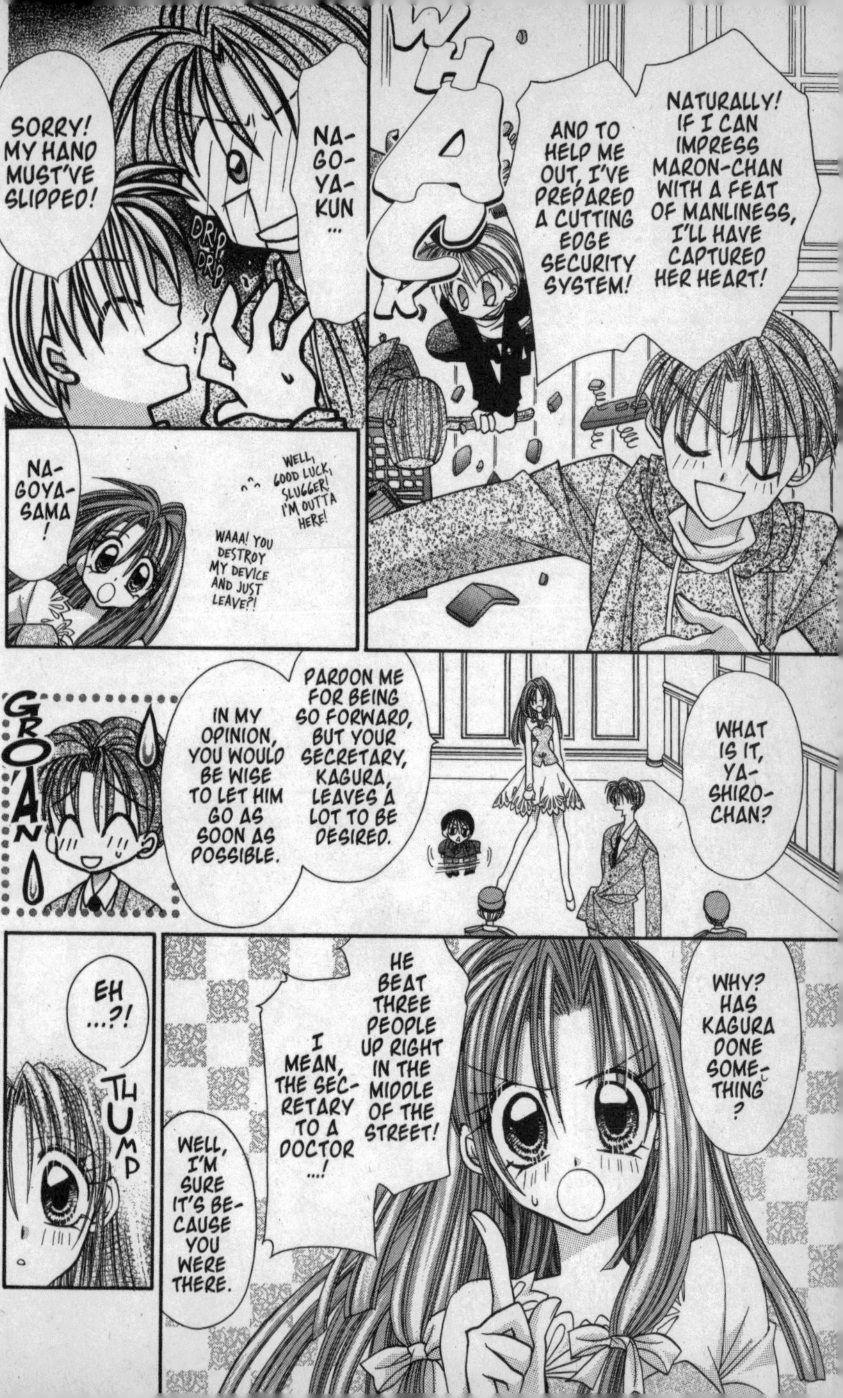
NATURALLY! IF I CAN IMPRESS MARON-CHAN WITH A FEAT OF MANLINESS, I'LL HAVE CAPTURED HER HEART!
AND TO HELP ME OUT, I'VE PREPARED A CUTTING EDGE SECURITY SYSTEM!
WHACK
NA-GO-YA-KUN ...
SORRY! MY HAND MUST'VE SLIPPED!
DRIP DRIP
NA-GOYA-SAMA!
WELL, GOOD LUCK, SLUGGER! I'M OUTTA HERE!
WAAA! YOU DESTROY MY DEVICE AND JUST LEAVE?!
WHAT IS IT, YA-SHIRO-CHAN?
PARDON ME FOR BEING SO FORWARD, BUT YOUR SECRETARY, KAGURA, LEAVES A LOT TO BE DESIRED.
IN MY OPINION, YOU WOULD BE WISE TO LET HIM GO AS SOON AS POSSIBLE.
GRO'AN
WHY? HAS KAGURA DONE SOMETHING?
HE BEAT THREE PEOPLE UP RIGHT IN THE MIDDLE OF THE STREET!
I MEAN, THE SEC-RETARY TO A DOCTOR ...!
WELL, I'M SURE IT'S BE-CAUSE YOU WERE THERE.
EH ...?!
THUMP

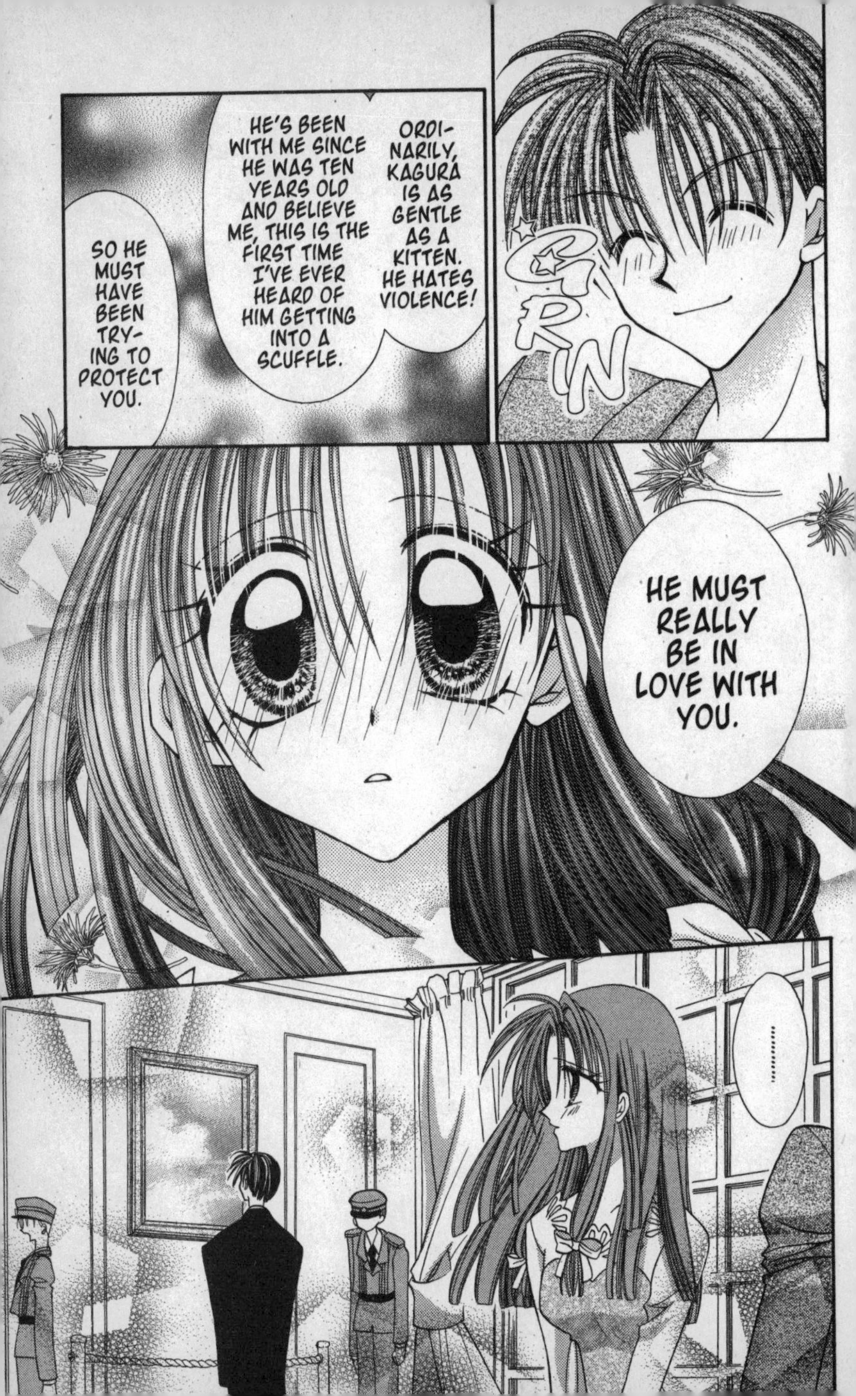
GRIN
ORDINARILY, KAGURA IS AS GENTLE AS A KITTEN. HE HATES VIOLENCE!
HE'S BEEN WITH ME SINCE HE WAS TEN YEARS OLD AND BELIEVE ME, THIS IS THE FIRST TIME I'VE EVER HEARD OF HIM GETTING INTO A SCUFFLE.
SO HE MUST HAVE BEEN TRYING TO PROTECT YOU.
HE MUST REALLY BE IN LOVE WITH YOU.
......

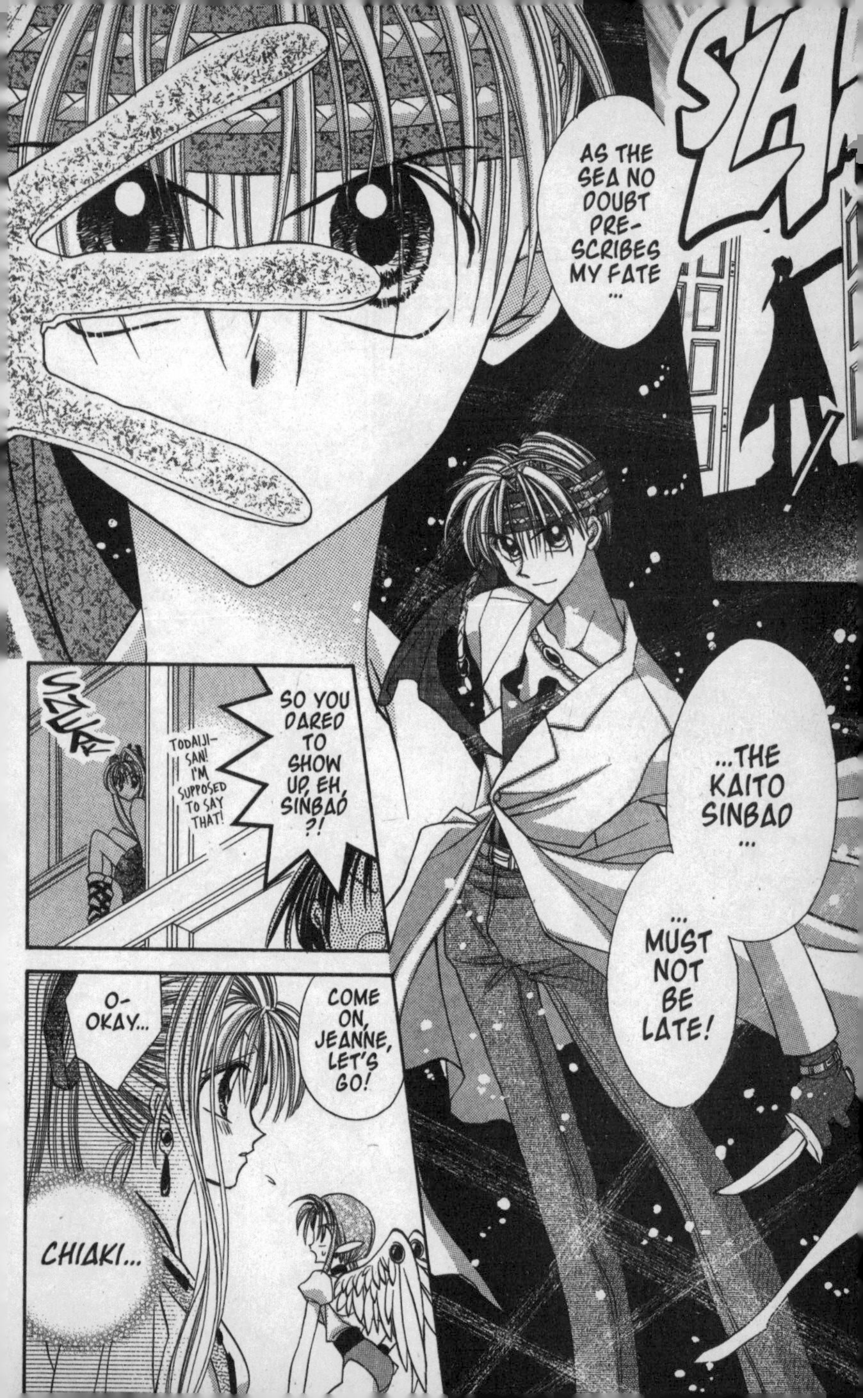
AS THE SEA NO DOUBT PRE-SCRIBES MY FATE ...
...THE KAITO SINBAD ...
... MUST NOT BE LATE!
SO YOU DARED TO SHOW UP, EH, SINBAD ?!
TODAIJI-SAN! I'M SUPPOSED TO SAY THAT!
COME ON, JEANNE, LET'S GO!
O-OKAY...
CHIAKI...

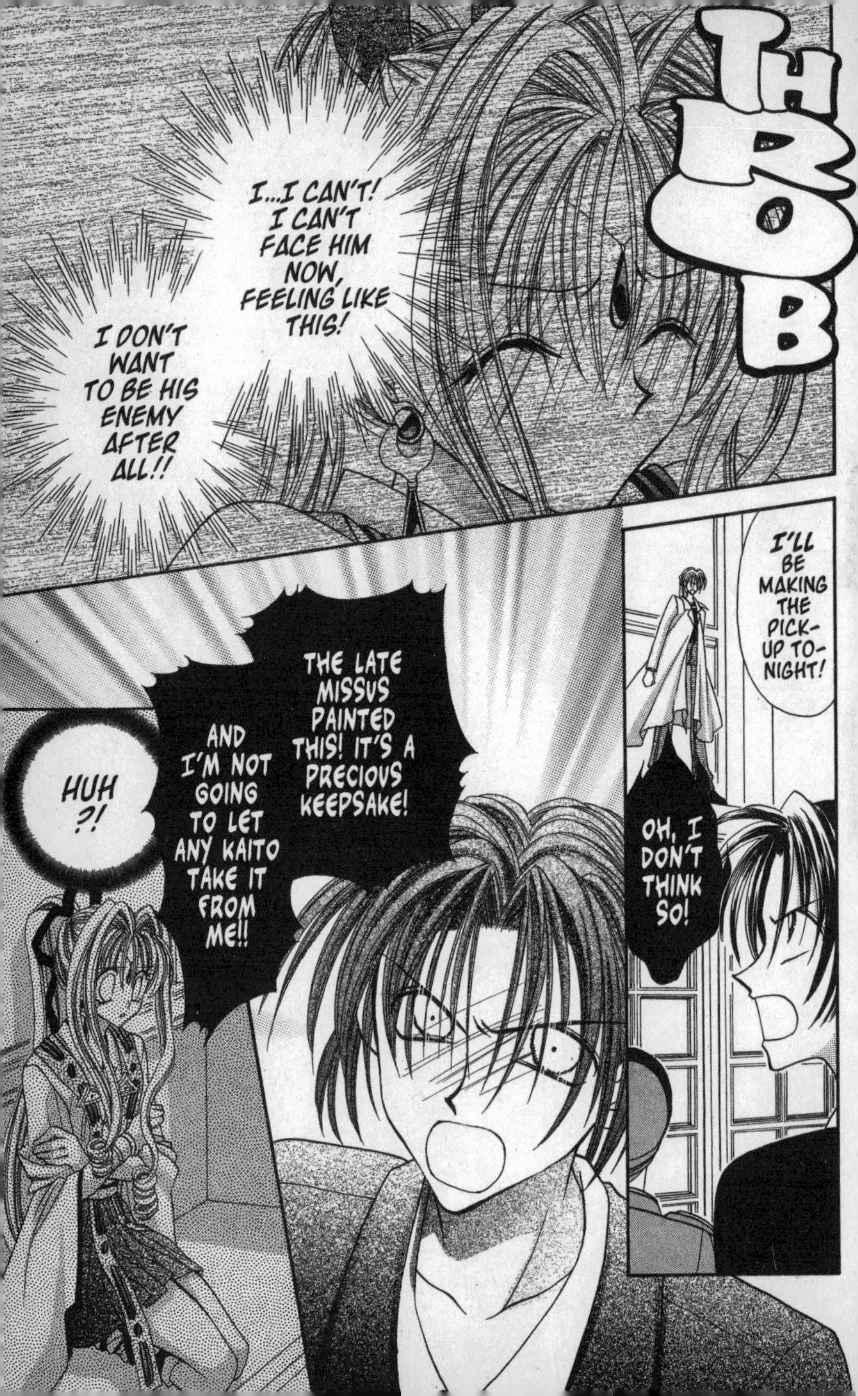
THROB
I...I CAN'T! I CAN'T FACE HIM NOW, FEELING LIKE THIS!
I DON'T WANT TO BE HIS ENEMY AFTER ALL!!
I'LL BE MAKING THE PICK-UP TO-NIGHT!
OH, I DON'T THINK SO!
THE LATE MISSUS PAINTED THIS! IT'S A PRECIOUS KEEPSAKE!
AND I'M NOT GOING TO LET ANY KAITO TAKE IT FROM ME!!
HUH ?!

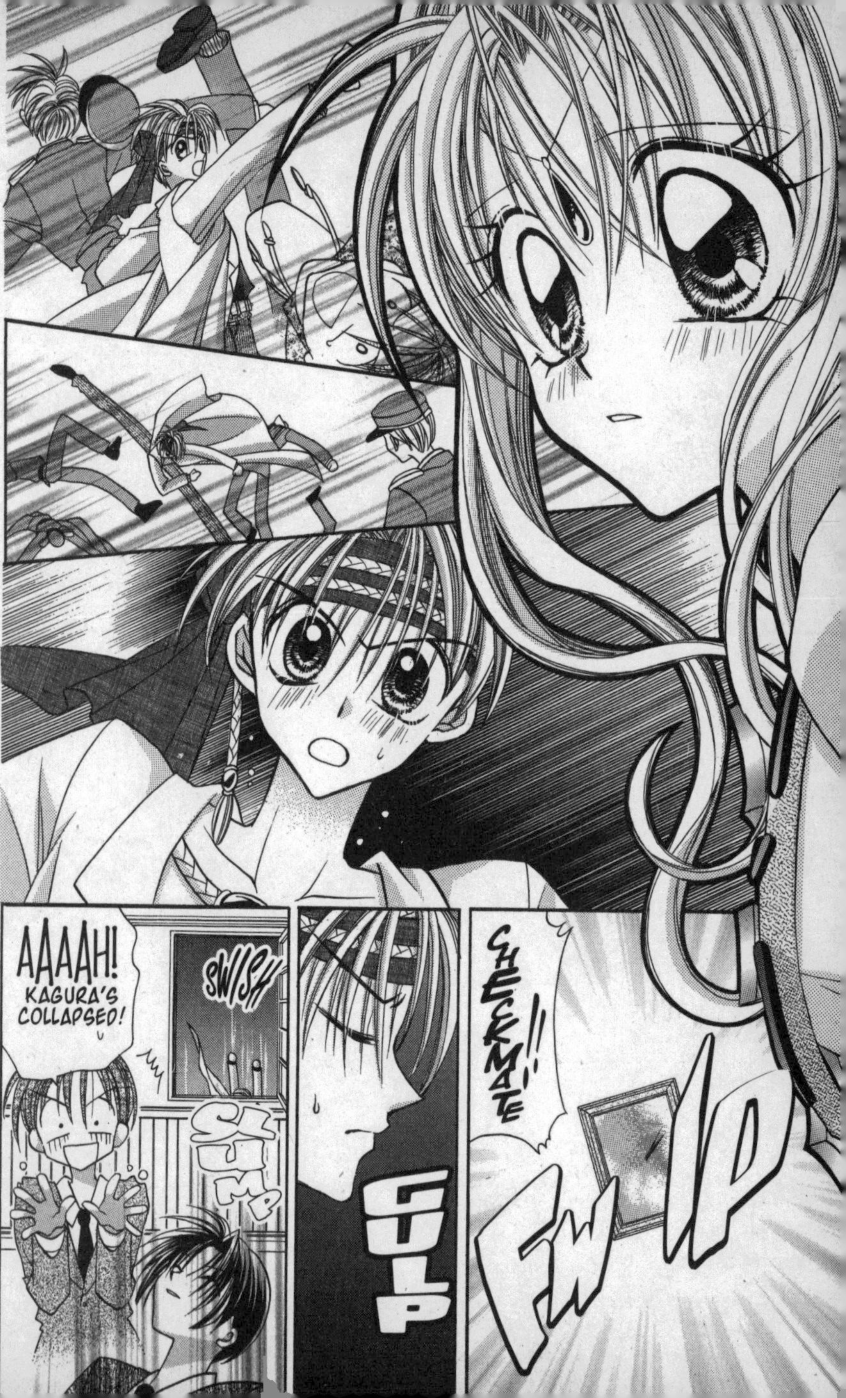
CHECKMATE!!!
FWIP
GULP
SWISH
AAAAH! KAGURA'S COLLAPSED!
SLUMP

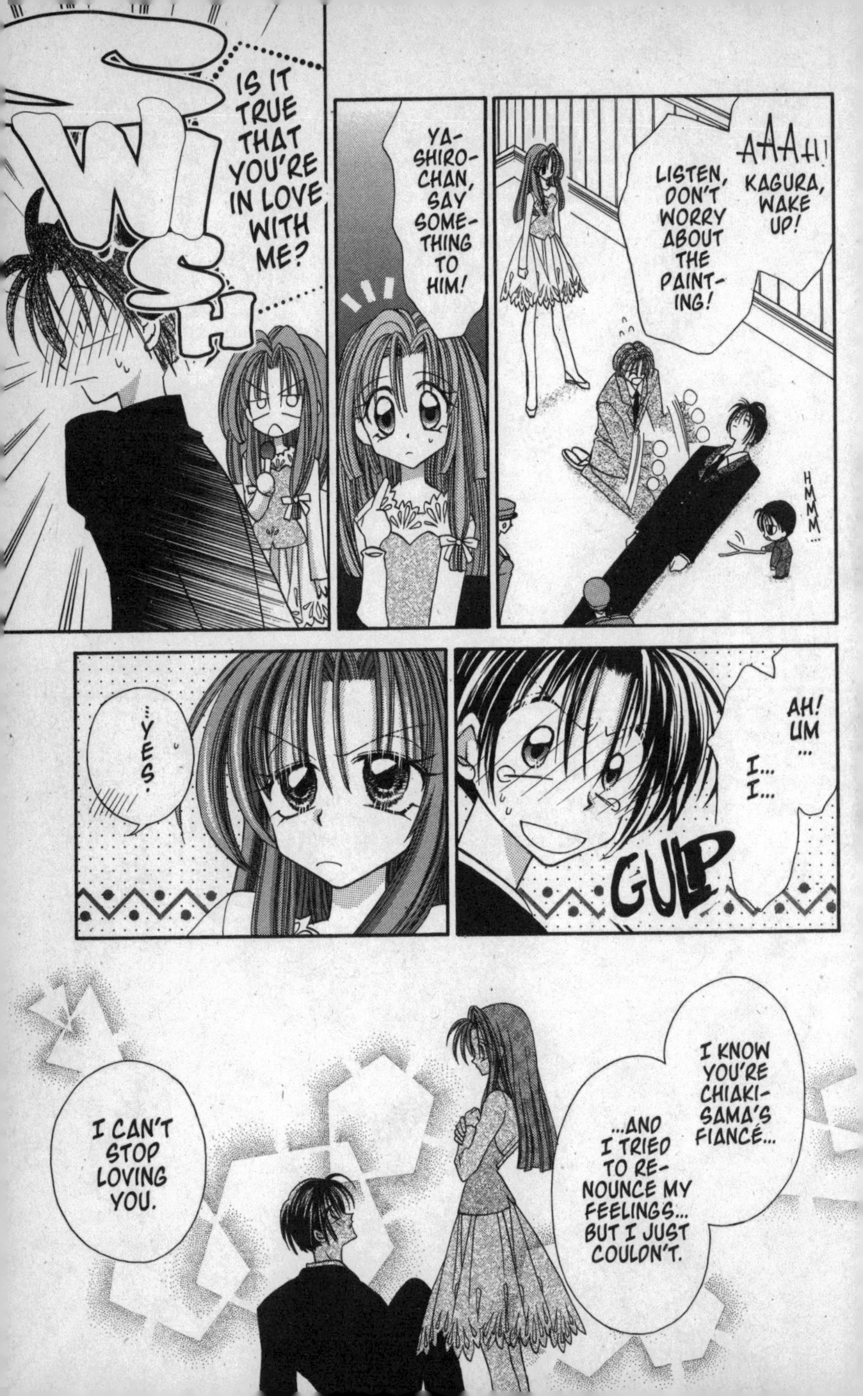
AAAH! KAGURA, WAKE UP!
LISTEN, DON'T WORRY ABOUT THE PAINTING!
HMMM...
YA-SHIRO-CHAN, SAY SOME-THING TO HIM!
WHSH
IS IT TRUE THAT YOU'RE IN LOVE WITH ME?
AH! UM...
I... I...
GULP
...YES.
I KNOW YOU'RE CHIAKI-SAMA'S FIANCÉ...
...AND I TRIED TO RE-NOUNCE MY FEELINGS... BUT I JUST COULDN'T.
I CAN'T STOP LOVING YOU.

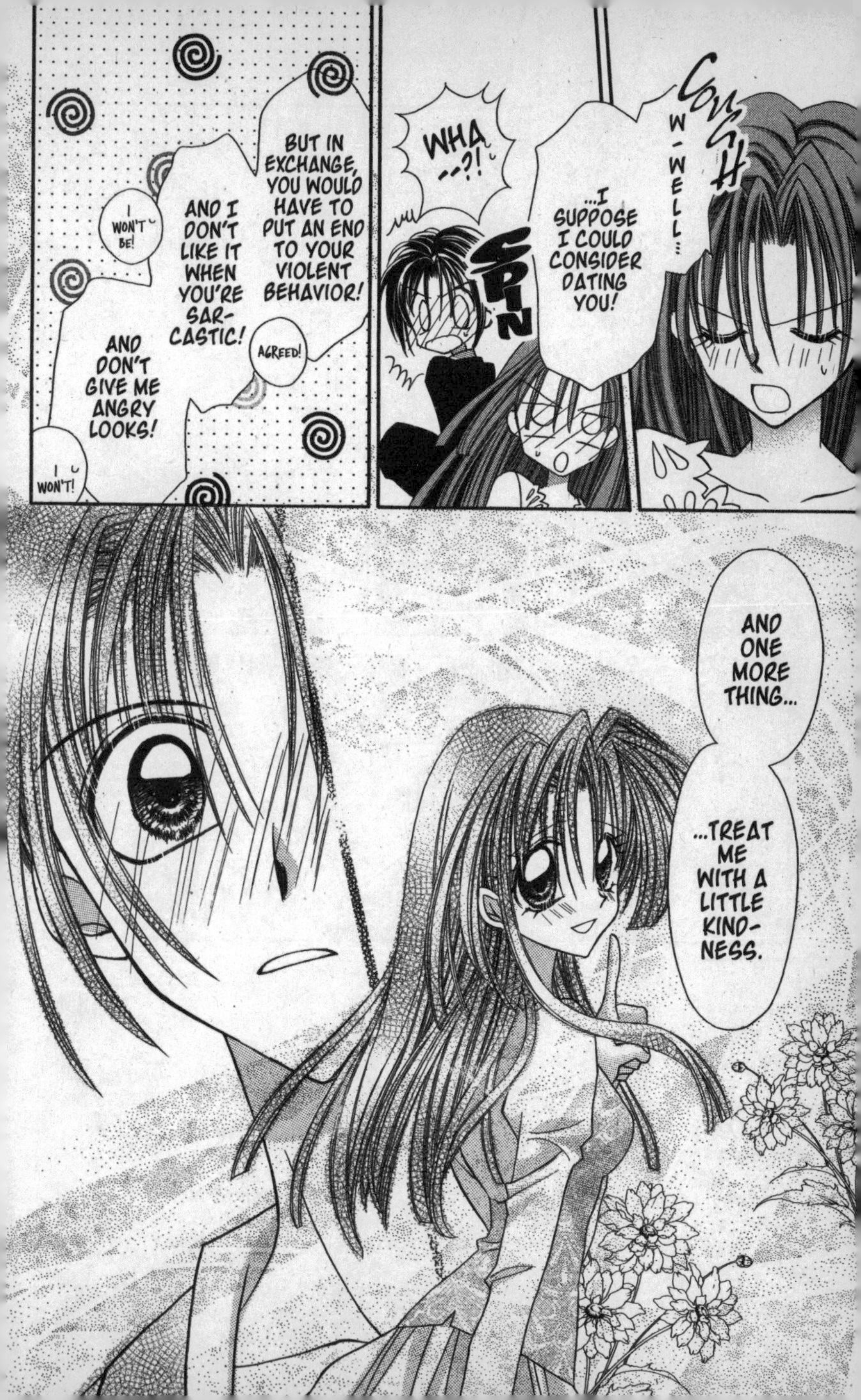
COUGH
W-WELL...
...I SUPPOSE I COULD CONSIDER DATING YOU!
WHA--?!
SPIN
BUT IN EXCHANGE, YOU WOULD HAVE TO PUT AN END TO YOUR VIOLENT BEHAVIOR!
AGREED!
AND I DON'T LIKE IT WHEN YOU'RE SAR-CASTIC!
I WON'T BE!
AND DON'T GIVE ME ANGRY LOOKS!
I WON'T!
AND ONE MORE THING...
...TREAT ME WITH A LITTLE KIND-NESS.

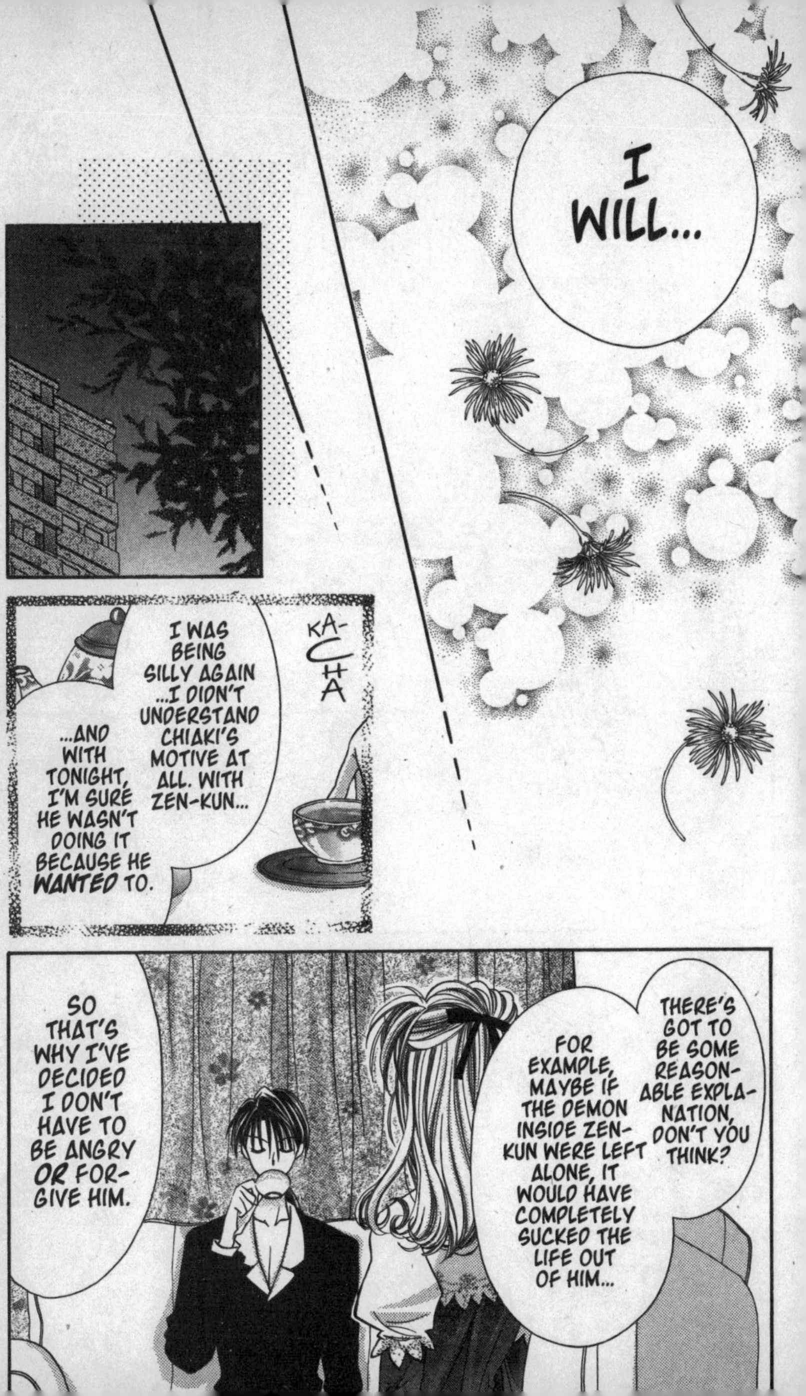
I WILL...
KA-CHA
I WAS BEING SILLY AGAIN ...I DIDN'T UNDERSTAND CHIAKI'S MOTIVE AT ALL. WITH ZEN-KUN...
...AND WITH TONIGHT, I'M SURE HE WASN'T DOING IT BECAUSE HE WANTED TO.
THERE'S GOT TO BE SOME REASONABLE EXPLANATION, DON'T YOU THINK?
FOR EXAMPLE, MAYBE IF THE DEMON INSIDE ZEN-KUN WERE LEFT ALONE, IT WOULD HAVE COMPLETELY SUCKED THE LIFE OUT OF HIM...
SO THAT'S WHY I'VE DECIDED I DON'T HAVE TO BE ANGRY OR FORGIVE HIM.

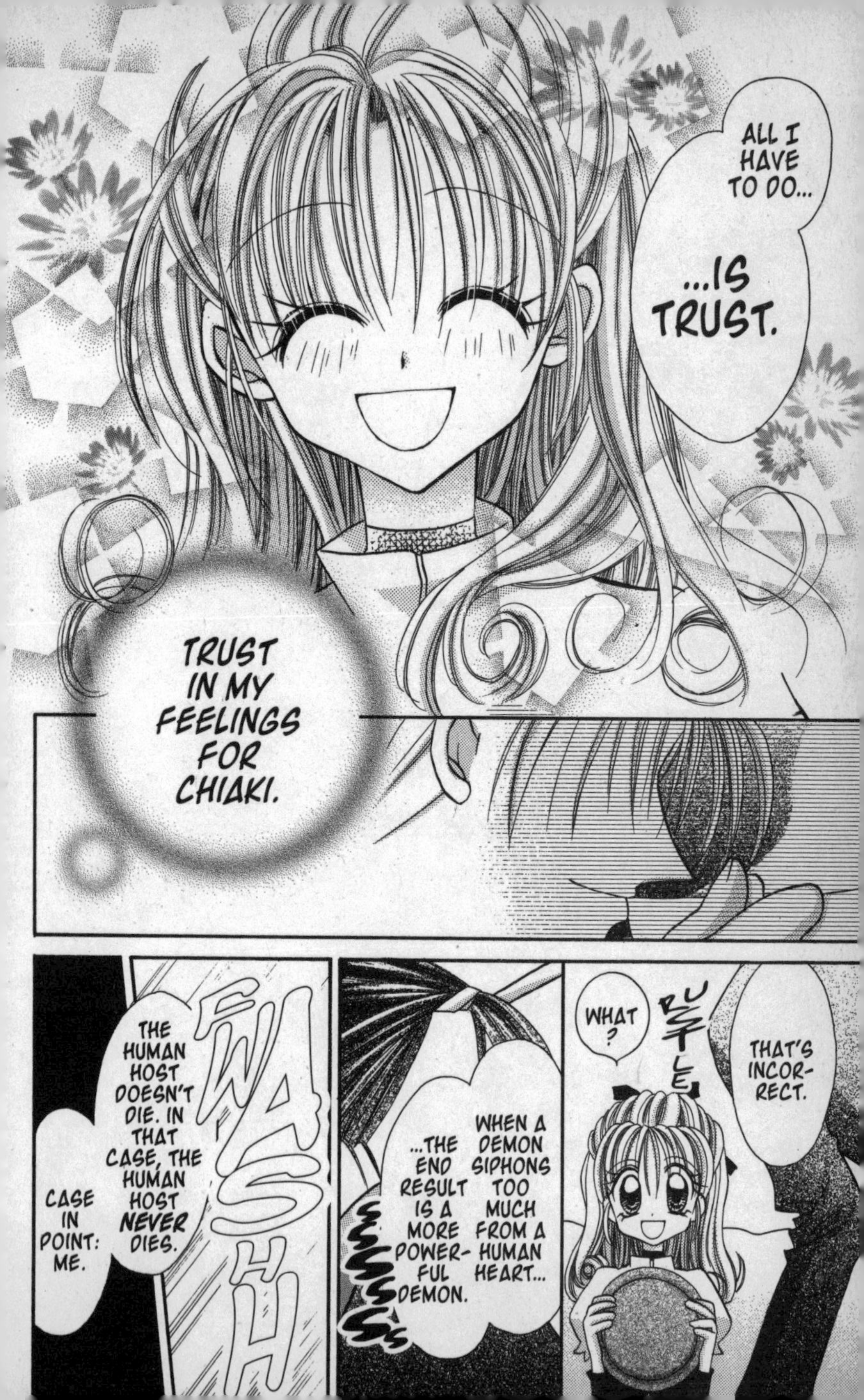
ALL I HAVE TO DO...
...IS TRUST.
TRUST IN MY FEELINGS FOR CHIAKI.
THAT'S INCORRECT.
RUSTLE
WHAT?
WHEN A DEMON SIPHONS TOO MUCH FROM A HUMAN HEART...
...THE END RESULT IS A MORE POWERFUL DEMON.
FWASHH
THE HUMAN HOST DOESN'T DIE. IN THAT CASE, THE HUMAN HOST **NEVER** DIES.
CASE IN POINT: ME.

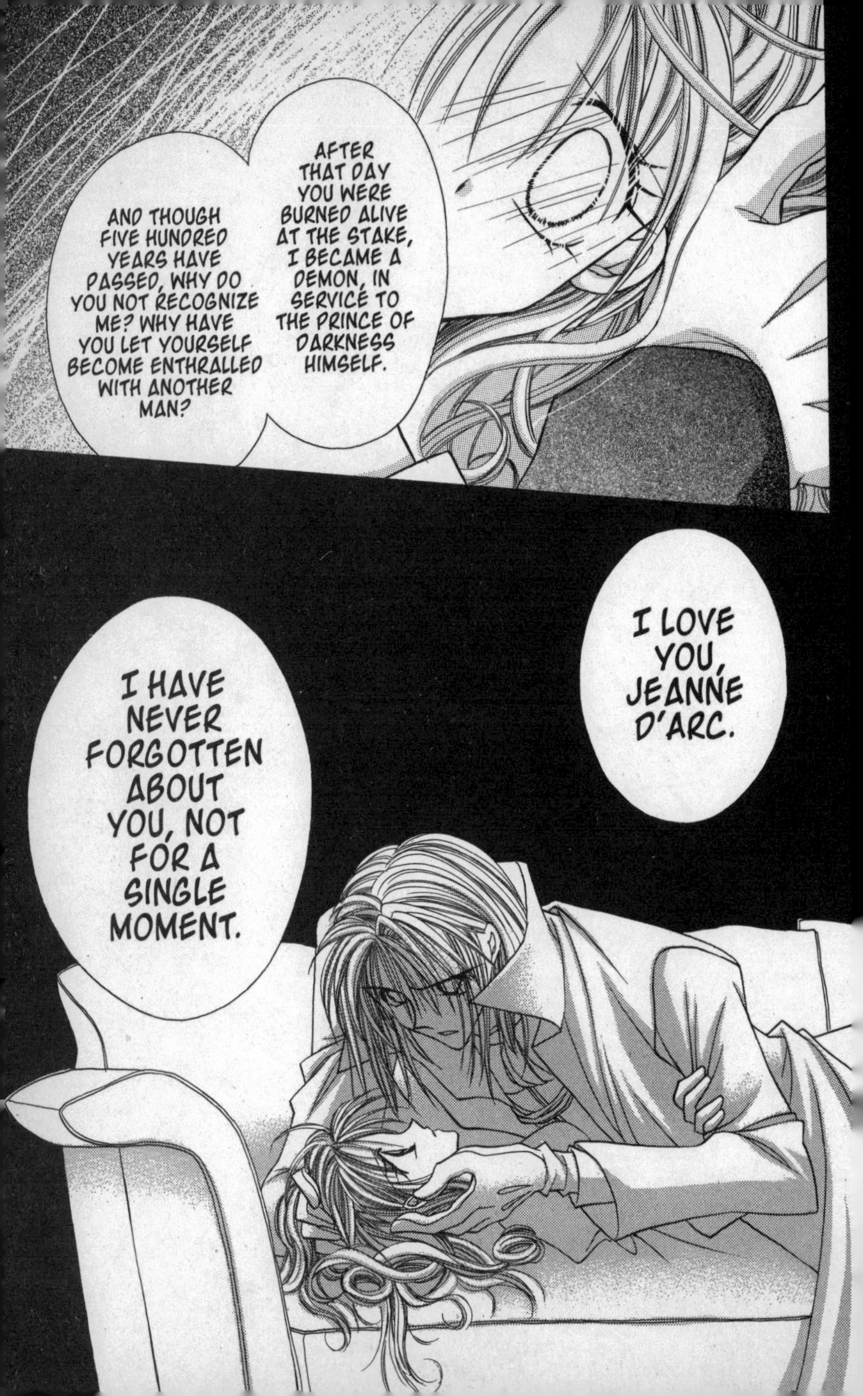
AFTER THAT DAY YOU WERE BURNED ALIVE AT THE STAKE, I BECAME A DEMON, IN SERVICE TO THE PRINCE OF DARKNESS HIMSELF.
AND THOUGH FIVE HUNDRED YEARS HAVE PASSED, WHY DO YOU NOT RECOGNIZE ME? WHY HAVE YOU LET YOURSELF BECOME ENTHRALLED WITH ANOTHER MAN?
I LOVE YOU, JEANNE D'ARC.
I HAVE NEVER FORGOTTEN ABOUT YOU, NOT FOR A SINGLE MOMENT.

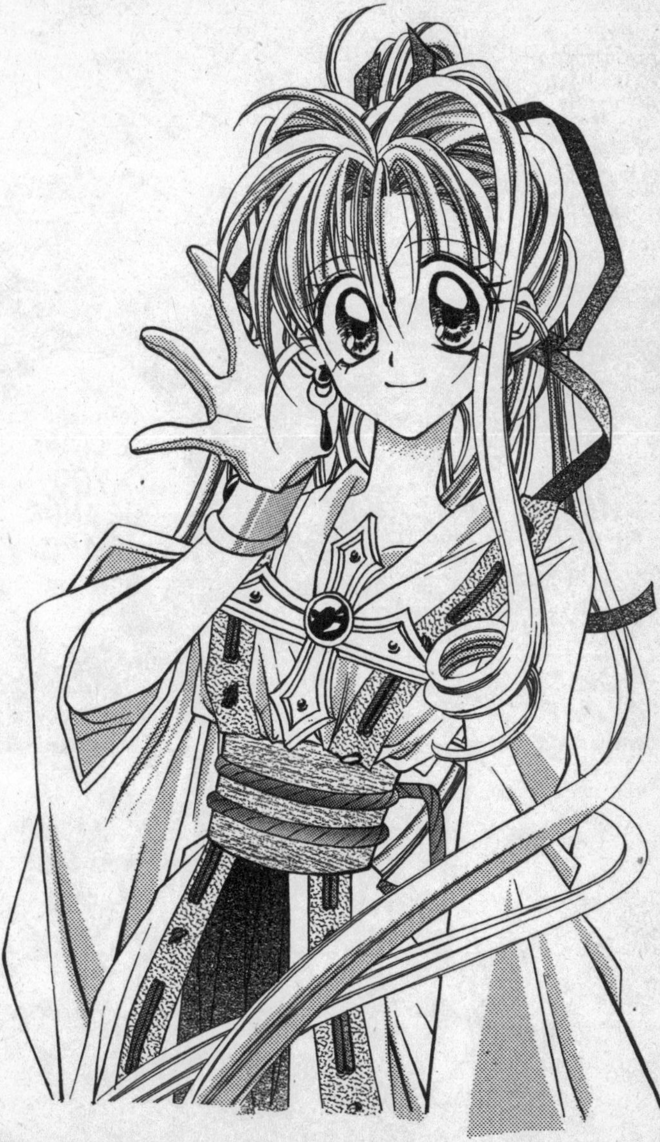

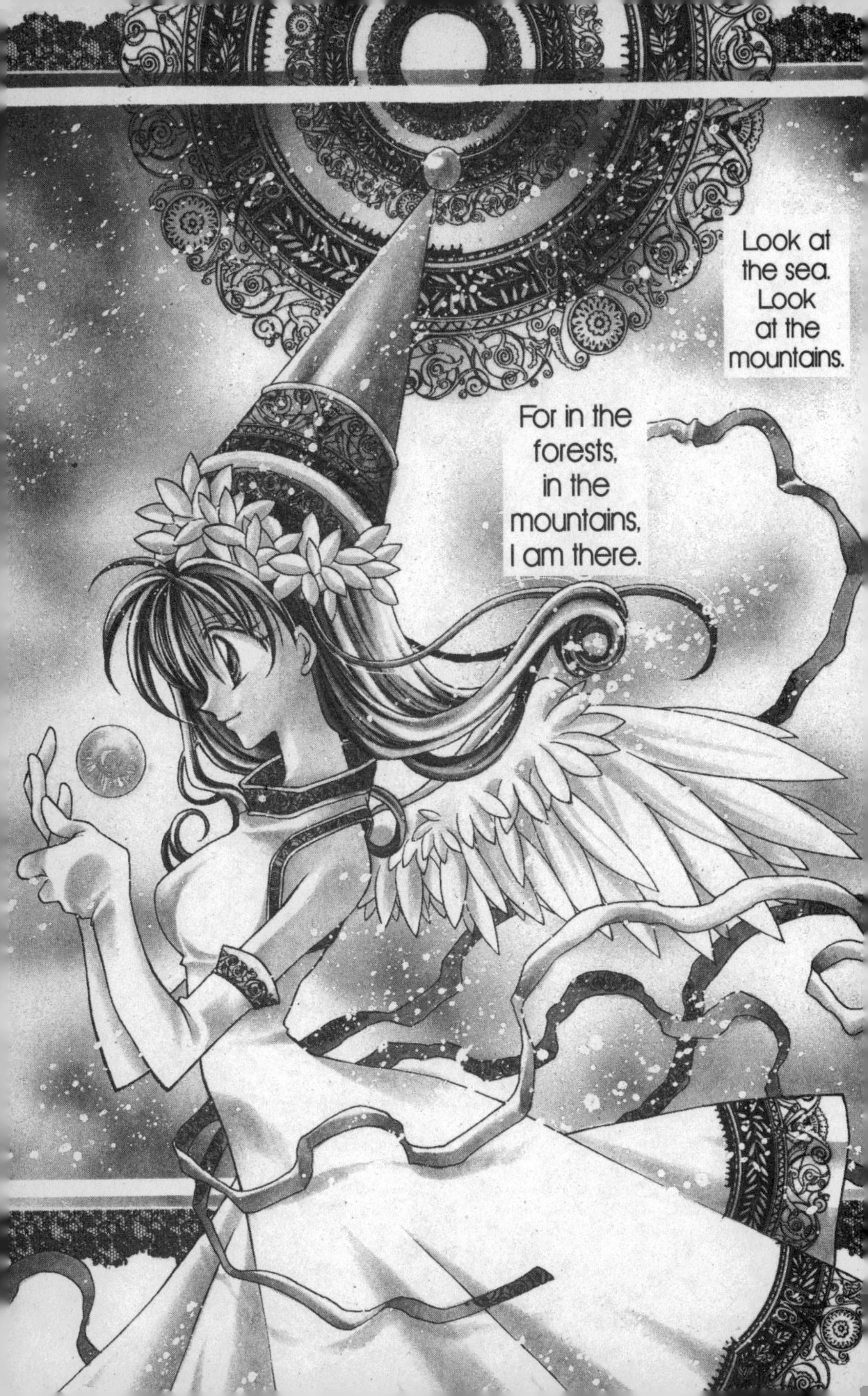
Look at the sea. Look at the mountains.
For in the forests, in the mountains, I am there.

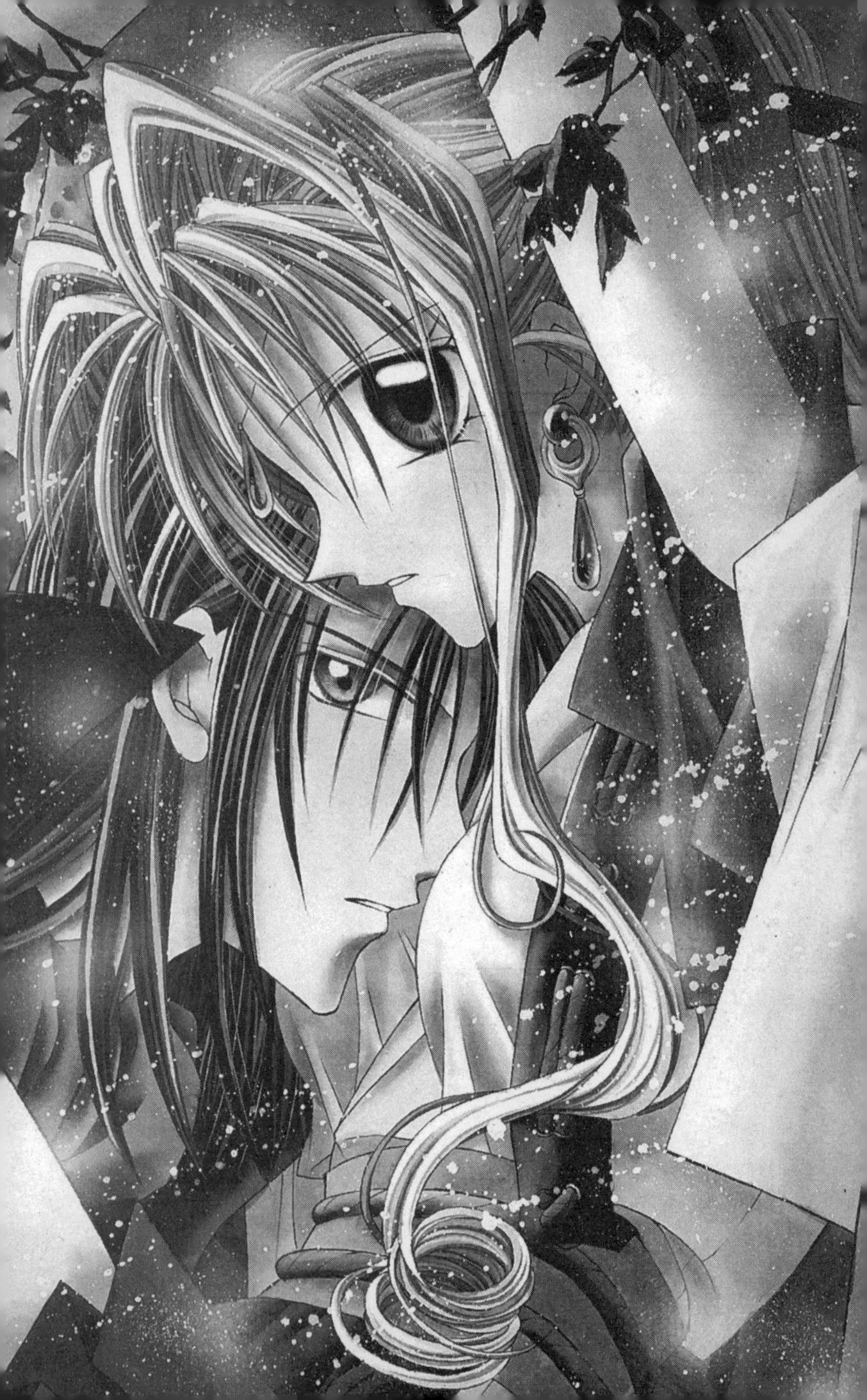

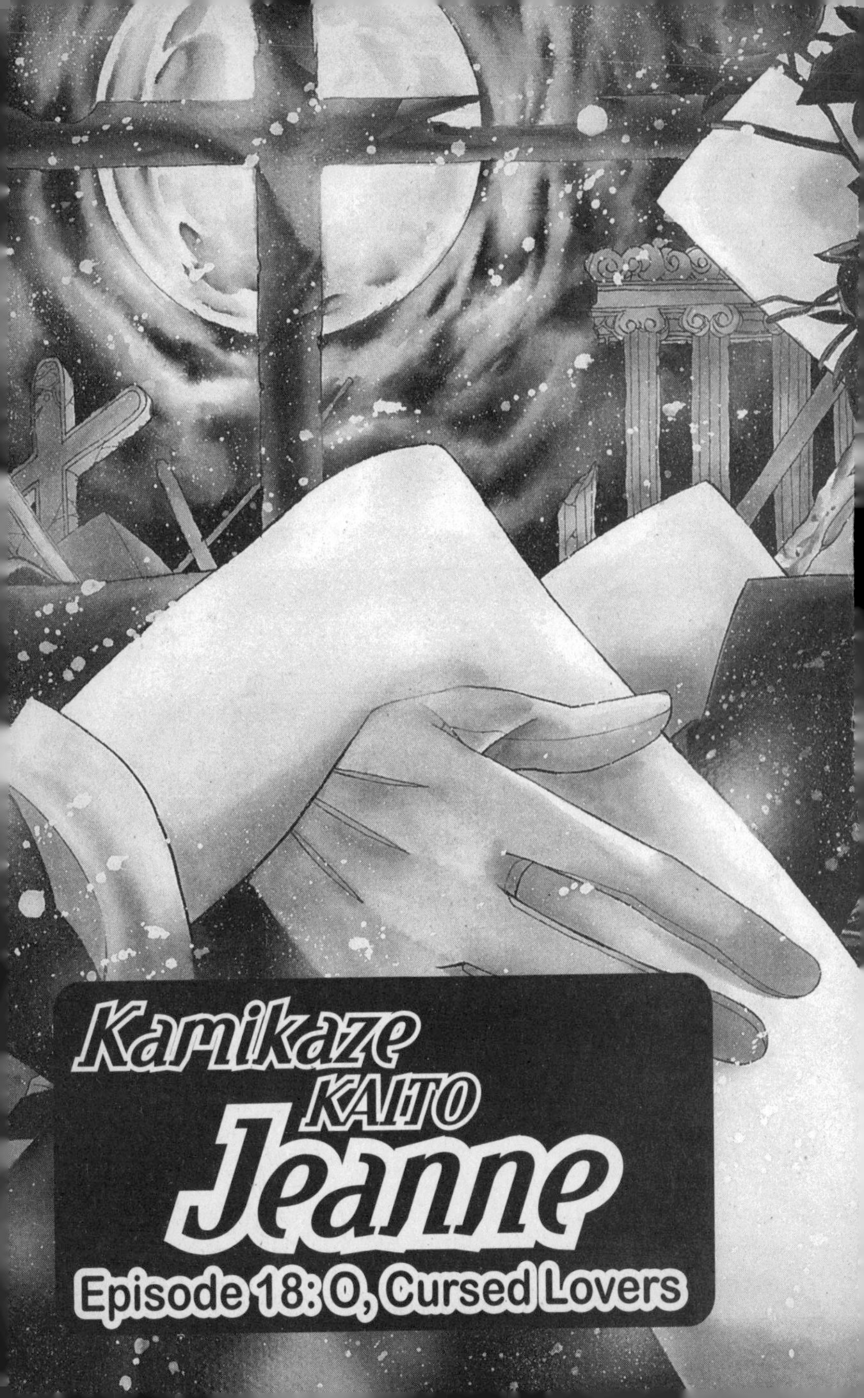
Kamikaze
KAITO
Jeanne
Episode 18: O, Cursed Lovers

Momokuri Momokuri ♪ Purikurishan ♫

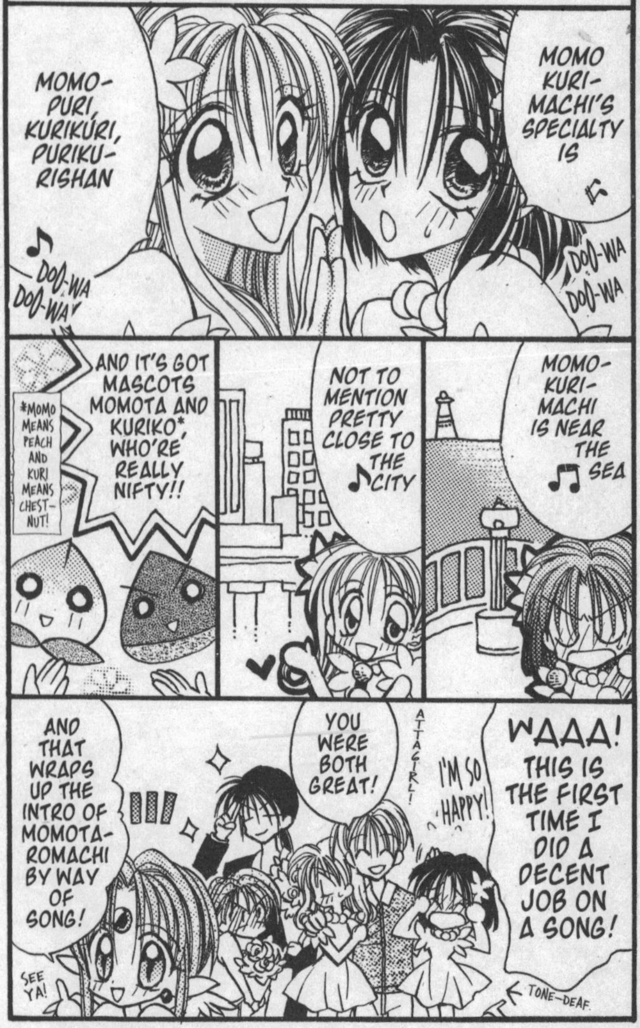
MOMO KURI-MACHI'S SPECIALTY IS
DOO-WA DOO-WA
MOMO-PURI, KURIKURI, PURIKU-RISHAN
DOO-WA DOO-WA
MOMO-KURI-MACHI IS NEAR THE SEA
NOT TO MENTION PRETTY CLOSE TO THE CITY
AND IT'S GOT MASCOTS MOMOTA AND KURIKO*, WHO'RE REALLY NIFTY!!
*MOMO MEANS PEACH AND KURI MEANS CHEST-NUT!
WAAA! THIS IS THE FIRST TIME I DID A DECENT JOB ON A SONG!
TONE-DEAF.
I'M SO HAPPY!
ATTAGIRL!
YOU WERE BOTH GREAT!
AND THAT WRAPS UP THE INTRO OF MOMOTA-ROMACHI BY WAY OF SONG!
SEE YA!

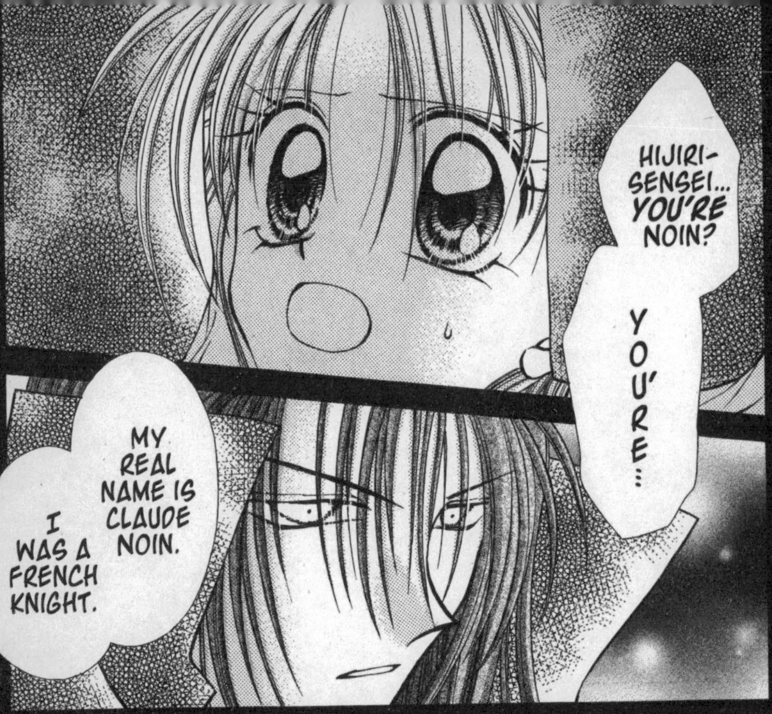
HIJIRI-SENSEI... YOU'RE NOIN?
YOU'RE...
MY REAL NAME IS CLAUDE NOIN.
I WAS A FRENCH KNIGHT.

Episode 18: "O, CURSED LOVERS" Tagline: "Is forgiveness necessary...?"

Mmm...Actually, I like the mood of this ep's title page art...(Yeah, I know it's got an erotic quality to it...♡Here, Noin's the biggest he's been in all of the title art, which kind of gets the point across that finally, we've gotten to his story. It was major work drawing this art, I mean, putting the two of them in close-up. (But that's why the art packs a punch. Every time I look at the title page art here, I give myself a mental pat on the back! I dunno, maybe it's strange to be praising myself so much over this...)

Story-wise, this episode is a continuation of episode 10 (see volume 3), but this time, I've finally crossed over to become an all-important Japanese erotic mangaka, or so I've been told. Even though I'm just a girl...Does this mean I'll never become a bride?

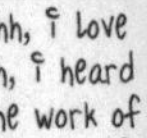

But like it or not, this part was really necessary for the story... Or maybe I tried to focus on drawing it so well that my seriousness backfired on me?...Eh-heh. Anyway, Noin's had a rough love life, too. With this episode, I felt a lot more sympathetic to him. What do you readers think of Noin? (Readers of Ribon magazine still weren't into him, even after this.) Another thing I like is the combo of Silk and Noin. My favorite image of Maron in this episode is on page 160, panel 3, the two-shot with Maron and Jeanne D'Arc seen from behind♡ I was also really happy this time to finally get another chance to draw a romantic scene between Maron-chan and Chi-sama♡ Ahhh, I love girls' manga!! It's the best!! Romantic!! ♡♡ Oops, I seem to have some excess space here. Oh yeah, I heard that recently an "Arina Tanemura" has been appearing on the internet (e-mail?), but it's allll the work of an impostor♡ (And you can believe me on this because I don't even own a computer.) And anyway, even if I do buy a computer in the near future, I'll use a different name for the internet. That's part of the fun. The impostor isn't saying anything malicious or anything, so I don't think he or she is a bad person...but still, lying is wrong. For those of you who believed it was really me, please don't get angry at the fake Arina.

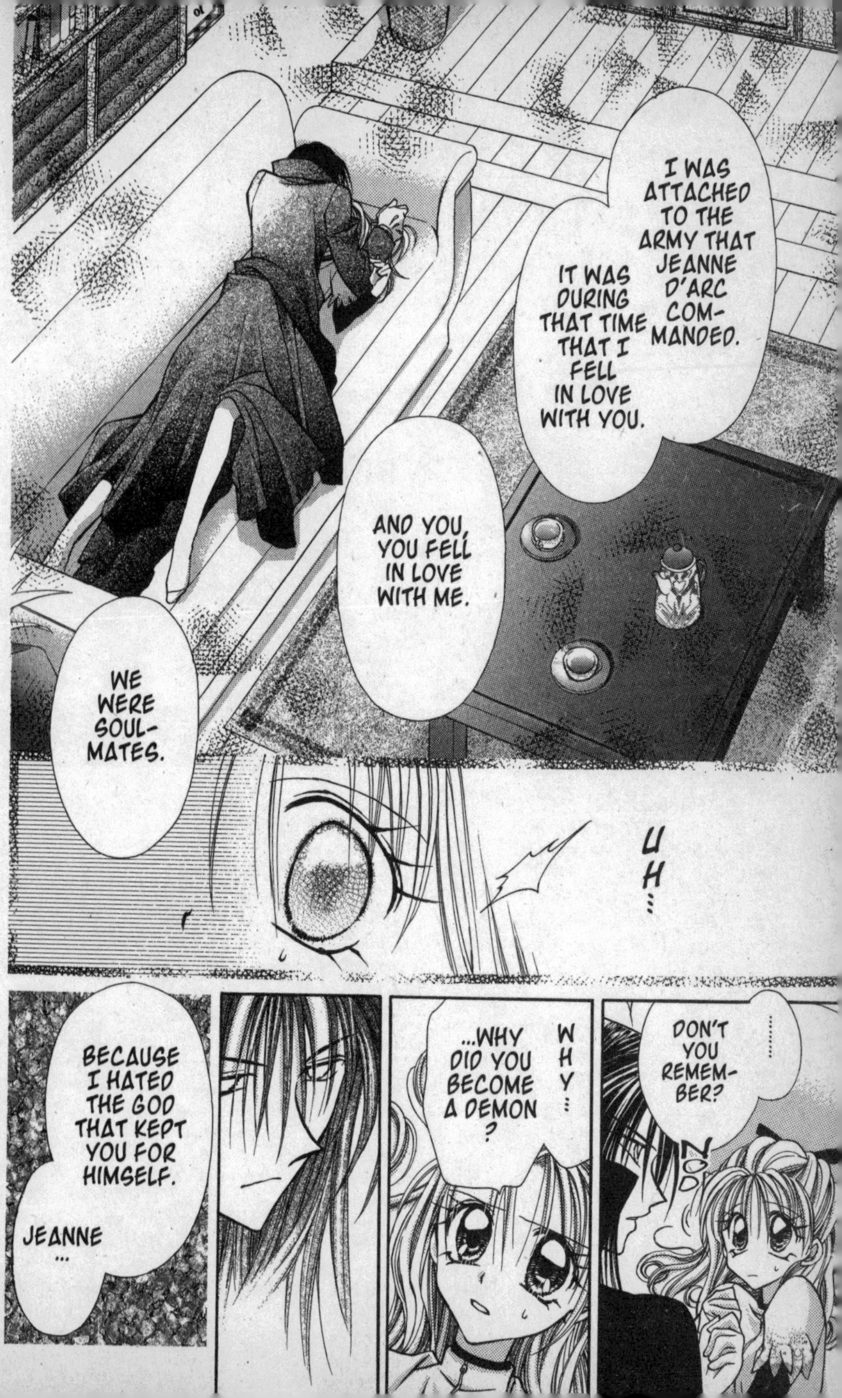

I WAS ATTACHED TO THE ARMY THAT JEANNE D'ARC COMMANDED.
IT WAS DURING THAT TIME THAT I FELL IN LOVE WITH YOU.
AND YOU, YOU FELL IN LOVE WITH ME.
WE WERE SOULMATES.
UH...
......
DON'T YOU REMEMBER?
NOD
WHY...
...WHY DID YOU BECOME A DEMON?
BECAUSE I HATED THE GOD THAT KEPT YOU FOR HIMSELF.
JEANNE...

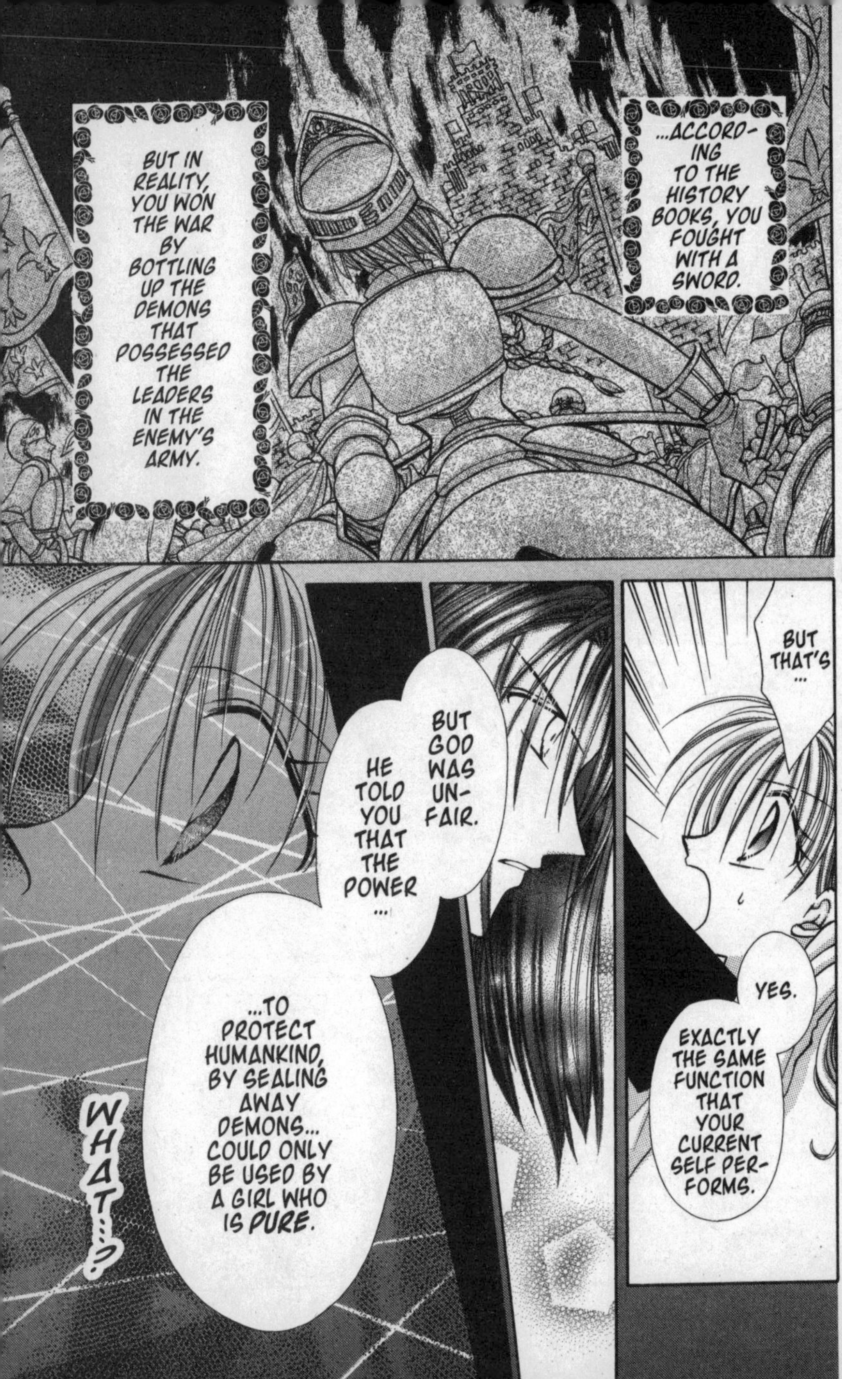
...ACCORDING TO THE HISTORY BOOKS, YOU FOUGHT WITH A SWORD.
BUT IN REALITY, YOU WON THE WAR BY BOTTLING UP THE DEMONS THAT POSSESSED THE LEADERS IN THE ENEMY'S ARMY.
BUT THAT'S...
YES.
EXACTLY THE SAME FUNCTION THAT YOUR CURRENT SELF PERFORMS.
BUT GOD WAS UNFAIR.
HE TOLD YOU THAT THE POWER...
...TO PROTECT HUMANKIND, BY SEALING AWAY DEMONS... COULD ONLY BE USED BY A GIRL WHO IS *PURE*.
WHAT...?

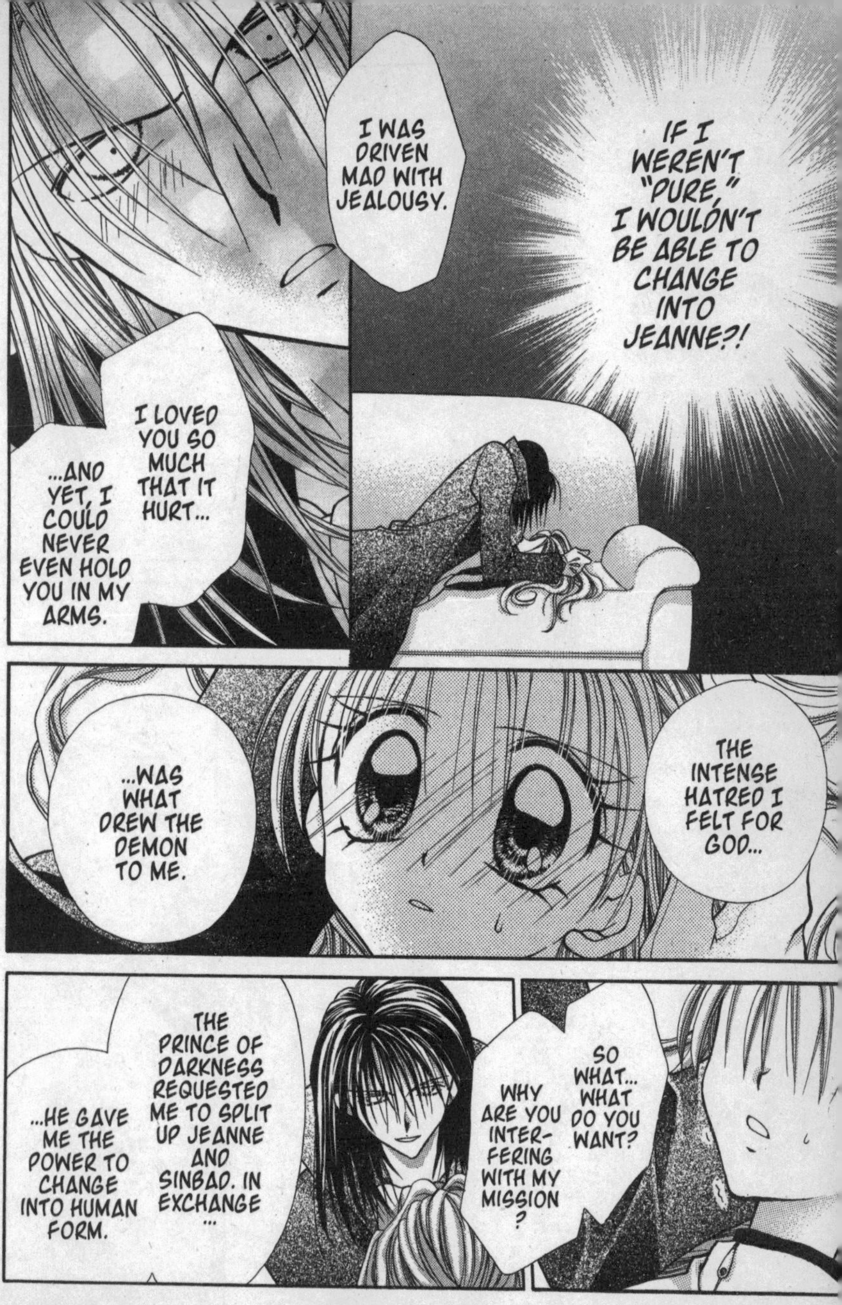
IF I WEREN'T "PURE," I WOULDN'T BE ABLE TO CHANGE INTO JEANNE?!
I WAS DRIVEN MAD WITH JEALOUSY.
I LOVED YOU SO MUCH THAT IT HURT...
...AND YET, I COULD NEVER EVEN HOLD YOU IN MY ARMS.
THE INTENSE HATRED I FELT FOR GOD...
...WAS WHAT DREW THE DEMON TO ME.
SO WHAT... WHAT DO YOU WANT?
WHY ARE YOU INTER-FERING WITH MY MISSION?
THE PRINCE OF DARKNESS REQUESTED ME TO SPLIT UP JEANNE AND SINBAD. IN EXCHANGE...
...HE GAVE ME THE POWER TO CHANGE INTO HUMAN FORM.

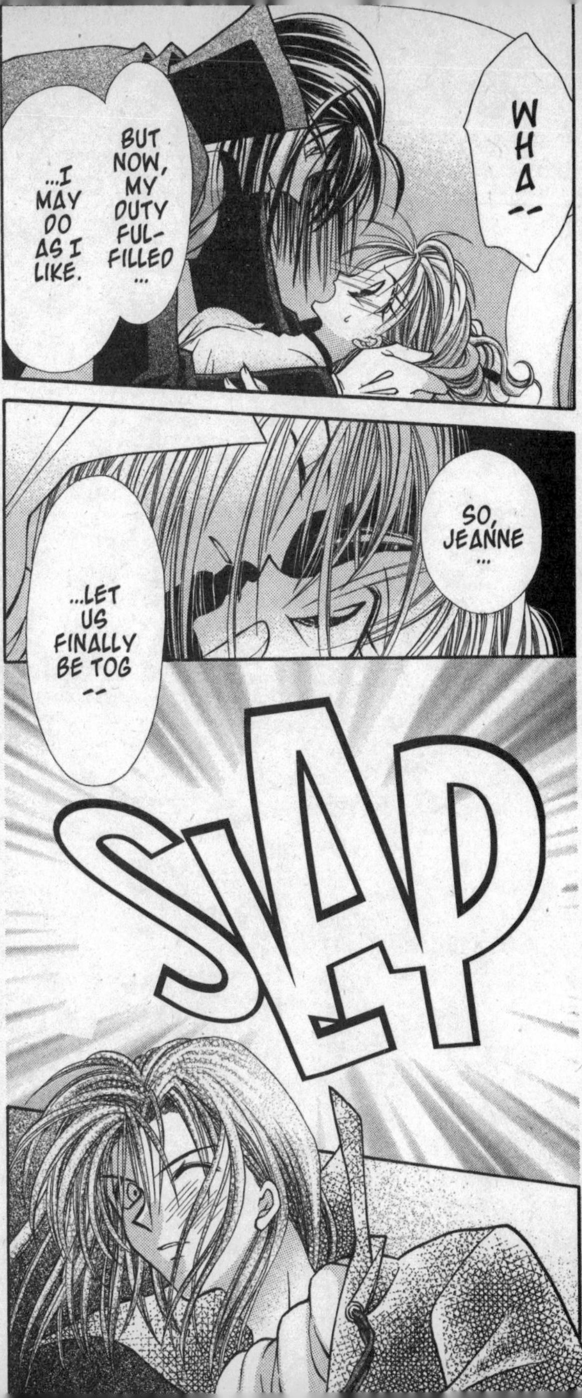
WHA--
BUT NOW, MY DUTY FUL-FILLED...
...I MAY DO AS I LIKE.
SO, JEANNE...
...LET US FINALLY BE TOG--
SLAP

ARINA TANEMURA'S "LIKE PULLING TEETH WITH PLIERS"

NUMBER 23: HOW ARINA EATS CANDY APPLES!!!

OLLOW THESE SIMPLE INSTRUCTIONS AND YOU'LL NEVER FEAR EATING A CANDY APPLE AGAIN!

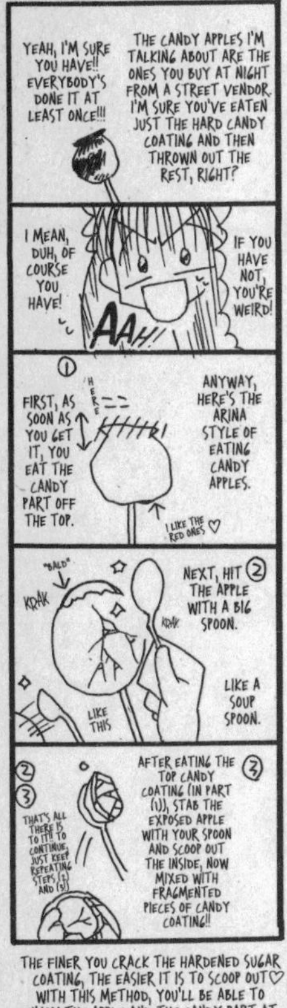
THE CANDY APPLES I'M TALKING ABOUT ARE THE ONES YOU BUY AT NIGHT FROM A STREET VENDOR. I'M SURE YOU'VE EATEN JUST THE HARD CANDY COATING AND THEN THROWN OUT THE REST, RIGHT?
YEAH, I'M SURE YOU HAVE!! EVERYBODY'S DONE IT AT LEAST ONCE!!!
IF YOU HAVE NOT, YOU'RE WEIRD!
I MEAN, DUH, OF COURSE YOU HAVE!
AAH!
ANYWAY, HERE'S THE ARINA STYLE OF EATING CANDY APPLES.
①
HERE
FIRST, AS SOON AS YOU GET IT, YOU EAT THE CANDY PART OFF THE TOP.
I LIKE THE RED ONES ♡
NEXT, HIT THE APPLE WITH A BIG SPOON. ②
"BALD"
KRAK
KRAK
LIKE A SOUP SPOON.
LIKE THIS
③
AFTER EATING THE TOP CANDY COATING (IN PART (1)), STAB THE EXPOSED APPLE WITH YOUR SPOON AND SCOOP OUT THE INSIDE, NOW MIXED WITH FRAGMENTED PIECES OF CANDY COATING!!
②
③
THAT'S ALL THERE IS TO IT! TO CONTINUE, JUST KEEP REPEATING STEPS (2) AND (3)

THE FINER YOU CRACK THE HARDENED SUGAR COATING, THE EASIER IT IS TO SCOOP OUT♡ WITH THIS METHOD, YOU'LL BE ABLE TO ENJOY THE APPLE AND THE CANDY PART AT THE SAME TIME ALL THE WAY THROUGH TRY ♡ IT, YOU'LL LIKE IT!♡

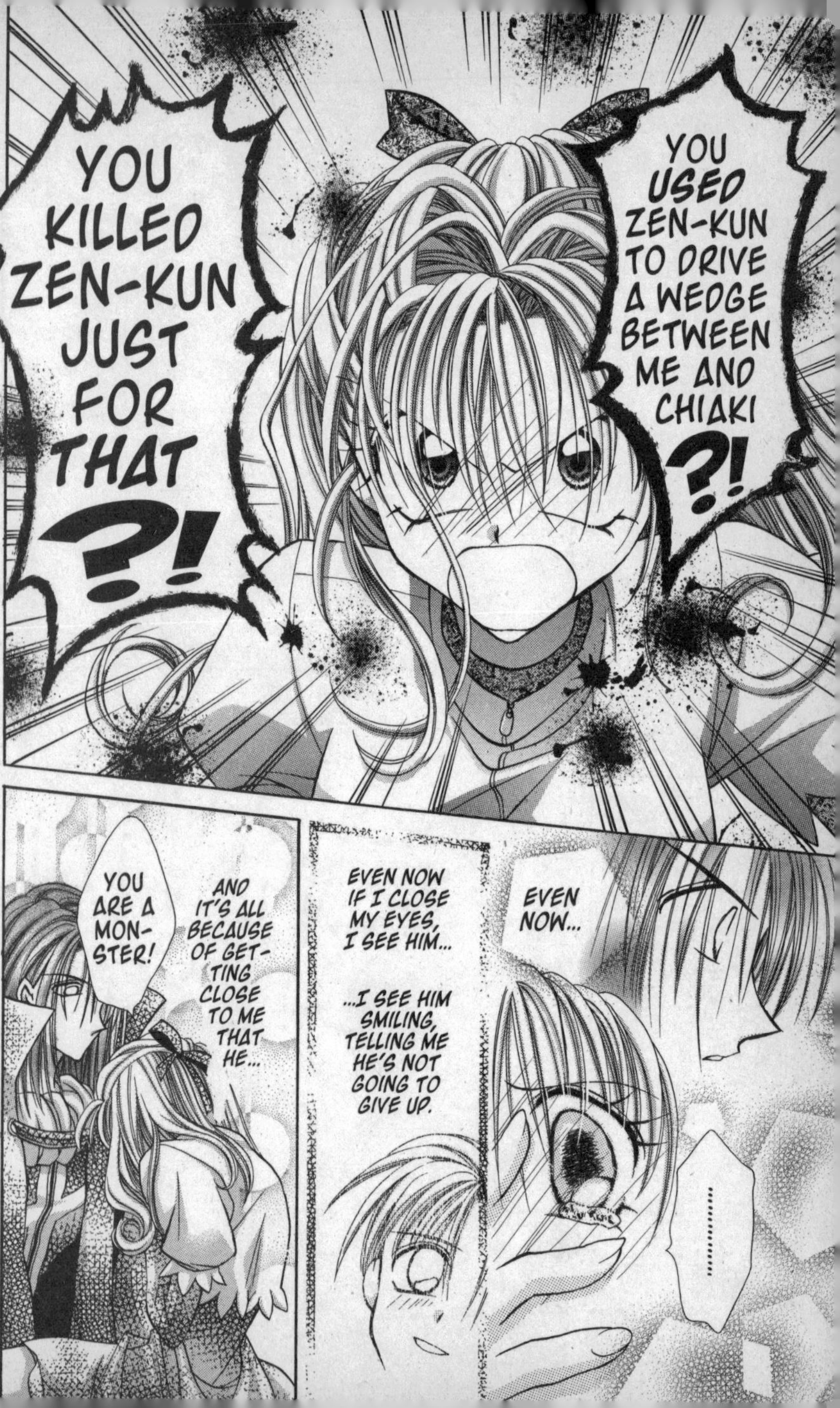
YOU USED ZEN-KUN TO DRIVE A WEDGE BETWEEN ME AND CHIAKI ?!
YOU KILLED ZEN-KUN JUST FOR THAT ?!
EVEN NOW...
......
EVEN NOW IF I CLOSE MY EYES, I SEE HIM...
...I SEE HIM SMILING, TELLING ME HE'S NOT GOING TO GIVE UP.
AND IT'S ALL BECAUSE OF GET-TING CLOSE TO ME THAT HE...
YOU ARE A MON-STER!

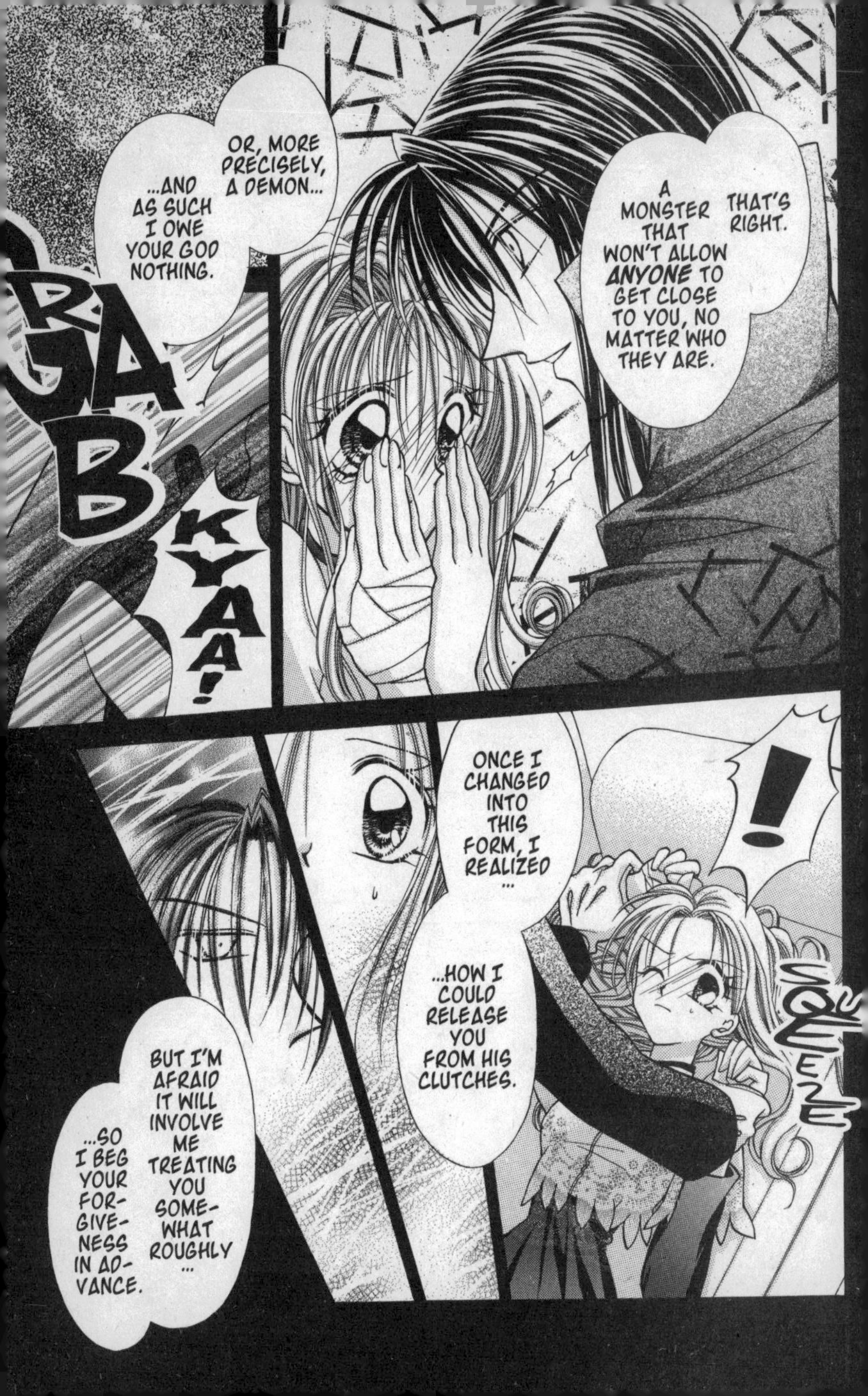
THAT'S RIGHT.
A MONSTER THAT WON'T ALLOW ANYONE TO GET CLOSE TO YOU, NO MATTER WHO THEY ARE.
OR, MORE PRECISELY, A DEMON...
...AND AS SUCH I OWE YOUR GOD NOTHING.
GRAB
KYAA!
!
SQUEEZE
ONCE I CHANGED INTO THIS FORM, I REALIZED...
...HOW I COULD RELEASE YOU FROM HIS CLUTCHES.
BUT I'M AFRAID IT WILL INVOLVE ME TREATING YOU SOME-WHAT ROUGHLY...
...SO I BEG YOUR FOR-GIVE-NESS IN AD-VANCE.

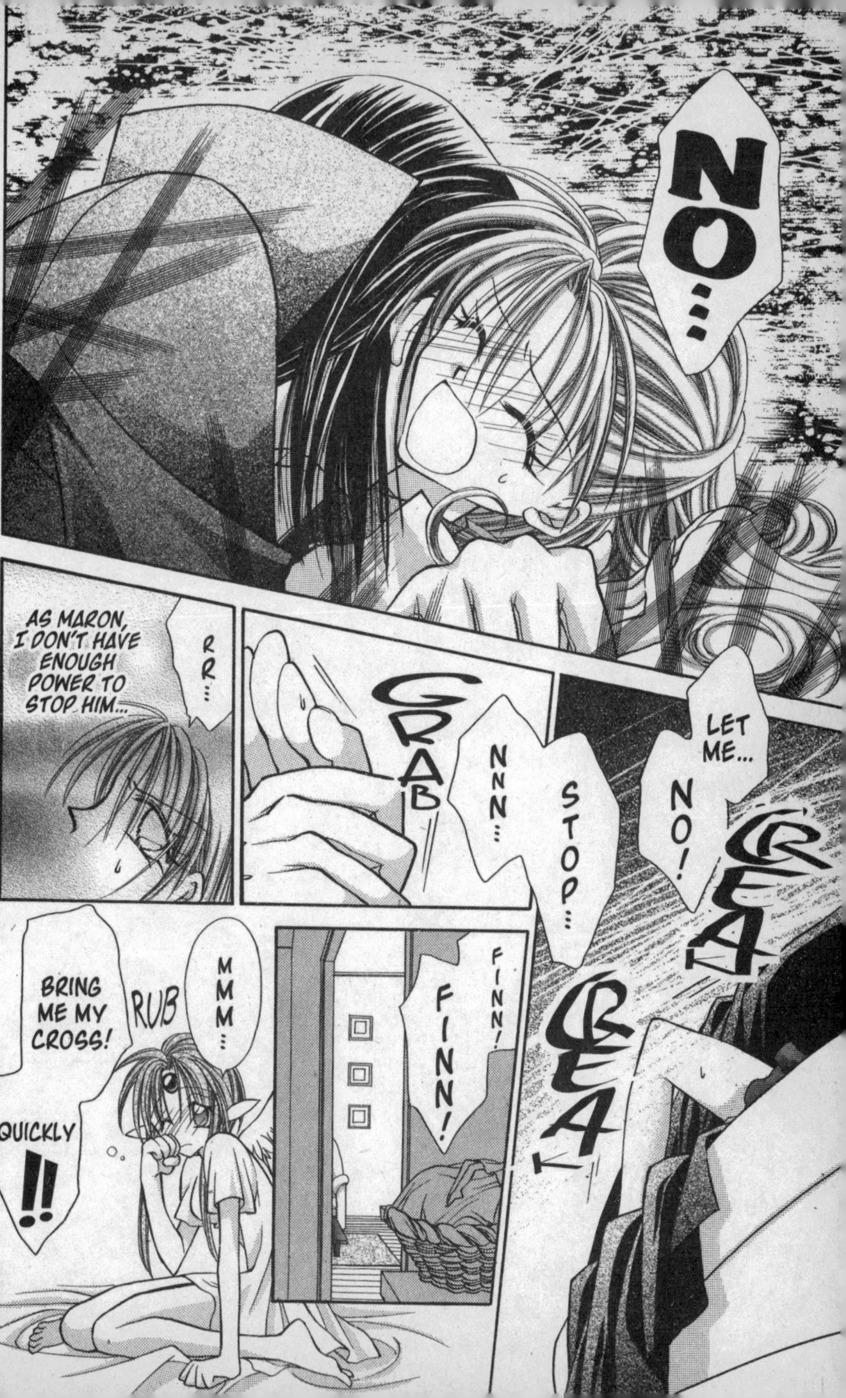
NO...
LET ME...
NO!
CREA
CREA
STOP...
NNN...
GRAB
RR...
AS MARON, I DON'T HAVE ENOUGH POWER TO STOP HIM...
FINN!
FINN!
MMM...
RUB
BRING ME MY CROSS!
QUICKLY!!

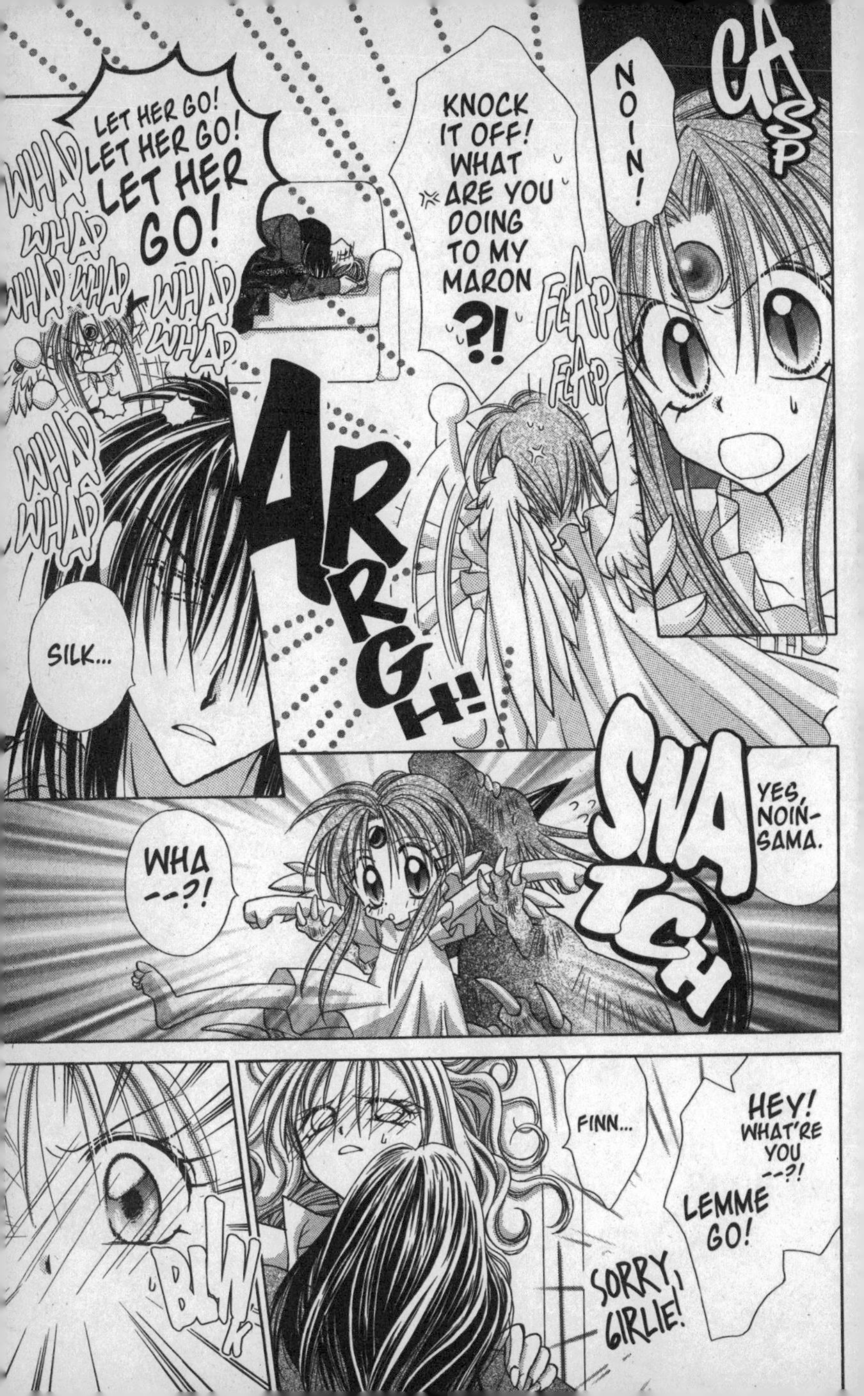
GASP
NOIN!
KNOCK IT OFF! WHAT ARE YOU DOING TO MY MARON ?!
FLAP FLAP
LET HER GO! LET HER GO! LET HER GO!
WHAP WHAP WHAP WHAP WHAP WHAP WHAP WHAP
ARRGH!
SILK...
SNATCH
YES, NOIN-SAMA.
WHA--?!
HEY! WHAT'RE YOU--?!
LEMME GO!
SORRY, GIRLIE!
FINN...
BLINK

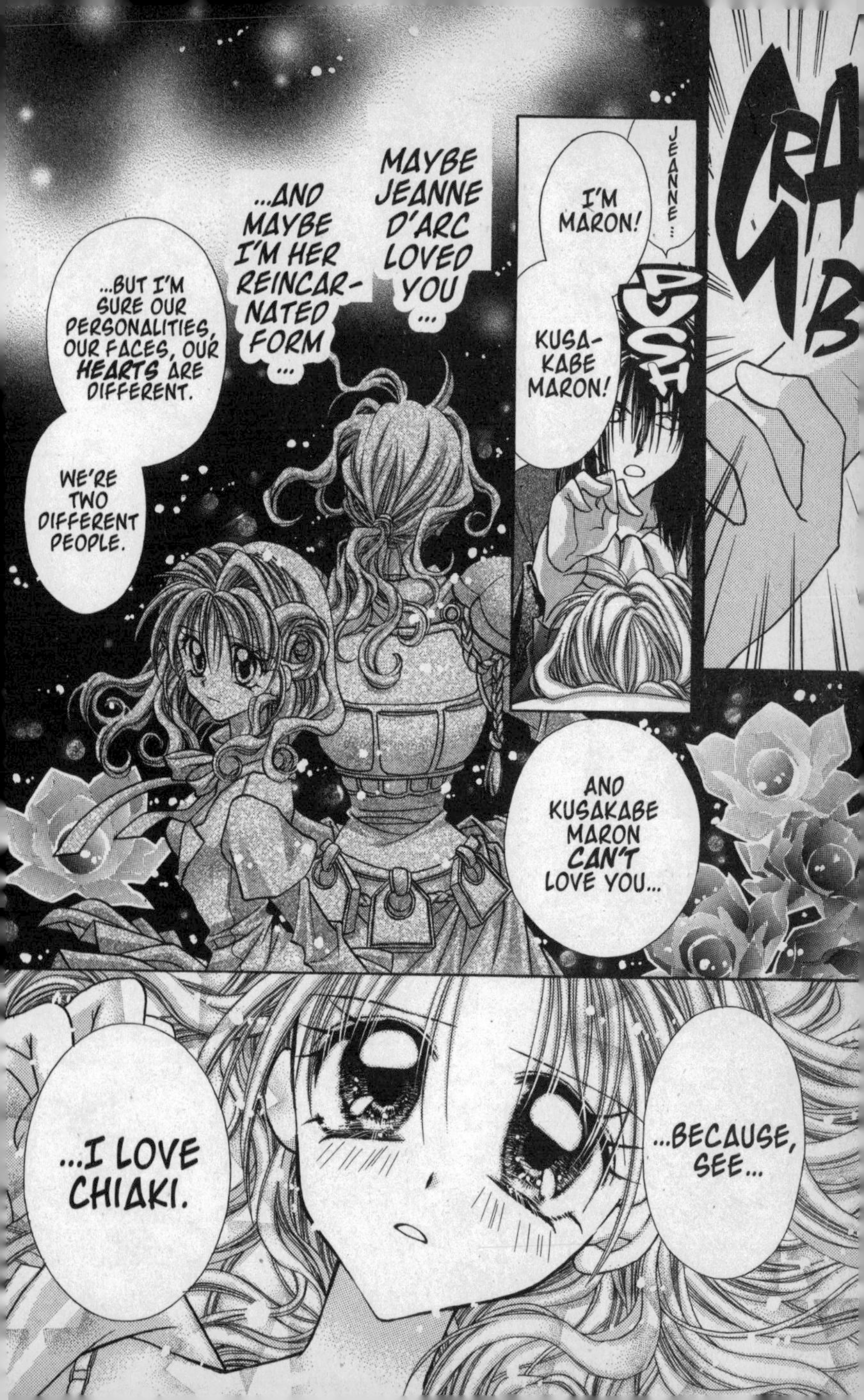
GRAB
JEANNE...
I'M MARON!
PUSH
KUSAKABE MARON!
MAYBE JEANNE D'ARC LOVED YOU...
...AND MAYBE I'M HER REINCARNATED FORM...
...BUT I'M SURE OUR PERSONALITIES, OUR FACES, OUR **HEARTS** ARE DIFFERENT.
WE'RE TWO DIFFERENT PEOPLE.
AND KUSAKABE MARON **CAN'T** LOVE YOU...
...BECAUSE, SEE...
...I LOVE CHIAKI.

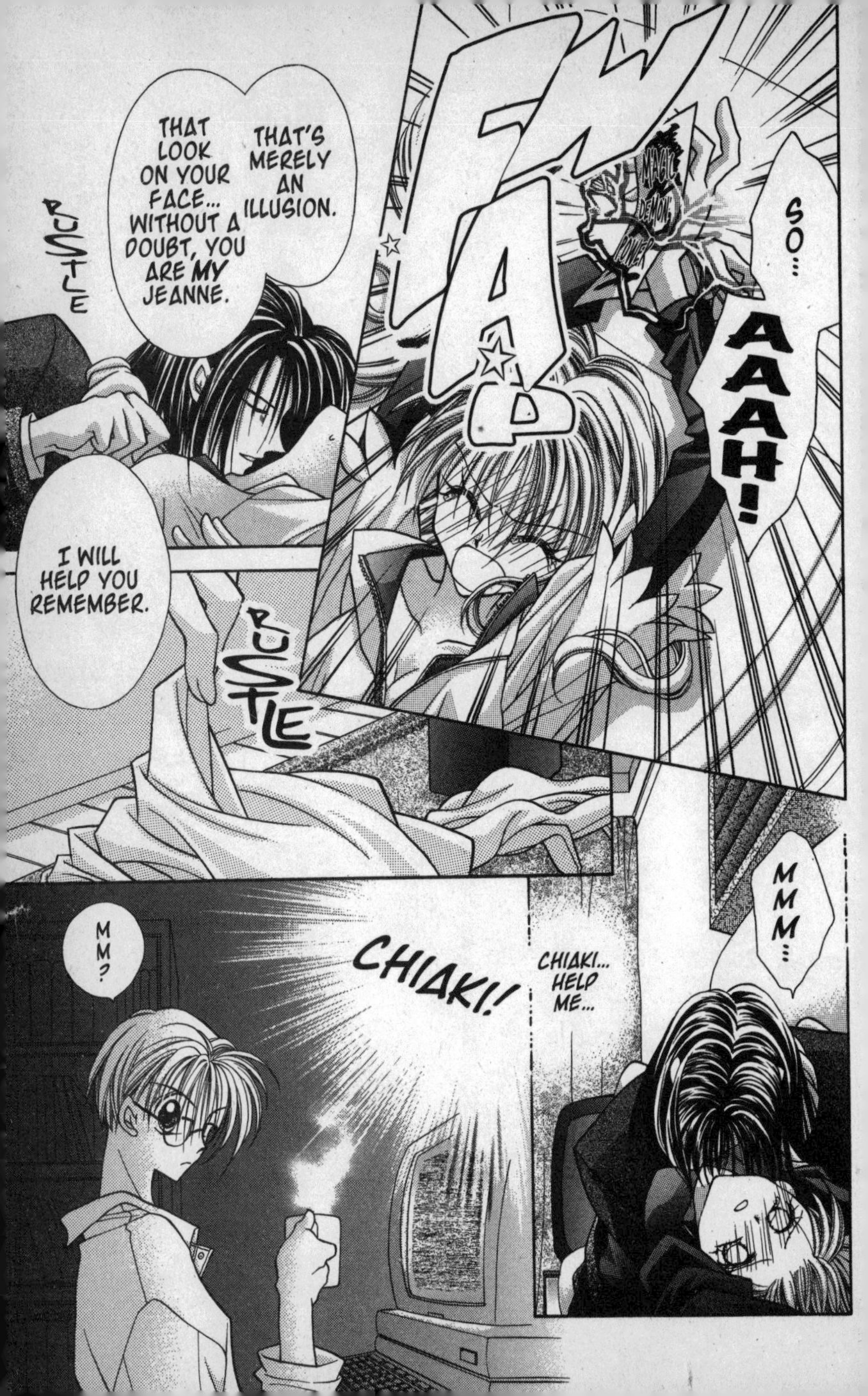

SO...
AAAAH!
FWAP
MAGIC DEMON POWER
THAT'S MERELY AN ILLUSION.
THAT LOOK ON YOUR FACE... WITHOUT A DOUBT, YOU ARE MY JEANNE.
RUSTLE
I WILL HELP YOU REMEMBER.
RUSTLE
MMM...
CHIAKI... HELP ME...
CHIAKI!
MM?

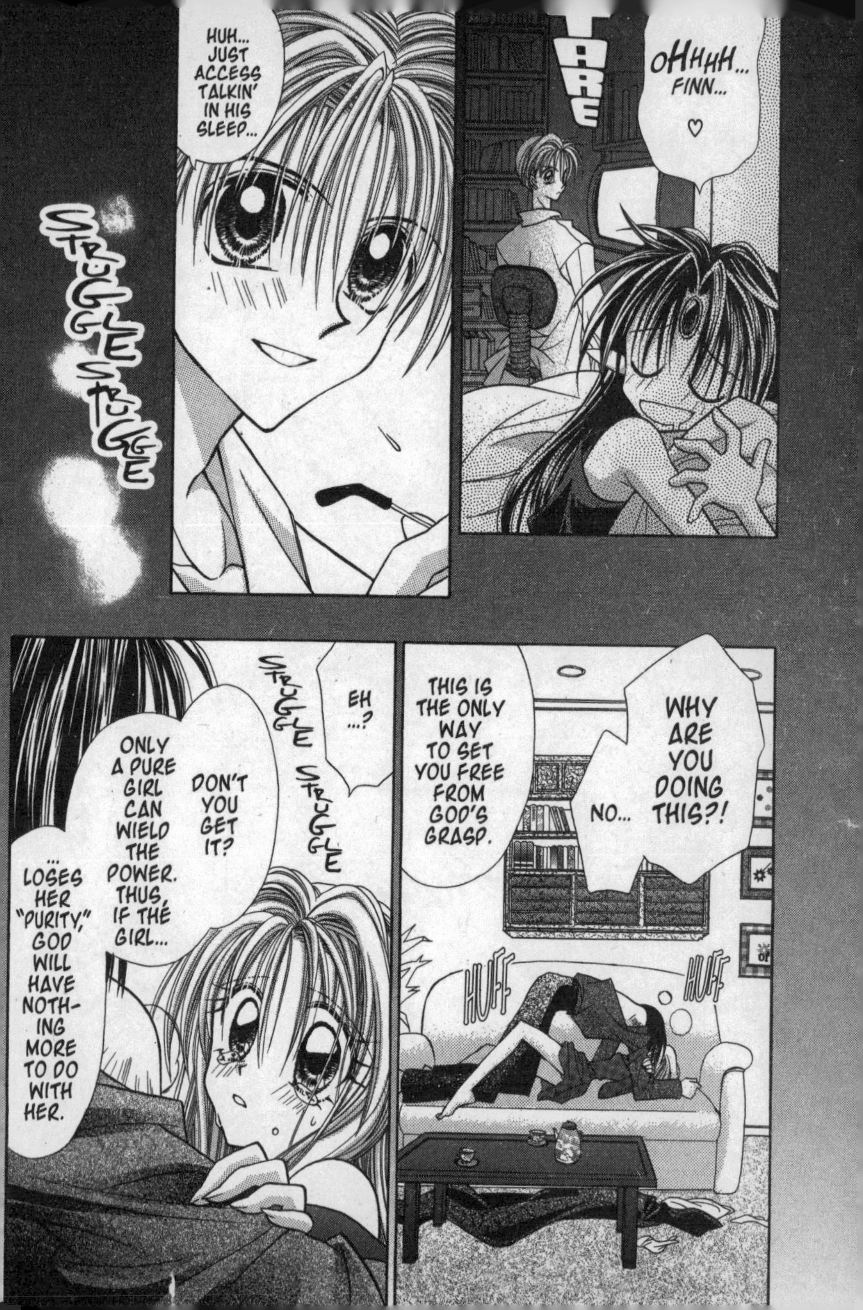
ARE
OHHHH... FINN... ♡
HUH... JUST ACCESS TALKIN' IN HIS SLEEP...
STRUGGLE STRUGGLE
WHY ARE YOU DOING THIS?!
NO...
THIS IS THE ONLY WAY TO SET YOU FREE FROM GOD'S GRASP.
HUFF HUFF
EH ...?
STRUGGLE STRUGGLE
DON'T YOU GET IT?
ONLY A PURE GIRL CAN WIELD THE POWER. THUS, IF THE GIRL...
... LOSES HER "PURITY," GOD WILL HAVE NOTHING MORE TO DO WITH HER.

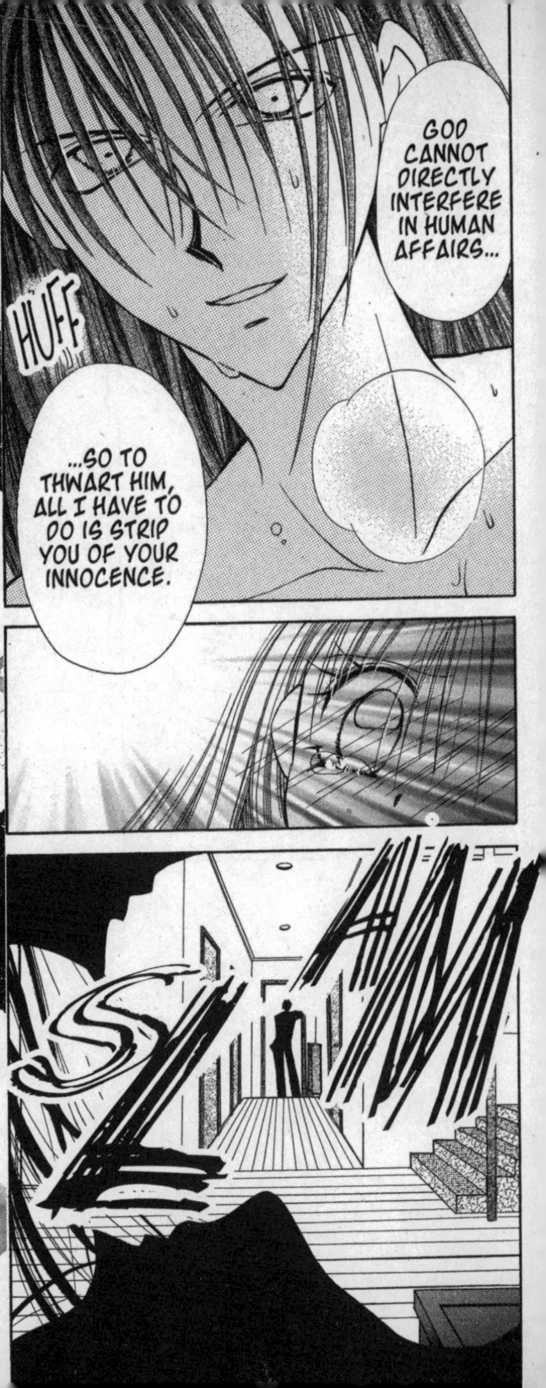
GOD CANNOT DIRECTLY INTERFERE IN HUMAN AFFAIRS...
HUFF
...SO TO THWART HIM, ALL I HAVE TO DO IS STRIP YOU OF YOUR INNOCENCE.
SLAM

BIG SERVICE FOR ARINA FANS

A Sketch Made Public!!!

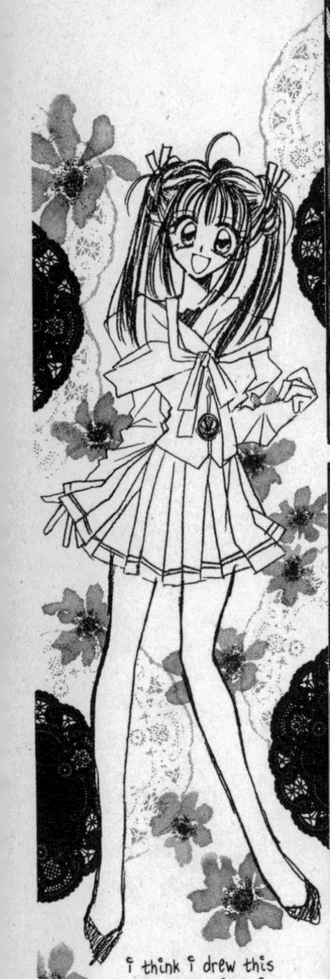

I think I drew this one right after I finished "I.O.N." Actually, I had planned to use this character in a one-shot story. Maybe I'll get around to using her...someday.

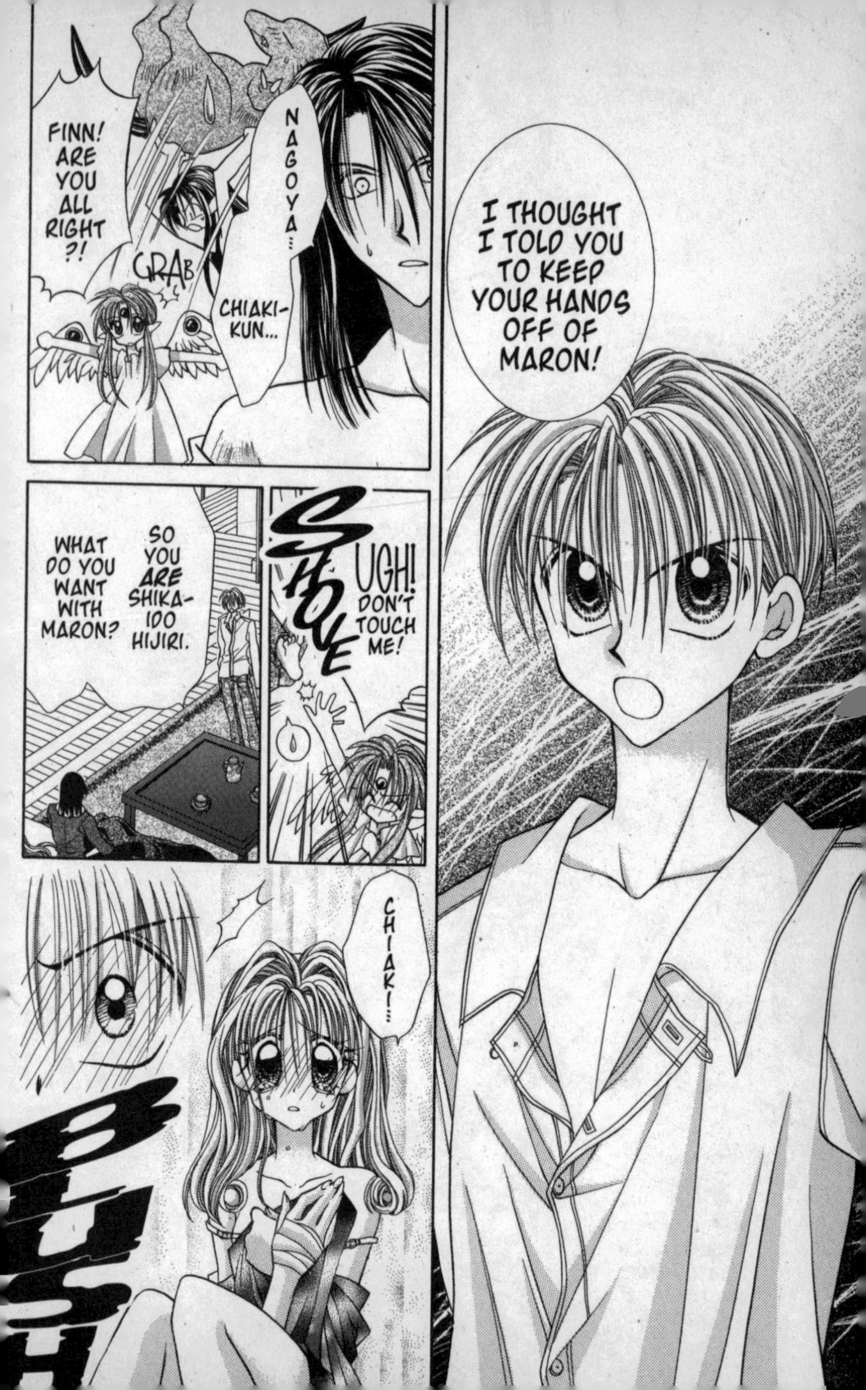
I THOUGHT I TOLD YOU TO KEEP YOUR HANDS OFF OF MARON!
NAGOYA...
CHIAKI-KUN...
FINN! ARE YOU ALL RIGHT ?!
GRAB
SHOVE
UGH! DON'T TOUCH ME!
SO YOU ARE SHIKA-IDO HIJIRI.
WHAT DO YOU WANT WITH MARON?
CHIAKI...!
BLUSH

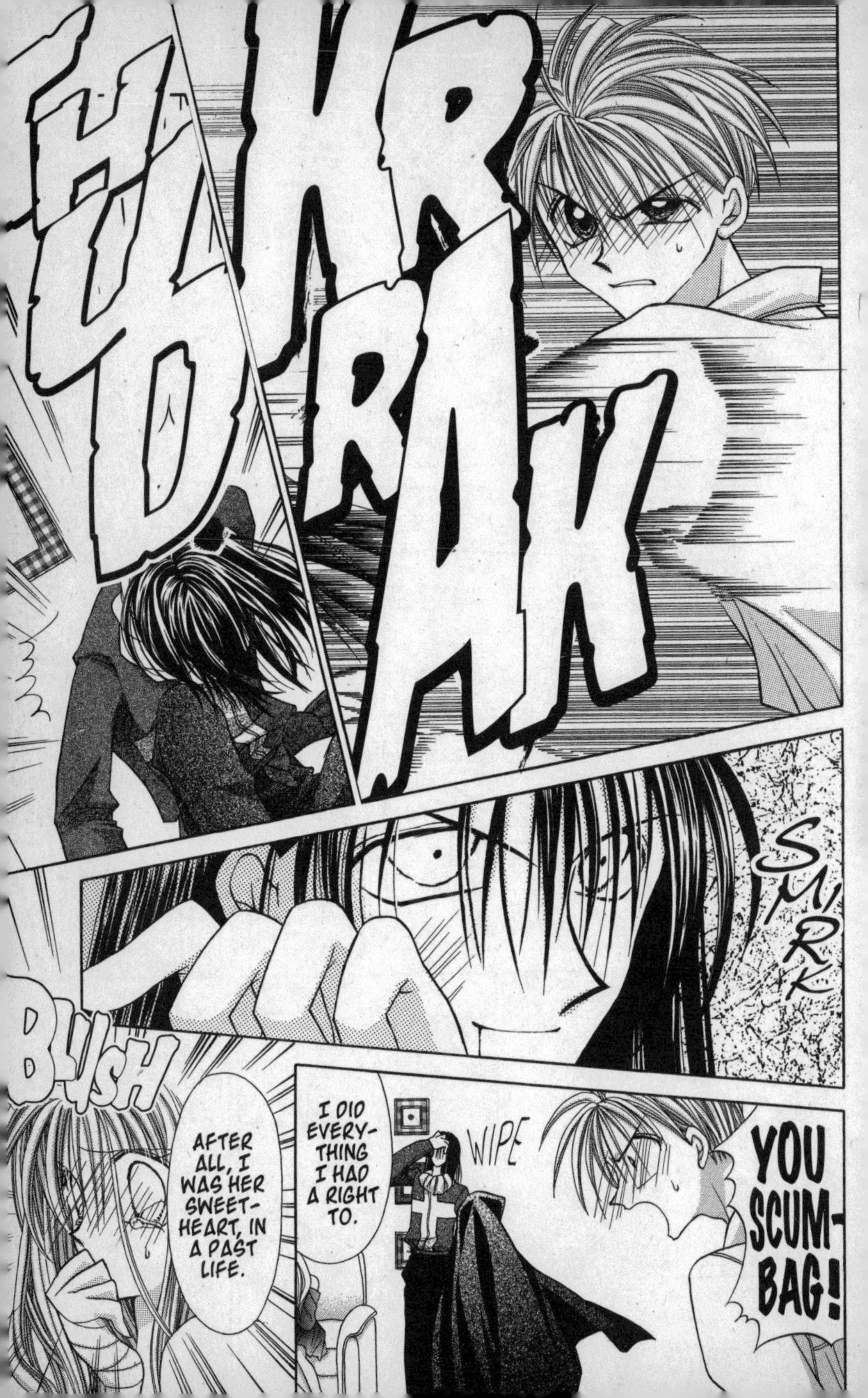
SMIRK
YOU SCUM-BAG!
WIPE
I DID EVERYTHING I HAD A RIGHT TO.
AFTER ALL, I WAS HER SWEETHEART, IN A PAST LIFE.
BLUSH

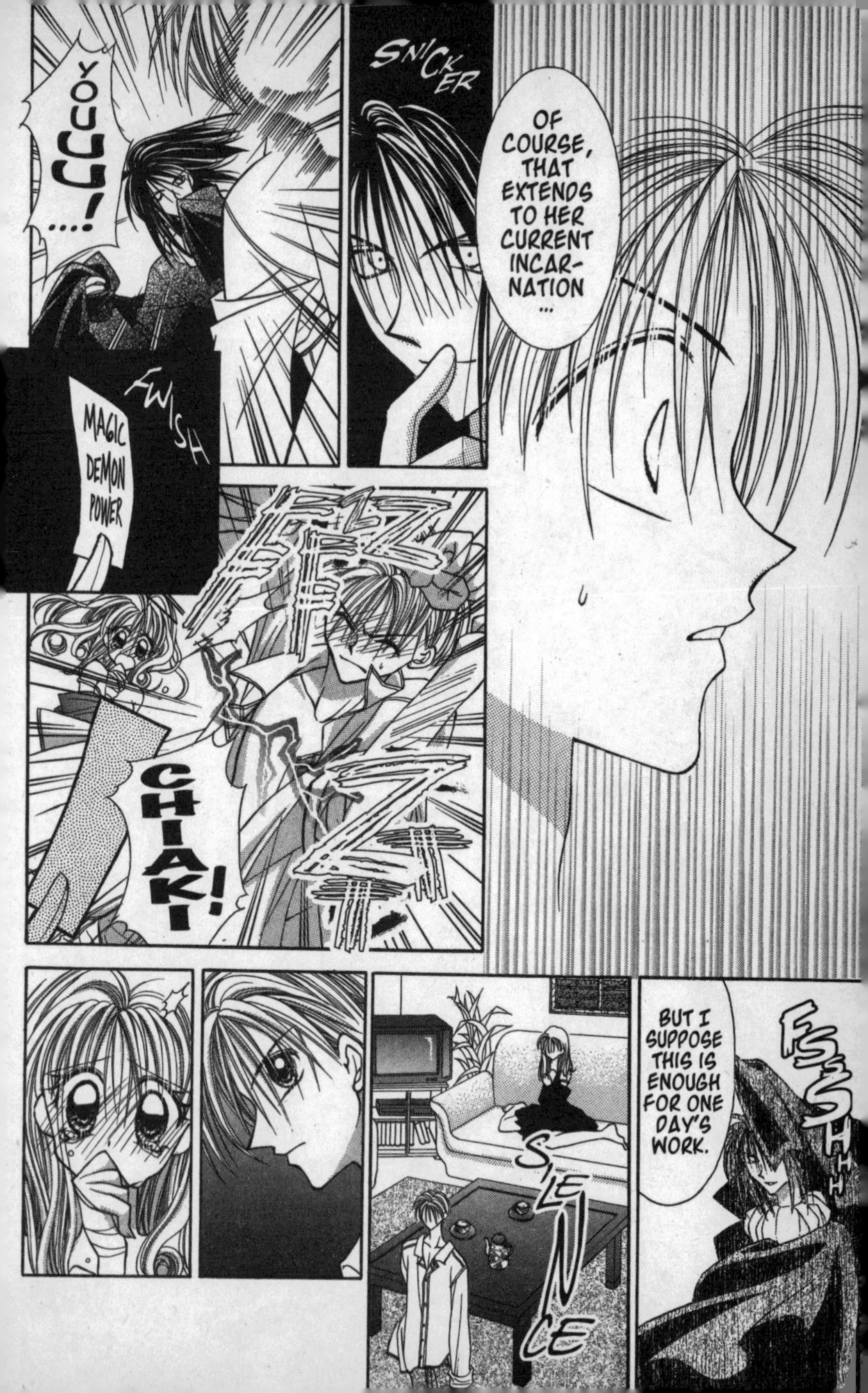
OF COURSE, THAT EXTENDS TO HER CURRENT INCARNATION ...
SNICKER
YOUUU...!
FWISH
MAGIC DEMON POWER
CHIAKI!
BUT I SUPPOSE THIS IS ENOUGH FOR ONE DAY'S WORK.
FSSHHH
SILENCE

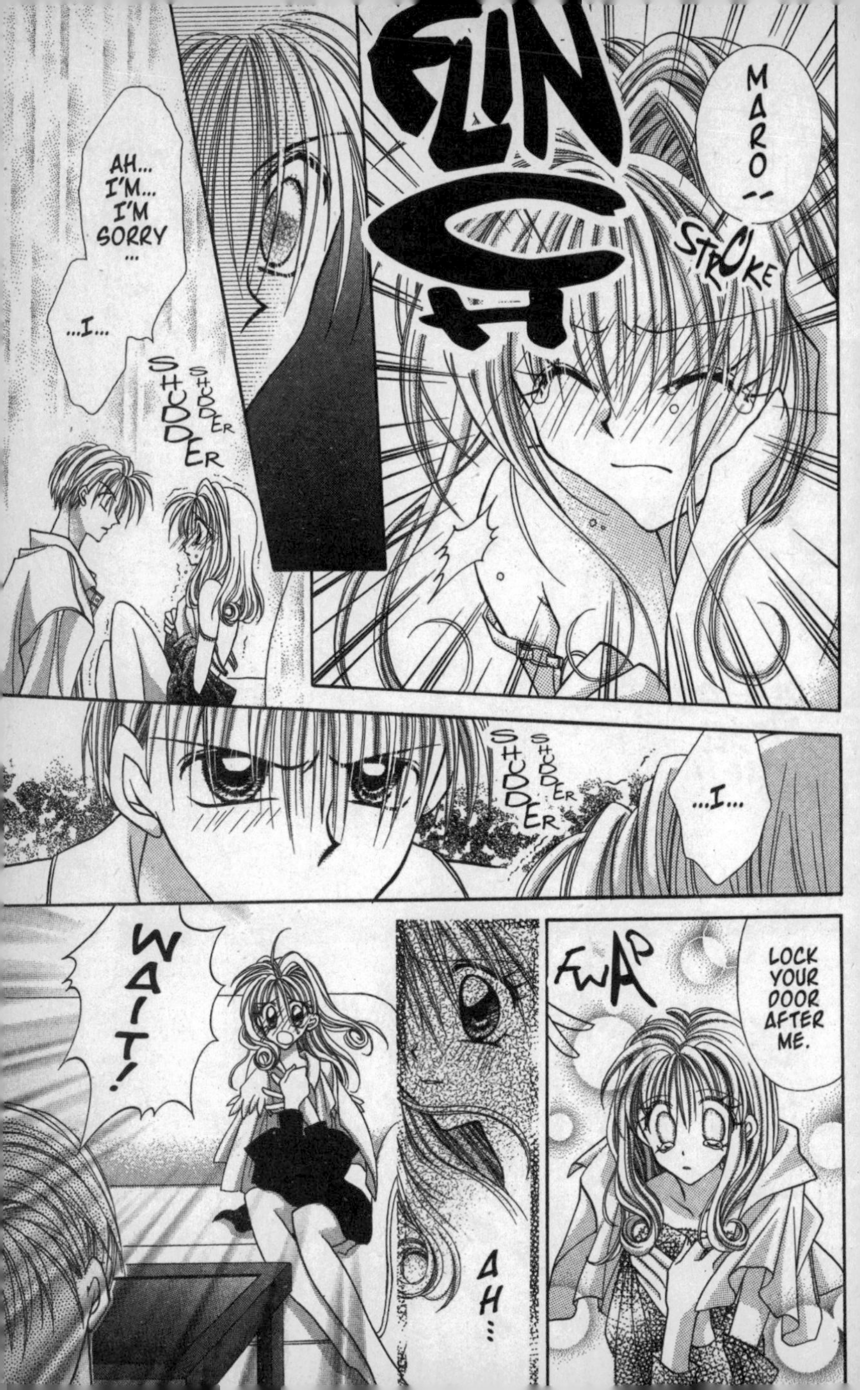
MARO...
STROKE
CLING
AH... I'M... I'M SORRY ...
...I...
SHUDDER SHUDDER
...I...
SHUDDER SHUDDER
LOCK YOUR DOOR AFTER ME.
FWAP
AH..
WAIT!

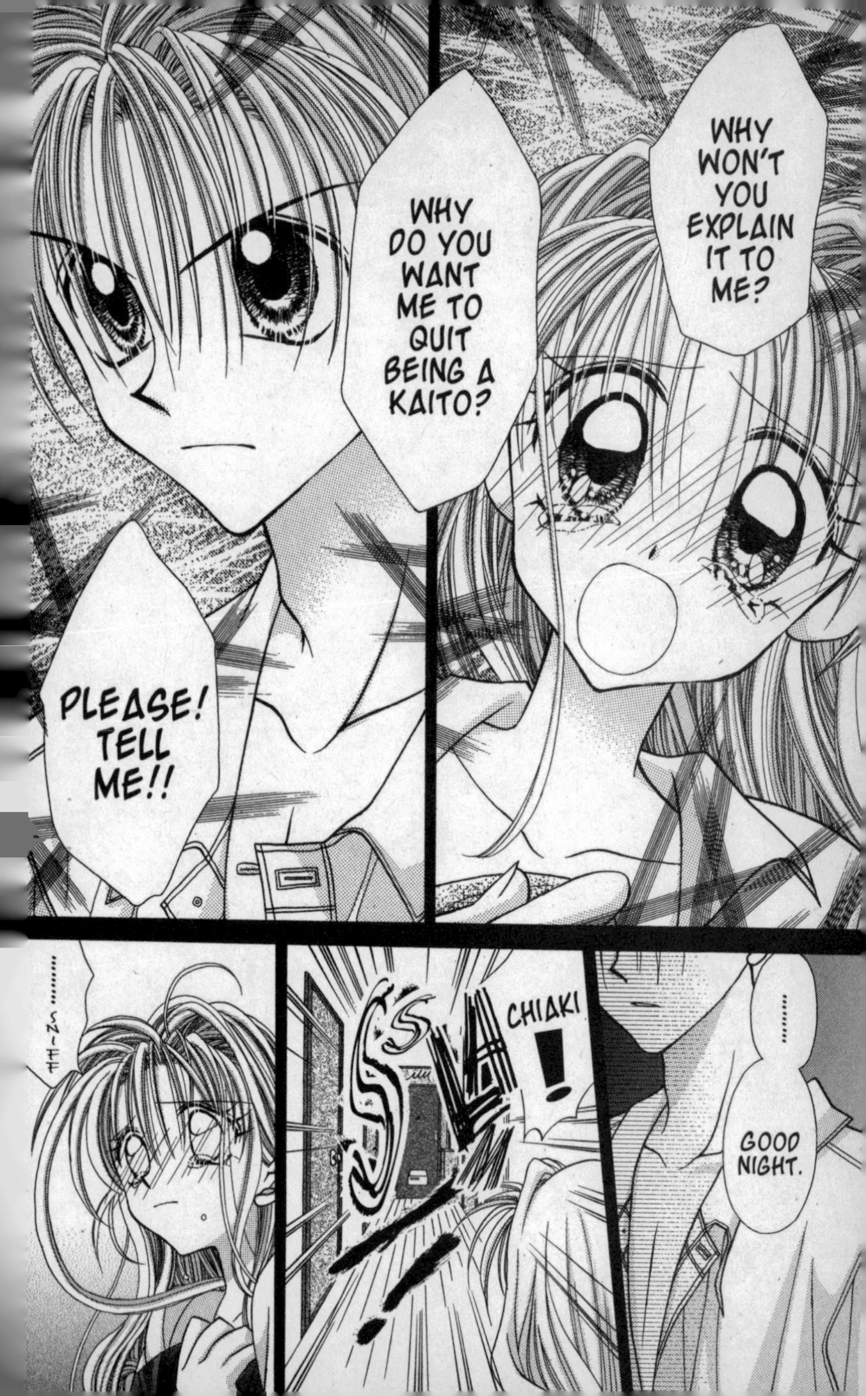
WHY WON'T YOU EXPLAIN IT TO ME?
WHY DO YOU WANT ME TO QUIT BEING A KAITO?
PLEASE! TELL ME!!
......
GOOD NIGHT.
CHIAKI!
SNIFF ....

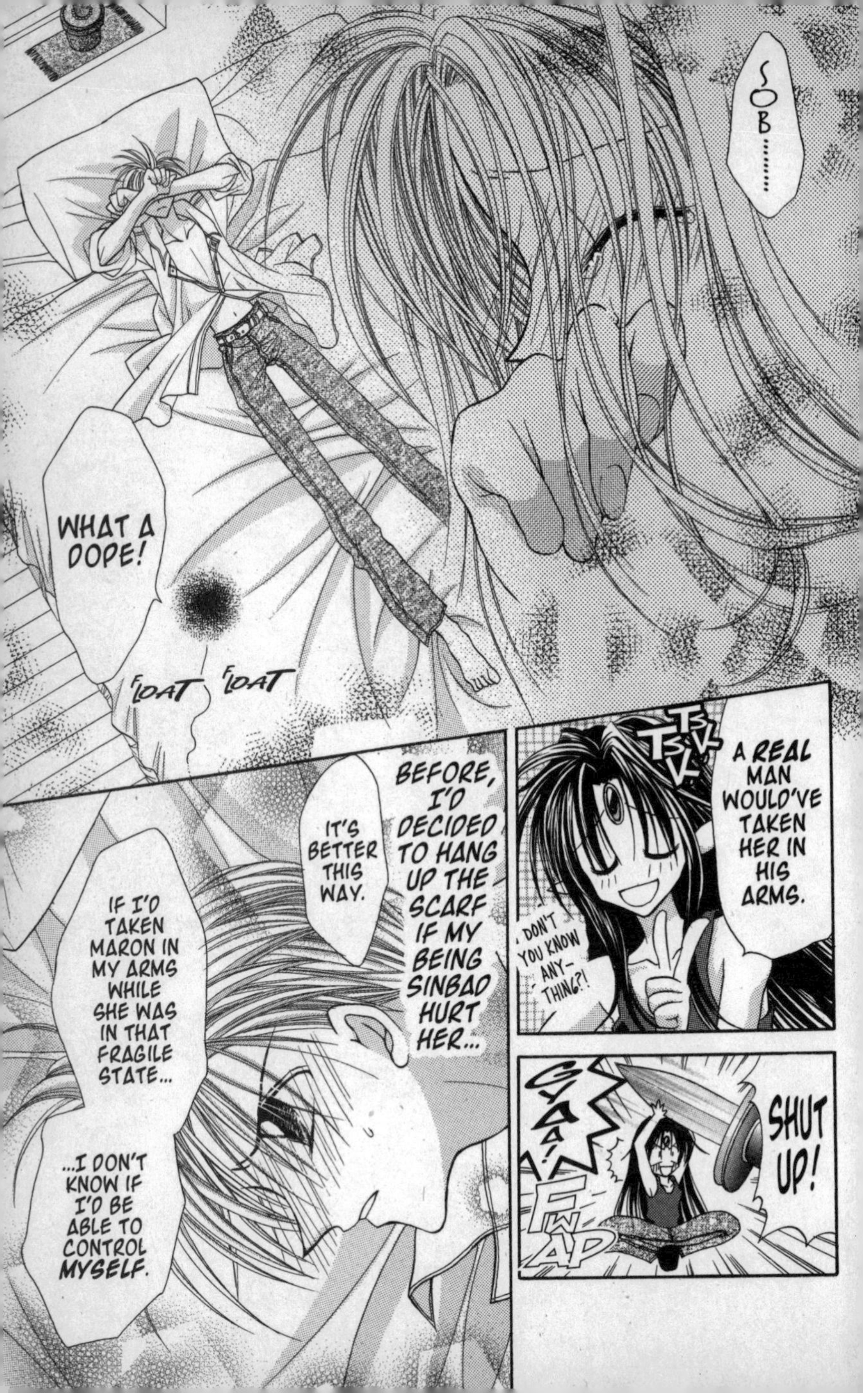
SOB......
WHAT A DOPE!
FLOAT FLOAT
TSK TSK
A REAL MAN WOULD'VE TAKEN HER IN HIS ARMS.
DON'T YOU KNOW ANY-THING?!
SHUT UP!
GYAA!
FWAP
BEFORE, I'D DECIDED TO HANG UP THE SCARF IF MY BEING SINBAD HURT HER...
IT'S BETTER THIS WAY.
IF I'D TAKEN MARON IN MY ARMS WHILE SHE WAS IN THAT FRAGILE STATE...
...I DON'T KNOW IF I'D BE ABLE TO CONTROL MYSELF.

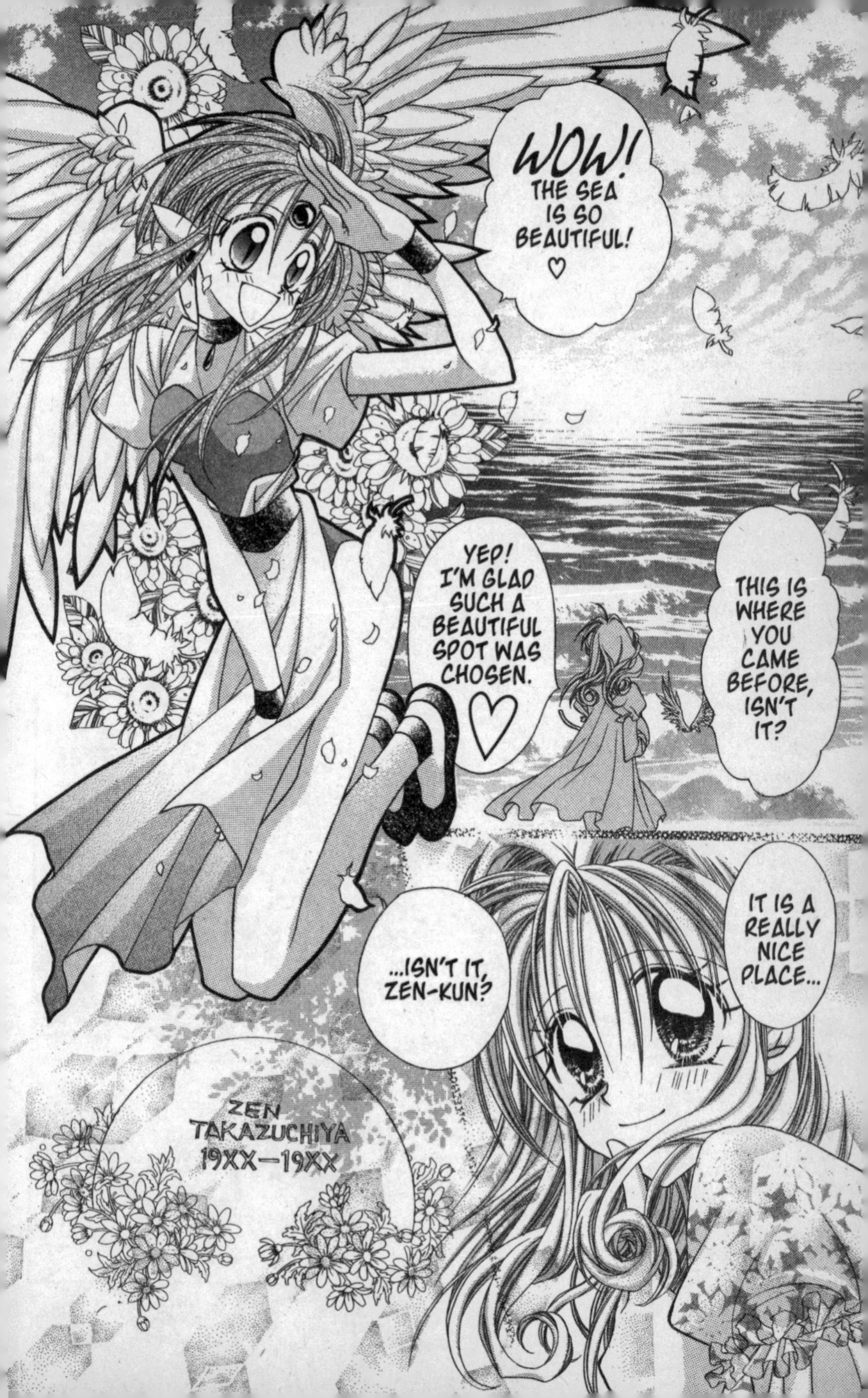
WOW! THE SEA IS SO BEAUTIFUL! ♡
THIS IS WHERE YOU CAME BEFORE, ISN'T IT?
YEP! I'M GLAD SUCH A BEAUTIFUL SPOT WAS CHOSEN. ♡
IT IS A REALLY NICE PLACE...
...ISN'T IT, ZEN-KUN?
ZEN TAKAZUCHIYA 19XX–19XX

FAREWELL

Well, this is the last column for this here volume! Because I've been so busy, I'm afraid I've cut a lot of corners re: the column extras this time around, but I'm happy that I filled the space up one way or another ♡ I apologize for not writing much about radio this time.

(Takahashi-san doesn't have a dirty mind! He's a really nice guy...or at least that's what Nao-niisan told me!)

Keep listening to the radio because you never know, you could be hearing me on the airwaves again! Check out Takahashi-san's show every week! ♡ (Believe me, his show is hilarious to listen to, which is why I want all of you to give it a chance! ♡ Of course, I never miss it!!) If you live outside the Tokyo area, the show will probably be on a different station, so check for your local listing in an anime magazine (or in a newspaper).

SORRY FOR THE INCONVENIENCE!

SPECIAL THANKS

AI MIZUSE (Commutes from Hiroshima every month!) ASANO KYAKYA (Also makes the trek from Hiroshima every month!) KAZUKI RUKA (Comes from Nagoya...not as long a haul as Hiroshima...but still, I'm impressed!) NAKAMURA CHIHO-SAMA, OOIMA YASUTO-SAMA, KAKEGAWA NARUTO-SAMA, SEISO NIKI-SAMA, TATENO-SAMA, my editor, OBAYASHI-SAMA and my big sister, YUKI-RIN.

Okay, see you next volume (...I hope it comes out! ♡) BYE-BYE!

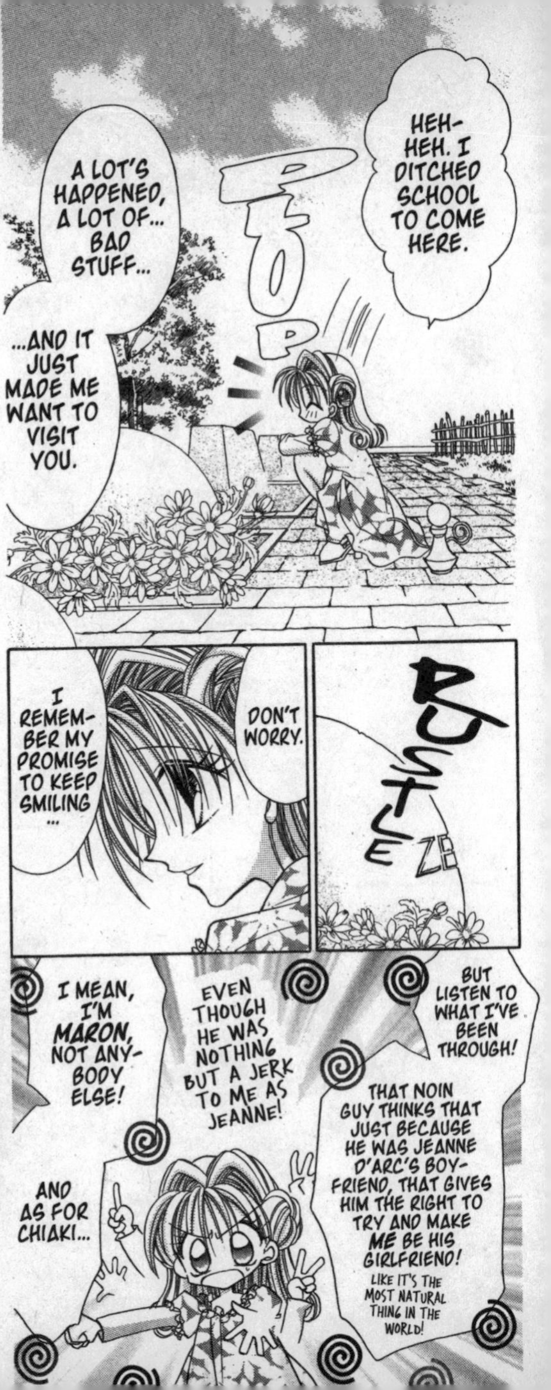
HEH-HEH. I DITCHED SCHOOL TO COME HERE.
POP
A LOT'S HAPPENED, A LOT OF... BAD STUFF...
...AND IT JUST MADE ME WANT TO VISIT YOU.
RUSTLE
ZE
DON'T WORRY.
I REMEMBER MY PROMISE TO KEEP SMILING...
BUT LISTEN TO WHAT I'VE BEEN THROUGH!
THAT NOIN GUY THINKS THAT JUST BECAUSE HE WAS JEANNE D'ARC'S BOYFRIEND, THAT GIVES HIM THE RIGHT TO TRY AND MAKE ME BE HIS GIRLFRIEND!
LIKE IT'S THE MOST NATURAL THING IN THE WORLD!
EVEN THOUGH HE WAS NOTHING BUT A JERK TO ME AS JEANNE!
I MEAN, I'M MARON, NOT ANYBODY ELSE!
AND AS FOR CHIAKI...

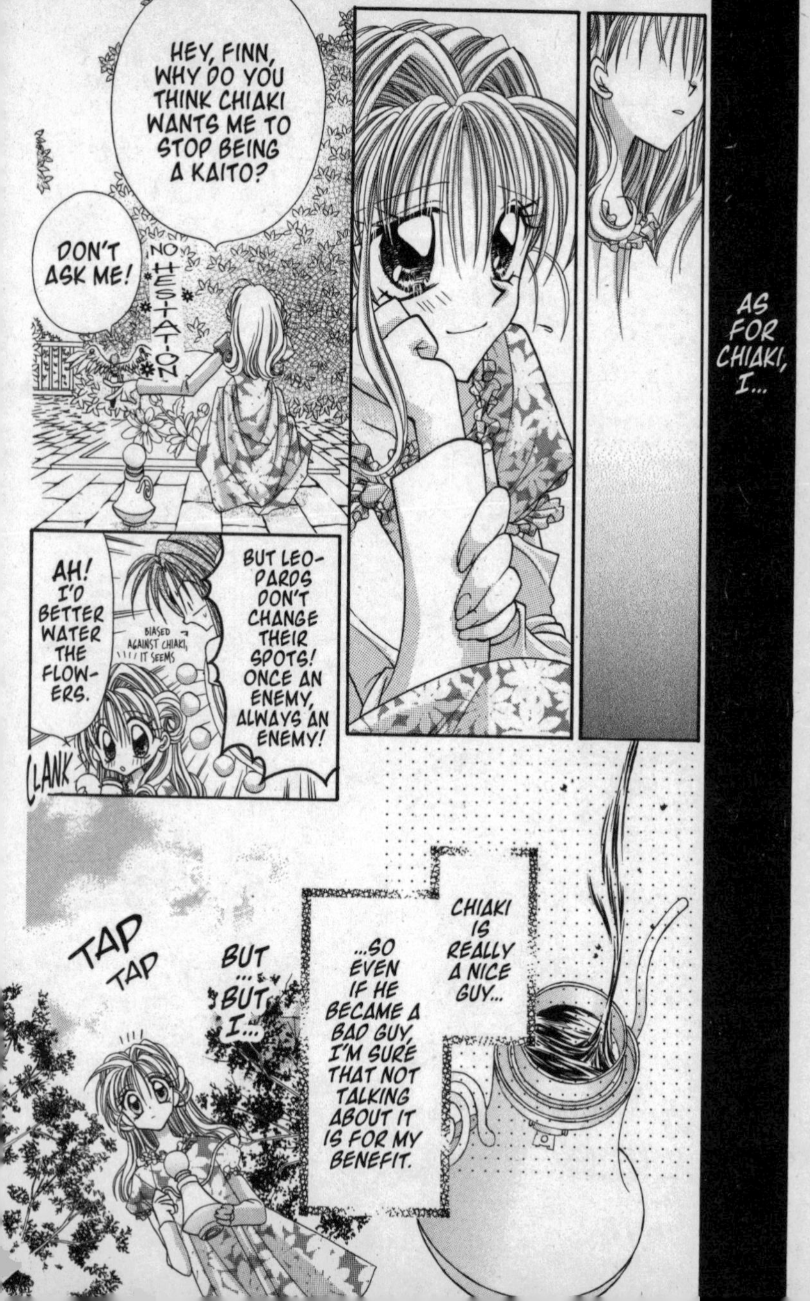
AS FOR CHIAKI, I...
HEY, FINN, WHY DO YOU THINK CHIAKI WANTS ME TO STOP BEING A KAITO?
NO HESITATION
DON'T ASK ME!
BUT LEOPARDS DON'T CHANGE THEIR SPOTS! ONCE AN ENEMY, ALWAYS AN ENEMY!
AH! I'D BETTER WATER THE FLOWERS.
BIASED AGAINST CHIAKI, IT SEEMS
CLANK
CHIAKI IS REALLY A NICE GUY...
...SO EVEN IF HE BECAME A BAD GUY, I'M SURE THAT NOT TALKING ABOUT IT IS FOR MY BENEFIT.
BUT ... BUT I...
TAP TAP

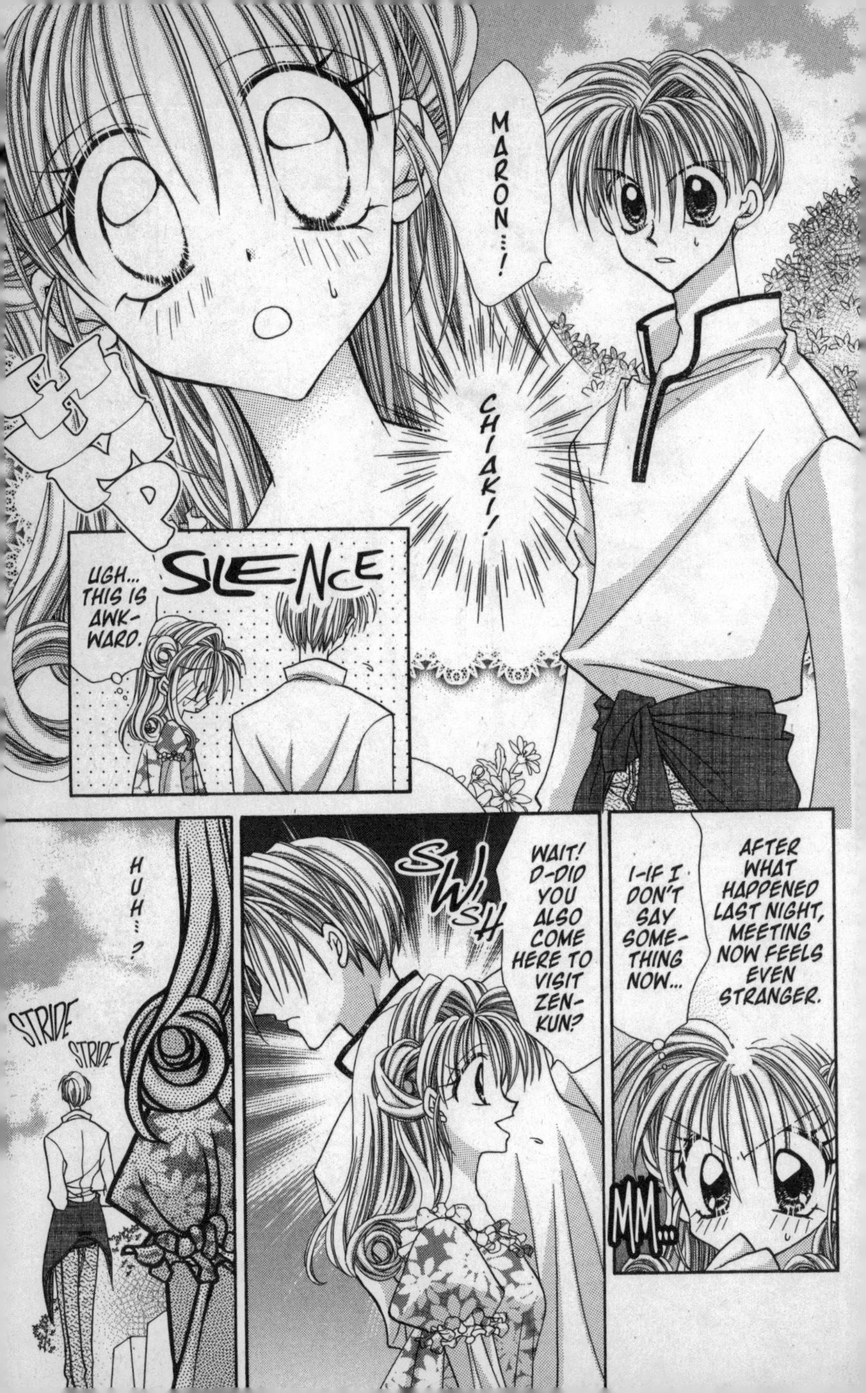
MARON...!
CHIAKI!
SILENCE
UGH... THIS IS AWK-WARD.
AFTER WHAT HAPPENED LAST NIGHT, MEETING NOW FEELS EVEN STRANGER.
I-IF I DON'T SAY SOME-THING NOW...
MM...
SWISH
WAIT! D-DID YOU ALSO COME HERE TO VISIT ZEN-KUN?
HUH...?
STRIDE
STRIDE

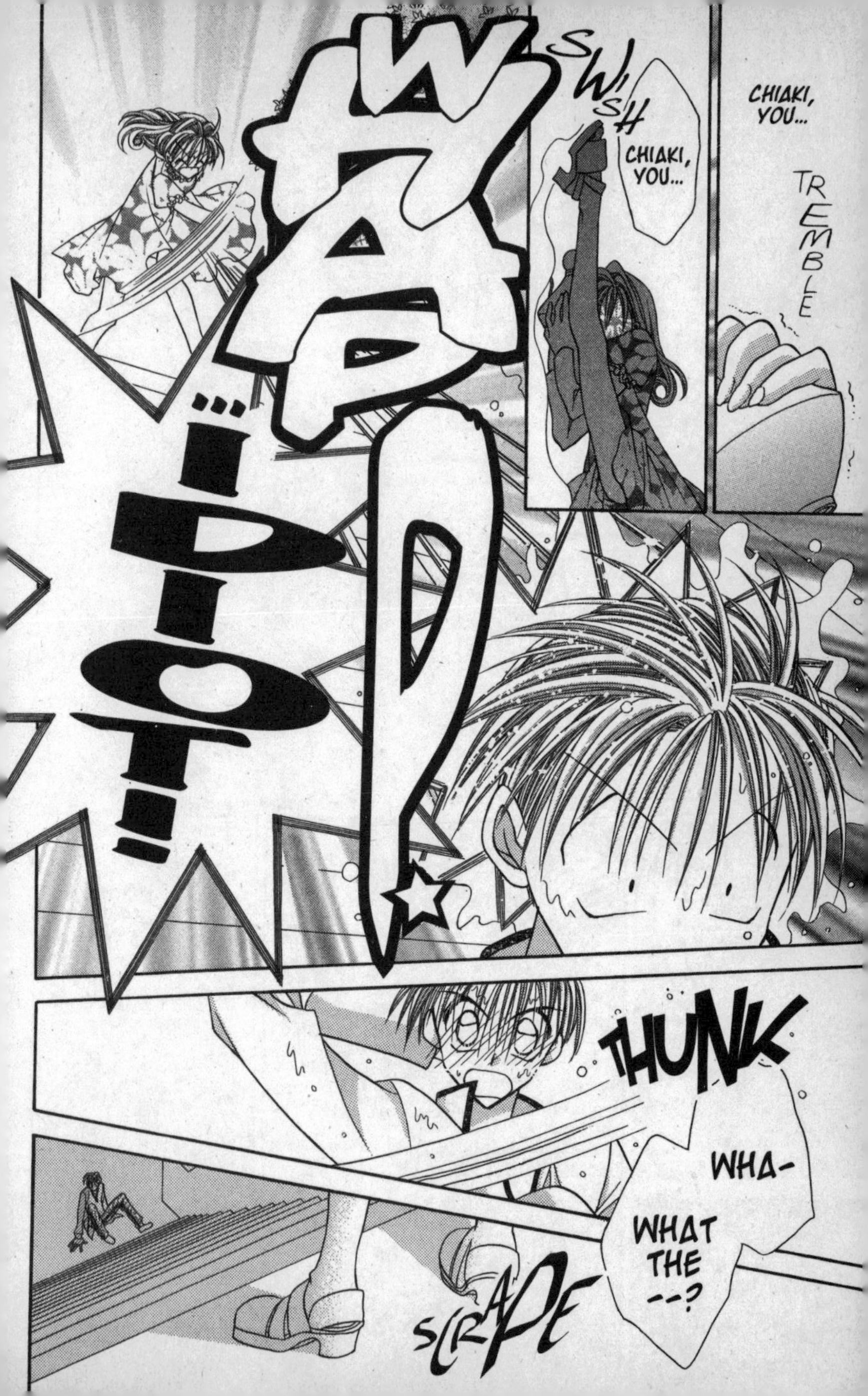
CHIAKI, YOU...
TREMBLE
SWISH
CHIAKI, YOU...
WHAP
IDIOT!!
THUNK
WHA-
WHAT THE --?
SCRAPE

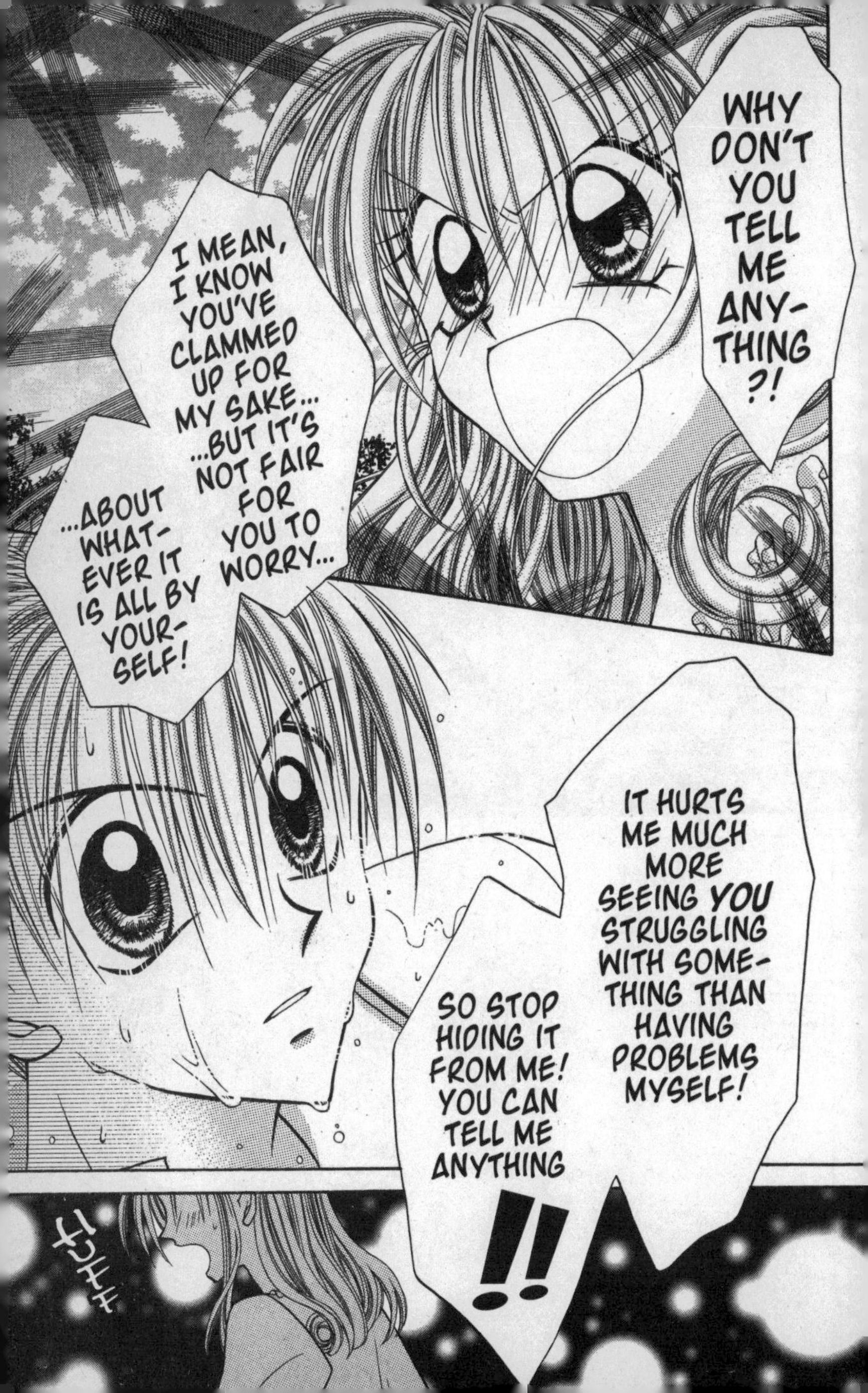
WHY DON'T YOU TELL ME ANYTHING?!
I MEAN, I KNOW YOU'VE CLAMMED UP FOR MY SAKE...
...BUT IT'S NOT FAIR FOR YOU TO WORRY...
...ABOUT WHATEVER IT IS ALL BY YOURSELF!
IT HURTS ME MUCH MORE SEEING *YOU* STRUGGLING WITH SOMETHING THAN HAVING PROBLEMS MYSELF!
SO STOP HIDING IT FROM ME! YOU CAN TELL ME ANYTHING!!
HUFF

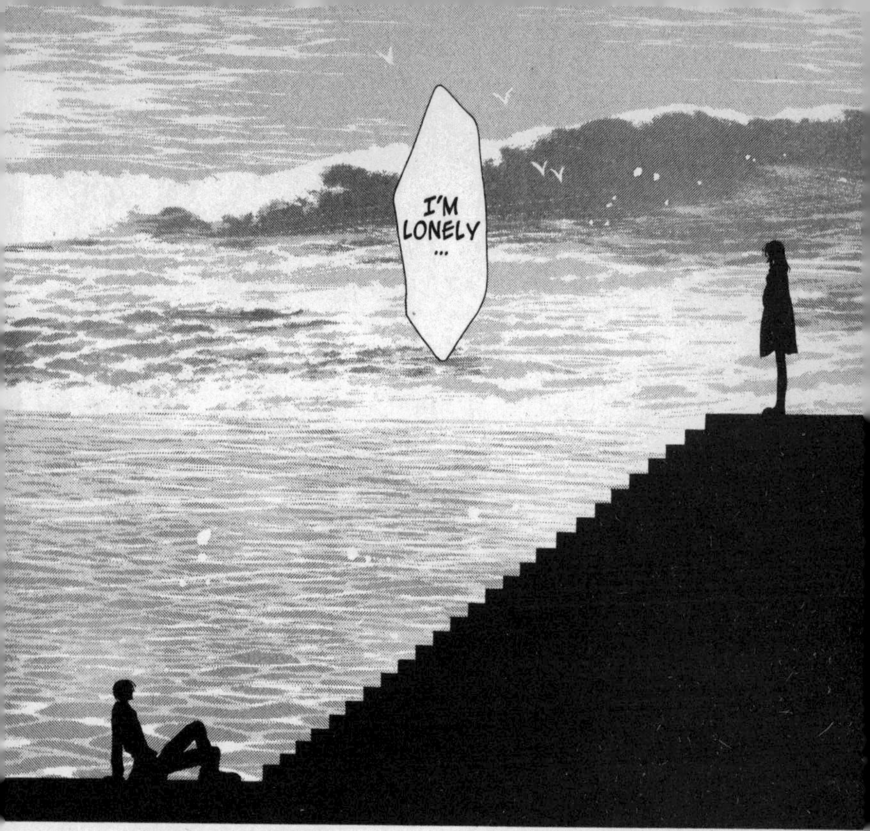
I'M LONELY ...

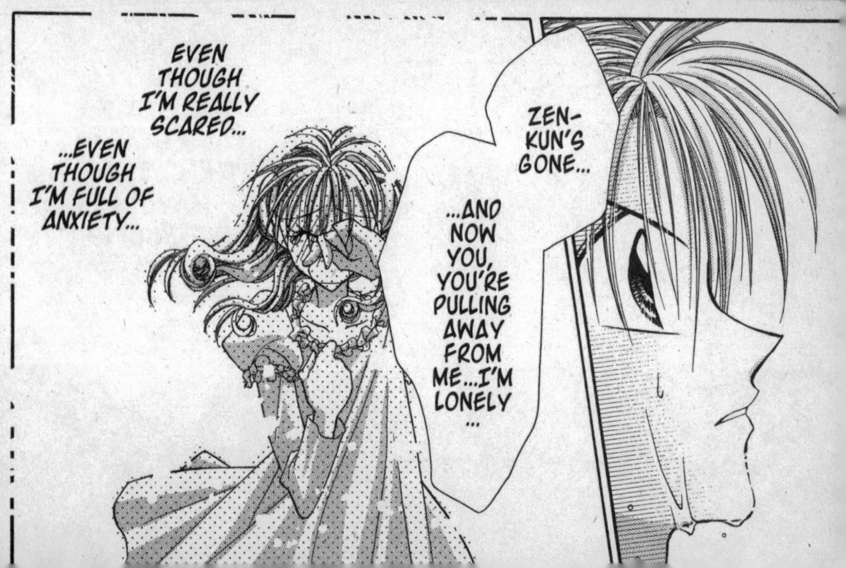
ZEN-KUN'S GONE...
...AND NOW YOU, YOU'RE PULLING AWAY FROM ME...I'M LONELY ...
EVEN THOUGH I'M REALLY SCARED...
...EVEN THOUGH I'M FULL OF ANXIETY...

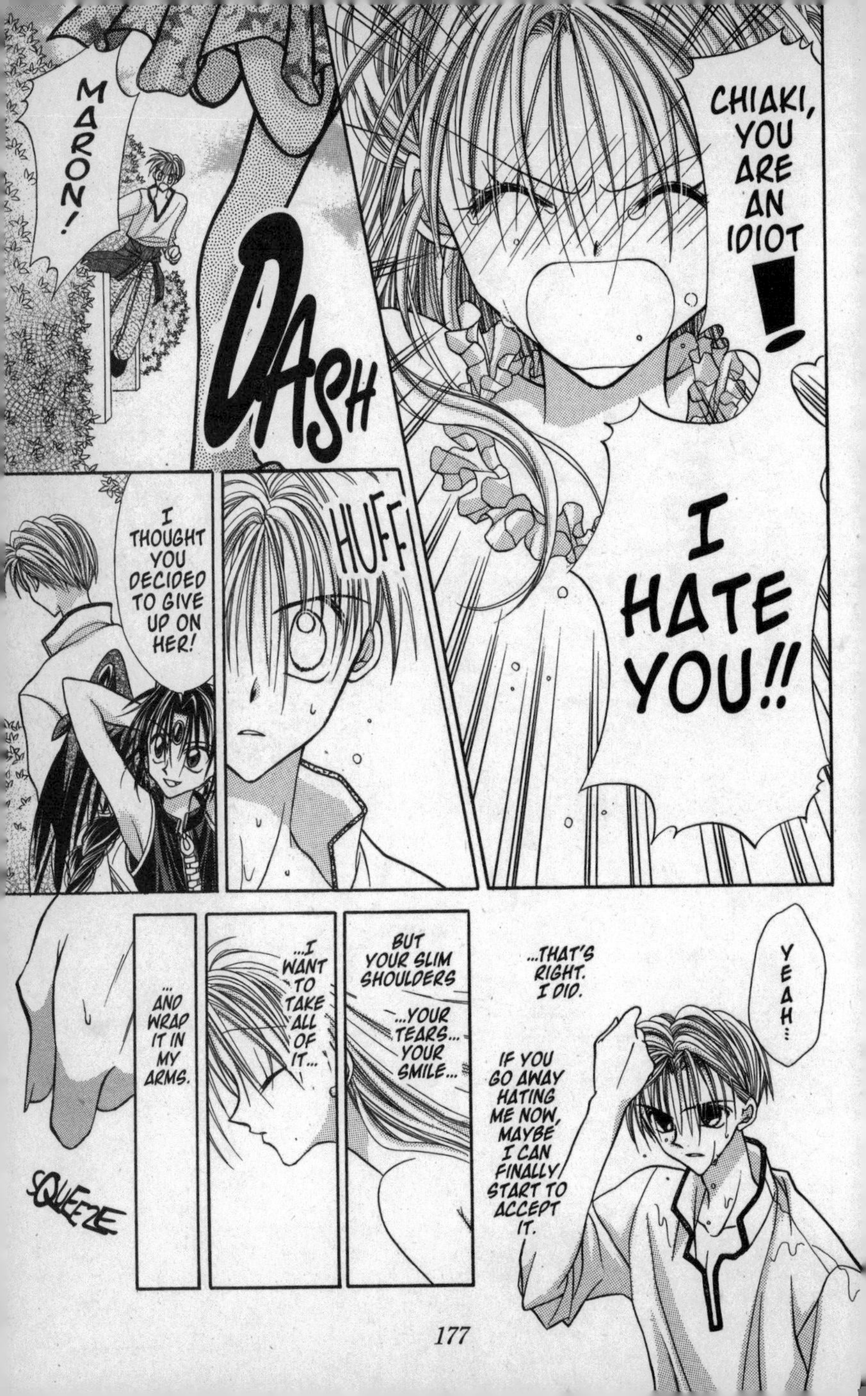
CHIAKI, YOU ARE AN IDIOT!
I HATE YOU!!
MARON!
DASH
HUFF
I THOUGHT YOU DECIDED TO GIVE UP ON HER!
YEAH...
...THAT'S RIGHT. I DID.
IF YOU GO AWAY HATING ME NOW, MAYBE I CAN FINALLY START TO ACCEPT IT.
BUT YOUR SLIM SHOULDERS
...YOUR TEARS... YOUR SMILE...
...I WANT TO TAKE ALL OF IT...
...AND WRAP IT IN MY ARMS.
SQUEEZE

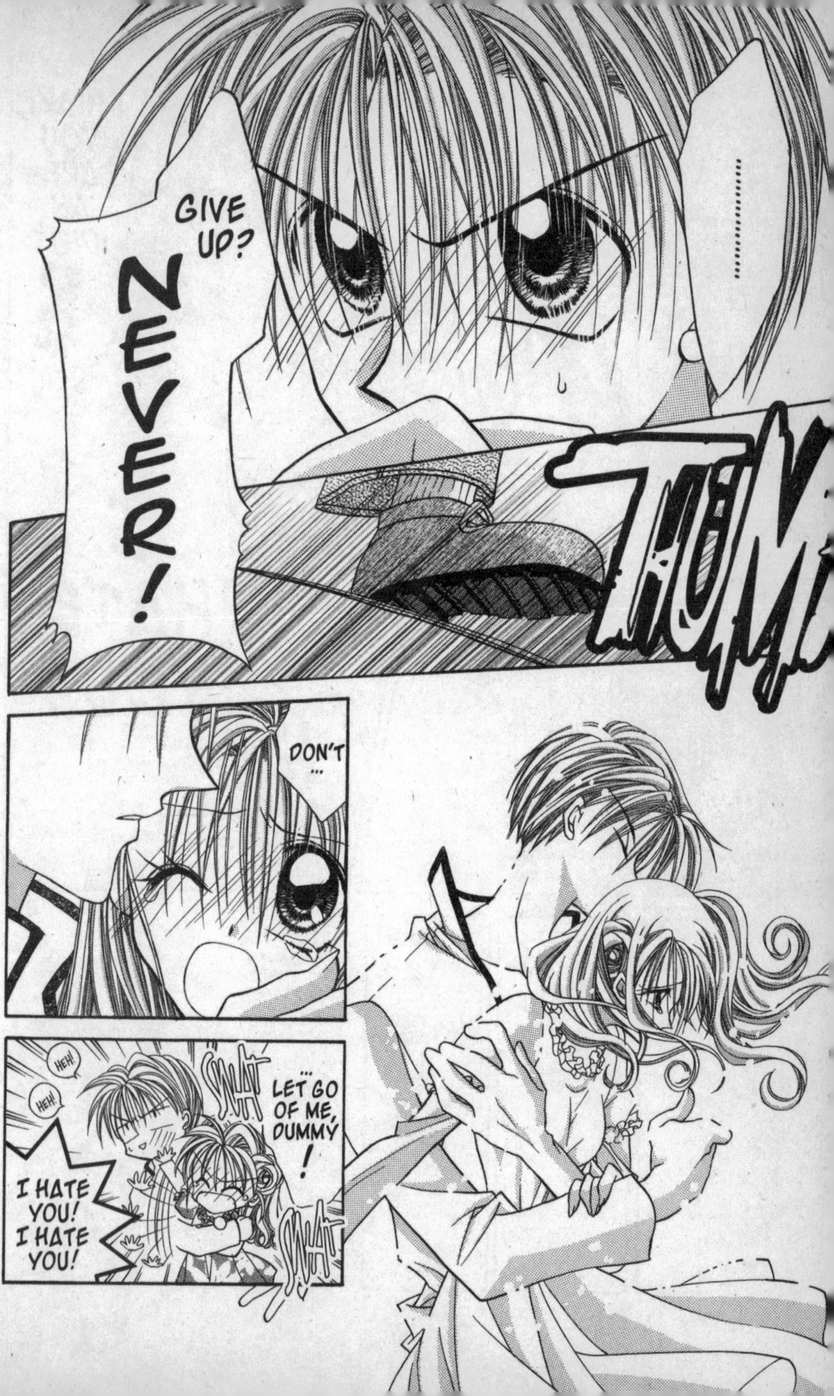
......
GIVE UP?
NEVER!
TOM
DON'T ...
... LET GO OF ME, DUMMY!
HEH!
HEH!
I HATE YOU! I HATE YOU!

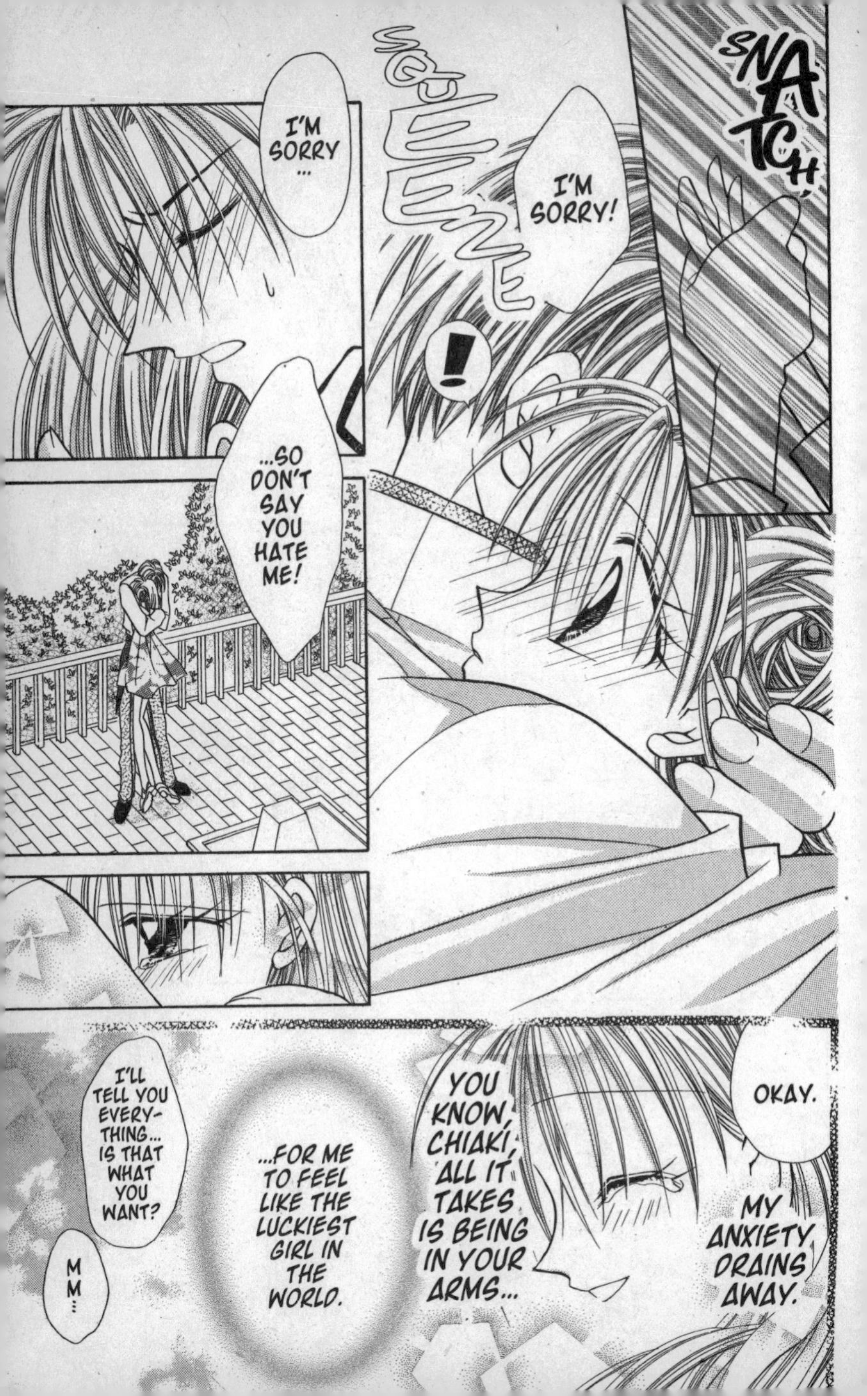
SNATCH
SQUEEZE
I'M SORRY!
!
I'M SORRY...
...SO DON'T SAY YOU HATE ME!
OKAY.
MY ANXIETY DRAINS AWAY.
YOU KNOW, CHIAKI, ALL IT TAKES IS BEING IN YOUR ARMS...
...FOR ME TO FEEL LIKE THE LUCKIEST GIRL IN THE WORLD.
I'LL TELL YOU EVERYTHING... IS THAT WHAT YOU WANT?
MM...

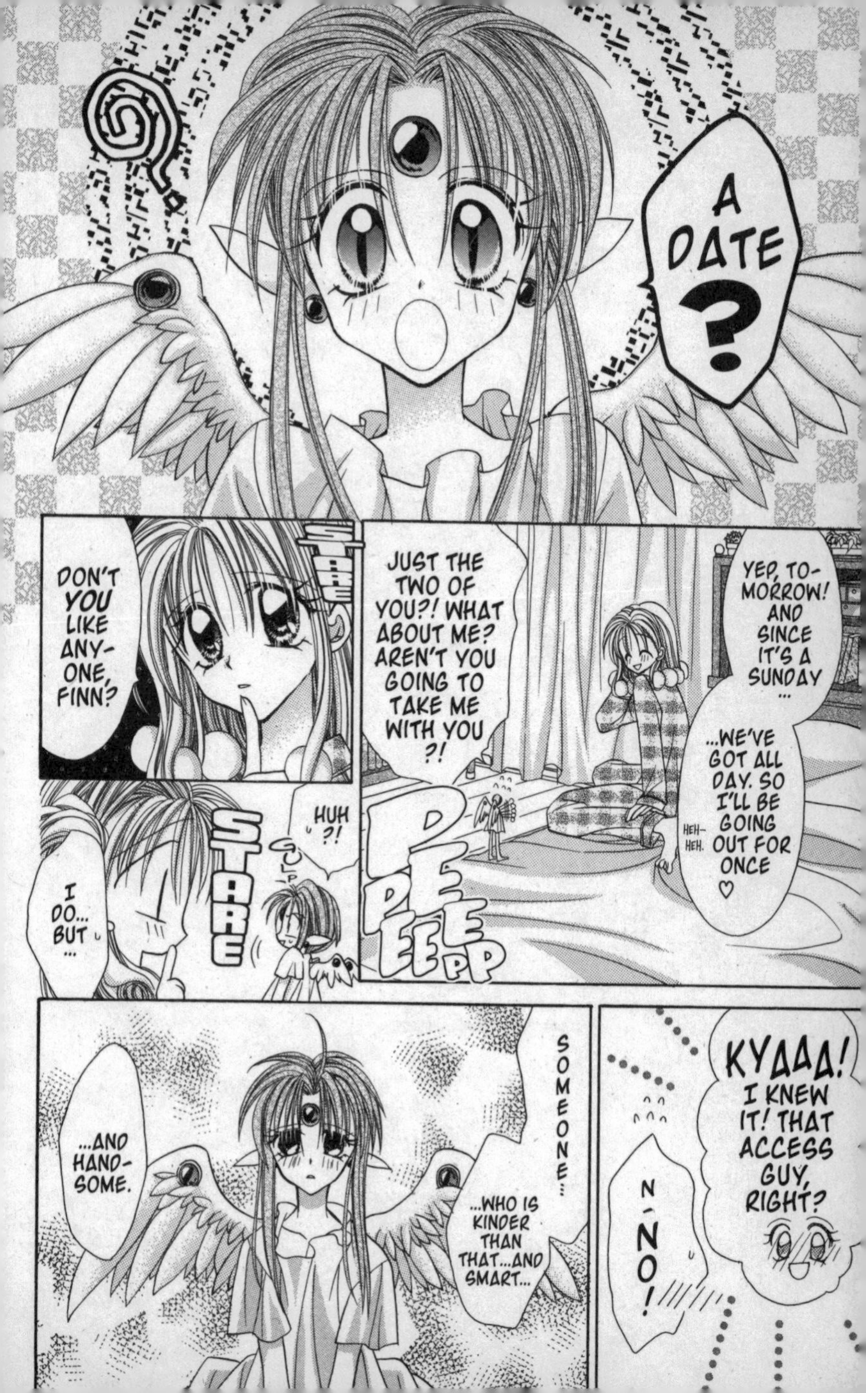
A DATE?
YEP, TO-MORROW! AND SINCE IT'S A SUNDAY ...
...WE'VE GOT ALL DAY. SO I'LL BE GOING OUT FOR ONCE ♡
HEH-HEH.
JUST THE TWO OF YOU?! WHAT ABOUT ME? AREN'T YOU GOING TO TAKE ME WITH YOU?!
STARE
DON'T YOU LIKE ANYONE, FINN?
HUH?!
GULP
STARE
I DO... BUT...
KYAAA! I KNEW IT! THAT ACCESS GUY, RIGHT?
N-NO!
SOMEONE...
...WHO IS KINDER THAN THAT...AND SMART...
...AND HANDSOME.

OYAYUBIHIME ∞ INFINITY

Volume 1

By Toru Fujieda. A group of friends from the past has been reincarnated together in the present day. Each one carries a butterfly-shaped birthmark on their thumb. When the marks touch, they catch a glimpse of their shared past, though what they see doesn't always match. Follow the gang as they try to reconcile their ties to the past with their present desire for fun and romance.

ADD TO YOUR CMX COLLECTION–
PICK UP THIS SERIES STARTING IN AUGUST!

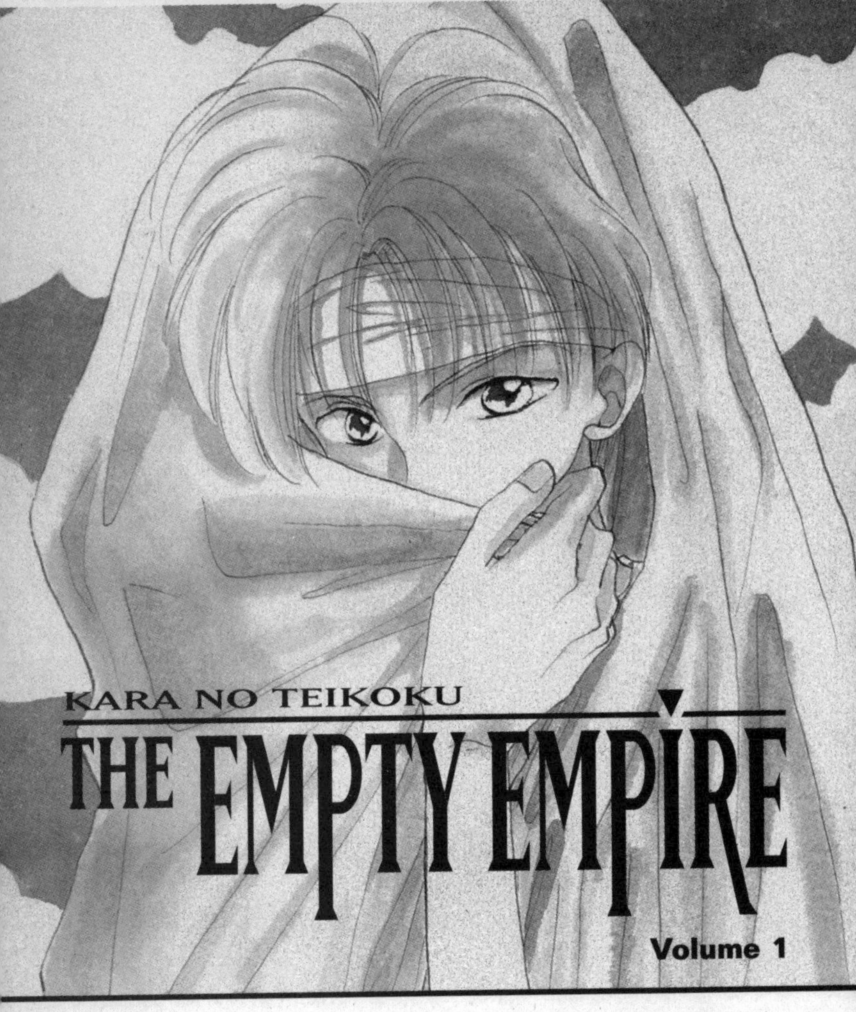
KARA NO TEIKOKU
THE EMPTY EMPIRE
Volume 1

By Naoe Kita. A boy with no memory finds himself on the run. Rescued by a girl who is a guardian of the imperial palace, he is named "Rose" due to the mysterious, flower-shaped scar on his forehead. Rose bears a striking resemblance to the recently departed, beloved emperor and may in fact be his clone! One faction wants the reluctant Rose to assume the mantle of leadership; another wants to put their own clone on the throne instead...and eliminate Rose in the process!

CMX

CHECK OUT THIS TITLE!

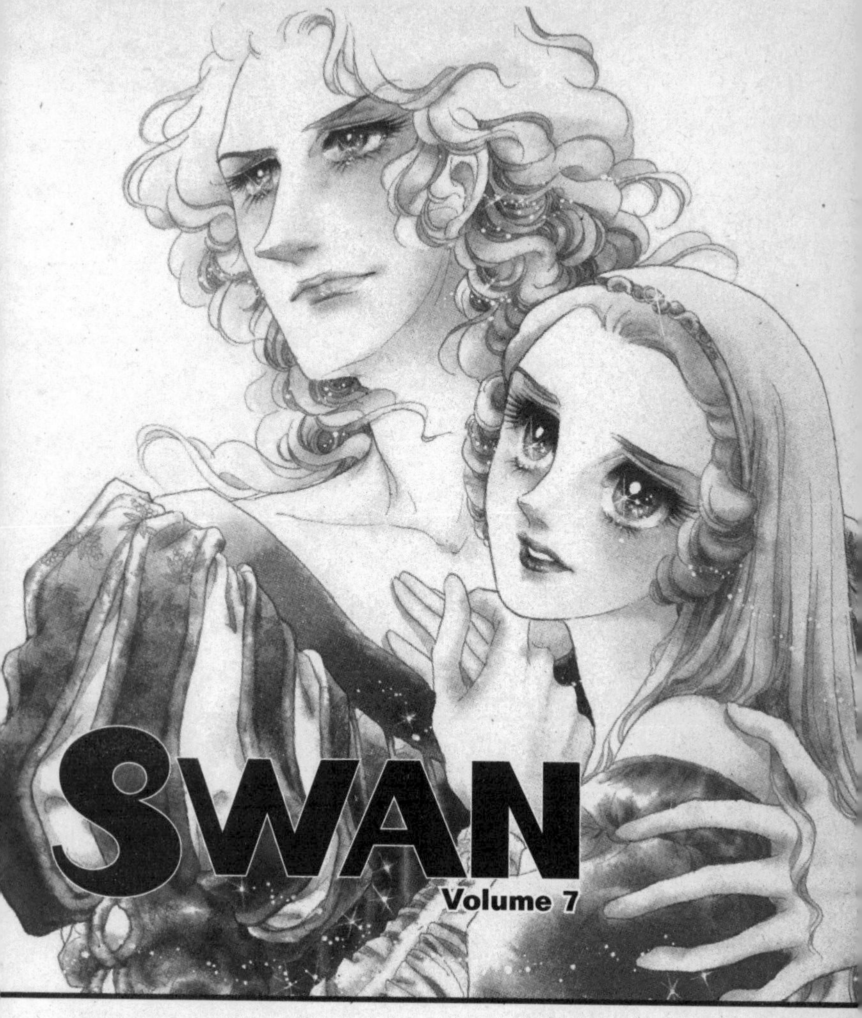
SWAN
Volume 7

By Kyoko Ariyoshi. Now that Masumi has leapt ahead of her mentor Sayoko, the pressure is on to win the lead in the latest dance competition. But her newest opponent has a connection with her late mother's past. Can Masumi stay focused on her goal, or will this unexpected link to her mother be too big a distraction?

IF YOU LIKE KAMIKAZE KAITO JEANNE, YOU'LL LOVE THESE SERIES, TOO!

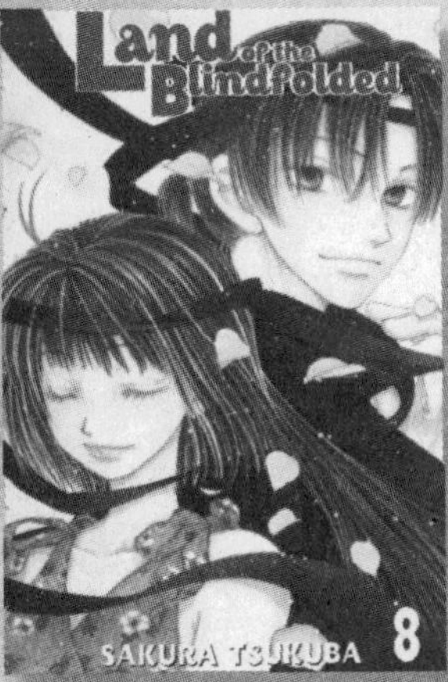

Land of the Blindfolded
SAKURA TSUKUBA
8

By Sakura Tsukuba
8 Volumes Available

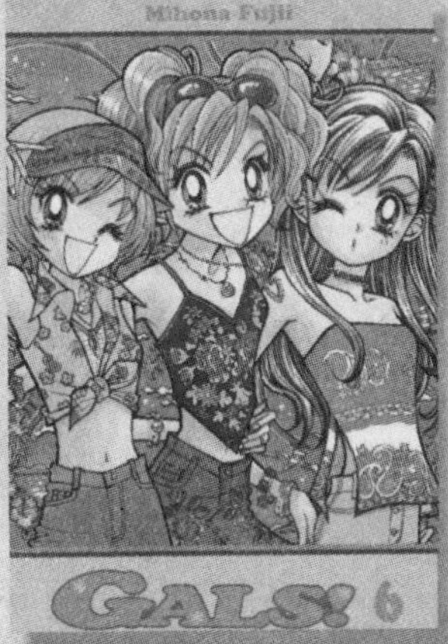

Mihona Fujii
GALS! 6

By Mihona Fujii
6 Volumes Available

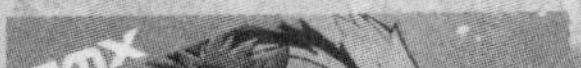

cmx
CHIKYU MISAKI
IWAHARA YUJI
1

By Iwahara Yuji
Entire Series Available!

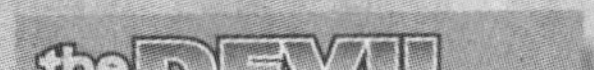

the DEVIL DOES EXIST
Mitsuba Takanashi
6

By Mitsuba Takanashi
6 Volumes Available

For more information and sneak previews, visit cmxmanga.com. Call 1-800-COMIC BOOK for the nearest comics shop or head to your local book store.

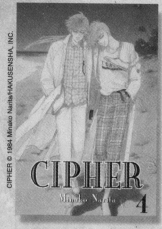

CHECK OUT MORE OF OUR CMX TITLES!

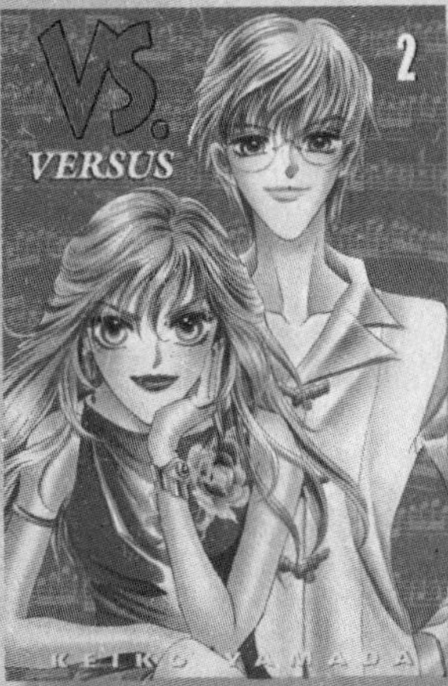
VS.
VERSUS
2
KEIKO YAMADA

By Keiko Yamada
2 Volumes Available

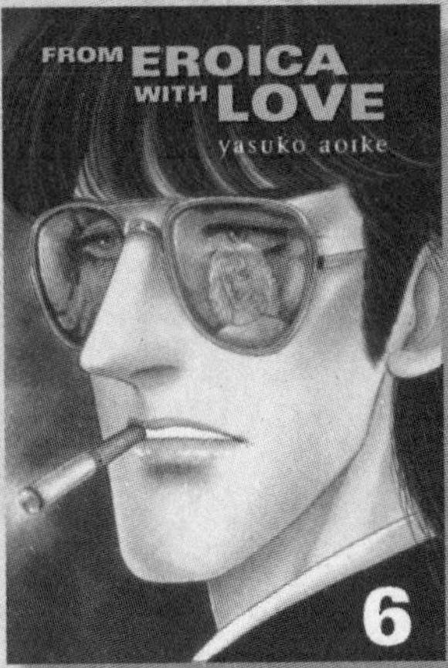
FROM EROICA WITH LOVE
yasuko aoike
6

By Yasuko Aoike
6 Volumes Available

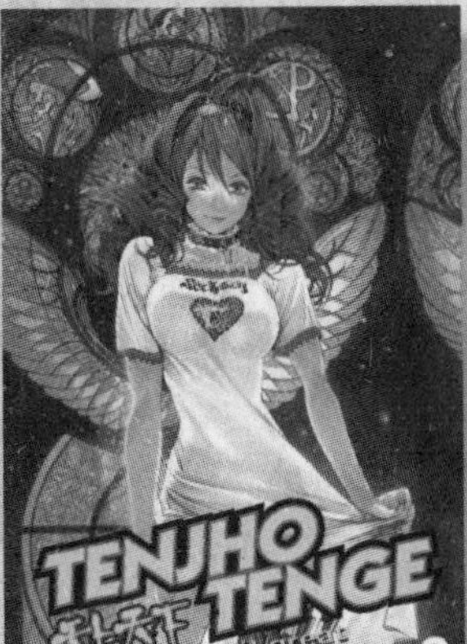
TENJHO TENGE
Oh! great
8

By Oh! great
8 Volumes Available

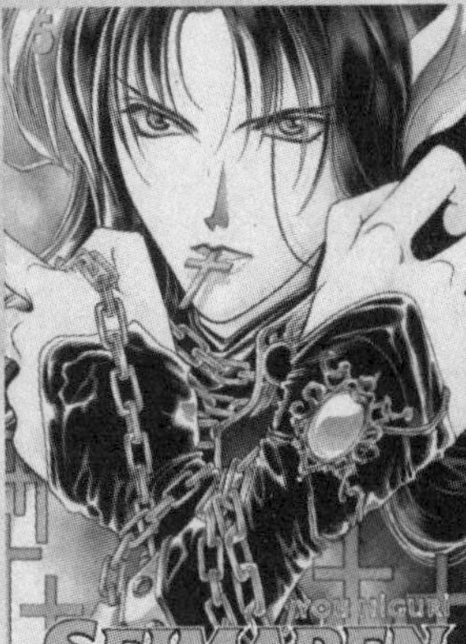
YOU HIGURI
SEIMADEN

By You Higuri
5 Volumes Available

For more information and sneak previews, visit cmxmanga.com. Call 1-800-COMIC BOOK for the nearest comics shop or head to your local book store.

KNOW WHAT'S INSIDE

With the wide variety of manga available, CMX understands it can be confusing to determine age-appropriate material. We rate our books in three categories: EVERYONE, TEEN and MATURE. For the TEEN and MATURE categories, we include additional, specific descriptions to assist consumers in determining if the book is age appropriate. (Our MATURE books are shipped shrink-wrapped with a Parental Advisory sticker affixed to the wrapper.)

EVERYONE

Titles with this rating are appropriate for all age readers. They contain no offensive material. They may contain mild violence and/or some comic mischief.

TEEN

Titles with this rating are appropriate for a teen audience and older. They may contain some violent content, language, and/or suggestive themes.

MATURE

Titles with this rating are appropriate for mature readers. They may contain graphic violence, nudity, sex and content suitable only for older readers.